ANNE CATHERINE EMMERICH

LIFE

OF

ANNE CATHERINE EMMERICH

VERY REV. K. E. SCHMÖGER, C.SS.R.

VOL. I.

TAN BOOKS AND PUBLISHERS, INC.
Rockford, Illinois 61105

APPROBATION.

The first volume of the work entitled " Life of Anne Catherine Emmerich," by Father Schmöger, C.SS.R., presented to us in manuscript, contains nothing contrary to the teachings of the Catholic Church, either as to dogma or morals, and, as it seems conducive to faith and piety, we cheerfully give it the approbation solicited by the author.

✠ PETER JOSEPH,
Bishop of Limbourg.

Limbourg, Sept. 26, 1867.

Reprinted from the 1968 edition of Maria Regina Guild, Los Angeles, California, itself reprinted from the English edition of 1885.

ISBN: Volume 1—0-89555-059-8
      Volume 2—0-89555-060-1
      The Set—0-89555-061-X

Printed and bound in the United States of America.

TAN BOOKS AND PUBLISHERS, INC.
P.O. Box 424
Rockford, Illinois 61105

1976

DEDICATION

To the Immaculate Heart of the Virgin Mary, Mother of God, Queen of Heaven and Earth, Lady of the Most Holy Rosary, Help of Christians, and Refuge of the Human Race.

CONTENTS

OF VOL. I.

Contents.

PREFACE TO THE ENGLISH EDITION.

The life of Anne Catherine Emmerich is already well known to thousands in Germany, Italy, and France. Its publication in those countries was hailed by numbers who have profited by its perusal. It will be no small recommendation in its favor to state that His Holiness, Pius IX. of blessed memory, ordered the Italian translation to be made from advanced proof-sheets of the German. The French, also, as we are told by Canon de Cazalès in his preface, was taken from the original proofs furnished by the author himself, Very Rev. Carl Erhard Schmöger, C.SS.R.

The present translation from the edition of 1870 was undertaken in the conviction, that the work is calculated to edify English readers not less than those of other nationalities. We were likewise actuated by the persuasion that it would be pleasing to Almighty God to publish the wonders of His workings in chosen souls; for if it is good to hide the secret of the king, it is also honorable to confess the works of the Most High (Tob. xii. 7).

The disciples of Antichrist never weary of publishing book after book, each more pernicious than the preceding, with the design of perverting the mind and corrupting the hearts of millions; they employ every effort, every stratagem to spread around by means of the press and in every possible form the deadly poison of hell.

Should the children of Holy Church, they who have it in their power to counteract these diabolical designs by the publication and circulation of good books, remain idle ? Should they fancy themselves exonerated from further efforts in a contrary direction by the mere utterance of useless lamentations whilst, at the same time, they behold the tide of evil gaining fresh strength as it sweeps along bearing with it innumerable souls to ruin ? Can too much be done to stem the torrent, to avert the danger before it is too late ?

May we not, also, whilst offering an antidote to the deadly effects of so much of our current literature, supply the spiritual wants, and gratify the varied tastes of many souls hungering for fresh and more suitable nourishment ?

Much has already been done in English Catholic literature, both in defence of Catholic principles and to lay before the public the lives of numerous saints and servants of God. But much still remains to be done, and it ought to be accomplished as carefully, as conscientiously as so noble an object deserves.

As every bad book tends to mislead the mind and corrupt the heart of its reader; so every good book is a cherished companion, a faithful teacher, whose lessons are often more telling on the interior life than the most eloquent sermons.

Should we have to-day a St. Ignatius Loyola had he, when convalescing after his wound at Pompeluna, been supplied with novels by way of entertainment instead of the legends of the saints ? Where would be our great St. Teresa had she continued her secret perusal of those dangerous romances which she found in the paternal home ? Should we be called upon to lament the spiritual ruin of so many of our young people, had they not imbibed principles of infidelity and licentiousness from the pages of those miserable publications whose only aim is to depict vice in its most vivid colors, and to spread it broadcast throughout the land ? Earnest Catholic parents, good Catholic schools, zealous priests, are indeed rich blessings for our Catholic youth; but let some dangerous book fall into a child's hands, and the efforts of parents, teachers, and priests will soon be frustrated.

May the present work, the "Life of Anne Catherine Emmerich," open in the future, as it has done in the past, a source of multiplied graces to its readers ! May its perusal prepare them for that of another most intimately connected with it; viz., the "Life of Our Lord Jesus Christ and His Blessed Mother," compiled from the revelations made to this holy religious !

If some of our readers find it difficult to lend credence to the extraordinary favors conferred upon this privileged spouse of Christ, let them remember that they are facts not met in every-day life, consequently, facts to the contemplation of which the mind must be gradually trained as to any other subject of thought and reflection. Let them understand that *the arm of the Lord is not shortened :* that He who bestowed so many extraordinary favors on His servants both of the Old and the New Law, has the same power, the same freedom to show forth in our own day for the benefit of mankind His marvellous gifts in those whom He has selected and prepared for them.

To those of our readers who may feel an interest in the opinion of theologians concerning the present biography, we can afford evidence not to be lightly put aside.

Even in her lifetime, after she had been subjected to the test of a most rigid examination, sound theologians approved Anne Catherine Emmerich's supernatural state; after her death sound theologians wrote and examined her life, and distinguished ecclesiastical authorities set their seal of approbation upon it. Among the first class, we may mention Mgr. Clemens Auguste, Count von Droste-Vischering, Coadjutor-Bishop of Münster, later Archbishop of Cologne, who suffered so much, even two years' imprisonment, for defending and upholding the rights of the Church against the encroachments of the government. We mention the renowned Bishop Michael Sailer, of Ratisbon, and his coadjutor, the saintly Bishop Wittman, (1) one of the greatest prelates of our age. Some hours before the death of the latter, as we read in *Schmöger's Lebensbild*, he earnestly exhorted the Pilgrim (Brentano) to publish his manuscripts relating to the servant of God. "O my beloved friend," said he, "labor faithfully, labor faithfully for the

(1) Mgr. Wittman (1760-1833) was during the greater part of his life Director of the Seminary at Ratisbon, Bavaria. He was a man of extraordinary learning, eminent holiness, and untiring activity. Besides his position as Director of the Seminary and professor in several branches, for twenty-five years the administration of the Cathedral parish was intrusted to him. In this capacity, he gave thirty-seven hours catechetical instructions weekly, preached generally twice on Sundays, visited the hospitals, the prisons, and the poor-house every week, breaking to the afflicted inmates the Word of God and affording them spiritual consolation. Five o'clock every morning found the good priest in his confessional, where he often had an opportunity to exercise the peculiar facility bestowed upon him to reconcile inveterate enemies. Amid all these labors he still found time to compose a number of excellent works particularly adapted to the use of the clergy. His day was divided as follows: seven hours of prayer; seven hours of study; seven hours' work; and three hours' sleep taken on a plank with a book for his pillow. He died in his seventy-third year, lying on the floor under a crucifix, as preconized Bishop of Ratisbon. His death was lamented by all that knew him, but most of all by the poor, to whom he was a real father and benefactor. His name is held in veneration by the Catholics of southern Germany.—Taken from Herder's Lexicon.

honor of Jesus Christ! Go on courageously!"—So spoke
the dying Bishop as he blessed Brentano, and congratulated
him in the hearing of all around upon having noted down
the visions of Anne Catherine, to the publication of which
he had in their very first interview urged him. Nor must
we omit Sister Emmerich's extraordinary confessor, the
pious and learned Dean Overberg, for a time Director of
the Seminary at Münster. We shall often meet his name
in the following pages. To the foregoing illustrious
names may be added those of Count von Stolberg and
Joseph Goerres who, though not in the ranks of the priesthood, so excelled in theological learning and sound judgment that their words were received as oracles in their
time

All these distinguished men knew Anne Catherine Emmerich personally and, like innumerable other witnesses of
her life, pronounced her a true spouse of Christ, a chosen
soul endowed with extraordinary graces and privileges.

Let us now turn to the second class of witnesses, to the
sound theologians that wrote and examined her life at a
later period The notes taken by Clement Brentano at
the bedside of the ecstatica during his six years' stay in
Dülmen, were at his death bequeathed as a precious legacy
to Christian Brentano, his brother. The latter handed
them over to the Abbot Haneberg, later Bishop of Spires,
with the understanding that they should at some future day
be arranged and published But the pious Abbot, a sincere
admirer of Sister Emmerich and fully conscious of the
treasure in his possession, could not find the time necessary

for the accomplishment of so great a work ; viz., the publication of the Life of Christ with that of the venerable
Sister herself.

Almighty God called another to undertake the task, one
eminently competent, one who united deep learning with
solid piety. This man was Very Rev. Carl Erhard Schmöger, C.SS.R., who had in 1850 entered the Congregation
of the Most Holy Redeemer as a secular priest of more
than ordinary learning. His Superiors soon discovered his
extraordinary talents and uncommon love for the study of
theology. He was, consequently, engaged for years as professor in its different branches, dogmatic, hermeneutic,
and exegetic, besides which he for some time taught
philosophy. As he was constantly enriching his mind by
the reading of the Holy Fathers, his keen eye could detect
at a glance the least inaccuracy in any author respecting
Catholic faith or tradition. This was an excellent preparation for Father Schmöger's later providential mission.

Gladly and with noble generosity, Abbot Haneberg delivered Brentano's manuscripts to such a man, to one whom
he considered so well qualified for the work, and by whom
that rich treasure of God's mercy was to be opened to the
faithful. Meanwhile, Divine Providence favored the undertaking. Father Schmöger found access to many documents concerning the civil and ecclesiastical trials to which
Sister Emmerich had been subjected, and this enabled him
to give a still more correct picture of her interior and exterior life. The task was begun in obedience to the command of Superiors. Encouraged by men like Abbot Hane-

berg and Very Rev. Frederic Windischmann, Vicar-General of Munich, and supported by the prayers of many pious souls, Father Schmöger continued and accomplished t only after years of hard and oft-interrupted labor ; or during the latter part of his life, he held the office of Provincial of his Congregation in Bavaria. Although himself a renowned theologian, he never failed to submit the result of his careful researches to other theologians and authorities upon whose learning and solidity he could safely rely. And so the Life of Anne Catherine Emmerich was published for the first time in 1870, with the approbation of the Bishop of Limbourg and the permission of Father Schmöger's Superior, the General of the Redemptorists at Rome.

The fact that not one voice was raised against his works after their publication by the Catholic press ; the fact that his books found their way unmolested into the houses of thousands, as the " Dolorous Passion," the only compilation from Sister Emmerich's revelations published during Brentano's lifetime, had previously done ; the fact that the Life of the Stigmatisee was immediately translated into French and Italian with the approbation of orthodox Bishops; the fact that in Germany a second edition of the said Life soon followed the first, and that new demands now render a third necessary—these facts might, we think, be accepted as sufficient proofs of God's blessing on the work.

But when great men like Dom Guéranger, Abbot of Solesmes, and Very Rev. F. Windischmann of Munich, whose names are known throughout the Catholic world, speak in

the highest terms of it, have we room to fear not being in
harmony with Catholic faith and teaching if we lend to it
our meed of praise? Dom Gueranger (whose word, as
Rev. Frederic Windischmann tells us, is of more weight
with him than that of a thousand others) expresses his conviction that Anne Catherine Emmerich had a mission from
God and that she faithfully fulfilled the same; otherwise
God never would have lavished so abundant and so extraordinary favors upon her.   It was hers to bring before the
mind of the German nation the Gospel in its most minute
details just at a time when the Divinity of Christ and the
Gospel truths were most strenuously denied by the philos-
ophers so-called of the day.   And here the learned Abbot
expresses his astonishment at the way in which she fulfilled
her mission.   That a poor, uneducated peasant-girl in the
heart of Europe should describe in their smallest details the
various characters and languages, manners and customs of
different and far-off countries ; that she should do all this
with perfect accuracy with respect to the varied circumstances of geography, topography, and archæology of times
long passed, is certainly sufficient to astound even the most
prudent and learned.

Rev. F. Windischmann, himself a warm friend of Father
Schmöger, considers it something very wonderful that in all
Sister Emmerich's descriptions of the various circumstances
and situations in which the Sacred Person of Our Lord
figures ; viz., at meals, at marriage-feasts, on journeys, etc.,
we find not the least trace of anything unworthy of Him.
All and everything He does or says is animated by a cer-

tain nobleness indicative of His Divine Personality. This, he concludes, Anne Catherine could never have done had her work been a mere human invention.

These facts would seem proof sufficient to establish the truth of Sister Emmerich's revelations. But we have still some others to bring forward.

Rev. Alban Stolz, Professor in the Seminary of Freiburg, and a famous German author, mentions in the description of his journey to Jerusalem that a certain Franciscan, Father Wolfgang of Jerusalem, told him that for six years he had made the statements of Anne Catherine Emmerich respecting the Holy Land, as given in Brentano's " Dolorous Passion," a point of special study. The result of his observations was, that they are perfectly correct in all their details. Rev. Stolz tells us on the same page that one Professor Hug, a man known to be not over-credulous on the subject of visions or revelations, one day expressed to his pupils his surprise that the statements of the nun of Dülmen agree so exactly with those of the Jewish historian Josephus. (1)

Rev. Anton Urbas, Parish-priest and Canon of the Cathedral of Laybach, Austria, published a book in 1884, entitled *"Die Reiche der Heiligen Drei Könige."* He mentions in the preface that he had read Anne Catherine Emmerich's Life, Visions, and Revelations for a considerable time without being able to harmonize many points that he found therein. Some things seemed to him very beautiful, useful, and correct ; but others were hard to accept. Instead

(1) See " Sem, Cham, and Japhet," by Alban Stolz.

of denouncing the whole as the pious dream of a good nun,
he set himself to the task of studying the geography of Asia
in all its details.   As he studied he compared his researches
with the statements of A. C. Emmerich.   The result of
his earnest and honest investigation was, that he publicly acknowledged Sister Emmerich to be the most correct geog-
rapher, topographer, and archæologist in the world, and
that his first difficulties were to be attributed rather to a
want of knowledge on his own part than to any fault on that
of the wonderfully enlightened Sister.

St. Paul writes to the Corinthians (I. Cor. i. 28, 29), " God
has chosen the foolish things of the world that He may confound the wise, and the weak things of the world God has
chosen that He may confound the strong . . . . . that no flesh
should glory in His sight."   Are not these words here literally verified ?

Canon Urbas says, moreover : " The works of Sister Emmerich are a rich mine.   Some few remarks often throw
much light on certain subjects.   Like cross-road signs,
they point out the right way.   Their power to move and
vivify the soul is especially noticeable.   Here, as in no
other book outside the Holy Scriptures, do we find words
of eternal life."

But coming nearer home, we could cite many distinguished ecclesiastics as stanch supporters of Sister Emmerich and her revelations.   We shall limit ourselves to
two whose rank in the sacred hierarchy lends greater
weight to their authority ; viz., the saintly John N. Neu-
mann, Fourth Bishop of Philadelphia, and the lately de-

ceased Bishop Tœbbe, of Covington, Ky. That the former favored her works, may be seen by a reference to his Life. In it we read that among others books which he imported from Europe in the early days of his ministry, he called particularly for those of A. C. Emmerich; the latter, Bishop Tœbbe, showed his appreciation of the same by heartily approving the new edition of the "Life of Jesus," compiled from her revelations. (1)

But as some critic may object that even great theologians may be deceived in such matters, we shall refrain from arguments of our own in its defence, referring our readers to the rules of Pope Benedict XIV. which Rome follows in the canonization of such souls as were favored in life with visions and revelations. By the application of these rules (which may be found in the author's preface) any fair-minded Catholic may judge whether such visions and revelations are from God or not.

If the life of Anne Catherine Emmerich may be tested by these rules, we may safely conclude that her extraordinary gifts were indeed from God; for what is considered by the Holy Father and his Cardinals a sufficient guaranty of truth in the process of canonization, ought to be sufficient also to satisfy the inquiries of the severest critic. Let the reader study without prejudice the Life of this favored soul, let him apply to it the aforesaid rules, and then only let him form his judgment of the same.

In conclusion, we beg leave to state that the translation

---

(1) " Das arme Leben und bittere Leiden unseres Herrn Jesu Christi und seiner heiligsten Mutter Maria," published by Fr. Pustet & Co.

of the present work was undertaken with the sole view to extend the reign of Jesus Christ in hearts and to further the coming of His kingdom upon earth. Our aim has been to reproduce carefully and conscientiously from the original every word that fell from the lips of the stigmatisée ; whilst, to suit the taste of English readers, the accompanying matter has been somewhat condensed, though not to the detriment of the author's meaning. Like the original it has been submitted to the judgment of competent persons and been thoroughly revised by an able theologian.

February 5, 1885.

PREFACE TO THE SECOND EDITION.

One of the hopeful signs of our times, despite a spirit of worldliness and polite sensualism, is the growing interest which is being manifested in the study of the lives of the mystics. It is evidence of how far the Church of God has lifted society out of the dross of materialism, when her great heroes and heroines of virtue, whose hearts were so unreservedly and passionately set upon things not of this earth, and never appealing to anything but the highest and noblest in their fellow men, are receiving a recognition so sincere and so profound. Nor is this recognition confined to the children of the " household of the faith." The " mystical " literature of the Catholic Church is read by a great number of non-Catholics who are engaged in a sincere search after truth. The writer has in mind the testimony of more than one devout convert, who owes the first dawning of the Light to the reading of the life of a saint. And this is but natural. The blending of the potential perfections of heaven with the actual experiences of earth, so impressively illustrated in the lives of the saints, brings the well disposed mind into such close touch with the supernatural, that all worldly concerns appear dwarfed and pale. The tree is judged by its fruit, and the conclusion is, that a church which can produce such exalted characters must have within her the divinity of the Gospel and the truth as it has been revealed by Jesus Christ.

Considering these facts, it is with joy and edification we hail this second English edition of the life of Anne Catherine Emmerich. Already her name is well known to the whole Catholic world. When the record of the wonderful

visions accorded her first appeared, it provoked a great deal
of adverse criticism.   But time, which is the one great test
of genuineness, has caused that adverse criticism to disappear and to give way to the highest approval.   An illustrious evidence of this fact is shown by the following letter from
a canon of the Cathedral of Loybach, Bavaria : "At first
I did not believe Catherine Emmerich's statements. I
wondered how the Bishop of Limbourg could approve the
publication of such a book. I went to work to find out all
the falsehoods she was telling, and to my surprise, I found
that in the light of tradition, geography, topography, and history, Anne Catherine Emmerich knew more than all our
so-called savants.   After Holy Scripture, there is no book
that contains so many words of eternal truth and life than
the revelations of A. C. Emmerich."

To this we must add the testimony of the eminent theologian, Dr. Rohling, who writes in an Appendix to his
Medulla Theologiæ Moralis : "I cannot refrain from
adding my voice of commendation to that of all who have
written on the life and visions of Anne Catherine Emmerich, and I earnestly commend them. I desire to mention
in particular her visions on the Life and Passion of Our
Lord, since I am convinced that every priest who studies
them will be so inflamed with zeal for souls and longing
for his own salvation, that it will be impossible for him to
be lost. He will find Our Lord therein portrayed in colors
so lively, and he will receive so clear a perception of His
goodness, that he will gladly renounce all worldly pleasure,
and daily participate in a new outpouring of God's Holy
Spirit, thus becoming ever fitter to move the hearts of
worldlings and lead them to penance."

A perusal of the Life of Catherine Emmerich makes one
appreciate these impressive words of Dr. Rohling. Her

visions bring before the mind so vivid a realization of the mission and Passion of Our Redeemer that, when the reader finishes his study of them, he feels conscious of having undergone an unusual influence, and he is moved to voice his feelings in the exclamation of the two who met the Saviour on the way to Emmaus : " Was not our heart burning within us whilst He spoke in the way, and opened to us the Scriptures ? "

To learn the life of Our Divine Lord, is the chief study of every Christian. Catherine Emmerich is a notable aid to the performance of this duty. It was a commendable thought of the translator to place this work at the disposal of English readers, for whatever tends to bring the soul into close union with the Saviour is of supreme value. We read in the Gospels that a diseased woman once pressed through the crowd, touched the hem of the Master's garment, and by the power of her faith was immediately healed. Is not the loyal disciple, who gets still near enough to touch Him in spirit and draw forth the inspiring virtue He delivers, made spiritually whole ? This is the mission of Catherine Emmerich—to bring souls into touch with Christ. And in a day like ours, when so many hearts are waxing cold, and a spirit of irreligion seems to sway the minds of multitudes, who will deny that the mission of Anne Catherine Emmerich is a blessing to the world ?

All admirers of this great servant of God received with grateful hearts the blessed tidings that the process for her Beatification had actually begun in Rome. We pray that the day is not far distant when the Church will enroll her name in the list of saints. One thing is certain : we may safely venture the opinion that the influence she has had upon the history of the Church in the nineteenth century will increase as the years roll by, and continue till time is no more. Despite all that the haters of the Christian religion may say—and they are saying much that is blasphemous—the memory of Jesus and His Passion will endure to the end. Ah, how little did Pilate dream, as he led Him out, bleeding from the degradation of the scourge, and said to the multitude, " Behold the man ! "—how little did the infuriated mob dream that the voice of that silent sufferer would thrill the world forever, and the image of Him crucified would melt the heart of all posterity. Animated by a very different spirit from that which filled the soul of the worldly-ambitious Pilate, Anne Catherine Emmerich cries out to us, " Behold the Lamb of God that taketh away the sins of the world ! "

This work will no doubt, now and then, meet with half-veiled sneers and cynical warnings from those that cannot appreciate its merits. But it is comforting to know that such criticism will in no way lessen its effect upon those elect souls who are seeking encouragement and enlightenment in a life of prayer. And He who, while on earth, breathed such divinity of tenderness, such inexhaustible magnanimity of forbearing pity and love toward all men ; who from His throne in Heaven is now willing to give the pearl of great price purchased with His Precious Blood to the lowest child of humanity ; who in the agony of death on Calvary's Cross yearned over the broken malefactor by His side with the promise of Paradise, will not fail to bless and enlighten all who, in a rightful spirit, study the life and revelations of Anne Catherine Emmerich.

A word, in conclusion, as to the work of the translator. She has succeeded in producing a work that reads as if it had been originally written in English. One may say that she has literally put her heart into it. It ranks among the most valuable productions of the Catholic press, and none will read it without profit.

T. A. D.

Feast of St. Monica,—1903.

INTRODUCTION

The author of the present biography published eight years ago the last volume of the "Life of Our Divine Saviour," compiled from the visions of Anne Catherine Emmerich. He purposed issuing, as a supplement to the same, the life of the servant of God drawn from the most authentic sources; but the duties of his ministry, sickness, and the difficulties attendant on the undertaking itself, retarded its publication until the present.

If Clement Brentano, (1) who resided at Dülmen from the

(1) Clement Brentano, whose name will appear so often in the course of this biography, was born September 8, 1778. He was a poet of the highest genius. What others acquired only by long and hard study, he learned with ease. He was perfectly at home with the Greek and Latin authors, with Calderon, Dante, and Shakespeare, as well as with those of his own tongue. His wit and humor, his brilliant talents and exquisite poetical productions won for him the love and admiration of all who came in contact with him, and opened to him access to the highest literary circles. His religious education had been very much neglected ; still he believed in the existence of God as a remunerator of good and evil, and in Jesus Christ as a divine mediator. He was charitable to the poor. Like Solomon he saw the vanity of all created things, and like the great Augustine he longed for something higher than earthly glory and knowledge. His restless heart at last found peace in God in a general confession, 1817. A new world was now opened up before him, new friends gathered round him ; his religious fervor was great, although wanting in prudence and needing direction. This he found by the bedside of the poor and suffering Anne Catherine Emmerich, to whom Divine Providence had sent him in 1818. So attracted was he by the heroic virtue he there witnessed that the former idol of the fashionable world resolved to bury himself in the little town of Dülmen, and warm his heart at this furnace of divine love. But not for himself alone were the graces he there received. Brentano was to be the instrument for the accomplishment of God's design that the revelations with which the ecstatica was favored should be recorded for the benefit of mankind. Ardently desirous of doing something for the glory of God, and thereby to atone for the shortcomings of the past, Brentano readily accepted the pressing invitation of Dean Overberg to become the amanuensis of the favored stigmatisée. For nearly six years, despite the jeers and mockery of his friends, he daily committed to writing what he learned in that school of Christ Crucified. When A. C. Emmerich died, Brentano returned to his friends, not now to entertain them by his talents, but to astound them by his ardor in the service of God and his neighbor. The large sums realized from his literary productions were all devoted to this noble purpose. Catholic literature felt a new impulse,

fall of 1818 till the spring of 1824, daily making notes of
his observations, shrank from the task of compiling this life,
so simple in the exterior, so little calculated to strike the
senses, and yet so rich, so wonderful in its interior signification, the writer of these lines may surely believe himself
entitled to the indulgence of his readers for withholding it
so long. He deemed the sketch of Sister Emmerich's life
prefixed to the first edition of " The Dolorous Passion,"
published by Clement Brentano, in 1833, sufficient, until
his friend Dr. Krabbe, Dean of the Cathedral Münster,
procured him access to the original " Acts of the Ecclesiastical Inquiry of 1813," and also accompanied him to Dülmen, Coesfeld, and Flamske, to collect among her few surviving contemporaries some circumstances of her life,
which led to the present work. Gratitude demands the
mention of the late Herr Aulike, Privy-Councillor at Berlin, who kindly forwarded to the author the notices given
to the public at intervals from the year .1813 to that of her
death, 1824. The above-named gentlemen regarded her
with deep veneration, and eagerly awaited the publication
of her biography, which, however, neither lived to see.

Owing to the conscientious record of the Acts of the In-

good books were translated and circulated, sculpture and painting were raised to new
life by his religious energy. Encouraged by the pious and learned of his time, and we
may add in the very home of the famous Diepenbrock, afterward Cardinal-Archbishop
of Breslau, he published in 1835 the " Dolorous Passion of Christ," the first work compiled from the revelations of A. C. Emmerich. One edition succeeded another and
quickly prepared the public mind for other works from the same source. Brentano
died holily in 1842. With him a great and noble soul passed from earth to heaven.
His early failings he had long before blotted out by torrents of contrite tears. If charity
covers a multitude of sins, certainly his heroic love for God and his neighbor more than
atoned for the wanderings of his early career, wanderings that sprang rather from
ignorance than malice. His death was followed by the conversion of some noble souls
to whom in life he had earnestly pointed out the Catholic Church as the only secure refuge, the only safe harbor of salvation.—*Taken from " Sketch of Clement Brentano,"*
by REV. F. DIEL, S. J.

vestigation, wholly unknown to Clement Brentano, the author has been enabled to support this history on testimony so weighty that none more conclusive can be found in the life of any saint favored by similar graces, whilst the rich materials they afford give a clearer understanding of Sister Emmerich's mission.   In them we behold a fact whose significance is universally acknowledged by the Church, a fact known and appreciated in every age ; viz., that Almighty God at all times chooses certain souls, who, either secluded from the world or amid the hurry of secular life, serve as instruments in suffering and combating for the Church. The life and sufferings of such chosen ones are often widely dissimilar : for instance, Lidwina of Schiedam, or our own Domenica Lazzari appear as victims in the body, like the early virgin-martyrs ; whilst others, such as Magdalene di Pazzi, or Colomba di Rieti, combat and suffer for the Church spiritually ; though, inasmuch as their life is a perpetual sacrifice, a course of uninterrupted endurance in perfect abandonment to the will of God, they closely resemble one another.   They expiate the faults committed in the bosom of the Church and repair the wrongs she endures from her own children, or they atone for actual guilt, doing penance for the guilty.   By prayer, or rather by an extraordinary gift which converts prayer into action, they avert impending dangers from the Sovereign Pontiff and the clergy ; they obtain conversion for sinners ; an increase of faith for the weak ; zeal and intrepidity for pastors ; and, lastly, they wrestle for souls in danger of being lost through the negligence of others, chiefly of those entrusted with their spiritual guidance. Besides this duty of prayer and expiation, there is, moreover, the task militant, to be undertaken by some privileged souls, and which consists in actually embracing corporal and spiritual dangers, diseases, temptations, and evil inclinations. Here it is no longer simple suffering or sacrifice, the fruits of which are reaped by others; but there is question of exposing one's self, really and personally, to all the perils that menace the neighbor, of taking upon one's self sickness or temptation exacting of the substitute a real struggle, the fruits of whose victory are to be made over to another. One of the most sublime instances of such a task is found in Judith confronting Holofernes and his army to prevent the profanation of the Sanctuary and the opprobrium of God's chosen people. It may seem, perhaps, that prayer must be the only or. at least, the chief duty of these victims; but such is not exclusively the case, since the martyrdom of penance undergone by the innocent is precisely that which gives to prayer its efficacy and draws down upon the Church the richest benedictions. The expiatory task is never separated from that of combating, and both united to prayer are found to an extraordinary degree in the life of Sister Emmerich who, from her very infancy, had been prepared for her mission, her communications with her angel, her intuitive perception of the unseen, and the gift of contemplation bestowed at her birth contributing thereto.

Three great evils menaced the Church at the epoch in

which she lived : the profanation of sacred things, the dis-
semination of false doctrines, and the corruption of morals,
to meet which with the weapons of prayer and expiation
was Sister Emmerich's mission, to struggle in defence of
the Church delivered over, as it were, to the will of her enemies. It will, in no small degree, animate the pious reader
to renewed confidence in God when he finds in this biography so many proofs of His merciful protection over His
Church during those troubled times, and beholds the instrument employed for that end in the person of the poor little
shepherdess of Flamske. This was the consideration that
encouraged the author to resume his oft-interrupted task,
and to spare no trouble in the study of her life, diligently
comparing for this end the facts contained in it with those
presented in the biographies of others similarly favored by
Heaven.

They who are familiar with the rules laid down by Benedict XIV. and the great theological authorities to whom he
constantly refers in his work, *"De Servorum Dei Beatifica-
tione,"* will understand the author's anxiety in elaborating
a history like the one under consideration, and agree with
him in declaring Sister Emmerich's life a striking exempli-
fication of the virtues exacted by the Church as proofs of
the truth wherever there is question of the supernatural (1).

To be able prudently to pronounce upon so delicate a
question, consideration must be had on the one side to the

(1) The following lines, taken from Father Schmöger's Introduction to the "Life of
Christ," seem so suitable to the subject here treated that, conforming to the advice of
certain capable persons, among them a holy confrère of the author himself, we take
the liberty of incorporating them in this Introduction to the Life of Sister Emmerich.

virtue of the person under examination, and on the other to her manner of conducting herself both in and out of vision ; for which latter point, Benedict XIV., with the most distinguished doctors and theologians, has laid down twelve marks deserving special attention :—

I.—Has the person in question ever desired visions ; or, on the contrary, has she begged of God the grace of being conducted in the ordinary ways ? Has she received such visions only in the spirit of obedience ?—" To desire such favors," says St. Vincent Ferrier, " would be to nourish secret pride or reprehensible curiosity ; it would be a sign of weak, imperfect faith."

II.—Has she received from her confessor an order to communicate her visions to holy and enlightened persons ?

III.—Has she always shown absolute obedience toward her spiritual guides ? Has she in consequence of her visions made rapid progress in the love of God and humility ?

IV.—Has she willingly conferred with persons disinclined to credit her, or who tried and contradicted her ?

V.—Does she habitually experience peace and tranquillity of conscience ? Is her heart always inflamed with ardent zeal for perfection ?

VI.—Were her spiritual directors ever obliged to reproach her with imperfections ?

VII.—Has she received from God a promise to hear all her lawful and reasonable petitions ? Has she by her prayers obtained great favors from Him ?

VIII.—Have those who live with her, supposing their own

perversity no obstacle to her virtuous influence, been in-
cited to piety and the love of God ?

IX.—Have her visions been vouchsafed her after fervent prayer or Holy Communion ? Have they excited in
her a desire to suffer for the glory of God ?

X.—Has she crucified her flesh ? Has she rejoiced in
trials and contradictions ?

XI.—Has she loved retreat ? Has she fled the society
of creatures ? Is she despoiled of every natural attachment ?

XII.—Has she preserved serenity of soul as well under
adverse as under prosperous circumstances? Finally, have
learned theologians found nothing in her visions contrary
to the rules of faith, or which might appear reprehensible,
viewed in any light whatever ?

These twelve points laid down by Benedict XIV.,
fruits of the experience of the most holy and enlightened
Doctors, furnish sure and infallible rules in such cases ; and
the more closely a soul endued with the gift of vision is
conformed thereto, the more motives are there, according to
the holy pontiff, for accepting her testimony and visions as
true and real. Now, the reader will, without doubt, be no
less gratified than we in tracing the perfect and truly surprising correspondence between these rules and the
whole life of Sister Emmerich. He will agree with us in declaring that to find these different characteristics united in
the same degree in any one soul, he would be obliged to
search the lives of the most illustrious saints of the Church.
In the first place, Sister Emmerich never desired such fav-

ors. They entailed upon her so many trials and contradictions that she frequently conjured God to deliver her
from them. Again, the age at which she first received them
permits us not to suppose she could have desired them, for
when she did begin to speak of them, it was with the simplicity of a child ignorant of the precise meaning of what it
says. Secondly, she could be induced to communicate
her visions only by the reiterated instances of her angelic
guide, and not till the last ten years of her life did she find
any one willing to listen to them. Thirdly, as her confessors
suspected her visions and took the trouble not even to examine them, she did all in her power to hide them, to
stifle them, so to say, in her own breast. The struggle
thence arising with her invisible guide, who ceased not to
urge her to reveal them despite her confessor's aversion,
caused her indescribable suffering. Still she continued to
address herself to the same directors from whom, however,
she had naught to expect but stern rebuffs and bitter humiliations. She left to God the care of enlightening them
in His own good time upon the origin and character of
her supernatural gifts ; and she rejected, as far as in her
lay, all that could modify or ameliorate her painful position, testifying only charity, patience, and sweetness
toward the authors of her trials.

Passing over the other points, we shall limit ourselves to a
glance at the twelfth and last: viz., the conformity of Sister Emmerich's visions with the teachings of faith—a circumstance
of the utmost importance in visions containing revelations.

Benedict XIV. here supports his opinion chiefly upon Suarez, who establishes **as an incontestable** principle that, in the study of revelations, it is chiefly to be considered whether they are in perfect accordance with the rules of **Faith and sound morals,** rejecting as illusory and diabolical every pretended revelation in contradiction with Holy Scripture, tradition, the decrees of Councils, and the unanimous teachings of the Fathers and theologians. Even those revelations which, without contravening the Faith, contain evident contradictions and serve but to satisfy vain curiosity, which appear to be the result of a purely human activity, or which, in fine, are opposed to the wisdom of God or to any other of His divine attributes, are to be suspected.

And here the illustrious pontiff asks what should be thought of revelations containing statements apparently opposed to the common opinion of the Fathers and theologians, revelations which on some particular point, give details quite new, or which affirm as certain what has not as yet been pronounced upon by the Church ? Resting upon the most solid authority, he answers that this motive suffices not to reject without further examination revelations in which such things are found ; for, 1st, a fact which at first sight appears opposed to the common opinion may, if submitted to an earnest and conscientious examination, evoke in its favor weighty authority and excellent intrinsic reasons for belief ; 2d, a revelation should not be condemned as false merely on account of its containing circumstances in the

Life of Our Lord, or that of His Blessed Mother, of which no mention is made in the Sacred Writings, in tradition, or in the Holy Fathers ; 3d, a revelation may, without militating against the decisions of the Church, the Fathers, and theologians, explain a point unexplained by them or make known some detail on which they are silent ; 4th, it would be to place arbitrary limits to the almighty power of God to suppose that He cannot reveal to a private individual a point which, not yet pronounced upon by the Church, is still a subject of controversy.

If the reader desires to apply the foregoing rules to the revelations contained in this work (1), he will find therein absolutely nothing wounding to the principles of Christian faith ; on the contrary, he will be fully satisfied that there are few books which enable the soul to penetrate so easily into the mysteries of our holy religion, or which impart so speedily even to ordinary minds the knowledge of that *art of arts* which, according to the author of the *Imitation,* consists in the meditation of the Life of Our Lord Jesus Christ, *In vita Jesu Christi meditari* (2).

As impostors and hypocrites are often met in these our days who vaunt themselves the favored recipients of Heaven's special favors, and who occasionally gain credence with some, the author has given faithfully and in detail the investigations made on Sister Emmerich's case as he found them in the original documents.

(1) "*Life of Our Lord Jesus Christ.*" The above remark is equally applicable to many points in Sister Emmerich's own life.

(2) Extract from Introduction to *Life of Our Lord*, Schmöger.

Clement Brentano's friend, Edward Steinle, painted the portrait from which the engraving prefixed to this volume was taken. His models were the drawings sketched by Brentano himself at various periods of his sojourn in Dülmen. They who knew Sister Emmerich best testify to its fidelity.

In conclusion the author declares his unreserved submission to the decrees of Pope Urban VIII. of March 13, 1625, and June 5, 1634, in consequence of which he claims for whatever is extraordinary in this book but a purely human origin.

P. SCHMÖGER, C.SS.R.

CONVENT OF GARS, ON THE INN, BAVARIA,
　　September 17, 1867.

— LIFE —

OF

ANNE CATHERINE EMMERICH.

CHAPTER I.

MANNERS AND CUSTOMS OF WESTPHALIA AT THE COM-
MENCEMENT OF THE PRESENT CENTURY.

The baptismal register, St. James, Coesfeld, contains the
following record:—" On September 8, 1774, was baptized
Anne Catherine, daughter of Bernard Emmerich and Anne
Hillers his wife, God-parents, Henry Hüning and Anne
Catherine Heynick, née Mertins." The day of little Anne
Catherine's baptism was also that of her birth. She was
the fifth of nine children, six sons and three daughters.
Gerard, the youngest brother, never married. He was still
living in September, 1859, when the author visited the little
hamlet of Flamske, near Coesfeld, the birthplace of the subject of this biography. Gerard had little to say of his sister,
excepting that she was of a remarkably sweet disposition,
that she had been a lifelong sufferer, and that he had often
gone to see her at Dülmen after she became a religious.
" She was so kind and affectionate to us," he added, " that
it was a great pleasure to her family to visit her."

The venerable pastor of the church of St. James, Rev. F.
Hilswitte, was also alive and remembered having seen Anne
Catherine for the last time in 1812. He testified to her re-
putation for piety, but the particulars of her life were un-

known to him. " The period in which she lived," he remarked, " was not capable of either understanding or appreciating such a case as hers, and few, even among the
clergy, interested themselves in her; consequently, she
was more quickly forgotten in her native place than elsewhere. In distant cities she was better known through
Bishop Wittmann and Clement Brentano. The latter, after
his visits to Dülmen, excited public interest in her by the
account of the marvels he had seen."

Long before her death, Sister Emmerich had uttered the
following words : " What the Pilgrim (1) gleans, he will bear
away, far, far away, for there is no disposition to make use
of it here; but it will bring forth fruit in other lands, whence
its effects will return and be felt even here."

The humble abode in which she was born was yet standing, in 1859, in the same condition in which Clement Brentano had found it forty years before. It was a little old
farm-house, or rather a barn in which man and beast dwelt
peaceably together. The worm-eaten door opened into a
small room whose only floor was the well-trodden ground;
this was the common room of the family. To the left were
spaces cut off from the main room by rough board partitions,
and strewn with the hay and grain scattered by the cattle ;
these were the sleeping apartments. The chimney-place,
rude and primitive, consisted of a stone slab or iron plate
cemented into the ground; on it glowed the fire, and above
it hung the kettle from an iron bar. The smoke, after de-
positing its soot upon the rough beams and dingy chairs
and table, the handiwork of preceding generations, escaped
as best it could by any chink in the roof or walls. The
rest of the dwelling was given up to the cows, which were
separated from their owners only by a few stakes driven

(1) " The Pilgrim"—it was thus Sister Emmerich always designated Clement Brentano. We shall retain the title throughout this work.

into the gronnd. At a later period a small addition of two bedrooms was annexed to the principal building. In front of this humble abode stood some aged oaks, beneath whose shade the wonderful little girl of whom we write often sported with her village companions.

Clement Brentano paid a visit to Sister Emmerich's birthplace during her lifetime. And the following are his impressions of the customs of that period in the country of Münster:—

" I went three leagues from Dülmen to the hamlet of Flamske,to visit Anne Catherine's early home, then occupied by her eldest brother Bernard and his family. Dülmen belongs to the parish of St. James, Coesfeld, a city about half a league distant. I longed to see the place of her birth, the cradle of her infancy. I found it an old barn, with mud walls and a moss-covered thatched roof. The rickety door stood invitingly open, and I entered to find myself in a cloud of smoke through which I could scarcely distinguish a step ahead. A look of surprise from Bernard Emmerich and his wife greeted my unceremonious entrance. But when I introduced myself as the bearer of messages and compliments from their sister, they received me most cordially, and the little ones, shy at first, came forward on a sign from their father and kissed their tiny hands in welcome. I saw no other room than the one I had entered, a corner of which was partly partitioned off. In it stood a rude loom belonging to one of the brothers. Several old chests blackened by smoke displayed when opened the novel sight of straw beds furnished with feather pillows. Opposite this room was the still more novel spectacle of the cows behind their stacks.

" The furniture was scanty enough. Cooking utensils garnished the walls and from the rafters hung straw, hay, and tow black with soot. Here in this dingy atmosphere, in this disorder and poverty, was born and reared that favored child, so pure, so enlightened, so surpassingly rich in intellectual gifts; here was her baptismal innocence preserved untarnished. It recalled to my mind our Saviour's crib at Bethlehem. From a wooden block before the door, which served as a table, I ate a slice of brown bread and drank a mug of milk whilst conversing with Bernard Emmerich, whose genuine piety shone forth in his words, his favorite expression being, ' With God's help !'

" An old discolored picture of Our Lady hung over the spot in which Anne Catherine used to take her rest. With the owner's leave I replaced it by another, and took it with me along with some acorns from the old oaks before the door as a memento of my visit. On bidding farewell to these good people, they told me that I was the first who had ever taken so much interest in their sister's birthplace. Thence I went half a league further to Coesfeld, to visit the church in which she had received the marks of the Crown of Thorns. It was here, in the parish church of St. James, that she had received holy Baptism, September 8, 1774, which day, the Feast of Mary's Nativity, was also that of her birth (1). My visit to this beautiful old church filled me with the sweetest impressions. From it I went to see the old pastor, Father Hartbaum, whom I found still quite vigorous, despite his years. He did not seem fully to appreciate his former parishioner, and he expressed surprise at the interest manifested in her. He struck me as one of those who would willingly see things remain always the same, who care not to deviate from their daily routine, whose horizon extends not beyond the range of their own intellectual vision.

(1) Clement Brentano himself was born Sept. 8, 1778.

"I next visited St. Lambert's, the principal church, wherein is preserved the miraculous crucifix, known as the 'Crucifix of Coesfeld,' before which when a child Sister Emmerich used to spend long hours in fervent prayer, receiving in return abundant graces. It is forked like that which, at a later period, was imprinted upon her own breast. Tradition says it was brought from Palestine in the eighth century. Here it was that Sister Emmerich received the Sacrament of Confirmation. I afterward went to the Jesuit church in which, at the age of twenty-four, probably in 1798, the Crown of Thorns was laid upon her brow by her Heavenly Spouse, as she prayed toward mid-day before a crucifix in the organ-loft. It saddened me to think that this beautiful church had partly fallen into Protestant hands since the Count von Salm's residence here. The so-called communion-table stood in front of that altar from whose tabernacle had issued the apparition of the Saviour to Anne Catherine; the feast of the Reformation, that triumph of apostasy, is here annually announced from the pulpit; and the grand old organ, near which she prayed at the time of the miraculous favor, has been replaced by one of more recent make. At present, the church is used by both Catholics and Protestants, and I was told that the Countess von Salm, as if she were sole mistress, had tried to deprive the former of their right to worship in it. She also arrogated to herself the privilege of quartering her people on the Capuchins whose monastery is not far off, and she loudly complained of the annoyance caused her by the sound of the morning bells calling the faithful to Holy Mass. This church, capable of seating two thousand, is one of the most devotional I have ever seen. The whole interior is in perfect harmony, the carving of the altar, the communion rail, and the furniture most elegant and elaborate. Some might wish it a little more lofty, but that is its only defect. The beautiful floor looks as if covered with a rich carpet. As soon as it shall have passed entirely into the hands of the Protestants, they will destroy its richly carved altars as too suggestive, perhaps, of the honor once paid the God of the Eucharist.

" Coesfeld was little Anne Catherine's Jerusalem. Here she daily visited her God in the Blessed Sacrament. Thither she lovingly turned whilst working in the fields, tending her flocks, or praying by night in the open air; and from Coesfeld it was that the bells of the little convent of the Annonciades struck upon her ear, awakening in her soul a longing desire for the cloistered life. This same convent now stands dismantled and deserted.

" For several years, Sister Emmerich lived at Coesfeld with a pious mantua-maker, and for three more in a choir-master's family with a view of learning to play on the organ, hoping by this means to facilitate her entrance into some convent; finally, it was from Coesfeld that she went to accomplish her pious design. It is not surprising, therefore, that she took a lively interest in the little city, and that she was deeply afflicted at the decay of Catholic piety, even among its clergy, owing to Protestant influence and the diffusion of the so-called enlightenment of the age. Piety and morality still prevail, however, throughout the country of Münster, preserved among the youth less by the education they receive than by the frequent use of the Sacraments. The Holy Scriptures are not, indeed, found in every family, nor are quotations from them common, but the practice of their sacred lessons is plainly visible. Instruction for the people adapted to the wants of the age, began with the present generation, the teachers both male and female having been formed in the school of Dean Overberg (1), who is everywhere honored as a saint and the common father of all. His praises are heard on all sides and his zeal and simplicity shed a blessing over all his undertakings ; yet none dare affirm that his efforts have rendered them more pious and faithful than their forefathers. Though Sister Emmerich entertained the greatest veneration for him, yet she often declared her opinion, corroborated by her visions, that the poor old village schoolmasters, sometimes obliged to follow also the trade of tailoring to gain a sufficient support, received more abundant helps from God as pious instructors of youth than their modern co-laborers puffed up by successful examinations. Every work bears its own fruit. When the teacher takes complacency in his labors, when he finds therein a certain personal gratification, he consumes, so to say, the best part of the blessing accorded him for his task. This is the case nowadays when teachers say : ' We teach well; ' pupils, ' We learn well; ' and parents glory in their children's talent and education, whilst in all is engendered a seeking for empty show. Our people do, indeed, read and write much better than their forefathers; but with their improvement the devil daily sows bad seed in the way which springs up to choke piety and virtue. I feel convinced that the real source of the morality and piety still to be seen among the people of Münster lies more in their firm adherence to the traditions of faith and the customs of their religious forefathers, in the great respect for the priest and his benediction, in their fidelity to the Sacraments, than in the rapid spread of modern education. Early one morning, as I was passing along by a hedge, I heard a

---

(1) Dean Overberg (1754-1826) was a renowned priest, a great catechist, and an experienced confessor. He was the tutor of the Countess Gallitzin, and in 1809 held the position of Director of the Seminary of Münster. He wrote many books on Christian Doctrine for the use of both teachers and pupils. Dean Overberg lived and died loved and venerated by all.

child's voice. I drew near softly and peeping over I saw
a ragged little girl about seven years old driving a flock
of geese before her, a willow switch in her hand. With
an inimitable accent of piety and innocence she exclaimed :
' Good morning, dear Lord God ! Praise be to Jesus
Christ ! Good Father, who art in heaven ! Hail Mary,
full of grace ! I want to be good ! I want to be pious !
Dear saints of paradise, dear angels, I want to be good !
I have a nice little piece of bread to eat, and I thank you
for it. O watch over me ! Let not my geese run into the
wheat ! Let no bad boy throw a stone and kill one !
Watch over me, for I want to be a good girl, dear Father
in heaven !'—Doubtless, the innocent little one composed
her prayer from some old family traditions, but our modern school-mistresses would scarcely tolerate it. When I
reflect on the scanty education, the rusticity of many
among the clergy ; when I behold so little attention given
to order and neatness in many of the sacred edifices, even
in what directly appertains to the service of the altar ;
when I recall the fact, that the people all speak the Low
German, whilst sermons and instructions have been for
years delivered in the language of upper Germany ; and
when, notwithstanding, I daily perceive the purity, the
piety, the good sense of even the humblest of these people,
their aptitude for the truths of religion, I am forced to exclaim that the grace of Our Lord is more active in His
living members than in speech or in writing. It dwells
with creative force in the divine Sacraments, perpetuated
from age to age by the marvellous power attached to the
sacerdotal consecration. The Church herself is there with
her benediction, her salutary influence, her authority, and
her miracles. She has existed from all ages and she will
continue te exist to the end, for she is the work of God

Himself, and all that believe in Jesus and His Church share in her sublime gifts.

"The population of this district is scattered over a wide extent of country, a fact which greatly contributes to the preservation of morality, as well as of national character; for the people do not mutually entice one another to sin as happens in crowded cities. Each family, of which the cattle always form a part, has a house surrounded by clustering oaks which shelter it from the storms, and broad fields enclosed by hedges or embankments. Distant about a quarter of a league is another homestead similar in its surroundings, though perhaps of greater or less size. A certain number of these farms constitutes a hamlet, and several hamlets, a parish. Charming clumps of trees, verdant hedges, shady nooks lie scattered all around. As I journeyed from house to house through the green meadows, I could not restrain the exclamation: What sweet scenes for childhood's innocent years! What solitary nooks! What lovely bushes and luscious berries!—The household of the peasants and indeed that of the gentry also, in some degree, presents a character altogether patriarchal. It centres, so to say, around the fire in which quarter the very best arrangements in the house are to be found. The outer door opens directly into the kitchen, which serves also as the family sitting-room, in which is passed the greater part of their life. The beds occupy recesses in the walls, the doors of which are kept closed during the day. Sometimes in the kitchen itself, but oftener in an adjoining area, are seen to the right and left the cows and horses upon a ground floor, a few feet lower than that of the main building, their mangers being on a level with it; in feeding their heads often protrude beyond the stakes of their enclosure into the family room. A movable iron or

wooden trough conducts water from the pump to the huge
kettle over the fire, in which the food is prepared.   In one
house I saw a child turning round and round in a hole cut
in one end of a board, the other being fastened to a post by
a transverse rod —a primitive arrangement to prevent the
little one's falling into the fire.   At the further end of the
apartment, shut off by a gate, is a large open space in which
the wheat is threshed or the flax hatchelled ; overhead are
stored hay, straw, and grain.   The good wife can attend to
her culinary duties at the fireplace, and at the same time
command a view of the whole establishment.

" The narrow window panes are adorned with pictures
of events of olden times, pictures of the saints, of heraldry,
and   other   devices.   Goffine's 'Familiar Instructions,'
Overberg's Catechism, and a volume of sacred history are
either displayed to advantage on a wooden shelf, or
carefully stowed away in a chest with the Sunday clothes,
to which a couple of mellow apples are added for the sake
of their sweet perfume.   The cottage is guarded without
by stately old oaks, through whose boughs the wintry winds
whistle unheeded by the pious, simple-hearted occupants
within, who are ever ready to extend hospitality to the
wayfaring stranger.

" A degree of what one might call elegance is noticeable
in the household arrangements of the rich.   In summer
an enormous bouquet replaces the blazing fire on the hearth,
and little porcelain plates are ranged around as an additional
ornament.   Among the poor all is plainer and simpler, yet
stamped with the seal of domestic life and local custom.
One feature in their homes, which is however gradually
dying out, is the absence of a chimney.   In rainy weather
the smoke fills the dwelling like a dense vapor."

Such is Clement Brentano's account of his visit to
Flamske and the surrounding district.

CHAPTER II.

ANNE CATHERINE'S BAPTISM AND INFANCY.

Bernard Emmerich's little girl could like St. Hildegarde say : "From the dawn of existence when God awoke me in my mother's womb, breathing into me the breath of life, He infused into my soul the gift of contemplation. Before my frame with its nerves and fibres was knit together, my soul enjoyed uninterrupted visions "—for she, too, had been endowed with gifts so sublime that from her very infancy she had the use of her intellectual faculties. A few hours after her birth she was taken to Coesfeld to receive holy Baptism in the Church of St. James, and the various impressions made upon her by the persons and objects met on the way never faded from her mind. Besides the gift of sanctifying grace and the theological virtues, the light of prophecy was so abundantly infused into her soul by Baptism as to find a precedent in the Church's calendar only in a very small number of privileged souls. Toward the close of her life she alluded to it in the following words :—

"I was born on the 8th of September and to-day (Sept. 8, 1821) being the anniversary of my birth, I had a vision of the same, as also of my Baptism. It produced upon me a most singular sensation. I felt myself a new-born babe in the arms of my god-mother going to Coesfeld to be baptized, and I was covered with confusion at beholding myself so small, so weak, and at the same time so old! All the impressions I had experienced as an infant I now again felt, yet mingled with something of the intelligence of my present age. I felt shy and embarrassed. The three old women present, so also the nurse, were displeasing to me. My mother inspired very different sentiments, and I willingly took her breast. I was fully conscious of all that passed around me. I saw the old farm-house in which we dwelt with all its appurtenances, and some years later I could recognize the changes that had been made in it. I saw how the various ceremonies of Baptism ·enriched my soul with the graces which they symbolized, and my eyes and heart were miraculously enlightened and touched. The Mother of God was present with the little Infant Jesus, to whom I was espoused with a ring. I saw also my angel-guardian, and my holy patronesses Sts. Anne and Catherine.

" All that is holy, all that is blessed, all that appertains to the Church, was as perfectly intelligible to me then as now, and I saw marvellous things of the Church's essence. I *felt* the presence of God in the Most Blessed Sacrament. I saw the relics shining with light, and I recognized the saints who hovered above them. I saw all my ancestors back to the first one that had received Baptism ; and, in a series of symbolic pictures, I beheld the dangers that menaced me through life. The whole time I had most singular impressions of my god-parents, my relatives present, and above all of those three old women who were always a little repulsive to me. I saw how my ancestors had branched off into different countries. The first one baptized lived in the seventh or eighth century. He built a church. Several others became religious, and there were two who received the stigmata, but lived and died unknown to the world. Among them was a certain hermit, who had once held a high position and had had several sons. He retired into solitude and lived the life of a saint.

" On our way home through the cemetery, I had a lively perception of the state of the souls whose bodies lay there, and I was filled with veneration for some which shone with great brilliancy."

As other children experience heat and cold, pain, hunger, and thirst, so did this blessed little child perceive the relations and influences of the superior order into which holy Baptism had admitted her ; that is, the Church, the Communion of Saints, the mystical Body of Jesus. All was realized by her in the most perfect manner and, leaning from the nurse's arms, she dipped her tiny hands into the holy-water font to appropriate to herself its beneficial effects. Her dignity as child of the Church was as palpable to her as the existence of her own members and, before she could articulate, she understood the signification of feasts and of the pious customs and practices that regulated the life of her good parents, all which she observed as far as the weakness of infancy would permit. Her understanding was developed, her mysterious life regulated by her angel, who taught her to serve the triune God by the practice of the infused virtues, faith, hope, and charity. The first movements of her soul were directed toward its Creator, who took entire possession of her heart before any created good could claim it. In the splendor of baptismal innocence she belonged to that Spouse who had chosen her heart to be conformed to His own in purity, charity, and suffering. The Holy Spirit animated all the powers of her soul and directed its rapturous elevations on high. In her second year when able to pronounce a few words, she began the practice of vocal prayer with all the fervor of one long used to the exercise. Her pious father eagerly awaited the moment in which his little girl would utter her first words and, thanks to his watchfulness, they were those of the petitions of the Lord's prayer. Even in the last years of her life she gratefully recalled this fact.

"My father," she said, "took great pains with me teaching me how to say my prayers and make the sign of the Cross. He used to put me on his knee, close my hand, and teach me first the small sign of the Cross, then opening it he would guide me in making the large sign. When I was too young to say more than half the *Our Father*, I used to repeat the little I knew over and over, until I thought I had said the equivalent of the whole prayer."

To this interior light belongs the angelic virtue, holy purity, which was bestowed upon little Anne Catherine at Baptism and whose effects were shown forth even at her mother's breast. Never was she heard to cry, never was she seen in a fretful humor, but like Maria Bagnesi of Florence, or Colomba di Rieti, she was ever gentle and amiable. Her parents found their delight and consolation in their affectionate little girl, who soon became the darling of the simple-hearted peasants among whom her lot was cast. St. Catherine of Sienna's friends used to vie with one another for the possession of her when an infant, for the sight of her charmed all hearts; and Maria Bagnesi was so attractive a child that, when she was taken to see her sisters in the convent, the religious could not bear to let her leave them. It was the same with the poor little peasant-girl of Flamske; she was the joy of all around her. The lustre of purity which beamed in her whole person lent an irresistible charm to every glance, to every motion, to every word of the timid child. As she advanced in age it clothed her with a sacred character which, unknown to herself, exercised a sanctifying influence upon all that came in contact with her. When later she entered upon the most painful portion of her task of expiatory suffering, this purity of soul shone exteriorly in proportion as her pains increased; and the nearer she drew to the end of her mission, the more sensible became the mysterious power that emanated from her. When her stigmata were subjected to investigation, the ecclesiastics and physicians engaged in it rendered this same testimony; and the strongest impression received by Count Frederic Leopold von Stolberg (1) on his first visit to her, was that of her angelic innocence.

One result of this purity was that Anne Catherine preserved till death the naive simplicity of an humble, innocent child knowing nothing of herself or of the world, because her life was wholly absorbed in God. This simplicity was so pleasing to Him that it is shown us as the end of the wonderful operations of grace wrought in her soul. Her Divine Spouse ever treated her as a child and, in His wisdom, so ordered it that in the full light of supernatural knowledge flooding her soul she was always the docile pupil. With the heroism that sighed continually after fresh struggles, she evinced the most attractive timidity; in a word, her grand and arduous mission in life found her— in its accomplishment as at its commencement—a shrinking, artless child. With eyes still suffused in tears she would in an instant regain the joyousness of that age which knows not sorrow because it knows not sin, as soon as a ray of consolation mitigated the torments which like furious waves were unchained against her. These sunbeams were often pictures of her own infancy presented to her soul by the God of all goodness. Then she became once more a little

(1) Count von Stolberg was renowned in his day for the nobility of his family, the high position he held under government, his great talents and learning, and his numerous literary productions. In 1800, being then in his fiftieth year, he resigned all his offices of honor, renounced Protestantism, and became with almost all the members of his family a fervent Catholic. He was a noble champion of the faith in Germany, and with some others of his own stamp he gave new impulse to Catholic life throughout the country. He died in 1819. Among his most noted works are the following: A Translation of the Works of St. Augustine; The True Religion; The Practices of the Catholic Church; History of the Religion of Jesus Christ (in 15 vols.); History of Alfred the Great; and Meditations on the Holy Scriptures.—(Herder.)

child, a little peasant-girl in her father's house, light hearted and loving. She drew from the sight fresh energy and fortitude to push on in the way of the Cross, at every step more steep and rugged.

Although the gift of purity had been bestowed upon Anne Catherine in Baptism, yet she had to purchase its possession by mortification and penance; and, as its preservation and increase demanded an unrelenting struggle against self, the practice of patient suffering was the exercise she was destined to undertake even in the first year of her life.

" I remember," she said, " a heavy fall that I got in my first year. My mother had gone to Coesfeld to Church; but feeling that something had happened to me, she returned in great haste and anxiety. One of my limbs had to be stretched and bandaged so tightly that it became quite shrunken. I was unable to walk for a long time. It was not till my third year that I was cured."

The remembrance of this accident, as well as some of the consequences of it, Anne Catherine preserved all her life, which proves how perfect must have been her mental development at the time it happened. Guided as she was by her angel-guardian, we may presume that it was with her as with Maria Bagnesi whom she closely resembled in many particulars. Maria, too, whilst yet a tender infant, began her task of suffering by enduring the cravings of hunger. Entrusted to an unprincipled nurse, who gave her neither milk nor other nourishment, the poor child was often seen picking up with her tiny fingers the scanty crumbs that fell to the floor. She then laid the foundation for that life of wonderful mortification and suffering which rendered her, like our own little child, a source of benediction for innumerable souls.

As soon as she was able to refuse a gratification, impose

a penance, or gain a 'victory over self, Anne Catherine began so to exercise herself as far as her age permitted, following in this the never-failing direction of her angel with astonishing prudence and constancy. She had hung up in a corner a picture of the Blessed Virgin and the Infant Jesus, and put before it a block of wood for an altar. On this she laid the trifles given her from time to time, those little nothings that make children so happy. She firmly believed that these small sacrifices were highly pleasing to the Holy Infant, and she joyfully renounced in His favor every gift she received. She did it so simply and quietly that seeing nothing to remark in these apparently childlike actions, no one ever interfered in her little arrangements. As her offerings frequently disappeared, she had the happy assurance that the Infant Jesus had, indeed, taken them for Himself. The more her sacrifice had cost her, the greater was her joy on such occasions ; for with all her wonderful gifts of grace, she was still a child capable, like others of her age, of being tempted with fruit, cakes, etc. Flowers, pictures, ribands, wreaths, rings, toys, and such things of value in the eyes of a child, all had to be immolated to the holy rapture of her heart.

By such practices of mortification her purity of soul so increased that, in her third year, she offered to God this fervent prayer : "Ah ! dear Lord, let me die now, for when children grow up, they offend Thee by great sins !"

And did she step out of her father's cottage, she earnestly exclaimed :

"Rather let me fall dead on this threshold than live to offend my God !"

When she grew older and began to associate with children of her own age, she gave them, for the love of God, all that of which she could dispose ; and, if she showed a preference, it was for the poorest. A child herself of needy parents, she was bountiful in her gifts. She had not completed her fourth year when she was accustomed to deny herself at her meals, taking the worst of everything and eating so sparingly that her family wondered how she lived.

"I give this to Thee, O God," she said in her heart, "that Thou mayst divide it among those poor souls that have the most need of it."

The poor, the suffering, had so strong a hold on her affections that her first sorrows in life sprang from her great compassion for them. If she heard of any misfortune, she was so overcome that she sank down like one about to faint. Her parents' anxious questions as to the cause of her strange emotion recalled her to herself; but the desire to relieve her neighbor became so ardent that she offered herself to God, earnestly begging Him to lay upon her the miseries of others. If a beggar passed, she ran after him, calling out: "Wait, wait, I will run home and get you a piece of bread." And her good mother never refused her an alms for the poor. She even gave away her own clothing. Once she pleaded so earnestly that she obtained permission to bestow her only remaining undergarment on a poor child.

She could not see a child crying or sick without begging to suffer in its stead, and her petition was always heard; she endured the pain, and beheld the little sufferer relieved. Her prayer on such occasions ran thus: "If a poor beggar asks not, he receives not. And Thou, O my good God, Thou dost not help him who prays not and yet is unwilling to suffer! See, I cry to Thee for those that do it not for themselves!"

If she knew of a child that committed faults, she prayed for it; and to insure being heard, she imposed some punishment on herself. Years after, when asked to say how it was that at so tender an age she had thought of such things, she answered :

" I cannot say who taught me. Pity prompted it. I have always felt that we are but one single body in Jesus Christ, and my neighbor's pain is as sensible to me as if it were in one of my own fingers. I have always asked for the sufferings of others. I knew that God never sends affliction without a design ; there must be some debt to be paid off by it. And if these afflictions weigh so heavily upon us at times, it is because, as I reasoned with myself, no one is willing to help the poor sufferer to pay off his debt. Then I begged to be allowed to do so. I used to ask the Infant Jesus to help me, and I soon got what I wanted."

" I remember," she said on another occasion, " my mother had erysipelas in her face. She was lying in bed, her face all swollen. I was alone with her and greatly distressed at seeing her in such a state. I threw myself on my knees in a corner and prayed with all my heart. Then I bound a piece of linen round her head and prayed again. Soon I felt an intense toothache and my face began to swell. When my father and brothers came home, they found my mother entirely relieved, and I also soon got well."

" Some years later I again endured intolerable pains. My parents were both very ill. I knelt down by their bed near the loom and invoked Almighty God ; then I saw my hands joined over them and still praying, I was impelled to lay them upon them that they might be cured."

If she heard sin mentioned or saw it committed, she burst into tears. When questioned by her parents, she could give no satisfactory reason for her grief ; consequently, she was often rebuked for her unaccountable behaviour.

This did not, however, cool the ardor of her loving heart; she still continued to pray and do penance for her dear neighbor. One day, in her fourth year, she stood by the crib of a sick child, its mother by her side. The father, in a fit of drunken rage, hurled at his wife an axe which would have cleft the child's skull, had not Anne Catherine skilfully intercepted the blow, the axe grazing her own head as it shot by the crib. The child was saved, and the terrible consequences of the furious act prevented.

On another occasion, Anne Catherine saw some children violating modesty in their sports. She was stung to the quick, and threw herself among the nettles, begging God to accept that act in expiation.

She deeply compassionated the Jews.

"When I was a little girl," she said, "my father often took me with him to Coesfeld to make his purchases at the store of a Jew. The poor man always filled me with compassion. The thought of this hardened race, so obstinate in rejecting salvation, often brought the tears to my eyes. Ah! how much they are to be pitied! They have no idea of the holy Jews of olden times such as I see. The Jews of the present day are the descendants of the Pharisees. Their misery and blindness have always grieved me ; yet, I have often noticed that one can speak very well to them of God. Poor, poor Jews! They once had among them the living germ of salvation, but they did not recognize the fruit; they rejected it, and now they do not even seek it."

But the most astonishing of all Anne Catherine's mortifications was the practice of nocturnal prayer, begun in childhood and never after omitted. She commenced from her fourth year to curtail her hours of sleep in order to devote them to prayer. When the family was buried in slumber, she arose from her little bed and prayed with her angel two or three consecutive hours, sometimes even till morning. She loved to pray in the open air. When the weather permitted, she used to slip out to a little hill in front of the house. There she felt nearer to God, and there she knelt in prayer, her arms extended, her eyes turned toward the church at Coesfeld. We cannot suppose the child would have undertaken such a practice save through an inspiration of her angel guardian and in accordance with the designs of Almighty God who, desiring to be glorified by the prayer of so pure a creature, imparted to her the strength necessary. We must not, however, imagine that by reason of the special helps of grace bestowed upon her the practice was easy and, as it were, self-sustaining. Not at all! It was quite the contrary. It is a peculiar characteristic of such souls that they are forced to acquire little by little the perfection to which they are called, by a faithful co-operation with grace and a perpetual struggle against the weakness of nature. By virtue of this law, Almighty God permitted the latter daily to assert its rights over Anne Catherine ; her delicate frame imperiously exacted the repose indispensable to growth and strength. But the heroic little girl promptly obeyed the angel's call to prayer in spite of the involuntary shrinking of nature, in spite even of the hot tears that flowed from her eyes. She even had the courage to devise means for facilitating her rising at any hour of the night. She found none more efficient than the sharp chips and hard cords strewn on her bed purposely to render her rest uneasy, besides which she bound her waist with knotted cinctures woven by herself. It was from an increase of voluntary suffering she drew that strength which nature was not allowed to supply. God recompensed her generous efforts.

She gradually arrived at a state in which she was able to deny rest to her weary body and, up to the last moment of her life, she served her Lord, by day and by night, without repose or intermission.

Many will, perhaps, be more surprised at the fact of a child's being able to prolong her prayer two or three consecutive hours, at the tender age of four, than even at her power to deprive herself of sleep. They will ask, "What, then, was the subject of this protracted prayer?" The subject was as varied as were the objects for which God willed the child's petitions to be offered. She was shown in a vision every day the task to be accomplished by prayer. In a series of tableaux she beheld the corporal and spiritual miseries which she was to avert. She saw the sick impatient, captives dejected, the dying unprepared ; she saw travellers wandering or shipwrecked ; she saw her fellow-creatures in distress and despair, trembling on the brink of the abyss ; and, moreover, she saw that Almighty God in His mercy was ready to give them at her request help, consolation, salvation. She understood that, if she neglected penance and supplication, these souls in so great need would perish for want of assistance. Her angel sustained her in her prayer, and her burning love for her neighbor made her so confident, so eloquent, so persevering in her petitions that the hours seemed rather short than long.

At the breaking out of the French Revolution, her visions became especially varied and frightful. She was carried in spirit to the prison of Marie Antoinette, Queen of France, and told to beg strength and consolation for her. The impression she retained of this visit was so strong that she related to her family the queen's distress, and begged them all to pray for the unfortunate lady. But her friends, as might be supposed, could not understand her. They thought her dreaming, and told her quite plainly that a person who could be in two different places at one and the same time or who could see all that is going on at a distance, could be none other than a witch. Anne Catherine was so appalled at this information that she ran to confession to regain her peace of mind. She assisted, also, at many executions—helped and consoled the poor victims by her prayers. She was present in this way at the execution of the unfortunate monarch, Louis XVI.

" When I beheld the king and many other noble victims meeting death so calmly, so resignedly, I said to myself: Ah ! it is well for them to be taken from the midst of such abominations. But when I mentioned what I had seen to my parents; they thought I had lost my senses. I often knelt and with tears begged God to save such or such a person. I then saw that dangers, either impending or still remote, may be averted by the prayer of faith."

Some years later, when Anne Catherine was called upon to render to Dean Overberg, her director, an account of the prayer of her childhood, she said :—

" I always prayed less for myself than for others, that they might not sin, might not be lost. There was nothing I did not ask of God, and the more I obtained, the more I asked. I never had enough. I said confidently to myself : All things belong to God, and nothing pleases Him so much as to see me begging Him for something with my whole heart."

Dean Overberg tells us what purity of heart this wonderful little child attained by such practices. He says : " From her sixth year Anne Catherine knew no other joys than those she found in God, no other sorrows than those that pierced her heart at the thought of His being outraged by men. When she began to practise mortification of the senses, the love of God was enkindled in her heart with such intensity that she often cried out in the midst of her prayer : 'Were there no heaven, no purgatory, no hell, I would still love Thee, O my God, with my whole heart and soul !' "

The poor sufferers in purgatory shared largely in her spiritual alms, and they often appeared to her, claiming her pity. Even in winter she arose at night and went out in the snow to pray with extended arms for their relief, until frozen stiff with cold. Sometimes she knelt on a triangular block of wood whose sharp edge cut deep into her knees ; or, again, she forced her way through stinging nettles to discipline her innocent flesh, that penance might lend efficacy to her prayer. In return for her charity, she often had the consolation of receiving the thanks of the souls that she had delivered.

"When I was a little child," she says, "I was taken by a person unknown to me to a place which appeared to be purgatory. I saw crowds of souls in excruciating torments who earnestly begged for prayers. I thought I was in a deep abyss. I saw a great, broad space, frightful, pitiable to behold. In it were the poor souls, silent and afflicted, yet not without joy and hope in the mercy of God. I saw no fire, but I felt that the souls were racked by the most intense interior sufferings."

" Whilst praying for them, I often heard voices around me, saying : 'Thank you ! thank you !' Once, on my way from church, I lost a little bag that my mother had given me. I was very much concerned at my carelessness, and I forgot that evening to offer my accustomed suffrages for the dear souls. I had to go to the shed for wood, and as I went along a white figure covered with black spots, appeared before me, saying : ' Thou art forgetting me !'—

I was very much frightened, and began right off to say some prayers. The next day I prayed hard and found my bag in the snow.

" When I grew older, I used to go very early in the morning to hear Mass at Coesfeld. I always chose a lonely road, that I might pray without distraction for the suffering souls. When it was still dark, I used to see them floating before me two by two, like fiery sparks in a dull flame. The way was lit up before me and I rejoiced in their presence, for I both knew and loved them. They often came at night to beg help in their pains."

CHAPTER III.

Anne Catherine is Led by the Way of Visions.

When little Anne Catherine began to talk, the wonders revealed by infused light to her soul were soon made known to all around. Her father's favorite recreation, as he sat by the fire after his day's toil, was to take his little daughter on his knee and listen to the marvellous things she would relate at his bidding. "Anna Kathrinchen," he would say, "now here we are! now tell me something!" (1) Then she would describe to him the pictures shown her from the Old Testament, until the good man would exclaim, with tears in his eyes: "But, child, where did you get all that?" (2) And the little one would answer earnestly: "Father, it is all true! That is the way I saw it!" Whereupon the astonished father would become silent and forbear to question further.

No special time was chosen for the unveiling of these pictures before the eyes of her soul—all hours of the day, all occupations were the same. Anne Catherine thought that every one had visions, as well as herself; consequently, she used to speak of them quite freely. But when her little playmates contradicted or ridiculed her on the subject, she became pensive and silent. Once it happened that a hermit, who wanted to impress his hearers with the belief that he had been in Rome and Jerusalem, spoke of the Holy Places, but in a manner altogether incorrect. Anne Catherine, who had been silently listening by the side

---

(1) "*Anna Kathrinchen, nun bist du in meinem Kämmerchen, nun erzähle mir etwas!*"

(2) "*Kind, woher hast du das?*"

of her parents, could not long restrain her indignation. She boldly taxed the man with falsehood, describing the Holy Places herself as if perfectly familiar with them, until her parents checked her vivacity and she became silent.

Anne Catherine went to the village school taught by an old peasant. One day she described the Resurrection of our Lord as she had seen it in vision, for which she received a severe reprimand and an injunction never again to indulge such imaginations. This treatment sealed the lips of the frightened child, who ever after refrained from communicating what passed in her interior. Her visions, however, were not discontinued. The truths and mysteries of holy faith, linked together in grand historic pictures, passed in still greater numbers before the eyes of her soul; wherever she chanced to be, they formed the subject of her contemplation.

The Twelve Articles of the Apostles' Creed were presented to her during the course of the ecclesiastical year. She contemplated the creation of heaven, the fall of the angels, the creation of the earth and Paradise; she beheld Adam and Eve and their fall. In successive visions, she followed, through ages and generations, the development of the holy mysteries of the Incarnation and the Redemption. The scenes of Sacred History and the personages of the Old Testament were better known to her than those of her own life; and those saints who, by their relationship to the Sacred Humanity of Jesus Christ, appear more closely connected with the faithful, were shown her in vision as communicating directly with her. Among them were the holy families of Joachim and Anne, of Zachary and Elizabeth, with whom she kept up the most familiar and affectionate intercourse. With them she celebrated the feasts of the time of Promise, made pilgrimages to Jerusalem and other holy places, sighed for the Saviour's coming, hailed His advent, and adored Him at His birth.

The Temple of Jerusalem (1), the splendor and magnificence of the worship there offered to the Most High, the Ark of the Covenant and all it contained, the mysteries of the Holy of Holies, understood by so few, the chanting of psalms, the numerous ceremonies and observances of the Old Law, all were perfectly familiar to her even in their slightest details. She understood, likewise, the pious customs and traditions of the faithful Israelites in the fulfilment of the law and the government of their family.

These contemplations were not for her a vain show; she actually lived among the scenes and associated with the actors of a thousand years ago. In this she resembled St. Catherine of Sienna, who also had been prepared by visions for the important part she was to play in the history of the Church. Her abstraction of soul from the things of this life, her recollection in God were so great that even when surrounded by the tumult of the world, in the midst of Popes and princes, she was as inaccessible to every distraction as if in the sanctuary of her own cell. She had acquired this power in the school of the penitents of the Thebaid whom she contemplated for many years in so real a way that with them she wove baskets and mats, chanted psalms, fasted, performed penances, observed silence; in one word, practised with them those mortifications which elevated her

(1) The history of Jerusalem from the date of its foundation was unfolded before her in successive pictures; in her childhood she knew of the Knights-Templars. "The first time that I saw some soldiers passing through our country," she said, "I thought they surely must be the same that I had seen in vision, and I scanned them closely to discover some belonging to a religious Military Order. I would have known them by their dress, a white habit ornamented with crosses, and a sword hanging from a little belt. I saw some of them far, far away among the Turks. They had secret practices like the Free-Masons, and I saw that many perished at their hands. I was surprised at not seeing any such soldiers among the troops marching by, and I found out afterward that they for whom I looked in vain were the Knights-Templars, and that the Order had long ceased to exist.

to perfect union with God. St. Paul, St. Antony, St. Pacomius, St. Hilarion, were her models and teachers. She communicated as intimately with them as Anne Catherine with St. Joachim, St. Anne, and their holy predecessors.

Although Anne Catherine celebrated in spirit the feasts of the Old Law as if really contemporary with them, yet she was, at the same time, a child of our holy Catholic faith; since in these prophetic figures and mysteries, she contemplated their fulfilment, seeing in them both their actual celebration and the historical events that gave rise to them. Her marvellous intuition embraced the whole plan of Redemption. These were the visions of her early years; they were succeeded by others, no less comprehensive, on the life of our Holy Redeemer. This order was in conformity with the task imposed upon her. She was called to suffer for the faith at a time in which men, in their insensate malice, questioned even the possibility of divine revelation, denied the mystery of the Incarnation and Redemption, and blasphemed the prophets, the Apostles, and the saints with diabolical rage; a time in which the enemies of God daily gained fresh recruits even from the ranks of the priesthood. At this terrible epoch it was that God gave to Anne Catherine full and clear knowledge of the truths of religion. He called upon her to bear witness to the accomplishment of His eternal decrees, and the purity and ardent love of her heart indemnified Him in some degree for the outrages offered to His mercy.

Our Saviour Himself deigned to be her guide through the immense circle of visions granted her, and He communicated to her the light to understand His hidden mysteries. With Him she visited the places sanctified by His presence, and learned from His own lips the mysteries there enacted for the salvation of fallen humanity. His never-failing assistance gave her the strength to support the infinite variety of her visions, and to maintain her interior and contemplative life in harmony with the exterior. For whole days she was lost in contemplation, her soul perfectly abstracted from the things of sense ; but, in spite of this, the duties imposed upon her by her parents were as promptly and carefully fulfilled, as if she had no thought beyond. It was proper that no exterior affair should disturb her contemplation ; therefore, God bestowed upon her wonderful aptitude for manual labor and domestic duties. As soon as she opened a book, she could read its contents ; whatever work she undertook, either in the house or field, instantly succeeded ; it appeared as if her very touch imparted a blessing even to things inanimate. Her friends were so accustomed to her taking part in the most painful labors and accomplishing them well, that they respected her interior recollection, and never intruded upon her by inquisitive questioning.

The embarrassing task of rendering an account of her visions had not yet been imposed upon Anne Catherine ; she had not yet been called upon to confine in the narrow compass of human language the spiritual riches lavished upon her. She herself could gaze upon them only by the prophetic light shed upon her soul; she saw them not under a form capable of being clothed in words. Although pain and suffering were - her constant companions, yet they could not ruffle the profound peace and recollection in which her days glided by. In after years she often sighed for the silence and solitude of her childhood. She used to say : " When I was a little girl, I was continually absorbed in God. I performed all my duties without interfering with this abstraction. I was always in contemplation. Working with my parents in the fields, or engaged in any other labor, I was, as it were, lifted above the earth. Exterior things were like a confused and painful dream, within all was heavenly light and truth."

Our Lord deigned to be her teacher not only in the regions of contemplation, but also in the practice of piety. He played with her as a little child that He might lead her step by step to perfection, to the highest conformity with Himself. Sometimes He appeared to her as a child of her own age, a cross on His shoulders. He would stand and gaze at her in silence until she, in her turn, would snatch up a heavy log of wood and carry it after Him as far as she could, praying all the time ; or again, she beheld Him in tears at the treatment He endured from disobedient children, and at this sight, she would throw herself among the nettles to console Him by her own penance. When she made the Way of the Cross, He used to lay His own cross upon her shoulders. When she kept the cows in the fields, which she did when only five years old, He came to her under the appearance of a child looking for its little companions, eager to share their sports and labors. He wished thereby to teach her by word and example to turn all her actions to God. He endued her with intelligence to act only for His glory, and taught her to sanctify even her little amusements.

In connection with this subject, she used to relate some very pleasing little incidents.

" When I was a child," she said, " the Little Boy used to come and work with me. At the age of six I did just what I now do. I knew, though I cannot say how, that I was soon to have a baby brother, and I wanted to make my mother something for the child ; but I could not sew. The Little Boy came to my aid and showed me how to make a little cap and other things necessary for infants.

My mother was astonished at my successful attempts, and she gladly made use of the articles."

" When I first began to mind the cows, the Little Boy used to meet me in the fields, and so arranged matters that my cows took good care of themselves. Then we used to talk together about all kinds of holy things, that we wanted to serve God and love the Infant Jesus, and that God sees all things. These encounters often took place, and nothing appeared impossible to me when I was with Him. We sewed, we made caps and stockings for poor children. I could do whatever I wanted, and I had everything necessary for my work. Occasionally some of the nuns of the ' Annunciation of the Blessed Virgin' (1) joined us. There was one thing that puzzled me : I always thought that I myself was managing everything, whereas it was, in reality, the Little Boy who was doing it all."

The blessing emanating from such intercourse was communicated by Anne Catherine to all with whom she came in contact ; but it was chiefly among children of her own age that she practised the teachings she had received. She spoke to them so charmingly of the presence of God, of the Infant Jesus, and of their angel-guardian, that the little ones listened with delight. When she went with them to gather stubble along the roads, she arranged them in procession, reminding them of their holy angels who also were present.

" We ought," she said, " to imitate the blessed in heaven. We should do nothing bad ourselves and, when we can, we ought to keep others from doing it. If, for instance, we come across traps or nets set by idle boys to catch hares or birds, we ought to remove them, that such petty thefts may be prevented. We ought to begin, little by little, to lead a new life, a life of heaven upon earth."

(1) The Annonciades.

If she played in the sand with other children, her skil-ful hands piled it up in imitation of the Holy Places of Jerusalem such as she had seen in her visions. She after-ward said in allusion to this : " If I had had some one to help me, I could have made models of most of the roads and places of the Holy Land. They were always before my eyes; no locality was better known to me. When playing with my companions in the moist sand, I used to build up a Mt. Calvary, lay out a garden, and hollow out a sepulchre in it ; then I formed a brook with a bridge over it and houses on either side. I can remember how I joined the square houses and cut with a chip strange looking openings for windows. Once I was about to make figures to repre-sent our Saviour, the Blessed Mother at the foot of the Cross, and the two thieves, but I gave up the idea as irreverent. One day two children and myself were playing in the fields. We wanted a cross for the little mud-chapel we had built, to say our prayers before it, but we knew not where to get one. At last, I cried out : 'I know, I know! Let us make a wooden one and then press it down into the soft clay until it leaves a deep mark. I can get an old pewter lid we have at home. We'll melt it, pour it into the mark, and when it cools, we'll have a beautiful cross.' I ran to the house to get the lid and fire to melt it. But just as we were ready to begin our work, my mother made her appearance and I was punished."

St. John the Baptist also shared Anne Catherine's inno-cent amusements, appearing to her as a child such as he was when he dwelt in the desert under the guardianship of the angels, irrational creatures his only companions. When she went out with the cows, she used to call him : " Come, little John ! I want little John in his sheepskin," and he came im-mediately to keep the child company. His life in the desert was shown her in detailed visions, and he taught her to imitate that ineffable purity and simplicity which had rendered him so pleasing to God. Whilst celebrating with him the marvels of his birth, she was conducted into his paternal home, and introduced to the wide circle of his relatives. She knew them all well; she felt more at home among them than even in her father's house.

To what an extent this mysterious intercourse with the characters of Sacred History was interwoven with the outward life of the child, we may glean from her own words. When, shortly before her death, she related her visions on the life of Our Lord, she gave the following account of what passed within her respecting them :

" Every Advent since my childhood I have accompanied St. Joseph and the Blessed Virgin from Nazareth to Bethlehem. The solicitude I felt for the holy Mother of God, and my share in all the difficulties of the journey, were as real for me as any other incident of my life. I took a far greater interest in it all, I was more affected by it than I could possibly be by anything that might happen to myself; for Mary was the Mother of my Lord and my God ; she bore in her womb my salvation. The feasts of the Church were for me not only simple commemorations or subjects of attentive consideration ; my soul actually took part in them, as if the mysteries they celebrated were under my very eyes. I saw them, I felt them, as if present before me."

So lively an intuition could not lie dormant in her soul ; its influence marked her every action. Filled with tender love for Mary, she did with childish eagerness all she would have done had she really lived with the Holy Family; for instance, if she beheld Mary and Joseph journeying toward Bethlehem, she joined them in spirit ; if she went out to pray by night, she waited on the road for Mary, and she deprived herself of food that she might have something to offer the holy travellers wearied by their long journey. She took her own short repose on the bare ground, that her little bed might be free for the Mother of God; she ran out on the road to meet her, or waited for her in prayer under a tree, because she knew that Mary would rest beneath its shade. On Christmas Eve she had so distinct a perception of the Blessed Virgin's arrival in the grotto of Bethlehem, that she lit a fire to warm her and to enable her to prepare some food. All that she had to dispose of, she held in readiness to offer to the Divine Mother.

"Almighty God," she said one day, "must have been pleased with this good-will of a child, for, from my infancy to the present time, He has shown me every year during Advent all the circumstances of His coming, and always in the same way. I am always seated in a little corner from which I can see everything. When a child I was free and unrestrained with Him; but, when I became a religious, I was much more timid and reserved. At my earnest request, the Blessed Virgin often laid the Infant Jesus in my arms."

These tender and intimate relations with God and His saints awoke in the child's heart a desire, or rather an insatiable thirst for purity and penance which suffering alone could allay. The visions that nourished her soul wonderfully increased her exquisitely delicate perception of all that is pure and holy, and filled her with horror of sin and everything leading to it. This instinct was an infallible guide on which she could rely as unerringly as upon her angel-guardian. It increased in delicacy and power in proportion to her fidelity in following the impulse of the Holy Ghost, urging her to watch scrupulously over her senses and conscience by virtue of the abundant graces that enriched her soul. Before the world's corruption could sully her sight, her eyes had gazed in vision on the splendors of sanctifying grace and innocence as existing in paradise. She knew the infinite value of the merits of the Redeemer, who deigned to restore fallen man to his pristine purity, even before he was conscious of the dangers menacing his soul. Her love of purity was like a consuming fire ; it destroyed whatever could sully her soul before it had the power to touch her. Her director, Dean Overberg, renders the following testimony:—

" Anne Catherine never e⁻perienced a movement of sensuality, never had to accuse herself of even a thought against holy purity. When questioned as to this perfect exemption from every temptation to the opposite vice, she answered in obedience that she had been shown in a vision that her nature would have inclined her thereto; but that, owing to her early mortification, her efforts to repress her desires and to surmount all other vicious inclinations, she had rooted out these evil propensities even before they had made themselves felt.

This unerring instinct was manifested in her childhood in a singularly touching manner, as may be seen by the following communication made whilst relating her visions of paradise :

" I remember that when I was about four years old, my parents took me one day to church, where I was sure I would see God and meet people very different from any I knew. I thought they would be far more beautiful, indeed quite resplendent. I looked all around the church as I entered, but saw nothing of what I had pictured to myself. ' The priest there at the altar,' I said to myself, ' may, perhaps, be God, but where is the Blessed Virgin Mary ?' I expected, too, the whole heavenly court to be in attendance ;

but alas! I was disappointed. After awhile I saw two
pious-looking women, who wore beads and appeared more
devout than their neighbors. I thought, perhaps, they
were those for whom I was looking; but no, they were
not. I used to think that Mary wore a white robe, a sky-
blue mantle, and a white veil. I had had before this the
vision of paradise, so I now looked through the church for
Adam and Eve, hoping to see them as beautiful as they
were before their fall; but disappointed in this also, I said
to myself: 'Wait till you have been to confession, then
you will find them.' But alas! even then I found them
not. I saw a pious noble family in the church, the daughters all in white. I felt that they came a little nearer to
those whom I sought, and I conceived very great respect
for them. Still I was not satisfied. I felt that what I had
once seen so beatiful had now become sullied and deformed.
I was so taken up by these thoughts that I forgot to eat.
I often heard my parents say: 'What is the matter
with the child? What has happened to little Anne
Catherine?' Sometimes, too, I would complain to Almighty
God that He had done such or such a thing. I could not
understand how He, who is all powerful, could have allowed
sin to enter the world; and the endless duration of hell
torments seemed to me incompatible with His attribute of
mercy. Then I was instructed in visions on the infinite
goodness and justice of God, and I was soon convinced
that, if things were according to my ideas, they would
be very miserable."

After what we have thus far seen of little Anne Catherine,
we may lawfully apply to her the words of Prof. Sebastian of
Perouse, when speaking of Blessed Columba di Rieti:

" This child was born for a life elevated above the
senses; she was to be liquified in the fire of charity, to be

inflamed with the love of God and the neighbor. She was
so well grounded in her holy vocation that she could not be
disconcerted by the insinuations of the evil one, troubled
by pride, nor attacked by the sting of the flesh." And
how, indeed, could Anne Catherine's soul receive such illumination, did it dwell in a body which was not as pure
as a lily, in a body which knew no other law than that
which subjecṭd it wholly to God ?

CHAPTER IV.

Early Training and Education.

A closer acquaintance with the thrice-happy parents to whose care Almighty God had confided so precious a treasure, affords a fresh proof of the wonderful vigilance of Divine Providence in arranging even the least details connected with His chosen ones, that all things may concur in the fulfilment of the mission assigned them.

Anne Cathèrine was the child of truly pious souls who, contented in their poverty because it was consecrated to God, found a rich indemnification for the want of material goods in the heavenly blessings shed upon them. Their whole life presented to the child a perfect model of Christian faith, and she received, thanks to their gentle firmness, an education best suited to her high vocation. Her father's house was a school of piety for his children; even in her last years, Anne Catherine gratefully recalled the advice given her by her good parents and the pious and regular habits to which they had trained her. She loved to speak of them. Their whole life might be written from the words of their child.

"My father was very pious and upright, of a serious disposition, but by no means morose or inclined to sadness. His poverty obliged him to hard labor, but he was not actuated by the love of gain. He had a childlike trust in God and performed his daily toil like a faithful servant without anxiety or cupidity. His conversation was full of beautiful, homely proverbs, interspersed with pious, simple expressions. One day he told us the history of a great man named Hun,

who travelled all over the globe.   That night I dreamed
that I saw this great man wandering over the earth and
turning up with an immense spade good and bad soil.   As
my father was very laborious himself, he taught me to work
hard even in my childhood.   Summer and winter, I had
to go out to the fields before daybreak to catch a vicious
horse which kicked and bit and used to run away from my
father.   The vicious creature used to let me catch him; indeed, he sometimes came himself to meet me.   I used to
climb on a stone or mound, get on his back, and ride home
in triumph.   If he took a notion to turn his head to bite,
I would give him a blow on the nose, which made him trot
on quietly as before.   I used to haul manure and produce
with him.   I cannot now understand how I managed
him at all.

"We often went into the fields before daybreak.   At the
moment of sunrise my father used to uncover his head and
say some prayers; then he would speak to me of the great
God who made His sun rise so gloriously above us.   He
often said it was a shameful thing to lie in bed whilst the
sun rose high in the heavens, for it leads to the ruin of
whole families, countries, and nations.   Once I replied: 'Yes,
but that does not mean me, for the sun cannot get near my
little bed!' and he answered: 'Even if you cannot see the
rising sun, he sees you—he shines everywhere.'   I thought
over these words a long time.

"On another occasion, he said to me: 'See, no one has
yet trodden in the dew!   We are the first and, if we pray
devoutly, we shall draw down blessings upon the earth.   It
is good to walk on the morning dew before any one else has
touched it.   There is a blessing upon it then, entirely fresh.
No sin has yet been committed in the fields, no bad word
has been spoken.   When the dew has been trodden under

foot, it seems as if the freshness and beauty of morning had flown.'

"Although very small and delicate, yet I always had to work hard, either around the house or out in the fields with my brothers and sisters. Once I had to load a cart with about twenty sacks of corn. I did it without stopping to rest, and more quickly than a strong boy could have done it. In the same way I used to reap and mow.

"Sometimes I led the horse for my father, sometimes I harrowed the ground. I did all kinds of field labor. Occasionally when we paused a moment to rest, my father would exclaim: 'Ah! how fortunate! Look! We can see straight ahead to Coesfeld. There is the church! We can adore Our Lord in the Blessed Sacrament. He watches us and blesses our work.' When the bell rang for Mass, he would take off his hat and say a little prayer. Then he would say: 'Now we must follow the Holy Mass,' and still continuing his work, he would utter a few words from time to time, such as: 'Now the priest is at the Gloria, now the Sanctus—we must say such or such a prayer and make the sign of the cross,' and sometimes he would sing a verse from the Holy Scriptures, or whistle a tune. Whilst I went on harrowing, he would say: 'They make great account of miracles, and yet we live only by miracles and the pure goodness of God. See the grain of wheat in the ground! There it lies and sends up a long stalk that reproduces it a hundred-fold. Is not that a great miracle?'

"On Sunday afternoons he used to rehearse the sermon of the morning for us, commenting upon it in the most edifying manner, and end by reading aloud an explanation of the Gospel."

Anne Catherine's mother was equally good and pious. In twenty-one years of married life she had given birth to nine children, the first in 1766, the last in 1787. She was a happy, contented, and faithful wife. Her life of incessant care and toil had stamped her countenance with rather a grave expression, without, however, embittering her heart; that was kind and gentle toward all. The incessant struggle to procure a suitable maintenance never brought a complaint to her lips ; on the contrary, in a spirit of prayer, she looked upon the necessity to labor as a favor from Heaven, and thought only of being in the eyes of God a faithful stewardess. In after years, Anne Catherine thus spoke of her :

" It was my mother who gave me my first lessons in Catechism. Her favorite ejaculations were : ' *Lord, give me patience,* and then strike hard !'—' Lord, may Thy will, not mine, be done !' I have never forgotten them. When I played with my young companions, my mother used to say : ' If children play together innocently, the angels join them ; sometimes even the little Infant Jesus comes, too.' I looked upon this as literally true, and it did not in the least astonish me. I often cast a searching glance up at the sky to see if they were coming. I sometimes imagined them present, although we could not see them. That they might not fail to come, we always played innocent games. My mother taught me to walk last and to say my prayers on the way when I went out with other children to church or elsewhere. She said that by doing so I should neither hear nor see anything bad. When I made the sign of the cross on my forehead, lips, and breast, I said to myself that these crosses were the keys to lock up my heart against everything hurtful, and that the Infant Jesus alone should hold them. All goes well when He has charge of them."

Anne Catherine saw nothing in the whole life of her

parents that was not in accordance with the commandments of God and the Church. The only joys that
lightened their labors were those they found in the celebration of her festivals. These simple souls were well suited for
such happiness; for never was their work so pressing,
their fatigue so great, as to prevent their making any
sacrifice for the good of their neighbor. Bernard Emmerich after his long day's toil never neglected to remind
his little ones, as night closed in, to pray for travellers,
for poor soldiers, for their fellow creatures in distress, he
himself saying particular prayers for such intentions. During the three days of Carnival, the mother accustomed her
children to prostrate and with extended arms to say four times
the *Our Father,* in order to avert all attacks upon innocence during those days : " Children," she used to say to
them, " you do not understand it, but I know it well.
Pray !"

The following incident shows how God blessed the
words and example of these good parents :—

" When we were very small, my eldest brother and I
slept in the same room. He was very pious, and we often
prayed together, kneeling by our little beds, our arms extended in the form of a cross. I often saw the room
all lighted up. Sometimes, after kneeling a long while in
prayer, I was suddenly jerked up with violence by some
invisible force, and a voice cried : ' Go to bed ! Go to
bed !' This used to frighten my brother very much, but
its only effect upon me was to make me pray the longer.
My brother himself did not escape these attacks of the evil
one who often tried to trouble him during his prayers.
My parents once found him kneeling with his arms extended, perfectly stiff with the cold."

As these good people were too humble to look upon the

unremitting practice of their Christian duties as anything extraordinary, so neither did the phenomena they witnessed in their child arouse in them feelings of pride. They beheld with grateful emotion the gifts of grace with which she was endowed; but they concealed their wonder and continued to treat her as they did their other children. The mother chided her little Anne Catherine as severely for her faults as she did her brothers and sisters, and, even in her babyhood, she was not exempt from her share in the family duties. She was thus kept in happy ignorance of herself. Her simplicity and humility were never endangered by praise, admiration, or indiscreet curiosity. Her rich interior life remained hidden and unknown, expanding with ever-increasing beauty under the conduct of her angel-guardian, who regulated all her sentiments, thoughts, and words, and restrained her ardent nature by the constant practice of obedience.

Her parents, it is true, felt more than ordinary affection for this child, but it was contrary to their nature to manifest it by exterior marks or caresses. It was almost a necessity for Bernard Emmerich to have his winning, discreet little girl near him when he worked in the fields. Her childish remarks, her answers to his questions, her whole demeanor were so pleasing to him that he could not bear to have her absent from his side. Her mother was too much occupied with the care of her younger children to give as much of her attention to Anne Catherine as her husband. The father's sprightly disposition had been inherited by the child, who cheered his daily toil by her innocent sportiveness. She was naturally gay, as might be expected of one admitted to so familiar intercourse with God and His saints. Her forehead was high and well-formed, and the sweet light of her clear brown eyes shed an air of serenity over her whole countenance. Her dark hair was thrown back either in braids or coils around her head, and her silvery voice and vivacity of expression revealed the intelligence of her mind. She spoke with ease and fluency of things that seemed mysterious and unintelligible to her hearers; but her modest and humble reserve soon dispelled the impression produced by these unexpected flashes of superior gifts. She was so sweet, so kind, her eagerness to be of service to others was so charming that young and old flocked to little Anne Catherine to receive assistance and advice. Although ignorant of her high gifts, none could help loving her. These simple peasants knew well that there was no sacrifice that she would not make for their good, and they were as much accustomed to the blessings that emanated from her as to the perfume of the rosemary in their own gardens.

"When I was a child." she said, "the neighbors used to come to me to bind up their wounds, because I tried to do it carefully and gently. I was skilful at such things. When I saw an abscess, I used to say to myself: 'If you squeeze it, it will get worse; the matter must, however, come out in some way.' Then I sucked it gently and it soon healed. No one taught me that. It was the desire of rendering myself useful that led me to do it. At first, I felt disgust, but that only made me overcome myself, for disgust is not compassion. When I promptly surmounted the feeling, I was filled with tender joy. I thought of Our Lord who did the same for all mankind."

Sometimes her color changed from a bright red to a livid pallor, her sparkling eyes grew suddenly dim, her simple gayety was exchanged for gravity, and a shade of inexplicable sadness passed over her countenance —she was hardly recognizable. Her parents anxiously questioned each other :

' What is the matter with the child ?" The cause of this
sudden change lay in the sad sight of the miseries of mankind presented to her mind. As she could not hear the
name of God or a saint without falling into contemplation,
so neither could mention be made in her presence
of any accident or misfortune, without her soul's being
irresistibly borne to the scene of suffering by her desire to
relieve it at any cost. Her friends, as may be supposed,
could not account for her singular conduct, and her mother's
uneasiness soon gave way to displeasure on beholding the
child's languor disappear as quickly as it had come. She
ascribed these unaccountable changes to caprice, and thought
reproofs and punishments the best remedy to apply to
them ; therefore she sometimes chastised the little girl
severely when the latter, overwhelmed by interior sufferings, was scarcely able to stand. But the undeserved
treatment was received with such patience and submission,
the child was still so bright and loving, that the father and
mother gazed at each other in amazement, saying : " What
a strange child ! Nothing ever appears to intimidate her.
What will become of her !" It was not only the angel's
admonitions that influenced Anne Catherine to bear this
harsh treatment for the love of God, it was her own conviction that she deserved all kinds of punishment.

"In my childhood," she says, "I was irritable and
whimsical, and I was often punished on that account. It
was hard for me to repress my capricious humor. My
parents often blamed and never praised me; and, as I
used to hear other parents praising their children, I began
to look upon myself as the worst child in the world. What
disquieted me most was the fear of being an object of abhorrence in the sight of God also. But one day I saw some
children very disrespectful toward their parents, and,

though pained at the sight, yet I felt somewhat reassured, as I thought I might still hope, for I could never do so bad a thing as that."

Anne Catherine found the greatest difficulty in repressing her vivacity, crushing self-will, and submitting entirely to that of others. Her tender heart, her exquisite sensitiveness, ever alive to a thousand things which others would pass over unheeded, her ardent zeal for the glory of God and the salvation of her neighbor, obliged her to repeated efforts to acquire meekness founded upon self-forgetfulness and obedience so perfect that the first movements of resistance were stifled in their birth. Her courageous soul gained the victory, however, and her fidelity was so freely recompensed that she could say in later years : —

" Obedience was my strength, my consolation. Thanks to obedience, I could pray with a peaceful, joyous mind. I could commune with God—my heart was free."

She not only thought herself the least and last of creatures, she actually felt herself such and regulated her whole conduct by this inward conviction. Her angel tolerated no imperfection ; he punished every fault by reprimands and penances. In her fifth year, she one day saw through a garden-hedge an apple lying under a tree, and felt a childish desire to eat it. Scarcely was the thought conceived when her contrition for this covetousness was so great that she imposed upon herself as a penance never again to touch an apple, a resolution to which she ever faithfully adhered. On another occasion, she felt a slight aversion for a woman who had spoken disparagingly of her parents, and she resolved not to salute her the next time she met her. This resolve she acted on, though not without an effort. The next moment she was so contrite that she instantly turned back and begged pardon for her rudeness.

When she began to approach the Sacrament of Penance, her delicate conscience gave her no peace after faults of this kind until she had bitterly accused herself of them to her confessor and received penance and absolution.

That these early interior sufferings and her penitential life might not banish the innocent gayety of childhood from her heart, God in His goodness amply indemnified her by the joy she derived from the uninterrupted contemplation of the greatness and magnificence of creation and by her constant intercourse with irrational creatures. When alone in the woods or fields, she would call the birds to her, sing with them the praises of their Maker, and caress them as they perched familiarly on her shoulder. If she found a nest, she peeped into it with beating heart and spoke the sweetest words to the little ones within. She knew where the earliest flowers bloomed, and gathered them to weave into garlands for the Infant Jesus and His Mother. But her eye, enlightened by grace, saw far beyond the senses. Other children are amused by picture-books. They take more delight in painted flowers and animals than in the glowing colors of animated nature. But for Anne Catherine creatures were themselves the pictures in which she exultingly admired the wisdom and goodness of the Creator. She knew their nature and varied properties, as she intimates in her account of her visions of St. John the Baptist:—

" What John learned in the desert of flowers and animals never surprised me ; for, when I myself was a child, every leaf, every tiny flower, was a book which I could read. I perceived the beauty and signification of color and form ; but when I spoke of it, my hearers only laughed at me. I could entertain myself with everything I met in the fields. I understood everything, I could even see into the flowers and animals. O how charming it all was ! I had a fever when

I was young which, however, did not prevent my going
about. My parents thought I would die, but a beautiful Child came and showed me some herbs which
would cure me if I ate them. He told me also to suck the
sweet juice of the bind-weed blossom. I did both, and I
was soon quite well. I have always been exceedingly fond
of camomile flowers. There is something agreeable to me in
their very name. Even in my childhood I gathered them
and kept them in readiness for the sick poor who came to
me in their ailments. I used to think of all sorts of simple
remedies for them."

The beauty of the sacred discipline of the Church was
also manifested to her, as the following lines will prove :—

"The sound of blessed bells has always been to me like
a ray of benediction which banishes hurtful influences
wherever it reaches. I think such sounds terrify Satan.
When I used to pray at night in the fields, I often felt and,
indeed, saw evil spirits around me ; but, as soon as the bells
of Coesfeld sounded for matins, they fled. I used to think
that, when the voices of the clergy were heard at a great
distance, as in the early ages of the Church, there was no
need of bells ; but that now these brazen tongues were
necessary. All things ought to serve the Lord Jesus, pro-
mote our salvation, and protect us against the enemy of our
soul. God has imparted His benediction to His ministers
that, emanating from them, it may penetrate all things and
make them subservient to His glory. But when the Spirit
of God withdraws from the priests and the bells alone diffuse
His benediction and put the evil one to flight, it is like a
tree which appears to flourish. It receives nourishment
through its bark, but the heart-wood is rotten and dry. The
ringing of blessed bells strikes me as essentially more
sacred, more joyous, more animating, and far sweeter than

all other sounds, which are in comparison dull and confused ; even the music of a church organ falls far short in fulness and richness."

The language of the Church made a still more lively impression upon her. The Latin prayers of Mass and all the ceremonies of the divine service were as intelligible to her as her mother-tongue, and it was long before she discovered that all the faithful did not understand them as well as herself.

" I was never conscious of any difference," she said, " between my own language and that made use of by the Holy Church. I understood not only the words but even the various ceremonies themselves."

She had so keen a perception of the power and beneficent influence of the priestly benediction, that she could tell when a priest was passing the house. She felt herself involuntarily drawn to run out and get his blessing. If she happened to be minding the cows at the time, she quickly recommended them to her angel-guardian, and set off in pursuit of the priest.

She always wore around her neck, in a little bag, the Gospel of St. John. On this point she says :

" The Gospel of St. John has ever been for me a source of light and strength, a real buckler. When frightened or in any danger, I used to say confidently : *And the Word was made flesh and dwelt among us.* I never could understand how some priests could call these words unintelligible, and yet I have really heard them say so."

As Anne Catherine was keenly alive to whatever had received the blessing of Holy Church, she was, on the contrary, seized with horror at the approach of anything evil or accursed. She was immediately impelled to prayer and penance on such occasions. She relates the following incident of her youth :

" At a short distance from our house, lying in the midst of a fertile field, was a little piece of ground where nothing would grow. When I was a child, I never crossed it without a shudder. I used to feel myself pushed by some invisible power, and sometimes I was even thrown down. Once I saw two black shadows wandering about, and I noticed that the horses became uneasy at their approach. I felt that there was something sinister about the place and I tried to get information concerning it. Fearful stories were told of it, and many pretended to have seen strange sights there; but this was all false. At last my father told me that at the time of the ' Seven-Years' Wars,' a Hanoverian soldier had been condemned by a military tribunal and executed on that spot. The poor man was innocent; two enemies had been the authors of his misfortune. I did not hear this till after my First Communion. I went by night to pray there with my arms extended. The first time I had to force myself, I was so afraid; the second time a horrible phantom appeared to me in the form of a dog. It stood at my back resting its head on my shoulder. If I turned my head, I could see its snout and flaming eyes. I was terror-stricken, but I tried to hide my fear. I said in my heart: ' Lord, when Thou wert in agony on the Mount of Olives, Thou didst pray the longer! Thou art by me!' The evil spirit could not harm me. I began to pray and the horrible figure disappeared. On another occasion, whilst praying in the same place, I was lifted up violently as if about to be cast into the ditch close by. I renewed my confidence in God, and exclaimed: ' Satan, thou canst not harm me!' He ceased his attacks, and I went on with my prayers. I never again saw the two shadows, and from that time all appeared quiet.

"I often felt repugnance for places in which there had once

been pagan graves, although I had never heard anything about them. A short distance from home there was a sand-hill in the middle of a meadow. I never liked to keep my cows there, for I always saw a black, ugly-looking vapor, like the smoke of smouldering rags, creeping over the ground. A strange obscurity hung over the spot, and sombre figures, enveloped in darkness, moved here and there and, at last, disappeared underground. I used to say to myself, child that I was, 'It is well the thick grass is above you, for that keeps you from hurting us!' When houses are built over such places, a curse issues from the pagan bones resting beneath them, if their occupants do not lead lives sancti-fied by the benediction of the Church and so counteract its baneful effects. If they should happen to make use of superstitious means condemned by the Church to rid them-selves of the curse, they enter, though without knowing it perhaps, into communication with the powers of darkness, which then acquire fresh strength. It is hard for me to make this understood. I see it really, with my bodily eyes, but my hearers can only see it in thought. It is far more difficult for me to comprehend how it is that so many peo-ple see no difference between the holy and the profane, the be-liever and the unbeliever, the pure and the impure. They see only the external appearance. They do not trouble them-selves as to whether it is lawful to eat certain things or not, whether they may turn them to profit or not; but I see, I feel quite differently. That which is holy, that which is blessed, I see all luminous, diffusing light and benediction; while that which is profane, that which is accursed, I see spreading around darkness and corruption. I behold light or darkness springing like corporeal things from what is good or bad, each producing its own fruits. Once, on my way to Dülmen, I passed the hermitage near the grove

in which the peasant H— dwelt. Before it stretches a
heath. As I drew near with my companion, I saw rising
from it a vapor which filled me with horror and disgust. In
the middle of the heath several such currents arose and
floated in waves over the ground, but I could see no fire.
I pointed them out to my companion, saying : 'What
smoke is that over there ? I see no fire.' But she could
see nothing. She seemed astonished at my question ; she
thought something was the matter with me. I said nothing more although I still saw the vapor and felt my terror
increasing. As we approached nearer the spot, I distinctly
saw a similar vapor rising from the opposite side. Then I
understood that unhallowed bones were interred there, and
I had a rapid view of the abominable, idolatrous practices
that had formerly been carried on in the place."

CHAPTER V.

ANNE CATHERINE MAKES HER FIRST COMMUNION.

About the seventh year of her age, Anne Catherine went with the other school children to make her first confession for which she had prepared most earnestly. Her contrition was so great that, on her way to Coesfeld, her strength gave out, and her little companions had to carry her to the church. Her conscience was burdened not only by some childish transgressions long before expiated, but also by her uninterrupted visions, for which she had so often been reproached as for "imaginations and dreams." As her mother was incessantly warning her against idle fancies and superstition, her anxiety on the subject was proportionately great, and she laid these "day dreams" clearly and fully before her confessor to receive his advice and direction. Here let us pause to admire the designs of Almighty God. Having given Anne Catherine the gift of contemplation for the good of the Faithful, He now willed to submit this gift to the decision, to place it under the guardianship of the Church. Whilst examining her conscience before confession, Anne Catherine feared above everything else that self-love or false shame would lead her to conceal or palliate her sins. To encourage herself, she often repeated these words : " What the devil has taken he may keep. If he took away shame before sin, he may keep it now. I will not take it back before confession."

She dreaded self-love more than the demon himself, for she

had seen in vision that Adam would not have fallen so low, had he not cast the blame on Eve who, in turn, threw it on the serpent ; consequently, she accused herself with intense sorrow, looking upon her offences as mortal and unwilling to accept any extenuation from the lips of her confessor. She had once quarrelled with a playmate and replied to another by a sarcastic speech, which faults she thought mortal, since the school-master had told his pupils that God commanded us, if struck on one cheek, to turn the other.

Dean Overberg states that it was her greatest delight to be able to testify her affection to one who had offended her. She confessed her so-called mortal sins, therefore, with hearty contrition, trembling lest the priest would refuse her absolution. The Father said to console her : " My child, you are not yet capable of mortal sin," whereupon she burst into tears and had to be taken from the confessional. Her parents had given her seven pence to buy white bread, as the children were accustomed to do after their confession ; but she gave them all in alms that God might pardon her sins. Her parents always allowed her the same sum and for the same purpose when she went to confession. She used to make the little purchase, but not for herself; she took it all home to those dear parents. On another occasion, she was much troubled when approaching the tribunal of penance. She had heard her mother talking to one of her friends of a certain deceased person whose soul, she said, was not at rest. This news touched her with pity. She constantly thought of the poor, uneasy soul and almost involuntarily sought other intercessors for it. One day she was on the point of communicating what she had heard. She began : " The poor woman has no . . . .," when she became so terrified that she could not utter another word. The thought had suddenly

presented itself that she would be unable to repair this
sin of detraction, that she could not ask pardon of the dead,
and she could get no peace until she had confessed her
inadvertence. This fright of hers was no exaggerated
scruple, but the effect of great purity of conscience. The
following fact will bear witness to this :—

" When she began to read," says her father, " she loved
to sit on the ground near the fire and, gathering together
the burning embers, read her prayer-book by their light.
Once I was repairing a bench for a neighbor and using for
the purpose a piece of new wood. Anne Catherine gathered up the shavings for the fire, but only those from the
new wood. I asked her why she did not take the old
wood, too. She answered: ' I only pick up the new, because the old chips that fall from the bench do not belong
to us.' I was struck at her words and, turning to her
mother, I said : ' She is, indeed, a most singular child !' "

When her parents had retired for the night and the fire
was smouldering on the hearth, the little girl sometimes
hunted up the ends of candles by which to read her prayer-
book. She saw no harm in it at the time, but she confessed it later with true contrition, and never again made
use of the least thing without permission.

Anne Catherine was in her twelfth year when she made
her First Communion. From the day of her Baptism, she
had been powerfully attracted toward the Most Blessed
Sacrament. When before It, her joy shone exteriorly.
She never entered the church without her angel-guardian who taught her by his own example the homage
due to the Eucharistic God. Our Lord Himself had made
known to her in vision the grandeur and magnificence of
His mysteries. This inspired her with such reverence
for the priesthood that no dignity appeared to her com-

parable to it. We shall see later on that there were no offences expiated more rigorously by her than those committed by the ministers of the altar. When kneeling in church, she dared not look either to the right or to the left ; her heart and eyes were fixed upon the Most Blessed Sacrament. The silence of the holy place was equalled only by the profound recollection of her soul. She spoke to Jesus in the Eucharist with confidence and fervor, and on feast days she sang to Him the hymns of the liturgy ; but as she could neither go to church as often as she desired nor when there remain as long as she wished, she turned almost involuntarily in her nocturnal prayer in the direction of the nearest tabernacle.

Even in her babyhood she knew how to make spiritual communion ; but when the time came for actually receiving the Holy Eucharist, she thought she could never do enough. Her desires were equalled only by her efforts to make ready the poor house of her soul for the coming of her Celestial Guest. She reviewed her short life over and over in her anxiety to appear pure in the eyes of her God. She feared now even more that at her first confession, having some stain on her soul, and she was tormented by the thought of not having confessed as fully and sincerely as she should have done. She looked upon herself as the worst child in the world, and earnestly begged her parents to help her examine her conscience, saying :

" I want no secret, no fold in my heart. Could I discern the slightest concealment in an angel, I should not hesitate to declare that he had dealings with the evil one who lurks in the by-places of hearts." She kept her eyes closed going to church on the day of her Communion, that she might see nothing to disturb the recollection of her soul, and she repeatedly offered herself as a sacrifice for the

salvation of others. Dean Overberg says on this point :
" Anne Catherine did not ask for many things at her First
Communion. She begged Our Lord to make her a good
child, such as He Himself desired to see her, and she devoted herself to Him entirely and unreservedly."

We may judge of the child's earnestness and of God's
pleasure in the same by the surprising effects the Holy
Eucharist produced in her heart. She was all on fire with
the love of her God. It impelled her so powerfully that she
began at that early age a life of mortification and renunciation such as the most rigorous rule never prescribed to a penitent in the cloister or a monk in the desert. Did we possess no other testimony than Dean Overberg's on the effect of
her First Communion, it alone would suffice to prove something truly extraordinary in the inspiration, the heroic energy,
and the ardent love of this child, who, in her twelfth year,
without direction, under the blessed influence alone of the
Divine Sacrament, could impose upon herself so entire a
renunciation, could persevere in it as unflinchingly as did
Anne Catherine. She closed her senses against everything
that might allure her from God. He alone who had
deigned to enter her heart, He alone should possess and
govern it. Dean Overberg says :—

" From the day of her First Communion, her efforts to
mortify and renounce self became even more persevering
than before. She was convinced of the truth that without
mortification it is impossible to give one's self entirely to God.
Her love had taught her this. She used to say : ' The love
of creatures impels men to great and difficult undertakings.
Why, then, should not the love of Jesus lead us to the
same ? " She mortified her eyes, turning them away from
curious or beautiful objects ; in church especially she
kept them under continual restraint, addressing to herself

these words : ' Do not look around. It would distract you, or be, perhaps, too much of a gratification. And why would you indulge your sight ? Restrain it for the love of God.' If an occasion presented itself of hearing something strange or amusing, she would say : ' No, I have no ears for that. I will be deaf to it for the love of God.'

" She mortified her tongue, imposing silence upon it when she wished to speak. She ate nothing pleasing to her taste. When her parents noticed this, they ascribed it to caprice and insisted upon her eating. She mortified her feet when inclined to go where duty did not call her. ' No,' she said, ' I will not go there. It will be better to stay away for the love of God. If I went, I might have cause to regret it.' It was customary with her to make the long Way of the Cross at Coesfeld barefoot. She refused herself many little pleasures she might have innocently enjoyed. She disciplined her body with nettles, she wore penitential cinctures, she slept on a wooden cross, or on a kind of frame formed of two long beams with two shorter transverse pieces."

After Holy Communion, the child had a vision in which she assisted at the Sacred Mysteries in the Catacombs in company with St. Cecilia.

" I knelt," she said, " in a subterranean hall which seemed to be cut out in a mountain. Many people were kneeling around on the bare ground. Flambeaux were fastened to the wall, and there were two upon the stone altar which had a tabernacle, likewise of stone, and a door. A priest was saying Mass, all the people answering. At the end of it he took a chalice from the tabernacle. It looked like wood, and from it he distributed the Blessed Sacrament to the people, who received it on little white linen cloths spread carefully on their breast. Then they all dispersed."

This vision was a pledge that God had heard her and had accepted the sacrifice of her whole being. Her purity of heart and austerity of life rendered her worthy of figuring in the sacred cohort of early Christians who had drawn from the Most Blessed Sacrament their strength in the midst of torments. Her own life was to be a perpetual martyrdom and she, too, was to draw strength and courage from the same divine source. Like St. Cecilia she was to suffer for the Faith at a time of persecution, unbloody, it is true, but not the less dangerous to the Church. She, too, with heroism not inferior to that of the virgin-martyrs, was to confess her Redeemer denied and abandoned by the multitude.

Dean Overberg tells us that the little girl divided the time between her Communions into two parts: preparation and thanksgiving. She intreated the saints to join their prayers to hers, and conjured Almighty God, by His love for Jesus and Mary, to prepare her heart for His well-beloved Son. On the morning of her second Communion, a little incident occurred which seemed to indicate her own intimate communication with the Blessed Sacrament and the graces received from It for herself and others. She was to set out with her mother before daylight for Coesfeld. Her best clothes were carefully kept in the family chest. When she went to get them, she found it filled with fine white loaves so numerous that she could not count them without taking them out. At first she thought her mother had put them there to try her. She had scarcely time to replace them when her mother, impatient at the delay, came after her and hurried her off so quickly that she forgot her neckerchief. She did not miss it until some distance from home. She dared not return for it, but ran on after her mother, in dread all the time of being discovered, and praying earnestly to God to help her out of her difficulty. At last they came to a muddy crossing and, just as the mother turned to help her over, the child felt a kerchief placed by invisible hands around her neck. Anne Catherine was so agitated at this speedy answer to her prayer as to be scarcely able to follow her mother, who chided her a little for her strange conduct. When she reached the church, she tearfully confessed the curiosity that had led her to take the loaves from the chest. Her longing for the Holy Communion became like a flame; her breast and tongue seemed to be on fire. In her humility she looked upon this as a punishment for her curiosity, and the thought almost deprived her of consciousness. To get some relief, she touched her tongue with a little picture of the Five Wounds. When she approached the Holy Table, she distinctly beheld the Sacred Host fly toward her under a luminous form and enter her breast, whilst, at the same moment, the priest laid another Host on her tongue. Again did the divine fire burn more intensely than before, and she tried to cool her parched mouth as she returned home by pressing to it her cold gloves. At the spot on which she had miraculously received the neckerchief, her former un-easiness returned on noticing for the first time that it was much more beautiful than her own : " It has fringe !" she cried in trepidation. " What will my mother say !" When she reached home, she took it off tremblingly and laid it on her bed ; but, on turning again to look at it, it was gone ! She was greatly relieved at its having escaped her mother's eye.

The little loaves, visible only to Anne Catherine, were symbolical of the rich gifts she was to receive as a reward for her fervent preparation for Holy Communion and which she was to distribute as spiritual nourishment to the needy. They were hidden under her apparel as a sign that she was herself to multiply and distribute them. The greater part she gave to the most necessitous, the suffering souls in purgatory, for whom she offered all her actions; in return they testified their gratitude by prayers and assistance. It was to them she was indebted for the neckerchief so opportunely presented.

Her confessor at this time was a venerable old Jesuit of Coesfeld, Father Weidner. She says :

"My confessor was Father Weidner who lived with his two sisters at Coesfeld. I used to go to the first Mass on Sundays and then attend to the cooking, so that the rest of the family might go to church. Coffee was not so common then ; and, when I had a couple of stivers, I used to go after early Mass to Father Weidner's sisters, pious girls who sold coffee. I liked to go there, the old gentleman and his sisters were so good and kind. When my parents returned from church and found the coffee ready for them, they were greatly pleased."

CHAPTER VI.

SNARES OF THE EVIL SPIRIT.

As soon as Anne Catherine had become sufficiently strong to resist the open attacks of Satan, Almighty God allowed her to be tormented by him. But the evil one tried in vain to draw her from the path of perfection along which she was walking so courageously. She despised his cunning, his malice, and his power. The more humble she became, the more difficult was it for her to comprehend how he could intimidate a soul. His first attacks were directed against her life. She tells us herself :—

" When a child my life was repeatedly in danger, but by the help of God I was always saved. I knew very well that these perils were not accidental; I knew they came from the evil spirit. They generally happened when I was not thinking of the presence of God, or when I had negligently committed some fault. I never could attribute them to chance. God always protects us if we do not wander from Him. His angel is ever at our side, but we must render ourselves worthy of His care. Like grateful children, we ought never to leave Him. We ought constantly to beg His assistance, for our enemy lies in wait to destroy us. When I was only a few years old, my parents went out one day and left me at home alone, my mother charging me to stay in and mind the house. Presently an old woman came in who, for some reason or other, wanted to get rid of me for awhile. ' Run,' she said; ' run get some pears off my tree ! Run fast before your mother comes back !' I yielded to the temptation, forgot my mother's orders, and ran to the old woman's garden in such haste that I stumbled over a plough half-hidden in the hay and, striking my breast violently against it, I fell unconscious to the ground. My mother found me in this state, and brought me to by a smart correction. I felt the effects of this accident a long time. Later I was shown that the devil had made use of the old woman to tempt me to disobedience through gluttony and that, by yielding to the temptation, I had endangered my life. This gave me horror for the latter vice, and I saw how necessary it is for man to deny himself."

When Anne Catherine began her nocturnal vigils, the attacks of the evil spirit became bolder and more frequent. He tried to frighten her from her prayers by terrible noises and apparitions, even by blows. She often felt icy-cold hands grasping her by the feet, casting her to the ground, or lifting her high in the air; but, though terror-stricken, the child never lost countenance. She continued her prayer with redoubled fervor till Satan was forced to withdraw. She even returned to the place in which she had been maltreated, saying : " Miserable wretch ! thou shalt not chase me away. Thou hast no power over me ! thou shall not hinder my prayer ! "

These attacks were renewed whenever she prayed for the souls in purgatory or performed penances. But as she was always instructed how to resist the enemy, and the beloved souls were often visible thanking her for the relief she gave them, they served but to animate her courage and nerve her to fresh exertions.

Sometimes she went at night to pray before a rustic Crucifix which stood toward the middle of the hamlet. The road was crossed by a narrow by-path upon which there often stood facing her a horrible beast like a dog with an enormously large head. At first she used to shrink back some steps in horror ; but quickly summoning courage, she would say to herself : " Why flee before the enemy ?" Then with the sign of the cross, she would boldly push by the monster. But she trembled violently, her hair stood on end, and she flew rather than walked over the road that led to the crucifix, the brute running along by her side, sometimes even brushing up against her. However, she speedily surmounted her fear, and walked on bravely by her enemy who, unable to endure his own discomfiture, soon took to flight.

As the devil could not force her by apparitions to desist from penance, he instigated a wretch to attack her near the crucifix ; but, aided by her angel, she courageously defended herself and forced him to retire. Owing to the angel's protection, she was delivered from innumerable dangers. Once the evil spirit tried to hurl her down a ladder ; again he pushed her into a deep ditch, plunging her repeatedly to the bottom in order to drown her. But her angel drew her out and placed her on the brink safe and sound. These attacks have a deep signification which may not, perhaps, be understood at first. We discover in them not only the rage and malice of hell aiming at the destruction of God's chosen instrument, but also an essential part of the mission assigned her. This was, indeed, to draw upon herself hell's fury, to expose herself to its assaults, thus to avert them from certain other souls whose sins rendered them powerless to resist. She took the place of those who had incurred chastisement ; she suffered for those who exposed themselves to the danger of being lost ; and she paid off their debt by her own combats. As she took upon herself the corporal maladies of her neighbor in order to deliver him from them, so also did she bear for him the attacks of the demon, sustain the struggle in his stead, and gain for him the victory. She not only took the place of the members of the Church, but she also guarded the treasures that had been confided to her pastors, and which were now exposed to the fury of hell. Her painful exercises, her vigils, etc., were not dependent on her own will; they were all regulated by her angel, by instructions received in vision. Her own choice does not move her to make the long Way of the Cross at night, or to pray in the open fields—all forms part of the task marked out for her. Its accomplishment demands that she should traverse the lonely road that led to the centre of the hamlet to expiate the negligence of a slothful pastor who sleeps whilst the wolf breaks into the sheepfold ; she must struggle with the rapacious animal and prevent his devouring the flock. Is she dashed from a ladder, or thrown into a ditch ?—it is for a soul in mortal sin whom she snatches from the demon at the moment in which he thinks himself sure of his prey. If frightful visions and phantoms fill her soul with horror, they are the terrors from which she delivers the dying, that they may prepare in peace for the hour of death.

These attacks of Satan were redoubled whenever her prayers confounded the efforts of his malice, or disconcerted his plans.

"Once," she said, " I was going to church in the dark when a great dog passed me. I stretched out my hand, and received so violent a blow in the face that I staggered. My face and hand swelled up in church and both were covered with blisters. When I reached home I was unrecognizable. I was cured by bathing with baptismal water. On the road to the church was a hedge over which I had to climb. When I came to it early on St. Francis's day, I felt a great black figure pulling me back.

I struggled and succeeded in crossing. I was not frightened. He, the demon, used to station himself in the middle of the road to force me to turn aside, but he never succeeded."

The devil now sought to perplex her by more artful and subtle attacks. The mortification of her early years which had acquired for her such strength to resist, was hateful to him. He tried to tempt her to some little self-indulgence, but she only redoubled her austerities as soon as she discovered the artifice. Then, taking the opposite course, he urged her to carry her penances to excess; but she with the advice of her director immediately moderated them.

It will be seen further on that although Satan never desisted from tormenting Anne Catherine in every conceivable way, yet he could never excite in her the slightest movement opposed to perfect purity. He dared not present this temptation to a soul endowed with the gift of prophecy and confided to the visible guardianship of her angel. Hers was, indeed, to be a way of sorrows, but no stings of concupiscence were to spring up in her path. He did, it is true, sometimes place impure objects before her imagination, but never could he lead her to cast a glance upon them. He did, indeed, instigate his wicked slaves to attempt violence against the young virgin; but, with the courage of a lioness, she struck the wretches to the ground. " My Lord and my God does not abandon me!" she said. " He is stronger than the enemy!" This confidence in divine protection was her buckler, the shield that warded off every attack.

CHAPTER VII.

Her Communications with Her Angel.

The familiar intercourse that existed between Anne Catherine and her angel-guardian ever visible to her, is but a repetition of what all souls enjoy who have been raised to high contemplation. The gift of supernatural intuition is for man so weighty a burden, it is exposed to such risks in his possession, it exacts so great purity of soul that, for him to use it rightly, special assistance is necessary. He must follow a guide in the boundless spheres unveiled to the eye of contemplation. From his birth every man without exception is attended by an angel who watches over him, who directs him in the good use of the graces assigned him by the eternal decrees of the Almighty; that, by so doing, he may become a child of faith and in the end attain heavenly beatitude. The soul's capability of profiting by the angelic influence increases with its own purity and perfection. But nothing brings it nearer to its angel, or renders it more deserving of communication with him than the unsullied splendor of baptismal innocence. This was the surpassing, the indescribable charm in Anne Catherine that made the heavenly spirit, although belonging to the highest ranks of the celestial hierarchy, look upon his duty of enlightening and conducting her as a commission well suited to his high dignity. A child still in years and experience, she was however ripe for the understanding of eternal truths, and ready to become the depository of divine secrets.

The angel's first care was to instruct his charge in the Catholic faith, by intuition and symbolical images. She thus acquired an incomparably clearer view, a deeper knowledge of its mysteries than human teaching and reflection could bestow. To the light of faith was added the practice of the love of God which kept her in constant union with Him. It became, so to speak, a necessity for her to seek God in all things, to refer all to Him, to see all in Him. He was the first good that attracted her soul, and He possessed her so entirely that no creature could separate her from Him. The splendor emanating from the angel enshrouded her from the first moment of her existence, constituted the very atmosphere she breathed, and hid from her those seductions which engross and dissipate the affections of man. Her soul confirmed in charity regarded creatures but in God. Every look of the angel was a ray of light, a breath which fanned the flame of divine love, an impulse on to God. All the powers, all the movements of her soul were so well regulated that no wave of passion could ruffle its peace. She calmly endured the most intense bodily sufferings, and her soul, despite the keen sensitiveness of her sympathetic nature and the timidity consequent on childhood, was possessed of so great energy that she could instantaneously surmount terror or pain. The angel's jealous watchfulness suffered not the smallest attachment in her to anything earthly.

She felt that her whole being was laid open to his gaze, that he penetrated the inmost recesses of her heart; therefore she watched unceasingly to keep the mirror of her soul untarnished. She was all her life a child of wonderful simplicity and candor. Her artlessness alone would have sufficed to prove the origin of her extraordinary gifts, for even the gift of contemplation is of less value than that spirit of humility which hid the riches imparted to her. She never dreamed of her high privileges, the thought of self filled her with confusion and disquietude. Such an estimation of one's self can proceed neither from nature nor from the evil one, but only from a high degree of grace and extraordinary fidelity.

The angel's direction had been given Anne Catherine as a talent which she was to increase by the good use she made of it. The more she strove to become worthy of so great a favor, the more abundant light did she receive, the firmer and closer grew the bond that united her to her angelic protector. Now, this bond could be none other than obedience springing from the love of God; for there is none higher, none more meritorious. It is, in truth, the very one which unites the angel himself to God. From her earliest years Anne Catherine was exercised in perfect abnegation of her own will in the sacrifice of every power of soul and body to God. It was in this way she perpetually offered herself for others. God accepted her offering and so regulated her life through the ministry of her angel, that every action, even in the smallest detail, became a meritorious act of obedience for her. She abandoned her will to her angel that he might govern it, her understanding that he might enlighten it, her heart that he might keep it for God alone, pure and free from every earthly attachment. Docile to his interior instructions, she refused herself sleep and nourishment, chastised her body severely, and petitioned only for the pains and maladies of others. Her perseverance in such a course attracted upon her the blessings of heaven, which richly indemnified her for all the privations attendant upon it.

In consequence of her great charity for her neighbor, she acted as substitute for those who could not endure their

sufferings, and she aided others who sued for mercy. It was
the angel who conducted her where she was most needed.
As the flame borne by the breeze first to one side then to
the other, her loving soul followed the angel's call when
he led her to the abodes of misery and sin. Guided by him
she was ever ready to succor the needy, to go wherever the
irresistible impulse of pity impelled, for compassion knows
neither time nor space ; no bounds can arrest the desires of
the soul. Like a flame mounting on high, enlightening all
things far and near, her charity penetrated the whole body
of the Church, bearing help and succor wherever her angel
led her. She said once, speaking on this subject :

"The angel calls me and I follow him to various places ;
I often journey with him. He takes me among persons
whom I know either well or slightly, and again among
others who are entire strangers to me. We cross the sea
as quickly as thought travels. I can see far, far away ! It
was he who took me to the Queen of France (*Marie Antoinette*) in her prison. When he comes to take me on a
journey I generally see first a glimmering of light, then
his luminous form appears suddenly before me like a flash
from a lantern opened in the dark. As we journey along
in the darkness, a faint light floats over our path. We pass
over countries familiar to me to far distant regions.
Sometimes our way lies over roads; sometimes across deserts,
mountains, rivers, and seas. I travel always on foot, and I
often have to climb rugged mountains. My knees ache from
fatigue, and my bare feet burn. My guide is sometimes
ahead of me, sometimes at my side. I never see his feet move.
He is silent, he makes few motions, but sometimes he accom-
panies his short replies by a gesture of the hand or an inclination of the head. O how bright and transparent he is ! He is
grave but very kind. His hair is smooth, flowing, and

shining. His head is uncovered, and his robe long and dazzlingly white like that of a priest. I address him freely,
but I can never look him full in the face. I incline before
him. He gives me all kinds of signs. I never ask him
many questions ; the satisfaction I take in being near him
prevents me. He is always very brief in his words. I
see him also in my waking moments. When I pray for
others and he is not near, I call to him to go to the angel of
those for whom I am praying. I often say to him when he
is by me : ' Now I shall stay here, but do thou go to such or
such a place where thy help is needed,' and I see him going.
When I come to broad waters and know not how to cross,
I find myself all at once on the other side, and I look back
in wonder. We often soar above cities. I left the
church of the Jesuits at Coesfeld late one winter evening
in a heavy storm of snow and rain to return home over the
fields to Flamske. I was frightened, and I began to cry to
God. Suddenly I saw a light like a flame on before me. It took
the form of my guide in his robe. The ground under my
feet became dry, it cleared overhead, neither rain nor snow
fell upon me, and I reached home not even wet."

Anne Catherine's communications with the souls in purgatory were also carried on through her angel who took her
into that prison of mercy that she might refresh the dear
captives with the fruits of her penance.

"I was with my guide," she says, " among the poor souls
in purgatory. I saw their desolation, their inability to help
themselves, and the little assistance they get from the living.
Ah, their misery is inexpressible ! Whilst contemplating
their state, I saw that a mountain separated me from my
guide. I sighed for him like one famished, I almost swooned
with desire. I saw him on the opposite side, but I could
not reach him. He said to me : ' See, how thou sighest

for help ! The poor souls are always in the state in which thou now art ! ' He often took me to pray before caverns and prisons. I prostrated, I wept, my arms extended, and I cried to God for mercy. My angel encouraged me to offer all kinds of privations for the poor souls. They cannot help themselves, they are cruelly neglected. I often sent him to the angels of certain persons in suffering, to inspire them to suffer their pains for them. They are instantly relieved by such offerings ; they become so joyous, so grateful ! Whenever I do something for them, they pray for me. I am terrified to see the riches the Church holds out in such abundance neglected, dissipated, so lightly esteemed, whilst the poor souls are languishing for them."

From her earliest childhood, Anne Catherine had always begged God to keep her from sin, to treat her as a loving father treats his little child, to teach her to know and fulfil His holy will. And Almighty God mercifully heard her prayer. He guarded and enlightened her through the ministry of her angel in her long journey through a life of toil and suffering. He showed her all that was in store for her in symbolical pictures, that she might be ready for any emergency. He prepared her for sufferings, that she might ask for strength to embrace them. Every incident, every encounter which was to happen, either to herself or those connected with her, was shown to her in advance. She received precise instructions as to her behavior toward all with whom she came in contact, whether she was to treat them with frankness or reserve. The angel even prescribed, at times, the words she was to use.

She lived in two worlds : in the external, visible to the senses, and in the invisible and hidden one. She acted in both and for the good of both. The immense task imposed upon her by Almighty God, demanded that she should fulfil per-

fectly all the duties of the common life, in the midst of difficulties and sufferings sufficient of themselves to fill a whole
lifetime ; and to this was added her interior action for the
good of the universal Church. The sufferings of Christianity, the dangers threatening the faith, the wounds endured,
the sacrilegious usurpation of church property, the profanation of holy things—all were placed before her, and she
was so absorbed by the labors resulting therefrom, that days
and weeks passed in this state of spiritual abstraction. She
retained, meanwhile, entire control over her senses and faculties, that she might fulfil the duties of everyday life in that
world from which she was daily more and more removed.
How would she have been able to satisfy its demands,
how would those with whom she lived have been able to endure her, had not the angel watched over this double life, had
he not aided her in such a way that all she did received a
blessing, had he not, in fine, harmonized these diversified
operations ?

Whilst yet too young to fall under the direction of the
pastors of God's flock, her angel was her only guide. But
when she began to approach the Sacraments, the respect
and submission paid by her to the angel then became the
rule of her communication with the priest, the angel himself
setting her the example by submitting his own direction to
that of the minister of God. He now was, as it were,
merely the treasurer and dispenser of the gifts granted his
pupil for the benefit of the faithful. Whilst the Church, in
the person of her priests, assumed the guidance of Anne
Catherine, she was herself to work out her salvation by
means common to all the faithful. God's wonderful gifts
were not to form the end of her life, but only a means of
fulfilling her mission of expiatory suffering for the Church ;
consequently, these gifts were to fall under the judgment

and decision of her Ecclesiastical Superiors. The immense power of the priesthood is hereby undeniably proved, since we see the angel himself bowing to the decisions of lawful authority. It was the angel who transmitted to her the word of obedience from her confessor or superiors when, transported in spirit to other worlds, she lay like one dead, wholly insensible to every outward impression. One word from either was sufficient at such moments to recall her instantaneously to consciousness.

Once she said: " When in contemplation, or in the discharge of some spiritual labor, I am often suddenly recalled into this world of darkness by a sacred and irresistible power. I hear the word ' *obedience,*' as if uttered from afar. It is a sad sound to me at such moments, but obedience is the living root of the tree of contemplation."

Nevertheless, the confessor's voice could not have reached her but for the angel who regarded the practice of obedience as more meritorious for his charge than the highest flights of contemplation. Although his unexpected and peremptory order pierced her soul like an arrow, yet he never delayed to recall her to consciousness at the word of her superiors.

We shall see, further on, the priest's direction opposed in many instances to that of the angel; but never shall we see the least departure from the order prescribed by God for the preservation of faith in its purity—an order by which no vocation, no privilege can exempt a soul from submission to superiors. No grace, no degree of sanctity surpasses in intrinsic dignity and grandeur the sacerdotal character. Between God, the invisible Head of the Church, and the faithful there exists no other mediator than the priest; hence the treasures of mercy bestowed upon the Church in the persons of His chosen ones must fall under the supervision

of the priesthood, must be received by them in trust for the
wants of the faithful at large. Thus it was with Anne
Catherine Emmerich. Her angel omitted nothing to make
her a source of benediction to the Church. This benediction was to be diffused only by God's minister, and according to the use made of this power was to be its fruit.

CHAPTER VIII.

ANNE CATHERINE'S VOCATION TO THE RELIGIOUS STATE. SHE IS PREPARED BY SPECIAL DIRECTION.

The desire of living for God alone went on increasing in the heart of the wonderful little child. She dreamed but of the state which would most surely lead her to its fulfilment. For a long time she entertained the thought of secretly quitting her home to seek in some distant land a spot in which she might, unknown to all, lead a life of penance. Her parents, her brothers and sisters were the only objects that shared her love with God ; yet she looked upon herself as wanting in fidelity as long as she remained in her native place. Her project was impracticable to one in her position; but the greater the obstacles that presented themselves, the more earnestly did she sigh after the contemplative life. The thought of it pursued her constantly, it formed the supreme end of all her youthful aspirations. She was unable to control her emotion at the sight of a religious habit, though she hardly dared hope for the happiness of ever being clothed in a similar manner.

Almighty God, who inspired her with this ardent longing, deigned Himself to guide her to the wished for term. If we consider the intrinsic character and exterior circumstances of this direction in connection with the situation in which the Church was at the time, we shall not fail to discover in it something very remarkable. We shall find therein the mysterious ways by which Almighty God aids the Church in her trials, and a consoling and encouraging proof that the miracles of His Almighty power are never wanting to her, even when her own members league with her enemies for her destruction. When Anne Catherine was called to the religious state there to exercise a most exalted influence, events had transpired which made such ravages in the vineyard of the Church that she could not, like a St. Colette, restore conventual discipline nor establish new communities. There remained to her only the far more arduous task of serving God as an instrument of expiation, as did Lidwina of Schiedam at a time equally disastrous. She was to satisfy for the sins of others, to take upon herself the wounds of the body of the Church, and thus apply a remedy.

God directed the child in accordance with her immense task. He condescended to woo her as His betrothed, and thus to fit her for the highest perfection. The Church regards every soul that makes the triple vows of religion as contracting thereby a spiritual betrothal with God; but the extraordinary vocation of this child, the multiplied favors bestowed upon her, her wonderful fidelity to grace, are proofs that her dignity was unparalleled, that she was specially chosen to repair the innumerable outrages offered to the Celestial Spouse of souls. God in His liberality ever holds in reserve a superabundance of spiritual favors for His elect; but, when His graces are despised or squandered, justice demands their withdrawal. This would follow as a necessary consequence, did He not in His mercy prepare some souls in whom to store these slighted treasures till more favorable times. Now, God wills that this guardianship of His graces should be meritorious ; consequently, He qualifies their custodian to acquire by labor and suffering more than is sufficient to discharge the debts contracted by the levity, the sloth, the infidelity, or malice of others. These instruments of God's mercy have never been wanting to the Church in any age ; and they are so much the more needful to her as the zeal of her priesthood, the mediators between God and His people, grows weak. The Church had never been so oppressed, the scourge of incredulity had never produced ravages so great, the enemies of the faith and their machinations for its destruction had never met with so little resistance as at the period in which Almighty God chose Anne Catherine for His betrothed. Poor, weak, lowly child ! she was called to war against powerful enemies. God placed in her hands the arms with which He Himself, in His most holy Humanity, had conquered hell, and He exercised her in that manner of combating which secures the victory. We see her led, not by the way of human prudence and foresight, but by that marked out by the impenetrable wisdom of Divine Providence.

She was in her fifth or sixth year when she received her first call to the religious state. She says on the subject :—

" I was only a tiny child, and I used to mind the cows, a most troublesome and fatiguing duty. One day the thought occurred to me, as indeed it had often done before, to quit my home and the cows, and go serve God in some solitary place where no one would know me. I had a vision in which I went to Jerusalem, where I met a religious in whom I afterward recognized St. Jane of Valois. She looked very grave. At her side was a lovely little boy about my own size. St. Jane did not hold him by the hand, and I knew from that that he was not her child. She asked me what was the matter with me, and when I told her, she comforted me, saying : ' Never mind ! Look at this little boy ! Would you like him for your spouse ?' I said : ' Yes !' Then she told me not to be discouraged, but to

wait until the little boy would come for me, assuring me
that I would be a religious, although it seemed quite un-
likely then.   She told me that I should certainly enter the
cloister for nothing is impossible to my affianced.   Then I
returned to myself and drove the cows home.   From that
time I looked forward to the fulfilment of her promise.   I
had this vision at noon.   Such things never disturbed me.
I thought every one had them.   I never knew any difference between them and real intercourse with creatures."

Some time after another incident happened which encouraged her to make a vow to enter religion.   She relates it
herself:—" My father had vowed to give every year a calf
to the nuns of the Annunciation of Coesfeld, and when he
went to fulfil his vow he used to take me with him.   The
nuns used to play with me, whirling me round in the turn,
giving me little presents, and asking me if I did not want
to stay with them.   I always answered : ' Yes,' and I never
wanted to leave them.   Then they would say : ' Next time
we'll keep you ! Next time !'—Young as I was, I formed
an affection for this house in which the Rule was still strictly observed, and whenever I heard its bells, I used to unite
with the good nuns in prayer.   In this way I lived in close
union with them.

" Once, about two o'clock, on a sultry summer day, I
was out with the cows.   The sky grew dark, the thunder
rolled, a storm was at hand.   The cows were restless from
the heat and flies, and I was in great anxiety as to how
I should manage them, for there were about forty
and they gave me no little trouble running into the copse.
They belonged to the whole hamlet.   As many cows as
each peasant owned, so many days was he obliged to herd
them.   When I had charge of them, I always spent my time
in prayer.   I used to go to Jerusalem and Bethlehem.   I was

more familiar with those places than with my own home. On the day in question, when the storm burst I took shelter under some juniper-trees that stood behind a sand-hill. I began to pray, and I had a vision. An aged religious clothed in the habit of the Annonciades appeared and began to talk to me. She told me that to limit the honor we pay the Mother of God to adorning her statues, to carrying them in procession, and to addressing fine words to her, is not truly to honor her. We must imitate her virtues, her humility, her charity, her purity. She said also that, in a storm or in any other time of danger, there is no greater security than to fly to the Wounds of Jesus; that she herself had had profound devotion toward those Sacred Wounds; that she had even received their painful impression, but without any one's ever knowing it. She told me that she had always worn on her breast a hair-cloth studded with five nails and a chain around her waist, but that such practices ought to be kept secret. She spoke, too, of her particular devotion to the Annunciation of the Blessed Virgin. It had been revealed to her that Mary from her tender infancy had sighed for the coming of the Messiah, desiring for herself only the honor of serving the Mother of God. Then she told me that she had seen the Archangel's salutation, and I described to her how I had witnessed it. We soon became quite at home with each other, for both had seen the same things.

" It was about four o'clock when I returned to myself; the bell of the Annonciades was ringing for prayer, the storm was over, and I found my cows quietly gathered together. I was not even wet from the rain. Then it was that I made a vow to become a religious. At first, I thought of the Annonciades; but on further reflection, I concluded that it would be better to be altogether separated from my family. I kept my resolution secret. I found out later that the religious with whom I had conversed was St. Jane. She had been forced to marry. I often saw her in my journeys to Jerusalem and Bethlehem. She used to go with me, as did also St. Frances and St. Louisa."

From this time Anne Catherine was firmly resolved to enter a convent. She saw no human possibility of fulfilling her vow, still less had she any idea as to where she would apply for admittance; but strong in the remembrance of what had been promised her, she felt sure that God would perfect in her what He had begun, that He Himself would be her guide. She tried, in her own way, to begin at once the life of a religious as far as circumstances permitted. Her parents and teachers she looked upon as her Superiors and she obeyed them most punctually. The mortification, self-renunciation, and retirement prescribed by conventual rules, she observed as perfectly as she could.

One of her companions, Elizabeth Wollers, deposed before ecclesiastical authority, April 4, 1813 :—

"I have known Anne Catherine Emmerich from childhood. We were much together; in fact, we lived for a time under the same roof. Her parents were strict, but not harsh. She was of a good disposition, very fond of her family, prudent and rather reserved. Even when she was a little girl she wanted to be a nun, having always an attraction to piety, caring nothing for companions or amusements. She generally left them and went to church. She was recollected, sparing of her words, active, laborious, cordial and affable toward all. Her winning ways often gained her little presents. She was good-hearted, but sometimes a little quick and impetuous, which gave her cause for regret. She was not fastidious about her dress, though she was very clean and neat."

In her twelfth year she entered upon service in the family of one of her relatives also named Emmerich. His wife made the following deposition, April 18, 1813 :—

" When Anne Catherine was twelve or thirteen years old, she came to my house and kept the cows. She was kind and respectful to every one ; no fault was ever found with her ; our intercourse was always agreeable. She never went to any assembly of pleasure. She preferred going to church. She was conscientious, industrious, and pious ; she spoke well of every one ; she was indifferent to the things of this world. Next to her person she wore a rough woollen garment. She used to fast continually saying that she had no appetite. When I advised her to give up the idea of becoming a nun, since she would have to sacrifice everything to do so, she used to say : ' Don't speak that way to me or we shall fall out. I must be a religious, I am re-solved to be one !' "

Anne Catherine met in this new home certain well-to-do peasants, a circumstance very pleasing to her parents, who hoped that, by being thrown more with others, she would gradually become less silent and reserved. They could not understand such aversion to the world in so young a child, and they feared besides that her retired life would injure her future prospects. But the more Anne Catherine saw of the world, the more did her disgust for it increase. She was always in contemplation, even in the midst of those exterior occupations which she knew how to discharge so skilfully. When at work in the fields, if the conversation turned on God, she would utter a few short words ; otherwise, she kept silence performing her share of the labor promptly, calmly, and systematically. If she were

addressed suddenly, she either did not hear at all or, like
one waking out of a dream, gazing upon her questioner with
eyes whose expression made even her simple-minded
companions suspect that they were not turned upon things
of sense, she gave an answer irrelevant to the subject.
But her winning artlessness, her cordial willingness to
oblige, soon dispelled the impression produced by her
manner.

After three years spent in the family of her relative she
was placed with a seamstress, her mother thinking this
would suit her delicate constitution better than hard labor.
Before she began her apprenticeship, however, she returned
home for awhile to help with the harvest. An incident occurred about this time which led to the disclosure of
her long-cherished design to enter the cloister. They
were all at work in the fields one afternoon when
the bell of the Annonciades rang for Vespers. Anne
Catherine had often heard it before, but this time the
sound so moved her soul that she almost lost consciousness.
It was like a voice calling to her: "Go to the convent!
Go at any cost!" She was unable to continue her work
and had to be taken home.

"From this moment," she relates, "I began to be sick.
I had frequent vomitings, and I was very sad. As I went
about languid and sorrowful, my mother anxiously begged
me to tell her the cause. Then I told her of my desire to
enter a convent. She was greatly vexed, and asked me
how I could think of such a thing in my poverty and state
of health. She laid the affair before my father, who
immediately joined her in trying to dissuade me from
the thought. They said that such a life would be a most
painful one for me, as a poor peasant-girl would only be
despised by the other religious. But I replied: 'God is

rich, though I have nothing. He will supply.' My parents'
refusal grieved me so that I fell sick and was obliged to
keep my bed.

"One day about noon, the sun was shining through the
little window of my room, when I saw a holy man with two
female religious approach my bed. They were dazzling
with light. They presented me a large book like a missal
and said : 'If thou canst study this book, thou wilt see
what belongs to a religious.' I replied : 'I shall read it right
away,' and I took the book on my knee. It was Latin, but
I understood every word, and I read it eagerly. They
left it with me and disappeared. The leaves were of parchment, written in red and gold letters. There were some
pictures of the early saints in it. It was bound in yellow
and had no clasps. I took it with me to the convent and
read it attentively. When I had read a little, it was
always taken away from me. One day it was lying on the
table when several of the Sisters came in and tried to take
it off with them, but they could not move it from its place.
More than once it was said to me : 'Thou hast still so
many leaves to read.' Years after when I was rapt in
spirit to the Mountain of the Prophets, I saw this same book
among many other prophetic writings of all times and places.
It was shown me as the share I was to have in these treasures. Other things which I had received on various occasions and which I had kept for a long time, were also preserved here. At present, Dec. 20, 1819, I have still five
leaves to read; but I must have leisure for it, that I may
leave its contents after me" (1).

This mysterious book was not merely symbolical, it was
a real book, a volume of prophecies. It formed a part, as
will be seen further on, of the treasure of sacred writings

(1) Sister Emmerich died in 1824.

preserved upon what Anne Catherine calls the "Mountain of the Prophets." These writings are transmitted miraculously to those who, by the infusion of prophetic light, have been rendered capable of reading them. The book in question treated of the essence and signification of the religious state, its rank in the Church, and its mission in every age; it also taught those to whom such a vocation was given what service they could render to the Church in their own time. What Anne Catherine read in this book was afterward unfolded to her in a series of pictures. When she recited a psalm, the Magnificat, the Benedictus, the Gospel of St. John, a prayer from the liturgy, or the Litany of the Blessed Virgin, the words unfolded, as it were, like the ovary which contains the seed, and their history and meaning were presented to her contemplation. It was the same with this book. In it she learned that the chief end of the religious life is union with the Heavenly Bridegroom, and in this general view she distinctly perceived her own duty with the means, the obstacles, the labors, pains, and mortifications which would further its accomplishment. All this she saw not only in what referred to her own sanctification, but also in what related to the situation and wants of the whole Church. She had not received the grace of religious vocation for herself alone. She was to be, as it were, a treasury for this grace with all the favors attached thereto, that she might preserve it to the Church at a time in which the Lord's vineyard was being laid waste; therefore, all that she learned in the prophetic book, and all that she did in accordance with its teachings, bore the stamp of expiation and satisfaction for the failings of others. Her spiritual labors were performed less for herself than for her neighbor; they were a harvest, a conquest, whose fruits and spoils were for the good of the whole Church.

The more closely Anne Catherine studied this mysterious book, the more extended became her visions, the more did they influence her whole inner and outer life. She saw the harmony of the pictures presented to her soul, whether with one another, or with her own mission; she saw that they embraced in their entirety the history of a soul seeking her Celestial Spouse. She sighs after Him, she tends toward Him, she prepares all that is needful for her espousals; but she is continually delayed and perplexed by the loss or destruction of many necessary articles, and by the malicious efforts of others to thwart and annoy her. From time to time impending events were shown her in symbolical pictures, which never failed to be realized. She was warned of the hindrances caused by her own faults and by her too great condescension to others; but this foreknowledge never removed difficulties from her path. It did, indeed, strengthen and enlighten her, but the victory was still to be won by many a hard struggle.

Anne Catherine's labors in vision bore reference to the nuptial ornaments of a maiden betrothed to a royal consort. All that a careful, judicious mother would do to prepare her child for such an affianced, was precisely what she did in her visions. She got all things ready as in common and ordinary life, but with a far more elevated significance and altogether different results. She prepared the soil, sowed the seed, rooted out the weeds, gathered the flax, soaked, hatchelled, spun, and wove it; lastly, she bleached the linen destined for the bride. After this she cut out, made, and embroidered the numerous pieces according to their varied signification. These spiritual labors were typical of the weariness, mortification, and self-victories of her daily life. Every stitch was symbolical of some pain patiently borne which increased her merits and helped her on to her end.

An imperfect act of virtue appeared in her vision as a defective seam or a piece of embroidery that had to be taken out and done over. Every act of impatience or eagerness, the slightest failings appeared in her work, as defects that had to be repaired or removed by redoubled exertions. Year by year these labors advanced from the simplest article of apparel to the festal robe of the bride. Each piece was finished off by some sacrifice and carefully laid away until the time of the marriage. The vision relating to this end became daily more extended. All the circumstances and influences that bore upon the Church at this epoch were therein depicted. All persons throughout the whole world, whether ecclesiastics or seculars, who either opposed or supported the Church's interests, were shown most clearly with their unanswered petitions, their unsuccessful enterprises, and their baffled hopes.

Anne Catherine's spiritual labors blended simply and naturally with her exterior life; one never interfered with the other, and she herself was conscious of no difference between the two actions. They were but one and the same for her, since similar views and intentions ruled both, and both were directed to the same end. Her spiritual labor preceded her exterior actions as prayer those of a pious Christian. He offers his works to God for His greater glory and the acquisition of some virtue. As he is accustomed to renew his intention during the course of the day, to strengthen himself in his good dispositions and designs, so too was it one and the same thing for Anne Catherine to obey her mistress or her parents and to follow the instructions received in vision. Once she explained it, as follows :—

" I cannot understand how these visions are connected with my actions; but it is in accordance with them that I

either punctually perform, or carefully shun whatever occurs
in the course of everyday life. This fact has always
been very clear to me, although I have never met any one
who could comprehend it. I believe the same happens to
every one who labors zealously to attain perfection. He sees
not the guidance of Almighty God in his own regard, though
another enlightened from above may do so. This I have
often experienced in the case of others. But, though the
soul sees not the divine direction, yet she fails not to follow
it as long as she obeys the inspirations of God made known
to her by prayer, by confessors, Superiors, and the ordinary events of life. On whatever side I look, I see that
humanly speaking my entrance into a convent is impossible; but, in my visions, I am ever and surely conducted
thereto. I receive an interior assurance which fills me with
confidence that God, who is all powerful, will lead me to
the term of my desires."

When Anne Catherine had recovered from her illness,
she went to a mantua-maker of Coesfeld, Elizabeth Krabbe,
her good mother anxiously hoping that this contact with
people of all classes would distract her a little and wean
her from her desire of the conventual life. But God so
ordered it that this very period of about two years should
be the most tranquil of her life. She did not have to
begin by learning. As she had formerly acquitted herself
creditably of all her duties without prejudice to contemplation, so now her skilful fingers plied the needle, her
mind turned toward other things. She could accomplish
the most difficult tasks without the least mental application,
her fingers moving mechanically. She at first took her
place at the work-table with uneasiness, knowing well that
it would be impossible to resist the visions that so suddenly
came upon her; she was tormented by the dread of attract-

ing the attention of her companions. She begged God's
assistance, and her prayer was heard. The angel inspired
her with the proper answers when unexpectedly addressed,
and watched over her fingers to prevent her work from
falling. She soon became so skilled in her trade that to
the close of her life she was able to consecrate her nights
of suffering not only to prayer and labor purely spiritual,
but also to sewing for poor children and the sick without
applying either mind or eyes to the work.

We can readily believe that the rough field-labors of her
younger days demanding, as they did, greater physical
exertion, rendered it much easier for her to resist a profound absorption in vision than when quietly seated at a
table employed in things which cost little effort or attention.
Her whole soul was now rapt in her contemplations. They
seized upon her more vehemently than did the scenes from
Sacred History, since their subject was almost always her
own life and the task she was to accomplish. God showed
her what great things He operates in a soul called to
the religious life, and the grace needful to a weak, incon-
stant creature to arrive at her sublime end in spite of failings and infidelities. Filled with gratitude, she praised
the touching bounty of God, who lavishes His inestimable
gifts on certain chosen souls, and the greater became her
sorrow at the sad situation of the Church, in which the religious state with its holy vows seemed fast dying out.
This was all shown her to animate her to prayer, suffering,
and sacrifice for the preservation of these graces to the
Church ; to rouse her to greater ardor in following her own
vocation and offering herself as a perpetual victim to atone
for the ingratitude and contempt with which it was everywhere treated.

The Saviour showed her all He had done and suffered to

confer upon His Church the jewel of the religious state.
He had placed it under the patronage and special care
of His most pure Mother ; and, to enhance that Mother's
glory, He had delegated to her the privilege of planting the
different Orders in the vineyard of the Church and of re-
forming them when necessary. It was to Mary that Anne
Catherine presented one by one the nuptial garments as she
finished them, to receive her approval or correction. When
we recall Anne Catherine's custom of disciplining herself
with thorns and nettles even in her fourth year when she
saw little children offending God, we may perhaps form
some slight idea of that love which now led her to indemnify
Him for the infidelity of His unfaithful spouses. This desire
increased in proportion as she more clearly understood the
high dignity of the religious vows. When she reflected
upon the merit and perfection communicated by vows to the
most insignificant actions, she longed for the privilege of
making them. She deemed a lifetime of labor and suffering insufficient to purchase so high a favor ; therefore, the
utter impossibility of at once accomplishing her desire had
no power to daunt her noble soul, though her physical
strength gave way under the constant pressure of interior
suffering, and she became so ill that she was forced to give
up her apprenticeship.

Her mistress, the mantua-maker, deposed the following
before ecclesiastical authority, April 14, 1813 :

" I first knew Anne Catherine Emmerich when she was
only twelve years old. She lived with her relative, Zeller
Emmerich, in Flamske, parish of St. James, Coesfeld. It
was from that situation she came to me at the age of fifteen
to learn mantua-making. She was with me only about two
years, as she fell ill, and before being quite recovered
went to Coesfeld where she remained.

" Whilst in my house she conducted herself in the most exemplary manner. She was very industrious, silent, and reserved, always ready to do what she was told. She stayed with me only on work-days, Sundays and holy-days being spent at home. I never saw any fault in her, unless, perhaps, that she was a little particular in her dress."

When Dean Overberg, April 21, 1813, asked Anne Catherine if it were true that in her youth she had been particular about her dress, she answered :—

" It is true I always wanted to be dressed properly and neatly, though not to please creatures ; it was for God. My mother was often unable to satisfy me on this point. Sometimes I used to go to the water or before a looking glass to arrange my dress. To be clothed decently and neatly is good for the soul. When I went very early to Holy Communion I used to dress as carefully as if it were broad day; but it was for God, and not for the world."

CHAPTER IX.

ANNE CATHERINE FROM HER SEVENTEENTH TO HER TWENTIETH YEAR AT COESFELD.

Up to the present, Almighty God had directed Anne Catherine by extraordinary means to the religious state. Now she was to follow the ordinary way, to overcome those difficulties against which all that are so called have more or less to struggle. As long as her soul was immersed in the contemplation of the supreme excellence and dignity of that state, her desire of embracing it was equalled only by her sorrow at beholding its lamentable decadence and the efforts of its enemies to destroy it. Her interior trials consisted, for the most part, in her painful attempts to control her ardent desire and her ignorance as to how she could triumph over obstacles apparently insurmountable. God willed that she should experience the weakness of a soul thrown upon its own resources, that she should prove her fidelity amid darkness, aridity, and contradictions.

At the age of seventeen a new period began in her direction which lasted till her twentieth year. She resided at Coesfeld, working at her trade of mantua-making, hoping by strict economy to lay up a sum sufficient to gain her admittance into a convent. But this plan was never realized. Her small weekly earnings were often disposed of the very day they were received, for all that she made belonged to the poor. Her desire to enter a convent, though truly intense, equalled not her love for the needy for whom she never hesitated to despoil herself. One day she met an old woman in rags. Without a thought she took off one of her garments (the only one of the kind she possessed) to clothe the beggar. The more painful the privation in her neighbor's behalf, the more readily she embraced it, hoping by this to regain the fervor she feared she had lost during her sojourn at Coesfeld. The consolations she had once tasted in her devotions had been withdrawn, and she fancied that she had grown cold in the love of God. This thought greatly tormented her, especially when she found her usual practices of piety become difficult and painful. She attributed it to her own infidelity, and esteemed herself wholly unfit for the religious vocation. No penance, she thought, could expiate her faults, and, notwithstanding her repugnance, she multiplied her austerities and devotions. In confession she could not accuse herself of even the least negligence or consent to her sudden antipathy to spiritual things, yet her feeling of guilt was so great that she dared not approach the Holy Table as often as usual, a positive command from her confessor being necessary to overcome her dread. Thus did she struggle for three years, when God again inundated her mind with light, her heart with peace and joy.

Her family at this time annoyed her in many ways in their efforts to divert her from entering a convent. The mantua-maker, at whose establishment she worked, formed such an affection for her that several times she offered to remain single and share all she owned with her if she would only promise never to leave her, if she would lead with her a life wholly dedicated to the service of God. She never embarrassed her young work-woman by indiscreet curiosity nor restrained her in anything. She was pleased when other young girls came to ask her advice in their practices of piety, hoping that Anne Catherine would look more favorably on her proposal when she saw in it an opportunity of doing good. But the latter could not be won over. She declined her benevolent offers with arguments so sweet and persuasive that the good understanding existing between them was never wounded.

It was more difficult to resist her parents who imagined she would lose her desire of the religious life if they could prevail upon her to take part in worldly amusements. Anne Catherine had always found it hard to refuse anything to her neighbor, and how could she continually repulse those good parents when they urged her to go to a dance or elsewhere with her brothers and sisters? Twice she yielded a reluctant consent hoping by this concession to secure herself from further remonstrances on the subject. She says :

" Once my eldest brother insisted on my going with him to a dance. I refused. He fell into a passion and left the house. But he soon returned weeping bitterly and knelt down in our parents' presence to ask pardon. We never disagreed before nor since.

" But one day when I had allowed them to persuade me to go to such an assembly, I became so sad that I was almost in despair. My heart was far from the gay scene. I endured the torment of hell, and I was so strongly urged to quit the place that I could scarcely control myself. I remained only through fear of attracting attention. At last I thought I heard my Divine Spouse calling me, and I fled from the house. I looked around, and there I saw Him standing under a tree, sad and displeased, His face pale and bloody. He said to me : ' How unfaithful thou art! Hast thou forgotten Me? How hast thou treated Me! Dost thou not recognize Me?' Then I implored pardon. He told me what I should do to prevent sin; viz., to kneel and pray with extended arms, and to go where my presence would hinder its commission.

"On another occasion I went, though reluctantly, to the same kind of a gathering. But again I was drawn away by an irresistible power, and I fled in spite of my companions who tried to detain me. I thought the earth would swallow me up. I felt as if I should die of grief. Hardly had I passed the city gate, when a majestic lady appeared before me and in a severe tone thus addressed me : 'What hast thou done? What conduct is this? Thou wast betrothed to my Son, but thou no longer deservest that honor!' Then the youth approached, pale and disfigured. His reproaches pierced my heart, when I reflected in what company I had been whilst he was awaiting me, sad and suffering. I thought I should die. I begged His Mother to intercede for me, and I promised never to yield again. She did so, I was forgiven, and I resolved never more to allow myself to be enticed to such places. After accompanying me some distance, they disappeared. I was wide awake, with full consciousness. They had spoken with me just like ordinary people. I returned home sobbing, sad unto death. The next day my friends reproached me for having left them, but they never again pressed me to attend such amusements. About the same time, a little book fell into my father's hands in which he read that parents are wrong in forcing their children to such places. He was so troubled that he shed tears, saying: 'God knows my intention was good!' I consoled him." Her parents' opposition did not, however, cease; indeed, it became only the more obstinate. At first sight it seems strange that these poor peasants, who could entertain no hope of ever seeing their daughter occupying other than a very humble position in life, should have so strongly opposed her becom-

ing a religious ; but when we reflect what a treasure she
was to them, we can no longer be surprised. She was
their joy and consolation. They had recourse to her in every
doubt. Her wisdom and intelligence guided them in every
emergency, they could not do without her. All that she
undertook received a blessing; nothing succeeded so well
when their favorite child was absent, and there was something so attractive about her that they could not bear to be
separated from her for any length of time. She was attentive to their wants, she sought to gratify their every desire.
They looked upon her as the support of their old age.
Although she had for some years been from under the
paternal roof, yet it was at so short a distance that
daily intercourse had not been interrupted ; but the cloister
once entered would deprive them of her presence altogether.
They knew her too well not to feel confident that, even were
she in a relaxed community, she would live as a perfect religious, scrupulously observing her Rule. They would have
been more pleased to discover in her an inclination for the
married-state, as that would not preclude their frequent communication with her. They also feared that her poverty would
be made a subject of reproach to their child in the miserable
condition to which convents were then reduced. Actuated
by these considerations, they implored her with tears, reproaches, and entreaties to abandon a design which they
represented as the effect of caprice and presumption, or as
a desire of escaping a life of poverty in the world. Her
affectionate heart was crushed by such arguments, and often
she knew not what to reply. Her only resource was prayer,
from which she drew the strength and light necessary to
carry out her resolution.

"My parents," she said to Dean Overberg, "spoke of marriage, for which I felt the greatest repugnance. Sometimes

I thought that my distaste to it arose from a dread of the
duties it imposes. 'If it be the will of God that I should
marry,' said I to myself, 'I ought to be willing to bear the
burden.' Then I begged God to take from me that feeling
of dislike, if it were His will that I should conform to my
parents' desires. But my longing for the convent only
increased.

" I laid my trouble before my pastor and my confessor,
and begged their advice. Both told me that if there were
no other children to take care of my parents, I ought not
to enter religion against their wishes; but that, as they
had several sons and daughters, I was free to follow my
vocation. So I persevered in my resolution."

It was a very remarkable fact that, although Anne Catherine had so often received in vision a positive call to the
religious state, yet she had to recur to ordinary means for
a confirmation of what had been extraordinarily communicated. As obstacles did not disappear miraculously, as
they had to be surmounted by her own efforts, so neither
did her supernatural illumination dispense her from the obligation of proving her vocation by the usual methods.
She was called to religion for the good of the Church, she
was to serve as a model for all in it, she was to show forth
at a time in which the religious state was in absolute decadence, what fidelity a soul can practise who has chosen
God for her spouse. For this it was that she was sent to
the representatives of God, the priesthood of the Holy
Church. Like the ordinary Faithful, her life was to be
regulated by their judgment and decision, and by this way
open to all, she was to attain the end marked out for her by
God. This submission to the guidance and discipline of the
Church was precisely the surest test of the truth of all that
was extraordinary in her. We shall meet in her life numer

ous facts which prove that the graces bestowed upon her were all destined to be placed under the guidance of ecclesiastical Superiors to receive from them their seal of authenticity.

She was in her eighteenth year when she received the Sacrament of Confirmation from the hands of Gaspard Max von Droste-Vischering, then suffragan Bishop of Münster. This sacred ceremony was performed during the period of her interior desolation ; hence, the call to receive the Sacrament was to her like a voice from heaven. She prepared for it most carefully, trusting through its efficacy, to regain that spiritual strength and joy for which she thought she had been striving uselessly during the past year. At her First Communion she had begged to be a good and docile child; now she asked for fidelity and love that she might suffer until death for God and her neighbor. Again she felt rise in her soul her former desire of burying herself in some distant land to serve God unknown and alone. One day, as she was conversing with an intimate friend, she said that a true imitator of Jesus Christ ought like the saints to quit all things for Him. These words made so deep an impression on her hearer that she declared her readiness to follow wherever she might lead in imitation of those servants of God. Anne Catherine joyfully accepted the offer and together they planned their flight into solitude; but they soon discovered that their pious design was not feasible.

The following is Anne Catherine's own account of her Confirmation :—

" I went to Coesfeld with the children of our parish to be confirmed. Whilst I stood at the church door with my companions waiting my turn, I had a most lively sentiment of the sacred ceremony going on inside. I saw those who came out after receiving Confirmation interiorly changed, but in various degrees. They bore an exterior mark. When I entered, the Bishop seemed to me to be all luminous, a band of heavenly spirits around him. The chrism was resplendent and the forehead of the confirmed shone with light. When he anointed me, a fiery dart shot from my forehead to my heart, and I felt the strength emanating from the sacred chrism. I often saw the suffragan Bishop after, but I would scarcely have known him."

We can judge of the effects of this Sacrament in Anne Catherine's soul from her own words. She declares that from this time she had to endure frightful apparitions and chastisements from invisible agency for the faults of others. This expiation was often performed under circumstances apparently accidental : for instance, she was sometimes thrown down, wounded, bruised, or scalded by the awkwardness of a companion ; or, again, she was suddenly seized by some unaccountable malady which every one ridiculed. She bore their bantering with patient sweetness, she silently endured contradiction, blame, harsh words, and unjust accusations. Naturally hasty, the interior struggle to control her feelings, pardon her persecutors, and, at the same time, to bear the chastisement due to them, was great. In the Sacrament of Confirmation, she received the strength to fulfil her mission. We shall see later on how rapid was her progress in perfection.

The corporal maladies that from this epoch unceasingly attacked her, bore the characteristic stamp of expiation under the most varied forms. They had a special reference, known to God alone, to the offences for which they atoned. The more faithful Anne Catherine was to the direction given in her great vision, the more worthy was she of holding before God the place of the Spouse *par excellence*, the Church ; but by the impression of the Sacred Stigmata of

Jesus Christ, her quality of representative reached perfect assimilation with her Beloved.

As in the sight of God she held the place of Holy Church, she was to bear the same wounds, incur the same dangers, undergo the same persecutions that menaced either the whole body or its individual members. At the age of four, she had intercepted the murderous axe hurled at the sleeping infant; now as a substitute she was to endure whatever threatened the Pope, ecclesiastics, or other influential personages, whose well-being in any way affected that of the Church. She expiated the spiritual maladies of such members by unspeakable sufferings; and she atoned by patience for those whose infidelity, negligence, or immorality would have drawn down upon the Church the chastisements of Divine Justice if not appeased by some such offering.

In Anne Catherine was wrought the same marvellous change as in the Apostles on the day of Pentecost when, as the catechism teaches, "They were so filled with the power of the Holy Spirit that they esteemed themselves happy to be judged worthy to suffer stripes, imprisonment, and even death for the name of Jesus Christ." One day she revealed the secret of her strength in the following words:—

"After my Confirmation, I could not refrain from petitioning to bear the punishment of every sin."

What a high idea of the sanctity and justice of God, what reverence for the Precious Blood, what horror of sin, what compassion for sinners, must have found a place in that heart which lived but to atone for its neighbor's faults!

Her love of penance ever increased. Her days were spent in labor, her nights in prayer and penitential exercises. From her infancy, though hiding it as much as possible from her family, she had been accustomed to the same; even now humility forbade her revealing all these practices to her confessor. Her mistress, the mantua-maker, had however informed him of it. When he questioned Anne Catherine upon the subject, she was covered with confusion ; she acknowledged all and afterward followed his advice most exactly. He again declared to her that she was called to the religious state. When she expressed her fear of not being received into any convent without a dowry, he recalled to her the power and goodness of God, and promised to interest himself for her with the Augustinians of Borken. He did so, and soon announced to her the welcome news that she might present herself to the Superioress of the Borken community, who was disposed to admit her on his recommendation. The Superioress did, it is true, receive her most kindly ; but Anne Catherine was suddenly overcome by mental anguish, tears choked her utterance. The sight supernaturally revealed to her of the spiritual state of the community, the Founder of the Order and even their holy Rule being almost entirely unknown to the religious, overcame her. The Superioress in surprise asked the cause of her tears, to which question Anne Catherine answered truthfully, but evasively : "I weep over my want of veneration for St. Augustine. I am not worthy to become an Augustinian ! " She took leave, saying that she would reflect on the matter ; but she could never resolve to return.

Dean Overberg speaks thus of her mortifications at this time :—

" Anne Catherine practised more austerities in the world than she did after entering the convent. She knew not at the time that for such things her confessor's leave was necessary. She wore chains and cords and a rough undergarment which she had made herself of the coarsest material she could find."

Among her other penances was that of the Stations of the

Cross, erected upon the confines of Coesfeld. It took at least two hours, pausing only a few moments at each station, to perform this devotion, since they were at a great distance apart, separated by intervening groves of fir-trees. Her labor began at daybreak and lasted till late in the evening; consequently, it was only at night she could make this exercise. She used to begin a little after midnight and, when the city-gates were closed, she had to climb over the broken wall. She was naturally timid and her retired life made her still more so. This nocturnal expedition was a very formidable undertaking for her, yet she never failed to perform it at the instance of the souls in purgatory, or on a command received in vision. No inclemency of the weather could prevent her. She was sometimes accompanied by a friend who shared her pious sentiments.

"Once," she says, "I went with my friend, about three o'clock in the morning, to make the Way of the Cross, and we had to climb the broken wall. On our return, we stopped awhile outside the Church to pray, when I saw the cross with all the silver offerings suspended from it leave its place and draw near to us. I saw it clearly and distinctly; my companion did not see it, but she heard the clinking of the silver objects. After this, I used to go behind the main altar to pray before the miraculous crucifix there, and I often saw the Saviour's figure inclining toward me. It made a strange impression on me."

On one occasion, she performed this devotion to ask for peace in a certain household.

"The hatred existing between a husband and wife at Coesfeld," she says, "afflicted me greatly. I often prayed for the poor people. On Good-Friday, after leaving the Holy Sepulchre, about 9 o'clock in the evening, I made the Way of the Cross for them. The evil spirit in human form attacked me and tried to strangle me, but I cried to God with my whole heart and the enemy fled. After this the husband treated his wife less harshly."

She often experienced similar opposition from the demon. She says :—

"I felt great compassion for a poor girl who had been deceived by a young man, who afterward refused to make her his wife. This great sin against God grieved me to death. I formed a little plan with two companions to make on Easter-night fifty-two turns around the cemetery of Coesfeld for the souls in purgatory, begging them to help the poor girl. The weather was bad, the night dark. We went barefoot, I between my two companions. As we were praying earnestly, the evil one in the form of a young man rushed upon me and dashed me several times from side to side. But I went on praying all the more fervently, for I knew that prayer is hateful to the demon. I know not whether my friends saw what I did, but they both screamed with terror. When we had finished our rounds, we were so exhausted that we could go no further. As we returned home, the same apparition cast me head foremost into a tan-pit twenty feet deep. My companions thinking I was surely killed, again screamed, but I fell quite gently. I cried out to them : ' Here I am !'—and, on the instant, I know not how, I was drawn out of the pit and placed on the ground. We began our prayers once more, and now went on unmolested. On Easter Tuesday the girl came full of joy to tell me that the young man had consented to marry her. He did so in effect. Both are still living (1818).

Another time, as a friend and myself were crossing a field before daybreak in order to go pray, Satan under the appearance of a huge black dog came bounding toward us on a little

path we had to cross. He wanted to prevent our going any further. Every time that I made the sign of the Cross he re-
treated a short distance and stood still. He kept this up
full fifteen minutes. My friend was trembling with fright.
She caught me and tried to hold me back. At last I went
boldly forward, saying : 'We will go in the Name of Jesus!
We have been sent by God and what we are going to do is
for God! If thou wert of God, thou wouldst not try to hinder
us. Go thy way, we will go ours!' At these words, the
monster disappeared. When my friend recovered from her
fright, she exclaimed : 'Ah! why did you not speak that
way at first ?' I answered : 'You are right, but I did not
think of it.' We then went on in peace.

"On another occasion, I was praying earnestly before the Blessed Sacrament, when the evil one threw
himself down so violently beside me on the kneeling bench
that it cracked as if split asunder. Cold chills passed over
me, I was so frightened ; but I continued praying, and he
soon left me."

For three long years, as before stated, Anne Catherine
patiently endured spiritual dryness. At the end of that
time the sun of consolation again shone upon her soul and
her intimate communication with the Celestial Spouse was
never afterward interrupted. Without such support she
would have been unable to fulfil the terrible expiatory task
of her life. O the mysterious ways of Divine Providence!
Anne Catherine now beholds her Redeemer almost constantly! She is enlightened, strengthened, consoled by
Him, the invisible Head of the Church! She receives
from Him the promise of assistance—but, at the same time,
all her efforts to enter a convent are futile! For three
years she had toiled to put by a sum for a dowry, and at
the end of that time she finds herself as poor as before,

for her Heavenly Betrothed sent her so many occasions of relieving the wants of her neighbor, that she could keep nothing for her own needs. But a still more serious obstacle stands in the way, one well calculated to crush her hopes, and that is her continued ill-health. She saw, indeed, in her visions, what she had to suffer and why she suffered; but the knowledge of these hidden causes was poor compensation for a life of daily sacrifice, for sickness so real, so sensible as to exhaust her vital energies. She could now with difficulty perform her usual duties; and when, after her unsuccessful attempt at Borken, she begged her confessor to speak for her to the Trappistines, of Darfeld, his reply was that he could not encourage one so weak and sickly as she to enter so severe an Order. On beholding her distress at this declaration, he consoled her by promising to ask admittance for her among the Clares, at Münster. These religious gave a favorable answer to his application, and Anne Catherine went to present her petition in person. But they informed her that, as their convent was poor and she could bring no dowry, they would admit her only on condition that she would learn to play the organ, and thus become useful to the community. She agreed to this, but her increasing debility made it necessary for her to return home awhile before beginning her new study.

The friend who accompained her to Münster on this occasion, made the following deposition before ecclesiastical authority, April 8, 1813 :—

"My name is Gertrude Ahaus, of Hammern, parish of Billerbeck. I have known Anne Catherine Emmerich for fourteen years. I became acquainted with her at Ccesfeld, and we were very intimate. She told me of her desire to become a nun, and I went with her to the Clares at Mün-

ster in which community I had two relatives. Her desire
was so great that, when I represented to her that
these houses would soon be everywhere suppressed,
she replied that if she could enter one although
with the certainty of being hanged eight days after, she
would still be too happy to do so. The most severe Order
was her attraction. I never saw any fault in her; she was
pious and upright. I had the greatest confidence in her.
Our conversations were always upon piety, and she instructed me in many things concerning the duties of a Christian,
relating traits from the lives of holy religious, St. Matilda,
St. Catherine, St. Gertrude, St. Clare, etc.

"She communicated on Sundays and feasts. When
she worked at our house, she used to kneel long in prayer
every evening. She had a particular devotion to the Five
Wounds of Jesus and to the three upon His Shoulder, from
which He suffered more than from all the others.

"She wore a red garment next her person. On Fridays
she fasted till mid-day, and if she could escape notice she
took nothing in the evening. She often went at night to
make the Way of the Cross and she spent Sundays and holy-
days in prayer.

"Her patience was wonderful. If I were sick, she consoled
me reminding me of the sufferings of Christ. Some said
it was through pride that she wanted to be a nun. But
Anne Catherine answered that she was pleased to be thus
spoken of, for her innocent Saviour also had been calumniated. She was prepossessing, kind to all, and very diligent.
She always worked hard at our house, and her conversation
did me much good. She was so generous that she gave away
all she had. She was frank and sincere in her words, although with most people she spoke but little."

We shall here give some other depositions made by Anne

Catherine's early companions concerning the period which forms the subject of the following chapter. They were made before Ecclesiastical Superiors in 1813 when the details of her life were collected. Their simplicity and truthfulness not only prove the wonderful benediction emanating from her, but they also present a striking and faithful picture of her. We shall give that of her eldest brother first, taken April 11, 1813 :—

"Anne Catherine Emmerich is my sister, and I am the eldest of the surviving children. She lived some years out of the family, but only at a short distance so that we saw her often. I always got along with her, although her disposition was like my own a little hasty ; but her earnest efforts to correct this defect were soon perfectly successful. She was by no means vain, though she liked to be well dressed. She kept aloof from parties and amusements of all kinds, and she was always respectful and affectionate to our parents.

"She spoke little on worldly things, but she was always glad to be able to instruct others on points of faith and morals. She often repeated the sermons she had heard or the lives of the saints, and tried by all means to make us love virtue. She was so kind-hearted that she gave away all she earned. She never allowed us to speak of our neighbors' defects, but often gave us sound admonitions on this score. When any one found fault with her, she said it was all true ; and, when we asked her how she could endure such injuries so sweetly, she used to answer : ' That is only what I ought to do. You can do the same if you try.' Much of her time was given to prayer. Long after the family had retired, she was still up reading or praying on her knees, her arms extended, and even when she worked she prayed.

"She fasted often, especially on days consecrated to the Sacred Passion. When we begged her to eat on account of her weak health, she replied that it was not necessary. She mortified herself in every way, and wore next her a robe of rough material. She strewed her bed with chips or thistles to do penance whilst she slept."

April 7, 1813, Clara Soentgen deposed :—

" Anne Catherine so distinguished herself among the other children at school that the master often told her parents that there was no question he could ask her which she could not answer, although she attended regularly only four months. She used to study during her leisure moments and whilst tending the cows. When the other children were playing, she sat off by herself with a book.

When she grew older she had to share the hardest labors ; and even then, though worn out after the day, she often spent half the night reading pious books after her parents had retired. Sometimes they had to order her to bed. She used to instruct the girls among whom she worked as seamstress telling them the beautiful things she had read. She was sought after by many, but chiefly by the young who confided to her their secrets and asked her advice. On Sunday afternoons she used to persuade them, especially when she knew they were wandering a little from the right path, to make the Stations of the Cross with her, she saying the prayers aloud. She often rose at night, slipped barefoot from the house, and made the Way of the Cross. When the city-gate was closed, she used to climb the wall. Sometimes she fell, but she never received any injury. Sunday was her joyous day, the day on which she could confess and communinate. When several feasts followed in succession, her confessor allowed her to receive Holy Communion on each. She fasted the last three days of Holy Week, touching nothing until dinner on Easter Sunday. But even when fasting, she performed the most fatiguing labor."

Anne Gertrude Schwering, St. Lambert's, beyond Coesfeld, deposed, April 16, 1813:—

"I have been intimate with Anne Catherine Emmerich for about fifteen years, and I always saw in her great virtue. She was very pious, her conversation always turning upon the Holy Scriptures, the lives of the saints, or the truths of faith. She never spoke of the defects of others or of worldly things. She was assiduous in her employment, and knelt long every evening in prayer. She was indulgent toward all, generous as far as her means would allow, and she never complained. I never saw any fault in her."

Mary Feldmann, St. James's, district of Flamske, beyond Coesfeld, deposed as follows, April 11, 1813 :—

"At the age of fourteen I went to Anne Catherine to learn to sew, and we were on as intimate terms as the difference in our age permitted. I was with her over two years and I loved her much because she was so good. She taught me so patiently, in spite of my dulness. I judged of her piety by the numerous prayers she said during the day, and by her quiet and retiring manners. She was already up and praying when I awoke in the morning, and at night when I fell asleep she was still on her knees, her arms extended in the form of a cross. I often saw little pieces of wood lying crosswise on her bed. She used to speak frequently of the Offices of the Church and instruct me in my faith. She never talked about her neighbor and always told me never to say anything uncharitable of any one and to return good for evil. She gave all she had to the poor. She rarely had any money since it all went as fast as it was earned. She never attended assemblies and only went out on business."

CHAPTER X.

ANNE CATHERINE'S ATTEMPT TO LEARN THE ORGAN—
THREE YEARS AT THE HOUSE OF THE CHOIR-LEADER.

When Anne Catherine had regained strength sufficient
to resume her occupations, she made every effort to earn
enough to cover the first expenses that her project of
learning the organ would entail. The needle never left
her fingers during the day, and at night she plied the distaff
to be able to take at least some linen with her to the convent. God blessed her efforts. In the course of a year,
she put by twenty thalers (about 15 dollars) earned by
her sewing, and a good supply of fine linen. This appeared to her so enormous a sum that she would not have
dared to keep it for any other purpose than that of entering religion. Her parents, meanwhile, renewed their entreaties to dissuade her from leaving them, her mother tearfully
representing to her that, being almost constantly sick, she
could not hope to discharge the numerous and painful duties to which her poverty would expose her.

" My dear mother," would she reply, " even if things
turn out as you say, even if I do have to work as you pre-
dict, still I shall escape the dangers of the world."

But the good woman understood not such reasoning, since
her child was even then so estranged from the world that
she could hardly imagine a more complete separation possible. She ceased not, therefore, her earnest entreaties ;
but her daughter replied so sweetly, so tenderly, and yet
so firmly, that the poor mother had no words in return.

She desisted from seriously opposing her when she saw her
settled in the family of the organist Soentgen, at Coesfeld.
A very important witness whom we shall often meet in
the course of our narrative, Dr. Wesener, of Dülmen, tells
us the following on this point:—

" I attended Anne Catherine's aged mother in her last
illness. She often told me with tears that she had, even in
infancy, perceived something extraordinary in her daughter,
and had always loved her with particular affection. It was a
great affliction to her that Anne Catherine, the eldest
of her daughters, who should have been the consolation of
her old age, desired so ardently to enter a convent. 'That
was,' she said, 'the only grief she ever caused me. I cannot
say the same of my other children !' When Anne Catherine
was eighteen she was sought in marriage by a young man,
the son of parents in easy circumstances. They greatly desired Anne Catherine's consent, for they knew her worth and
skilful industry in spite of her delicate health. ' But,' said
her mother, ' I could not part with her then. Her father's
health was bad and two of my other children gave me much
anxiety. I did not press her on that occasion. Some
years later a still more eligible proposal was made her, and
her father and I were very desirous that she should accept.
It seemed to us highly advantageous. But she pleaded so
earnestly against it that we had to yield assuring her, however, that we should never give her anything toward entering a convent. She had put by some pieces of linen, thinking that would facilitate her design ; but she was everywhere refused as too delicate. Then she obtained a situation at the organist Soentgen's of Coesfeld to learn the organ, hoping such an accomplishment would open to her the
door of a convent. Soon, however, she saw her mistake, for
she found in this family such poverty and distress that she

sacrificed her little all to relieve them. She gave them her linen, seven or eight pieces worth about twenty-four dollars. After she had lived with them some time, Clara, the organist's daughter, also began to think of beco ning a nun." Let us hear Anne Catherine's own remarks on the subject:—

" As to learning the organ," she said to Dean Overberg, " there was no question of such a thing. I was the servant of the family. I learned nothing. Hardly had I entered the house when I saw their misery, and I sought only to relieve it. I took care of the house, I did all the work, I spent all I had saved, and I never learned to play."

She could, however, have learned most readily. Her ear was so delicate, her appreciation of musical harmony so keen, and her fingers so skilful that she could find nothing difficult. Sometimes she would say :

" When I listened to singing or the tones of an organ, nothing moved me so much as the consonance of the different notes. How charming, I cried, is perfect harmony ! Since inanimate creatures accord together so sweetly, why do not all hearts do the same! Ah, how sweet this world would be if it were so !"

But God wished to initiate His chosen servant into harmonyof a more exalted order than that of the musical world, into perfect conformity with His own most holy will. She was now to walk by paths very different from those for which her heart sighed. Her plan, so carefully matured, so well carried out, proved a failure with respect to her study of music. The idea as we have seen, was abandoned even before it was put into execution.

" Ah ! I learned in that house what hunger is ! " did she once say. " We were often eight days together without bread ! The poor people could not get trust for even seven pence. I learned nothing, I was the servant. All that I had went, and I thought I should die of hunger. I gave away my last chemise. My good mother pitied my condition. She brought me eggs, butter, bread, and milk which helped us to live. One day she said to me : 'You have given me great anxiety, but you are still my child! It breaks my heart to see your vacant place at home, but you are still my child!' I replied : 'May God reward you, dear mother! I have nothing left, but it is His will that I should help these poor people. He will provide. I have given Him everything, He knows how to help us all!' Then my good mother said no more."

In the most austere Order, Anne Catherine would not have practised poverty so rigorously as she did in the Soentgen family. The more she relieved their wants, the further did she remove from the end in view, the more was her hope of arriving thereat disappointed and crushed. She spent her small savings, she served without wages, she was in absolute want ; and yet it all led to nothing. No attempt was made to teach her anything ; but her confidence in God remained unshaken.

Speaking of this period, she says : "I used often to say to myself : 'How can I enter a convent now ? I have nothing, everything works against me!' Then I would turn to God and say : 'I know not what to do ! Thou hast ordained it all! Thou alone canst free me from it!'"

She was then shown in a vision what a rich increase her bridal ornaments had received from all these trials and unsuccessful efforts. She saw the fruits of her self-victory, patience, and devotedness wrought into garments of exquisite beauty ; she saw them daily enriched by her renunciation and charity ; and she was told that her prayers and tears, her struggles and privations, emitted sounds more agreeable to God than the organ's most harmonious strains. But was it in accordance with the dignity of her Betrothed that she should attain to the nuptial union by such means? At this period, no attention was paid in convents to the signs of a supernatural vocation. Worldly advantages, external qualities, personal considerations decided everything, whence it followed that true religious were rarely met. It was this very indignity to the Divine Spouse that Anne Catherine was called upon to expiate. She had to open for herself in the most painful and humiliating manner access to a religious community in atonement for the slight put upon the religious vocation.

The organist Soentgen was grateful for Anne Catherine's disinterested charity and devotedness, and he promised to do all in his power to further her designs. He had a daughter of the same age, a skilful musician, who would be received anywhere. He resolved, therefore, to allow her to enter that convent only into which Anne Catherine would also be received, and his solicitude for his daughter's welfare gave strength to his resolution. He used to say to Anne Catherine: " My Clara shall not enter a convent without you. Convents are not so strict now as they used to be ; but if you are with Clara, you will keep her up to her duty."

The two young girls applied to several religious houses, but in vain. Some refused on account of their want of dowry, some would receive Clara alone. This was the case with the Augustinians of Dülman who were in need of an organist. But Mr. Soentgen was true to his word. He would not permit his daughter to enter without Anne Catherine ; so, at last, the religious reluctantly consented to receive her, too.

April 7, 1813, Clara Soentgen deposed, as follows, at

the request of the Vicar-General, Clement Auguste von
Droste-Vischering (1):—

"Anne Catherine Emmerich lived with us nearly three
years, and I noticed at meals that she always took what
was most indifferent. She wore a coarse woollen garment
next her person and under it a rough cincture, twisted and
knotted, which she bound so tightly around her waist that
the flesh became inflamed and swollen. When her confessor
heard of it he forbade her to wear it. She told me that
after obedience had deprived her of this cincture, there remained imprinted on the skin a mark like a red band. She
used to go out alone in the evening to pray and on her return I noticed her skin all torn as if by briers. On being
questioned, she was forced to acknowledge that she had disciplined herself with nettles. She once told me that a huge
black beast often rushed upon her to frighten her from her
prayer; but she took no notice of him. Then he would hang
his head over her shoulder, glare in her face with fiery eyes,
and disappear. The same apparition appeared to her one
morning on her way home after Holy Communion."

With regard to this incident and others of the same
nature, we shall give Anne Catherine's own words :—

" Whilst at the Soentgen's I kept up my old habit of praying

(1) Clement Auguste von Droste-Vischering, Archbishop of Cologne, was borne in 1773
and died in 1842. He was ordained to the priesthood in 1797 and later became Coadjutor and Vicar-General of the diocese of Münster. In 1835 he was appointed to the
Archbishopric of Cologne. His opposition to the Prussian laws respecting mixed
marriages, his condemnation of writings favoring heretical tendencies, and his disa-
vowal of certain professors of theology infected by heresy, aroused the animosity of
the government against him. He was, accordingly, declared guilty of 'obstinacy and
rebellion. Without formal process or investigation, the Archbishop was conducted by
a military force to the fortress of Minden as States-prisoner, Nov. 20 1837. This proceeding roused the just anger of all good Catholics throughout Germany. In an able
article, called " The New Athanasius," the great Goerres vindicated the rights of the
Archbishop.

After an imprisonment of two years, Clement Auguste was honorably released. He
resigned his position as Archbishop of Cologne and found at Rome, in the arms of the
Holy Father, ample indemnification for the wrongs he had suffered. He repeatedly
frustrated the intention of His Holiness to create him Cardinal. His death was announced to the Catholic world by Pope Gregory XVI. with a becoming eulogy.

Mgr. Clement Auguste was a hero of the faith who, by the splendor of his virtues,
became a spectacle to men and angels. He formed one of the literary circle of Münster in the time of the Princess Gallitzin.—(Herder's Kirchen-lexicon.)

by night in the open air. As usual, Satan tried to frighten me from it by horrible noises; but, as I only prayed the more fervently, he used to come behind me under the form of a hideous beast, an enormous dog, and rest his head upon my shoulder. I kept calm, by the grace of God. I stirred not from my position, but I said: 'God is more powerful than thou! I am His, I am here for His sake. Thou canst do me no harm!' I no longer felt afraid and the fiend vanished. He often seized me by the arm and tried to drag me out of bed, but I resisted with prayer and the sign of the cross. Once when I was ill, he attacked me furiously, opening his fiery jaws at me as if about to strangle me or tear me to pieces. I made the sign of the cross and boldly held out my hand to him: 'Bite that!' I said, and he instantly disappeared.

" One evening, Clara and I were praying for the poor souls. I said, 'Let us say some *Our Fathers* for your mother in case she needs them.' We did so earnestly. After each *Pater*, I said: 'Another, another!' As we went on in this way, the door opened and a great light streamed in. Several blows were struck upon the table, which frightened us both, especially Clara. When Mr. Soentgen came home, we told him of the circumstance, and he shed many tears."

" Often," continues Clara in her deposition, " after we had finished our prayers, never before, a pillow used to be pressed down upon our faces, as if to smother us, and repeated blows were struck with the fist on Anne Catherine's pillow. Sometimes impatient at this annoyance, she would run her hands over the pillow, but discover nothing. No sooner had she again settled herself to sleep than the noise recommenced. This was often kept up till midnight. Sometimes she arose and ran out into the garden to see if she could discover any clue to the noise, but in vain. It happened not only at our house but also in the convent where, at first, I occupied the same cell with her.

" After we retired to rest we used to pray for the souls in purgatory and once, as we finished our devotions, a brilliant light hovered near our bed. ' See! see! the bright light!' cried Anne Catherine to me joyously. But I was afraid, I would not look."

Reverend James Reckers, Professor at the Latin School, Coesfeld, was Anne Catherine's confessor. He deposed, as follows:—

" I was for about nine months, just before her entrance into the convent, the confessor of Anne Catherine Emmerich. She came to me sometimes out of confession to ask my advice with regard to her vocation. She appeared to me to be a person of great simplicity, uprightness, and goodness of heart. I know nothing unfavorable of her, except that her charity toward the poor sometimes led her to purchase what she could not immediately pay for. I must say in her praise that when able she assisted every morning at the Holy Sacrifice, confessed and communicated on Sundays and feasts, and that she was thought to be a very good, pious person. On several occasions, when her hopes of being admitted into a convent were frustrated, she showed unvarying and edifying submission to the will of God."

CHAPTER XI.

ANNE CATHERINE RECEIVES THE CROWN OF THORNS.—
HER ENTRANCE AMONG THE AUGUSTINIANS, OF DÜLMEN.

When Anne Catherine had completed her bridal outfit
by the practice of the most abject poverty and self-abnega-
tion, the Heavenly Bridegroom Himself added to it the last
and most precious jewel, the Crown which He had Himself
worn on earth. One day about noon, during the last year of
her residence in the Soentgen family, she was kneeling near
the organ in the Jesuits' Church, at Coesfeld. Clara was
by her side. Immersed in contemplation, she beheld the
tabernacle door open and her Divine Betrothed issue from
it under the form of a radiant youth. In His left hand He
held a garland, in His right a Crown of Thorns, which He
graciously presented to her choice. She chose the Crown
of Thorns. Then Jesus laid it lightly on her brow; and
she, putting up both hands, pressed it firmly down. From
that instant, she experienced inexpressible pains in her
head. The apparition vanished, and Anne Catherine awoke
from her rapture to hear the clicking of the sacristan's keys
as he closed the church. Her companion was wholly unconscious of what had happened. They returned home.
Anne Catherine, suffering acute pains in her forehead
and temples, asked Clara if she could see anything. The
latter answered in the negative. But the next day, the forehead and temples were very much inflamed, although there
was, as yet, no appearance of blood. That began to flow
only in the convent where she tried carefully to conceal it
from her companions.

As St. Teresa in her waking moments saw herself adorned with the jewels, the ring, and the girdle, received in vision, so too on days dedicated to the Sacred Passion the Thorny Crown was visible to Anne Catherine. She described it as composed of three different branches : the first was of white flowers with yellow stamens ; the second like the first, but with larger leaves; the third was like the wild eglantine, or sweet-brier. In the fervor of her prayer, she often pressed it down upon her head, and each time she felt the thorns penetrating more deeply. The wounds began to bleed in the convent and, at times, the red punctures were visible through the soaked bandages. The religious thought them mildew stains on the linen, and asked for no explanation. Once only did a sister surprise her wiping the blood from her temples, but she promised secrecy.

The moment was approaching for Anne Catherine to attain the long-desired end. The circumstances attending it were, in the sight of God, the most suitable termination to her persevering and laborious efforts, a proof of the fidelity with which the Bridegroom had waited for the bride. Some days before she bade adieu to the world, she repaired for the last time to Flamske to take leave of her parents. She thanked them with tears for their affection toward her, and begged their pardon and that of the rest of the family for the pain she gave them in following her vocation. Her mother replied only by tears. Her father, usually so indulgent, was quite overcome at the prospect of losing his child. When she humbly asked a little money for her journey, he answered bitterly: "Were you to be buried to-morrow, I should willingly defray the expenses of your funeral; but you shall get nothing from me to go to the convent."

In tears, poor, despoiled of everything, but interiorly

joyful, she quitted Flamske to follow the call of God. Next
day she and Clara were to start for Dülmen some leagues
distant from Coesfeld. But, at the last moment, fresh difficulties arose. The organist Soentgen needed ten dollars
and he could get the loan of this sum only on condition of
Anne Catherine's going his security. He explained his
embarrassment to her and ceased not his importunities until
she, trusting to Divine Providence, gave her signature for
the required amount. She had no money and only what
was absolutely necessary in the way of clothing. This with
her scanty bedding was packed in a wooden chest into
which her mother had secretly slipped a piece of linen for
her beloved child. When the latter discovered it, she would
not keep it, but gave it to Clara Soentgen in gratitude for her
admission to the convent. This generous act was richly rewarded. The mysterious book of prophecies was restored to
her, and she took it with her to Dülmen.

Never since its foundation had there entered this convent a maiden so poor in earthly goods, so rich in spiritual
treasures. She humbly begged the Reverend Mother to receive her as the last and least in the house and to employ her
in whatever she saw fit; but her gentle and retiring manners
could not calm the general discontent at the reception of a
subject so poor and, besides, in bad health. The very fact
of her asking such a favor proved, as was thought, her
audacity. Agnetenberg, the Augustinian convent of Dülmen, founded toward the middle of the fifteenth century (1)

(1) The Act of Foundation, still extant, runs as follows: "In the year of Our Lord
Jesus Christ, 1457, Hermann Hoken and Margretta, his lawful wife, gave this house and
its dependencies to be forever a house of religious Sisters. In consequence thereof the
Burgomaster and City-Council of Dülmen wrote to the Sisters of Marienthal, Münster,
to beg their acceptance of the above-named house and to send hither three religious to
begin the work. Margretta Mosterdes was sent as Superioress, and with her came Gertrude Konewerdes and Geiseke Tegerdes. Hermann Hoken and his wife Margretta,
named above, gave the house as a free gift to them and their successors that it might
be forever a house of religious, to the glory of God and the honor of Mary, His Mother.
The donors, with their respective parents, as also Mette, deceased first wife of the aforesaid Hoken, are to share in the good works performed therein at all times, especially
on the anniversary of the death of each of the aforesaid persons. Their patronal feasts

had received its first religious from the convent of **Marien-thal, Münster**. It remained up to the time of its suppression, under the spiritual direction of the Augustinian Canons of Frenswegen, and toward the last it was under the Canons of Thalheim, near Paderborn. It had always been in very straitened circumstances, and during the Seven Years' War it was in great distress. The community would have been forced to disperse, were it not for the alms of the people of Dülmen. Their circumstances did not improve with time. The convent was never again able to provide for the wants of its inmates, or to restore community life in its perfection. The religious supported themselves individually, some by their dowry, others by their labor. They who had not these resources, or who received no help from strangers, fared badly enough.

Under the spiritual direction existing at the time of Anne Catherine's entrance, the convent of Agnetenberg shared the same fate as most of the poor female cloisters throughout the whole country of Münster at that period. The Rule was no longer punctually observed, in truth, it was almost forgotten. The cloister, once so rigorously closed, was now thrown open to all visitors without distinction; the peace and silence of a religious house no longer reigned. The Sisters lived as persons whom chance had thrown together, each as best she could, rather than as members of a religious community strictly bound by vows and rules to a life of perfection. Custom and necessity indeed still kept up a certain order and regularity; but it was the habit

are, likewise, to be kept with the Masses and vigils as they occur in the calendar. In the year of Our Lord, 1471, the Saturday in the octave of St. Servias, Bp., the above-named religious house was solemnly cloistered according to the Rule of their holy Father and Patron, St. Augustine. The above-mentioned Margretta Mosterdes, Mother Superioress, and five other Sisters received the Rule and bound themselves to enclosure, to serve God, the Author of salvation, in all purity and the observance of the Commandments and doctrines of Jesus Christ, Our Redeemer. On the same day and year, four other Sisters were admitted to live outside the enclosure according to the Rule.

alone and not the spirit of religion that distinguished the inmates from their fellow-Christians in the world. Anne Catherine was introduced by Almighty God into the midst of this relaxation that she might attain the highest religious perfection ; but these unfavorable surroundings were to be no more an obstacle to that end than the fruitless attempts she had hitherto made to effect her entrance. Her expiatory mission had this one peculiar characteristic : all that might be for another an occasion of sin and damnation, became for her a means of proving her fidelity to God. The decadence of conventual discipline, the loosening of the bond of obedience, the absence of enlightened direction, in a word, all the miseries of communities at this period, miseries which called down the sentence of universal suppression upon them, became for Anne Catherine so many means of reaching perfection ; they did but arouse her zeal in the service of her God.

We now turn to a new page in her prophetic book. The vision of the espousals familiar to her from her sixteenth year and by whose direction she labored at her spiritual dowry, takes a new character. She sees herself in the house of the Bridegroom or, as she was accustomed to express it, in the Nuptial House, and thither also her bridal outfit was removed. She entered the convent with an empty purse and a scanty wardrobe, and her poverty, though dear to God, drew upon her the contempt of the nuns at large, who little knew that by this very treatment they were opening for the poor peasant-girl the door of the inner chamber of the Spouse. She no longer lives in the symbolical pictures which hitherto guided her, but really in a house of God, a religious house, in the midst of which He Himself dwells in the Most Holy Sacrament. From the tabernacle He calls upon the religious to serve Him by day and by night, in the holy Office and ceremonies of the Church; thence He regulates by the monastic constitutions not only their various practices of piety and mortification, but even their daily occupations. He notes every step, every look, every gesture, in a word, their whole life, upon which He stamps the seal of consecration to His service. Anne Catherine saw all this most clearly. The higher her estimation of the incomparable dignity of such a life, the more sensitive was she to each infraction of the Rule, every indication of indifference, indolence, or worldliness; and in corresponding proportion did she deem herself unworthy of so great a dignity. She indulged in no figure of speech when, on her entrance, she asked the Superioress to be treated as the last and least of all. We shall see that, by Almighty God's permission, her petition was fully granted.

CHAPTER XII.

ANNE CATHERINE'S NOVITIATE.

Anne Catherine passed her first months in the convent as a postulant in the secular dress, she and Clara Soentgen occupying the same cell. She had no security of being permitted to remain in the community, but God gave her during this time strength sufficient to render herself useful. She earned, besides, by her needle sufficient to supply her few necessities and to defray the expense of her reception to the habit. She thus escaped being sent away under the plea of uselessness, and on Nov. 13, 1802, she was clothed with the habit of the Order and formally admitted to the novitiate. The worst cell in the house was assigned her. It had two chairs, one without a back, the other minus a seat; the window-sill served as a table.

"But," she declared years after, "that poor cell of mine appeared to me so well furnished, so grand, that it was to me a perfect heaven!"

We can readily imagine what the spiritual training of novices would be in a community in which the exercises employed in happier times for this end had fallen into disuse. Anne Catherine sighed for the humiliation and obedience prescribed by the Rule, but there was no one to impose them. She knew that the humility that springs from obedience is infinitely more efficacious and meritorious than self-imposed penance. But such occasions of meriting would never have been hers had not her Divine Betrothed intervened as Master to conduct His pupil to the highest

perfection, and this He did precisely by those very circumstances which seemed so unfavorable to spiritual progress.
Everything was to be a means of attaining this end and, in
the same measure, a means of advancing the glory of God and
the good of His Church. A prudent mistress, one experienced in the spiritual life, would soon have discovered her
novice's sublime vocation and would have directed her in
accordance with it, tolerating in her no imperfection, no defect. Anne Catherine was naturally hasty. She had a keen
sense of injustice, and resented it accordingly ; but to the
mortification of these dispositions she could not attain without proper direction. Almighty God, however, furnished
the occasions for self-victory in these very points. From
the beginning of her novitiate, He permitted her to be
unjustly suspected, accused, reprimanded, and penanced,
all which she bore without murmur, excuse, or reply.

We shall cite one instance among many of the kind.
The convent possessed but a slender revenue from its lands ;
and in order to increase its funds, it boarded for a trifling
sum a few poor French nuns, émigrées, and an old gentleman, the brother of the Superioress. The nuns, learning
by chance that the old gentleman paid less than they,
grew dissatisfied and accused the Superioress of injustice. Then the question arose as to how the nuns
had come by this information. No Sister, of course,
acknowledged herself guilty, and so the blame fell
on the unfortunate novice, who was known to take a
lively interest in the destitute religious banished on account
of their profession. Anne Catherine could say most
truthfully that she knew not what either party paid and,
consequently, she had nothing to reveal on the subject.
But this was of little moment in the estimation of her
accusers. She was reprimanded by the Superioress

in full Chapter and she underwent the penance imposed. At once there arose loud complaints in the community against the galling ingratitude, as they styled it, of this miserable peasant-girl. The innocent victim of all this clamor had to bear not only unjust suspicion and severe punishment, but she endured also the bitterness of having been, although involuntarily, the cause of such uncharitableness. There was no one in the house to whom she might unburden her heart, no one to pour into her wound one drop of consolation. She overcame her feelings so far as not only to forgive them who had injured her, but also to render thanks to God for what she tried to look upon as a merited chastisement. The effort was, however, too trying on her delicate sensibilities. She fell seriously ill and recovered but slowly.

About Christmas, 1802, she felt around her heart acute pains which prevented her attending to her customary duties. In vain did she struggle against her sufferings, they did but increase ; it was as if she were being pierced by sharp arrows and she was, finally, obliged to keep her bed. In her humility, she dared acknowledge neither to herself nor to others the real cause of her malady, although she knew it from a vision vouchsafed her at the time of her clothing. The signification of the ceremony, as well as of every article of the religious dress, had been shown her. She had, in consequence, received it with deep respect and gratitude. St. Augustine, patron of the Order, had shown her his heart burning with love, had clothed her with the habit, accepted her for his daughter, promised her his special assistance. At this sight so great a fire was enkindled in her breast that she felt herself more closely united to the community than with her own blood-relations. The significance of the religious dress became then as real to her as the dress itself. She was actually conscious of the spiritual union it established between her and the rest of the sisterhood. It was like a current flowing through the whole body, but ever returning to herself as to its source. Her heart had become, so to say, the spiritual centre of the community. Hers was the terrible mission of enduring the wounds inflicted upon the Heart of the Bridegroom by the sins and imperfections of its members. She could advance but slowly in this way, for love did not render her insensible to pain and sorrow, and every infraction of vows or rules pierced her heart like a burning dart.

No one understood her state. The physician of the convent was called in. He pronounced her sufferings purely physical. It was the first time in her life that she had been subjected to medical treatment. In her own home certain simple herbs, of whose virtues she herself possessed the knowledge, and a little repose quickly wrought a cure; no one thought of having recourse to medicine. Now it was very different. The Rule imposed it as a duty to declare herself sick and to receive the care of the physician appointed. Although knowing her illness to be purely spiritual, to be relieved only by spiritual means, yet, as an obedient novice, she could refuse no remedy offered her. She quietly allowed herself to be treated, happy in having an occasion to practise obedience.

That her submission might be still more perfect, Almighty God permitted the evil spirit to lay all kinds of snares for her. He appeared as an angel of light, and exhorted her to return to the world. It would be sinful, he reasoned, to desire longer to bear a burden above her strength, and he pictured to her what she would have to endure from the Sisters, etc. But the sign of the cross put the tempter to flight even before he had finished his wily speech.

Again he sought to rouse her resentment and make her murmur against Superiors, or he tried to inspire her with such fear of them as to force her to leave the convent. One night he threw her into an agony of terror. It seemed to her that the Superioress and the Novice-Mistress suddenly entered her cell, reproached her in unmeasured terms, declared her absolutely unworthy of their holy vocation, and ended by saying she should be expelled from the community. Anne Catherine received their rebukes in silence, acknowledged her unworthiness, and begged them to be patient with her. Then the angry nuns left her cell, abusing her as they went. The poor novice wept and prayed till morning, when she sent for her confessor, told him what had occurred during the night, and asked him what she should do to appease the Superioress. But on inquiry, it was proved that neither the Superioress nor any other Sister had entered her cell at the time specified. The confessor saw in it an attack of the evil one, and the novice thanked God for the deep feeling of unworthiness by which she had overcome the tempter.

After some weeks the physician's visits were discontinued. The community thought her cured; but, in reality, it was not so. She was so weak and infirm that again the hue and cry was raised against the convent's burdening itself by the profession of such a member. " Send her away at once," they said; "do not incur the obligation of keeping her altogether." These whispers, although perhaps at the other end of the building, were heard by the poor invalid as if spoken in her cell. All the little plots, all the thoughts of her Sisters against her, pierced her soul like so many fiery sparks, like so many red-hot spears, wounding her to the quick. The gift of reading hearts which she possessed from her infancy, but which had never given her pain among the simple peasants, who all loved and reverenced her, now became for her a source of exquisite suffering. All this was in accordance with the designs of God. He willed that only by the perfection of virtue, should she surmount the obstacles she was to meet in her task of expiation. She saw the passions of her fellow-sisters, inasmuch as she had to struggle against them by her own prayer and mortification; and by humility, patience, and charity she had to disarm those who opposed her making the religious vows. If a word of complaint, a sign of dissatisfaction escaped her, she tearfully implored pardon with expressions of sorrow so touching that the Sisters became more kindly disposed toward her. Then she would run before the Blessed Sacrament and beg for strength to perform her duties. "She redoubled her efforts to render herself useful and stilled the anguish of her heart with these words: " I will persevere, even if I should be martyred !"

On a certain Friday in February, 1803, as she was praying alone before the Blessed Sacrament, there suddenly appeared before her a cross, eight inches in length, on which hung an image of the Saviour covered with blood.

" I was," she says, " greatly agitated by this apparition. I flushed and trembled, for I saw everything around me and the bloody crucifix before me. It was not a vision, I saw it with my bodily eyes. Then the thought struck me that by this apparition God was preparing me for extraordi nary sufferings. I shuddered !—but the pitiable sight of my blood-stained Jesus banished my repugnance, and I felt strong to accept even the most fearful pains if Our Lord only granted me patience to bear them."

The presentment was soon realized. The gift of tears was bestowed upon her that she might weep over the out-

rages offered her Divine Betrothed and find in it for herself a fruitful source of humiliation. Whenever anything
was presented either to her corporal or mental sight which
called for supernatural sorrow, it was impossible for her to
restrain her tears. When she considered the sufferings
and tribulations of the Church, when she saw the Sacraments conferred or received unworthily, her heart was so
wounded that torrents of bitter tears flowed from her eyes.
If she beheld spiritual blindness, false piety veiling evil
dispositions, grace despised or obstinately resisted, the truths
of faith set aside, her tears flowed involuntarily, bathing
her cheeks, her neck, her breast almost unknown to herself.   In the chapel, at Holy Communion, at meals, at
work, at community exercises, her tears would gush forth
to the extreme displeasure of the religious.   During Mass
and Holy Communion, all eyes were turned upon her.
This was all the notice she received, at first ; but, as her
tears became more abundant, she was taken aside and reproached for her singular behavior.   She promised on her
knees to correct; but soon, next day perhaps, it was remarked that during Mass even the kneeling-bench was
wet with her tears, a fresh proof as it was thought that
the novice was still indulging wounded self-love.   Again was
she reprimanded, again was she penanced ; but her humility and submission were such that the Superioress was
forced to acknowledge the poor novice's tears a greater
mortification to herself than to others. They were, in the
end, ascribed to constitutional weakness and not to discontent or caprice.   As to Anne Catherine, so far from looking upon them as supernatural, she anxiously examined
whether they did not proceed from some secret aversion to
the Sisters.   She dared not decide for herself, and disclosed
her fears to her confessor, who quieted her with the assurance

that they sprang not from hatred but from compassion.

She hoped that time would mitigate the intensity of her feelings and that her tears would cease to flow. But this was not the case; they rather increased than diminished. In her distress she applied to the other confessors appointed for the religious, but from all she received the same answer.

Dean Overberg says on this point:—

" Anne Catherine so tenderly loved her Sisters in religion that she would willingly have shed her blood for them individually. She knew that several were against her, yet she did all in her power to propitiate them and rejoiced when any one asked her assistance. She hoped by kindness to win them over to their duty.

" God permitted that she should not be appreciated by the Superioress and Sisters who saw in all that she did either hypocrisy, flattery, or pride, and they failed not to reproach her openly. At first she tried to justify herself; but afterward she merely replied that she would correct. She wept over the deplorable spiritual destitution of the religious; for whether at exercises of piety or other conventual duties, it was ever before her eyes.

" The tears she shed during the Holy Sacrifice were particularly displeasing to the nuns, and they held little whispered councils as to the most effective means of curing her of what they termed her sloth and caprice. All this added to her desolation, since she clearly knew what was passing in their inmost thoughts.

" She assured me that she knew all that was said or planned against her. ' I saw then even more clearly than I do now.' she said (April 22, 1813), ' what passed in souls, and sometimes I let them see that I knew it. Then they

wanted to know how I came by the knowledge, but I dared
not tell them, and they straightway imagined that some one
had told me. I asked my confessor what I should do. He
told me to say that I had spoken of it in confession and to
give no explanation on the subject."

On another occasion, she again alluded to her gift of
tears :—

" I would willingly have given my life for my sister-religious and, therefore, my tears could not be restrained
when I saw them so irritated against me. Who would
not weep at seeing himself a stumbling-block in the
house of peace, among the chosen of God ? I wept
over the poverty, the misery, the blindness of those whose
hard hearts languished amidst the superabundant graces
of our Holy Redeemer."

When, in 1813, Ecclesiastical Superiors demanded the testimony of the community of Agnetenberg concerning Anne
Catherine, the Superioress, the Novice-Mistress and five of
the other religious unanimously deposed as follows :—

" Anne Catherine was affable and cordial, very easy to
deal with, humble, condescending, and exceedingly pre-
venting. In sickness she was admirable, ever resigned to
the will of God. She quickly and cheerfully forgave every
offence against her, always asked pardon if she herself
were in fault, never harbored ill-will, and was always the
first to yield."

And Clara Soentgen told Dean Overberg :—

" Anne Catherine was never so happy as when serving
the Sisters. They might ask what they pleased, she never
refused; she gladly gave them even what she needed most
herself. If she had a preference, it was only for those that
she knew disliked her."

Dean Rensing of Dülmen deposed, April 24, 1813 :—

" I had been told of Anne Catherine's having rendered great services to one of the Sisters during an illness, and I asked her why she did it. She answered :—' The Sister had sores on her feet and the servants did not like to wait on her as she was hard to please. I thought it a work of mercy, and I begged her to let me wash her blood-stained bandages. She had the itch, too, and I used to make up her bed, as the servants were afraid of catching her disease. But I confided in God and He preserved me from it. I knew that this whimsical Sister would not thank me when she got well, that she would again treat me as a hypocrite as she had often done before. But I said to myself, 'I shall have so much the more merit before God,' and so I went on, washing her linen, making her bed, and taking the best care I could of her."

Anne Catherine understood so perfectly the signification of the religious vows, she so ardently longed to practise obedience in all things, that the fact of not being exercised in it by the commands of Superiors was a very grievous trial to her. She often begged the Reverend Mother to command her in virtue of obedience that she might practise her vow. But such requests were looked upon as singular, the effects of scruples, and she received no other reply from the weak and indulgent Superioress than : " *You know your duty*," and thus she was left to herself. This want of training afflicted the novice even to tears. It seemed to her that the blessing attached to the religious state was not for her, since blind obedience to Superiors, so pleasing to her Divine Betrothed, was not permitted her.

In 1813, the Superioress deposed as follows :—

" Sister Emmerich cheerfully and eagerly fulfilled the injunctions of obedience, especially when enjoined upon her individually."

The Novice-Mistress says :—

" She practised obedience perfectly. Her only regret was that Reverend Mother laid no commands upon her."

If occasions of practising obedience were for the most part wanting, she tried to supply the loss by her interior submission and untiring attention to regulate all her actions according to the spirit and letter of the Rule. She would not live in religion in the mere practice of the still existing observances; she aimed at moulding her whole interior and exterior life by its animating principle. With this view she made it a careful study, and so great was her respect for it that she read it only on her knees. Sometimes whilst thus engaged, the light by which she was reading would be suddenly extinguished and the book closed by an invisible power. She knew well by whose agency this was affected so, quietly relighting her candle, she set to work more earnestly than before. These attacks of the demon grew more sensible and violent, and amply indemnified her for the want of other trials. If he maltreated her for seriously studying her Rule, she applied thereto more assiduously ; if he excited a storm against her in the community, it only gave her an occasion to practise blind and humble obedience as the following incident will prove :

A rich merchant of Amsterdam had entered his daughter as a boarder in the convent. When about to return home, the young lady presented a florin to each of the nuns. But to Anne Catherine, for whom she had a special affection, she gave two, which the good novice immediately handed over to her Superioress. A few days after the whole house was up in arms. Anne Catherine was cited before the Chapter, accused of having received five thalers from the young Hollander, of giving only two to the Reverend Mother, and of having handed over the other three to the organist Soentgen, who had just paid a visit to his daughter. They appealed to her conscience, and Anne Catherine truthfully declared all that had passed. The nuns redoubled their accusations, but she firmly denied having received five thalers. Then sentence was passed upon the poor novice. She was condemned to ask pardon on her knees of each Sister. She gladly accepted the undeserved penance, begging God to grant that her Sisters might pardon not only this imaginary fault, but all they saw displeasing in her. Some months after the merchant's daughter returned, and the novice asked the Superioress to inquire into the affair. But she received for answer to think no more of what was now forgotten. She obeyed and reaped the full benefit of the humiliation.

We see by this circumstance how prone these imperfect religious were to dislike and suspect their innocent companion, and also how quickly the storm was lulled even when at its height. Their novice's demeanor produced impressions so varied upon them that we can scarcely wonder that, in their inexperience, their obtuseness to all beyond their every-day existence, they sometimes went astray. And, although Anne Catherine's sweetness and patience under such trials, her earnestness in begging pardon, could not fail to soften even the most exasperated, yet new suspicions, fresh charges soon arose against her. There was in the richness of her supernatural life, in the varied and wonderful gifts imparted to her, in a word, in her whole being something too striking to remain hidden, or to allow her to tread the beaten paths of ordinary life like the other religious. However great the simplicity and modesty of her bearing, there shone about her a something so holy, so elevated, that all were forced to feel, though they might not acknowledge her superiority; consequently, they regarded her as singular, tiresome, and disagreeable.

Anne Catherine was drawn to the Blessed Sacrament by an irresistible force. When some errand took her through the church, she fell as if paralyzed at the foot of the altar. She was ever in a state of contemplation and interior suffering which, in spite of every effort on her part, could not be wholly concealed. To all around her she was simply a mystery, to some quite insupportable.

Clara Soentgen deposed on this point as follows :—

" Anne Catherine did her best to conceal the attraction which impelled her to extraordinary devotion ; but nothing could escape me, I knew her so well. I often found her in the chapel kneeling or prostrate before the Blessed Sacrament. She was so powerfully attracted to contemplation that, even in the company of others, I could see that she was quite abstracted. She was much given to bodily mortification. At table I used to notice that she took the worst of everything, leaving dainty dishes untouched, or passing her share to her neighbor, especially if the latter had any ill-will toward her, and she was so pleased when a chance presented itself to do this that I was filled with astonishment."

The Novice-Mistress says :—

" Several times during Anne Catherine's novitiate, I removed little pieces of wood from her bed. She had put them there to render her rest uncomfortable, for she was much given to corporal mortification. I was sometimes obliged to make her leave the chapel at ten o'clock in winter and send her to bed ; otherwise she would have remained too long."

On various occasions, Anne Catherine herself spoke of her early days in the convent. Clement Brentano, who carefully collected all her communications and reduced them to writing, gives us the following :—

" From the very beginning of my novitiate I endured incredible interior sufferings. At times my heart was surrounded by roses and then suddenly transpierced by thorns, sharp points, and darts, which arose from my perceiving much more clearly than I do now every injurious thought, word, or action against me. Not one with whom I lived, no religious, no confessor, had the least idea of the state of my soul or the particular way by which I was led. I lived wholly in another world of which I could make nothing known. But, as on some occasions, in consequence of any interior direction, things appeared in me not in conformity with everyday life, I became a cause of temptation to many, a subject for injurious suspicion, detraction, and unkind remarks. These mortifying opinions and speeches entered my soul like sharp arrows. I was attacked on all sides, my heart was pierced with a thousand wounds. Exteriorly I was serene and cordial, as if ignorant of their cruel treatment ; and, after all, I really did not know much from without, for the suffering was all within. It was shown me in order to exercise my obedience, charity, and humility. When I failed in these virtues, I was interiorly punished. My soul appeared to me transparent ; and, when a new suffering assailed me, I saw it in my soul under the appearance of fiery darts, red and inflamed spots, which patience alone could remove.

" My condition in the convent was so singular, so perfectly abstracted from outward things that my companions can hardly be blamed for their treatment of me. They could not understand me, they regarded me with distrust and suspicion ; however, God hid many facts from them that would have perplexed them still more. As for the rest, in spite of these trials, I have never since been so rich interiorly, never so perfectly happy as then, for I was at peace with God and man. When at work in the garden, the birds perched on my head and shoulders and we praised God together.

"My angel was ever at my side. Although the evil spirit raged around me, although he heaped abuse upon me in the quiet of my cell and sought to terrify me by frightful noises, yet he could never harm me; I was always relieved in good time.

"I often thought I had the Infant Jesus in my arms for hours at a time ; or, when with the Sisters, I felt Him by my side and I was perfectly happy. I beheld so many things which roused feelings of joy or pain, but I had no one to whom I could impart them, and my very efforts at concealing these sudden and violent emotions caused me to change color frequently. Then the sisters said that I looked like one in love. They were, indeed, right for I could never love my Affianced enough, and when His friends spoke well of Him or of those dear to Him, my heart beat with joy."

CHAPTER XIII.

Anne Catherine makes Her Vows, Nov. 13, 1803.

The year of novitiate drew to a close, but the community had not yet decided upon admitting the novice to her holy profession. The Novice-Mistress could in all truth render the following testimony of her charge : "I remark in her constant submission to the will of God, but she is often in tears. She will not say why, because she dares not; otherwise I see nothing in her that deserves censure."

This testimony in her favor did not, however, satisfy the community. When the Chapter deliberated as to whether she should be sent away or allowed to remain, no other reason could be assigned for her dismissal than that she would soon become incapable of labor, a burden on the house ; yet the Reverend Mother was forced to acknowledge that the novice was very intelligent, that she possessed skill and aptitude, and that she would certainly be of great use ; a declaration which drew from her opponents the avowal that she always comported herself as a good religious and that, after all, there was not sufficient reason for sending her home.

These obstacles removed and the day appointed for the ceremony, a new difficulty arose on the part of the novice herself. She had not yet redeemed the security given to the organist Soentgen for ten thalers, and she had good reason to fear being held responsible for the debt. She explained her embarrassment to the Reverend Mother, who applied to the gentleman in question. But he declared his inability to release Anne Catherine from her obligation, as he was unable to discharge his indebtedness. The community resolved not to allow the novice to make her vows until she had freed herself from her engagement. What was now to be done? Anne Catherine turned to God. We shall give her own words on this subject:—

"I had not a single cent. I applied to my family, but no one would help me, not even my brother Bernard. All reproached me as if I had committed a crime in going security. But the debt had to be cancelled before I could make my vows. I cried to God for assistance and, at last, a charitable man gave me the ten thalers. My brother used to shed tears at a later period over his hard-heartedness toward me.

"This obstacle being happily removed and the preparations for the profession almost completed, another difficulty sprang up. The Reverend Mother told Clara and myself that we were still in need of something for which we should have to send to Münster, entailing an expense of three thalers each. I had no money, and where was I to get any? In my distress, I went to Abbé Lambert, who kindly gave me two crowns. I returned joyfully to my cell where, to my great delight, I found six thalers lying on the table. I ran with the two crowns to my friend who, like myself, had nothing and knew not where to procure her three thalers.

"Three years after I was again in need of money. Each Sister had to provide her own breakfast, and I had nothing at the time to procure mine. One day I entered my cell, which was locked, and found two thalers lying on the window-sill. I took them to the Superioress, who allowed me to keep them.

"Eight days before the Feast of the Presentation of the Blessed Virgin, 1803, on the same day on which one year before Clara Soentgen and I had taken the habit, we made

our profession as Augustinians in the convent of Agnetenberg, Dülmen, and from that day we were consecrated
spouses of Jesus Christ under the Rule of St. Augustine.
I was in my twenty-eighth year. After my profession my
parents became reconciled to my being a religious, and my
father and brother came to see me and brought me two
pieces of linen."

The Abbé John Martin Lambert, whom we now meet for
the first time, formerly a vicar in the parish of Demuin,
diocese of Amiens, had been like many other good priests
forced to leave his country on refusing to take the famous
oath of the Constitution. With recommendations from the
Archbishop of Tours and the Bishop of Amiens, he went
in 1794 to Münster, obtained faculties from the Vicar-General von Fürstenberg and was appointed confessor with a
small allowance to the house of the Duke von Croy, who resided in Dülmen. In the convent of Agnetenberg, which
had its own confessor, the Abbé held also the office of chaplain, a post which conferred upon the possessor the right
of a lodging within the convent grounds. When Sister
Emmerich had charge of the sacristy she became acquainted with him; his piety and deep recollection in saying holy
Mass impressed her favorably and she conceived great
confidence in him.

The unsisterly treatment she experienced from her companions distressed her sorely and failing to make herself
understood by the ordinary confessor, she resolved to open
her heart to the Abbé and ask his advice and assistance.
But, as the good father knew little German, their communications were, at first, necessarily very restricted.
Nevertheless, the pious and enlightened priest soon acquired
an insight into his penitent's state, and felt bound in consequence to help as far as possible a soul so highly favored

by God. He engaged the confessor to permit her to communicate more frequently, even to command it when
through humility she wished to abstain. And he it was
who at dawn of day held himself in readiness to administer to her the Adorable Eucharist when her desire of the
Heavenly Manna made her almost swoon away. Though
very poor himself, he was ever willing to assist her when her
distress made her consent to accept an alms from him, and
on her side she honored him as her greatest earthly benefactor. Later on we shall see her returning, as far as she
was able, his unvarying kindness.

We may readily conceive Anne Catherine's sentiments
when pronouncing at the foot of the altar the solemn vows
to which she had so long aspired. The same zeal, the same
desire with which sixteen years before she had prepared
for her First Communion, marked her preparation for this
solemn occasion. Multiplied prayers and penances, trials
and anxiety had exhausted her strength during the days
immediately preceding her profession; yet upon the
joyful day itself, she appeared to be endued with new
vigor. The joy of her soul manifested itself in her exterior;
she was, as it were, all luminous. She understood the real
signification of the ceremony, she perceived the meaning of
the trials that had beset her path since her first call to the
religious state, and her heart overflowed with gratitude for
all that God had operated in her and by her up to that
moment. She saw herself clothed in the festal robes and
bridal ornaments over which for years she had untiringly labored according to the directions given in her great visions;
every step, every self-victory, every sigh, was therein represented as a precious stone or an exquisite piece of embroidery. Now she saw how necessary all these trials had
been to prepare her for the nuptials at which her Divine

Betrothed assisted visibly with the saints of the Order of St. Augustine.

As at baptism she had seen herself espoused to the Infant Jesus by His holy Mother, so now it was by the Queen of Virgins she was presented to her Betrothed. Whilst her lips pronounced the words of holy profession, she beheld her solemn consecration to God ratified in a twofold manner. The Church Militant received her and the Heavenly Bridegroom deigned to accept her from the hands of Mother Church, sealing His acceptance by bestowing upon her His most magnificent gifts. She saw the exalted position in the Church to which the vows elevated her; she highly appreciated the abundant graces bestowed upon her and the dignity with which her quality of spouse invested her, a dignity which she ever after regarded in herself with respect. The same thing happened to her as to a pious candidate for Holy Orders. At the time of his ordination, his own soul became visible to him in all the splendor communicated to it by the indelible mark of the priesthood. Anne Catherine felt in what way she henceforth belonged to the Church, and through the Church to her Heavenly Bridegroom; as a consecrated gift she was offered to God body and soul. Like Columba di Rieti, Lidwina of Schiedam, and Blessed Colette, she understood the spiritual signification of her different members, as a spouse of God, and also their symbolical relation to the body of the Church.

No inmate of Agnetenberg had the slightest suspicion of these marvels, yet God willed that this day of spiritual nuptials should be for all supereminently a day of joy and peace. Anne Catherine, though in blissful tears that would not be kept back, exerted a gladdening influence on all her Sisters; and her reiterated thanks for admitting her irrevocably among them won even the most obstinate to smile upon her for that one day at least. A repast awaited the guests in the convent refectory, to which her beloved parents were invited after High Mass. The opposition of these good people and the suffering it had brought upon their daughter had had no other effect upon the latter than that of causing her to pray most earnestly that God would grant them the grace to make the sacrifice He demanded of them. Her prayer was heard at last. They were so deeply affected by the sight of their child on this day, the day of her espousals, that, uniting in her sacrifice, they gave her to God with all their heart. They testified their joy in so many ways and showed so much affection for her that, to the end of her life, the remembrance of this solemnity was always one of the sweetest.

The year 1803 opened most disastrously for the Catholic Church in Germany. It would, doubtless, have been utterly annihilated were its founder and defender other than God Himself. As formerly He had permitted the destruction of His holy city and temple as a punishment for the infidelity and apostasy of His people, so now the Church's powerful enemies were to be for her the instruments to separate the good from the bad grain. Whilst this sentence was being executed, whilst the " abomination of desolation" lasted, the Lord hid the holy things of His Church, as the priests of the Temple the sacred fire, until crime being expiated, it might be enkindled with greater brilliancy than before. The pits in which the sacred fire of the Christian Church was preserved were holy souls, few in number at this period. They hid 'neath the waters of tribulation those treasures which formed of old the delight and ornament of the Bride of Christ; treasures which were now abandoned by their custodians, pillaged and dissipated by those that ought to have guarded and defended them. Anne Catherine shared this task with a small number of faithful servants. The Lord made use of the fire of sufferings and the mallet of penance to make of her a vase, pure, strong, and sufficiently capacious to receive the incommensurable riches of the Church until the time for their restoration.

What now was the life that awaited Sister Emmerich in the convent? The favorable impression of the festal day was soon effaced from the hearts of her Sisters, and the poor child became once more what she had ever been, the unwelcome intruder among them. Almighty God had, as it were, procured her an entrance into this convent by force ; and from the very first she had contracted in the eyes of the religious, by her poverty and ill-health, a debt she could never discharge. The habit had been given her in the midst of dissatisfaction, and now she had taken her vows almost in spite of general opposition. A vessel of election, God's chosen instrument, she is forever to be a stumbling-block, an object of aversion to those for whom she entertained so warm an affection. This she knew and felt at every moment, owing to her gift of reading hearts, and thus she was in her own person treated precisely as the religious state itself was treated at that epoch by too many of its members. She had, moreover, not the faintest hope of being able to restore the strict discipline of former times by training active young members to it; for, after her entrance, the novitiate was closed forever. She was the last to make the religious profession in the convent of Agnetenberg, and she knew both from the political aspect of the day and her own visions, that this spiritual family would shortly be dissolved never again to be reunited. How admirable are the ways of God ! How contrary to those of the world! How different are the means that He employs from those of men! Anne Catherine combined, in a human view, qualifications eminently suited for rendering the highest services to the Church; but God demands of her no dazzling marks of loyalty. Incalculable sufferings, years of obscurity and humiliation, were the only remedies she was to apply to the deep wounds of His Spouse on earth. The further she advanced in her mission, the greater became her sufferings. We could scarcely support the frightful spectacle if her sweet, childlike simplicity came not as a gleam from Paradise to light up the dark sea of sorrows which bore her storm-tossed bark to the haven of rest.

CHAPTER XIV.

Corporal Sufferings.

"I gave myself to my Heavenly Spouse and He accomplished His will in me. To suffer in repose has ever seemed to me the most enviable state in this world, but one to which I never attained." In these words Sister Emmerich summed up the mystery of her whole life both in the convent and out of it, for sufferings never failed her. She accepted them gratefully from the hands of God, she welcomed them as a precious gift, but never was repose in suffering hers, never did a peaceful, hidden life fall to her lot. She was to arrive at perfect conformity with her Spouse. He consummated His mission amidst contradictions, tribulations, and persecutions—His servant was not to accomplish hers otherwise. From her infancy she had suffered for others; but now these sufferings assumed a more elevated, a more extended character. The wounds of the body of the Church, that is the falling off of whole dioceses, the self-will and negligence of ecclesiastics, the deplorable state of society —all was laid upon her to be expiated by varied and multiplied sufferings. Her infirmities resulted from spiritual wounds entailed upon the flock of Christ by the sins of its own members. In this she may be compared to Blessed Lidwina of Schiedam who together with Christina of Saint-Trond (*Christina mirabilis*) is, perhaps, the most wonderful instrument of expiation ever made use of by Almighty God for the good of the Church. A glance at her life will give us a clear insight into Sister Emmerich's mission (1).

(1) Blessed Lidwina's life was compiled by a contemporary, Brother John Brugmann, Provincial of the Friars Minor, in Holland, who died in the odor of sanctity. Communications were made for this end by Lidwina's confessor, Walter von Leyden, and John Gerlach, his friend. The Burgomaster and Council of Schiedam testified thereto, as also the blessed Thomas à Kempis.—See Acta Sanctorum, April 14th.

Lidwina, the daughter of a poor watchman of Schiedam, was born some weeks previously to the death of St. Catherine of Sienna and, by a special privilege, dedicated to the Mother of God to receive from her strength to continue the mission of suffering for the Church bequeathed to her by the saint. Catherine had been raised up by God in the fourteenth century, like St. Hildegarde in the twelfth, to aid Christianity by the spirit of prophecy. Her life counted but thirty-three years; for her heart, riven by divine love, could not longer endure the sight of the unhappy divisions in the Church caused by the election of an anti-pope opposed to Urban VI. A schism burst forth two years before her death, and St. Catherine shrank from no sacrifice to restore peace and unity, even imploring Almighty God to permit the rage of hell to be unchained against her own person rather than against the Head of the Church. Her prayer was heard. During the last three months of her life from January 19, 1380, Sexagesima, till April 30, fifth Sunday after Easter, hell did indeed make her its victim, as it had formerly done St. Hildegarde who for three consecutive years wrestled with the infernal cohorts for the good of the Church. On Palm Sunday, 1380, only a few weeks before the death of St. Catherine, Lidwina, the heiress of her sufferings and struggles, was born in Holland. From her very cradle she was a little victim of pain, the intolerable agony of the stone being her portion; yet, in spite of her ill health, she was so beautiful and presented so robust an appearance that her hand was sought in marriage at the early age of twelve. But long before she had consecrated her virginity to God by vow; and now, to free herself from suitors, she begged Him to deprive her of her beauty, a prayer most pleasing to the Author of all beauty. In her fifteenth year she fell ill.

On her recovery she was so disfigured as to be no longer an object of attraction. In this way she was prepared to be a vessel of sufferings, and the miseries which at that period afflicted the Church were laid upon her. Whilst skating on the ice a companion struck against her. Lidwina fell and broke a rib of her right side. An internal abscess formed which no remedies could relieve and from which she endured horrible pains. About a year after this accident, her father approached her bed one day to soothe and comfort her, when in a paroxysm of agony she threw herself into his arms. The sudden movement broke the abscess, the blood gushed violently from her mouth and nose, and she was in imminent danger of suffocating. From this moment she grew worse; the suppuration of the abscess hindered her taking nourishment and if she forced herself to eat, her stomach refused to retain the food. Burning thirst consumed her and when she dragged herself out of bed to swallow a mouthful of water, it was only to throw it off immediately. Nothing gave her any relief; and, what was still more deplorable, she was for years deprived of spiritual consolation and direction. Once a year, at Easter, she was carried to the church to receive Holy Communion, and that was all. Sometimes it seemed to her as if she could not possibly endure her state of suffering and abandonment longer; but sickness, even such as hers, could not at once crush her youthful buoyancy and she was often seized with a longing desire to be cured. A miserable little room on the ground floor, more like a cave than an apartment, was the one assigned her and the merry voices of the young people as they passed the narrow window intensified her feelings of utter abandonment. Three or four years passed away, and then God sent to her a holy confessor and director in the person of John Pot, who taught her how to meditate on the dolorous Passion of Christ, from which exercise she drew fortitude and re- signation. She was docile and faithful to his instructions, but perfect relief came to her desolate soul only when the gift of tears was granted to her, which happened one day after Holy Communion. For fourteen days her tears flow- ed constantly and uncontrollably over her former impa- tience and tepidity whilst, at the same time, her soul was inundated with consolation. From that moment she made such progress in prayer that all hours of the day and night found her absorbed in contemplation, and she regulated the time as precisely by her own interior admonition, as if by the sound of a clock. In the eighth year of her sickness, she could say : " It is not I who suffer ; it is my Lord Jesus who suffers in me !" and she continually offered her- self as a victim of expiation. Once upon Quinquagesima Sunday she asked for some special pain to atone for the sins committed during the Carnival ; whereupon she was attacked by pains in her limbs so excruciating that she no longer dared to make such petitions. Again she offered herself as a victim to avert the plague from her native city, and instantaneously two pestilential sores appeared on her throat and breast ; she begged for a third in honor of the Most Holy Trinity, and another appeared on her knee.

Soon the entire dismemberment and devastation of the Church were cast upon her. The three-fold havoc made at the time of the great schism by freedom of opinion, im- morality, and heresy, was represented in her by swarms of greenish worms that generated in her spine, attacked her kidneys and devoured the lower part of her body, in which they made three large holes. About two hundred of these worms, an inch in length, were daily generated. To protect herself in some degree, Lidwina fed them on a mix-

ture of honey and flour, or with capon fat spread on linen
and laid over the wounds.   This she had to beg as an alms;
and, if it happened not to be fresh, the worms attacked her
instead.   As infidelity, heresy, and schism spring from
pride of intellect and sins against the sixth commandment,
this triple evil had to be expiated in a manner analogous
in its nature, that is by putrefaction and worms.

What remained of the other internal parts of her body
after the action of the purulent abscess, was, at Lidwina's
own desire, buried and the cavity of the abdomen filled up
with wool.   She was attended by the physician of the
Duchess Margarite of Holland.   The agony she endured
from the stone, notwithstanding the decomposition of her
organs, reached at times such a degree of intensity as to
deprive her of consciousness.   This suffering was in
expiation of the abomination of concubinage even among
clerics.   Her kidneys and liver rotted away; purulent
tumors formed on her breasts, because of the milk of scandal
given to multitudes of children, instead of the nourishment
of pure doctrine; and, for the strife and discord that reigned
among Christian theologians, Lidwina endured the most
agonizing toothache, which was often so violent as to affect
her reason.   The unhealthy excitement agitating the body of
the Church was atoned for by a tertian fever that, like a withering blast, dried up her bones or shook her with icy chills.

Lastly, as Christianity for forty years was divided
between popes and anti-popes, so, too, was Lidwina's body
literally separated into two parts.   Her shoulders had to
be bandaged to keep them from falling asunder.   A split
extended vertically through her forehead down to the middle of her nose; her lips and chin were in the same condition; and the blood sometimes flowed so abundantly from
them as to prevent her speaking.

As the Pope could no longer guard the entire flock, Lidwina lost the use of her right eye, and the left was so weak
that she could not endure the light. The fire of revolt paralyzed the Sovereign Pontiff's power —and Lidwina's right
arm was attacked by St. Anthony's fire; the nerves lay
upon the fleshless bones like the cords of a guitar, the arm
itself being attached to the body merely by a tendon. With
the use of only her left hand she lay upon her back, heip-
less and motionless, and for seven consecutive years she
could not be moved lest she would literally fall to pieces.
Her body, deprived of sleep and nourishment, was like a
worm-eaten tree supported only by the bark; and yet there
daily flowed from her mouth, nose, eyes, ears, from all the
pores of her body so great a quantity of blood and other
fluids that two men would not have been able to carry it
away in the space of a month. Lidwina well knew whence
came this substitute for the vital sap which had entirely
dried up in her frame, for once being questioned as to its
origin, she answered: " Tell me whence the vine derives
its rich sap which in winter is apparently all dried up ?"—
She felt herself a living branch of the true vine, whose benedictions stream to the ground when they find no member
to receive them. Lidwina expiated this waste by the
blood which flowed from every pore, and which day by
day was miraculously replenished. The wonderful vase
of her body, notwithstanding its corruption and worms,
emitted a most sweet odor. It became at last a victim
so agreeable in the sight of Our Lord that He impressed
upon it the seal of His Sacred Stigmata.

For thirty-three years Lidwina presented this amazing
spectacle of suffering, utterly in contradiction to nature's
laws, and which no natural experience could explain.
When plied with questions such as these :—" How can you

live without lungs, liver, or intestines, and almost consumed
by worms ?"—she would quietly answer : "God and my
conscience bear witness that I have lost piecemeal what He
once gave me. You may well believe this loss was hard
to bear, but God alone knows what, in the fulness of His almighty power, He has done in me to replace that loss."

Lidwina's pious biographer, Francis Brugmann, Provincial of the Minorites, throws light upon these inexplicable
facts when he says that God, in miraculously preserving
the wasted body of His spouse, willed to manifest to all
ages the means by which He daily preserves the grace of Redemption to men who persecute the Church, her faith, and her
mysteries, as the worms, the fever, and the putrid matter
consumed the body of Blessed Lidwina.

That it might be evident to all that Lidwina bore in her
own person the wounds of the entire Church, God restored
her to her perfect state some time before her demise.
When Christianity again acknowledged one Head, Lidwina's task was accomplished, and she received once more
all that she had sacrificed for the interests of the Church.

We may now very lawfully inquire how life could possibly be prolonged in a body entirely destitute of vital organs,
and we find Lidwina on several occasions alluding to a supernatural nourishment. Her biographer says : " Curiosity impelled crowds to visit the pious virgin, some actuated
by laudable intentions, others coming merely to condemn
and blaspheme. All saw indeed but a picture of death ; yet
the former beheld also in this mutilated vase the balm of
sanctification ; in this disfigured image the wonder-working
Lord ; in this semblance of death the Author of life, the
most lovely among the children of men. Were Lidwina
asked in amazement what fever could lay hold of in her,
since she took no nourishment, she would answer : " You

are surprised that fever finds anything to feed upon in me—
and I, I wonder that I do not become like a barrel in a
month ! You judge by the cross you see me bearing, but
you know not of the unction attached thereto, you cannot
see the interior."

When holy persons expressed their surprise at seeing
her alive in such a state, saying : " You could not live if
God in His mercy did not preserve you "—she would reply : " Yes, I acknowledge that I do receive, though I am
unworthy of it, a sustenance which God pours out upon me
from time to time. Poor whelp that I am, I could not live
in such a body, if some crumbs from my Master's table fell
not to me; but it becomes not the little dog to say what
morsels it receives."

Sometimes indiscreet females tormented her with questions as to the reality of her taking no nourishment; then
she would answer sweetly : " If you cannot understand it,
yet do not join the number of the incredulous, do not despise
God's wonderful operations. He it was who supported
Mary Magdalen in her solitude and Mary of Egypt in the
wilderness. There is no question as to what you think of
me—but do not rob God of His glory."

Lidwina did not mean merely the unction communicated
by the gifts and fruits of the Holy Ghost. She alluded more
particularly to the relief received from the terrestrial
paradise, which invigorated her in a manner altogether
miraculous. The Fathers tell us that paradise still exists
in all its first beauty untouched by the waters of the Deluge.
Here Enoch and Elias were transported to await the coming of anti-Christ, at which time they will reappear upon
earth to announce to the Jews the Word of Salvation. St.
Hildegarde says : " Enoch and Elias are in paradise,
where they have no need of corporal food ; and, in like

manner, a soul rapt in the contemplation of God has no necessity whilst in that state of those things of which mortals make use (1)."

The terrestrial paradise was not created for pure spirits, but for man composed of soul and body ; consequently, it is provided with whatever is requisite not only for his sustenance but also for his *safeguard* against sickness and death, by virtue of the state of original justice in which he was first created.   The creatures of this magnificent abode, its animals and plants, belong to a higher order, as much elevated above those of earth as the body of Adam before his sin was superior to his fallen posterity.   And as the body of Adam was a real body of flesh and blood, not pure spirit, so, too, paradise is not a celestial or purely spiritual region, but a material place connected with human nature and with the earth itself.   This relation between the earth and paradise is clearly indicated in the Holy Scriptures. The manna in the desert revealed to the children of the Old Law the food prepared for man during his earthly pilgrimage.   St. Hildegarde says on this subject in her *Scivias*, Lib. I., visio II. :—" When Adam and Eve were expelled from paradise, a wall of light was raised around it, and the Divine Power effaced from it all marks of their sin. It was fortified, as it were, by this great light so that no enemy could reach it; but by this God also testified that the transgression which had taken place in paradise should in time be effaced by His mercy.   Paradise still exists, a region of joy, blooming in all its pristine loveliness, and imparting abundant fruitfulness to the sterile earth.   As the soul communicates life and strength to the body it inhabits, so the earth receives from paradise her supreme vitality ; the darkness and corruption of sin, which shroud this miser-

(1) Quaestio XXIX. ad Vibertum Gemblacensem.

able world cannot entirely check its beneficent influence."

Man's spiritual bond with paradise is the grace of Redemption, which not only restored him the high gifts possessed by Adam in that abode, but conferred on him besides that superior beauty, dignity, and worth which emanate from the Precious Blood of Christ. By virtue of baptismal innocence, God in every age bestows upon certain chosen souls many of those privileges which Adam received by virtue of original justice. Baptism confers a certain right to those extraordinary gifts, for its innocence is superior to that of paradise. St. Hildegarde wrote to the Cathedral Chapter of Mayence : " God who, by the light of truth leads on His elect to beatitude, has been pleased at various epochs to renew the spirit of faith among them by the gift of prophecy ; by its illumination they may, in a measure, recover that happiness possessed by Adam before his fall."

It is not a matter of surprise, then, that not only the spiritual but also the material favors of paradise, should be bestowed upon God's chosen ones as a recompense for their fidelity ; but such gifts are merited by sufferings and privations.

Man, even whilst living in the flesh, is conducted to paradise and its fruits are brought to him by pain and self-renunciation, and by the good works performed by souls in the splendor of unsullied innocence. The way to these heights is absolute self-denial open only to those who have been, as it were, spiritualized in the fire of affliction. No extraordinary natural faculty, no mysterious malady, no disarrangement between the functions of soul and body, only purity and heroic fortitude fit man though still an exile upon earth to enter the terrestrial paradise.

Rewards and punishments are meted out by Almighty God according to the nature and importance of good or evil

works; and so for every pain, every sorrow, for every
privation borne upon earth there blooms in Paradise a corresponding production which, as a flower or a fruit, as food
or drink, as consolation or relief, is communicated to souls
according to their special need, and this not merely spiritually, but really and substantially. This is the wonderful
repairer of their corporal life, this explains their miraculous
vitality.

It is related of Lidwina (1) that once a woman very
virtuous, but a prey to the deepest melancholy, came to
implore her help. Lidwina received her with kind words
and promised her relief. Some days later the poor sufferer was admitted with Lidwina herself to the earthly
Paradise, a favor obtained by Lidwina's prayers; but in
spite of the wonders she beheld on all sides, the poor woman
ceased not to lament and weep. Then Lidwina led her to
a certain locality which seemed to serve as the storehouse
of the whole world;—here were perfumes, health-giving
spices, and healing herbs, and here the poor sufferer was
finally cured and so inundated with celestial consolations
that, for several days after, she could not support even the
smell of food. As a reward for her docility to Lidwina's
advice and directions her melancholy entirely disappeared.

In the life of St. Colette (2), contemporary with blessed
Lidwina, it is related that during the whole of Lent, she
abstained from food excepting perhaps a few crumbs of
bread. On a certain Easter-day God sent her from Paradise a bird resembling a hen, one of whose eggs sufficed her
for a long time and, as she had need of some little recreation amid her great labors (she reformed the Poor
Clares) there was sent her from Paradise in reward for

(1) Acta SS., die XIV. Aprilis vita post: c. III.
(2) Acta SS., die VI. Martii, Chap. XIII.

her incomparable purity a charming little animal, dazzlingly white and perfectly tame when with her. It used to present itself at the door or window of her cell, as if craving entrance and, after a short time, disappear as mysteriously as it had come. Her sister-religious regarded it with intense interest and curiosity, but they could never succeed in catching it; for, if they happened to meet it in Colette's cell or any place about the convent, it instantaneously vanished (1). Colette entertained the deepest reverence for holy relics and, above all, for the Cross upon which the Saviour died, and as she ardently longed for a little piece of it, her desire was miraculously gratified. A small golden cross, not made by hand of man but a natural production, containing a particle of the True Cross, was brought her from the garden of paradise, and Colette ever after carried it on her person. Again, as she was one day conferring with her confessor on the reform of her Order, a cincture of dazzling whiteness descended from above and rested on her arm.

Lidwina often acknowledged that, without the help of divine consolation, she would have sunk under her accumulation of suffering. Her strength was daily renewed in those hours of rapture which transported her either to heaven itself or to the terrestrial paradise, and the sweetness she then tasted rendered the bitterness of her pains not only supportable but even delightful. Her guardian-angel, ever visible to her, was her conductor on these spiritual journeys. Before setting out, he used to take her to the parish church to an image of the Mother of God, whence after a short prayer they rose swiftly above the earth in an easterly direction until they reached the garden. The first time Lidwina made this aerial journey, she was

(1) Acta SS.. die VI. Martii. Ch. IX.

afraid to enter the beautiful gates. It was only on the angel's assuring her that her feet would not hurt the flowery carpet stretching out before her that she ventured in, holding the while her guardian's hand who went on before and gently drew her after him. When, at times, she paused in hesitating wonder at the height and luxuriance of the flowers which seemed no longer to afford a passage, the angel lifted her lightly over the fragrant barrier.

The meadows bathed in light, inaccessible to cold or heat, surpassed Lidwina's powers of description. She ate the luscious fruits presented by her angel, and inhaled their delightful perfume; and when returned to her little chamber, her family dared not approach her from the respect which her appearance inspired. She was wholly embalmed with the glory of another world. Her emaciated frame shone with light; perfumes unlike those of earth breathed around her poor couch; the hand held by the angel on their joyous expedition exhaled a peculiarly delicious odor, and a sensation was experiencd by one who approached her such as is produced by aromatic spices. On one occasion, the light surrounding her was so brilliant that her little nephew thinking her in flames ran away in terror.

Lidwina kept near her bed a stalk of dried hemp, light yet firm, with which she could with her left hand open and close the curtain to admit air to her feverish brow. A fire broke out at Schiedam on the night of the 22d of July, and in the confusion this stick was lost. Poor Lidwina was the sufferer, for she was now unable to procure even the small relief of a breath of fresh air. Her angel promised her assistance and, in a short time, she felt something laid gently on the coverlet of her bed. It was a stick about a yard and a quarter long. But in vain did she try to lift it, her poor hand refused its weight, and laughingly she exclaimed : ' Ah ! yes, now, indeed, I have a stick !'—Next morning she begged her confessor to whittle it for her and thus render it lighter. He did so or, at least, tried to do so ; but, even with a sharp knife, he could scarcely cut away a few chips, which shed around so delicious a fragrance that he dared not whittle any more of the precious wood. He took it to Lidwina, asking her where she got it, but she could answer only that she thought her angel had brought it to her. On August 8th, Feast of St. Cyriacus, being again conducted to Paradise, the angel pointed out to her a cedar near the entrance and showed her the bough from which he had broken a branch for her. He reproved her for not sufficiently honoring the precious gift, which possessed the power of expelling evil spirits. Lidwina kept this branch a long time. It lost its fragrance only in a hand stained by sin. On another visit to Paradise, Dec. 6th, of the same year, she was fed from a date-palm laden with magnificent fruit whose stones shone like crystals. We shall mention only one more of the gifts brought from Paradise to console and strengthen the patient sufferer.

" She was one day rapt to the choirs of the blessed and the Mother of God addressed her in the following words : ' My child, why do you not put on a crown and join these glorious spirits ? '—to which Lidwina answered simply : ' I came with my angel ; I must do what he tells me.' Then Mary gave her a beautiful crown with instructions to keep it herself for seven hours and then give it to her confessor, who was to hang it at Our Lady's altar in the parish church of Schiedam, whence it would be removed later. When Lidwina returned to earth, she remembered all that had passed ; but she dreamed not of taking it literally until she felt the crown of lovely flowers upon her head. When the seven hours had elapsed, she sent for her confessor at dawn, gave him the crown, which was hung at Our Lady's shrine according to order, whence it disappeared before full daylight."

After this digression, more apparent than real, we return to Sister Emmerich whose sufferings were of the same nature and signification as Lidwina's. Besides her interior torments, she endured a succession of cruel maladies most varied in form and opposite in symptoms, since she atoned both for the whole Church and her individual members. God had accepted the sacrifice of her whole being, and every part of her body offered its tribute of expiation, the natural order of things being entirely reversed in her regard—sickness and pain becoming health and strength to her whilst she lay consumed in the fire of tribulation. Her body was, so to speak, the crucible in which the Physician of souls prepared healing remedies for His people, whilst her soul was keenly alive to terror, sadness, anguish, dryness, desolation, to all those withering impressions which the passions of one man can cause another, or by which diabolical malice can assail its victims. She was burdened with the fears of the dying, the corruption of morals, with the consequences of wrath, revenge, gluttony, curiosity; with them she struggled, over them she gained the victory, the fruits of which she relinquished in favor of poor sinners. But these pains were nothing to the anguish she endured at the sight of the unprecedented degradation of the priesthood. The evil one succeeded in intruding many of his own servants into Holy Orders, men lost to the faith, members of secret societies who, with the indelible stamp of ordination upon their soul, shrank not from the blackest crimes against Christ and His Vicar upon earth. There was no attack made on the Church, her rights, her worship, her doctrine, and her Sacraments, that was not inspired by a Judas from among

her own. The Saviour felt His Apostle's treason more keenly than all His other sufferings; and, in like manner, the
sharpest wounds in the Church's body are ever from one
clothed with the sacerdotal dignity. The impious attacks
of heretics did not call for so grievous expiation as did the
crimes of fallen priests, and the latter were followed by far
more terrible consequences than the former.

If Anne Catherine's corporal sufferings did not seem so
violent, so frightful as Lidwina's, yet they were by no
means less excruciating. Sometimes she saw them as if
endured by another, when she would cry out in compassion:
"Ah! I see a poor little nun whose heart is torn to pieces!
She must belong to our own time, but she suffers more than
I! I must not complain!"

As the blood flows to and from the heart, so Sister Emmerich's pains taking their rise in this source, spread through her
whole person and returned to their point of departure, as if
to gather fresh strength to continue their work of expiation.
The heart is the seat of love. It is into the heart that the
Holy Spirit is poured there to form that sacred bond which
unites all the members of the Church into one body. Never
was love so much vaunted as at this period when both love
and faith were well-nigh dead, when the practice of Christian
piety and the observance of the evangelical precepts seemed
to have totally died out. It was at this time that the most
baneful and hypocritical sect that has ever risen up swept
as a devastating torrent over the vineyard of the Church—
the malicious sect of Jansenism with its so-called lights. Aided
and abetted by the secret societies, whose most zealous disciples were seated even in the ecclesiastical councils, it
sought in its blind hatred of the Blessed Virgin and the
Sovereign Pontiff, to separate irremediably her faithful
children from the heart of the Church by the introduction

of those heterodox elements which, under the cloak of "love and reform," attacked the very principles of faith and abolished those devout practices, those pious customs by whose extinction the most fatal wounds were inflicted upon Christianity. All things combined to further the cause of this diabolical sect : the Church was oppressed by secular power, her property pillaged, bishoprics vacant, religious orders suppressed, and the Pope fettered by Napoleon, whom Sister Emmerich often saw in her visions as an oppressor of the Church.

"Once," she said, " as I was praying before the Blessed Sacrament for the wants of the Church, I was transported into a large and magnificent temple, where I saw the Pope, the Vicar of Jesus Christ, anointing a king, a little yellow man of sinister aspect. It was a great solemnity, but it filled me with sorrow and dismay. I felt that the Pope should have firmly refused to perform the ceremony. I saw what harm this man would do the Holy Father and of what frightful bloodshed he would be the cause. I spoke to Abbé Lambert of this vision and of the fears it awoke in my heart, but he treated it lightly. When, however, we heard the news of Napoleon's coronation, by Pius VII., he said : ' Sister, we must pray and be silent.' "

Such was the epoch in which Anne Catherine bore the Church's sorrows imposed upon her, not as an undefined malady, but according to a certain order, as tasks which it was hers to fulfil perfectly one after another. They were shown her separately under symbolical forms that her acceptance might be for her a meritorious act of love ; she was called to labor daily in the vineyard, whilst the father of the family sent the workmen there but seldom. She received the order in vision and executed it without interfering with the regular routine of daily life, being perfectly alive to the hidden signification of her sufferings and their connection with the Church ; but her outer life contrasted so rudely with her inner that it was often more painful to her than the weight of spiritual sufferings that oppressed her. And yet, the former was the necessary complement of the latter ; it formed a part of the task assigned which could be looked upon as fully accomplished only inasmuch as it was fulfilled in the midst of exterior contradictions and interruptions. It was in the patient endurance of tribulations from without and sorrow from within that her merit lay This was the perfume she exhaled to God in an odor of sweetness. If we close our eyes to the economy of Divine Providence in the conduct of souls, her whole existence becomes to us an inexplicable enigma, an unmeaning fact. Many were touched on seeing her purity of soul, her superior supernatural intelligence, who, at the same time, were offended at her poverty and lowliness. They were scandalized at her surroundings, at the crowds of poor that thronged about her, at her helpless and abandoned condition. They understood not that the victim should not fare better than the Church whose wounds she bore, the Church tossed to and fro on the waves of persecution.

She would not have been able to support the trials of her holy Mother did she not also share in her supernatural life. A pilgrim upon earth and, at the same time, the companion of the blessed in heaven, the Church struggles under the pressure of present tribulations whilst bearing in her bosom the salvation of ages. Mourning the departure of her Divine Spouse to His Father, she daily unites herself to Him by the closest union ; and so, too, Anne Catherine, whilst weeping with that holy Mother, arose with her by contemplation above the vicissitudes of time and the bounds of space. The cycle of feasts was ever present to her,

ever unveiled and instinct with life, and she perfectly entered into the daily celebration of the mysteries of faith and
the truths of religion, which were more intelligible to the eye
of her mind than was the exterior world to that of her
body. She received from her Divine Spouse with the
tasks regulated according to the ecclesiasticial calendar, the
strength of soul necessary to fulfil them courageously.
Whilst in vision, she was able to understand the connection
between her various sufferings and her task of expiation;
but, in her waking state, she could not explain it intelli-
gibly. She dared not mention the subject before either
the physician or her Sisters, for they would have deemed
her delirious, if not quite demented; consequently she submitted silently to all prescriptions, to all attempts of science
to cure those sufferings which she well knew to be the very
object of her existence.

"Both in and out of the convent," she once remarked,
"I suffered intensely from the means employed for my cure,
and I was often in danger of death from too violent remedies. I knew the effect they would have, but I took them
in obedience. If through forgetfulness I failed to do so,
my attendants thought I did it purposely and that my sickness was feigned. The medicines were expensive. A
phial which cost a great deal was only half-empty sometimes when another was ordered, and all was charged to
my account, I had to pay for all. I cannot understand
where I got so much money. True, I sewed a good deal,
but I used to give all the proceeds to the convent which
toward the end paid half my expenses. I was often so
miserable that I could not render myself any service; but
if my Sisters forgot me, God helped me. One day I was
lying prostrate with weakness and bathed in perspiration,
when two female religious appeared, made up my bed, and

replaced me gently to my great relief. Shortly after, the Reverend Mother entered with a Sister, and asked me in astonishment who had arranged my bed so comfortably. I thought they themselves had done it, and I thanked them for their kindness; but they assured me that neither they nor any other Sister had entered my cell, and they looked upon what I told them of the two religious as all a dream; however, my bed had actually been made, and I felt better. I found out afterward that the two good nuns, who often rendered me kind and consoling services, were blessed souls who had once lived in our convent."

Clara Soentgen deposed to the above before ecclesiastical authority :—

"Sister Emmerich was very ill and I went one morning to her cell to see how she was. I asked who had made up her bed so early, or if she had had the strength to do it herself. She answered that Reverend Mother and I had come together to see her and that we had arranged her bed so nicely and expeditiously. Now, neither of us had yet been in her cell."

"At another time," says Anne Catherine, "whilst in the same state, I was again lifted gently out of my bed and laid in the middle of the cell by two religious. At the same moment one of the Sisters entered suddenly. Seeing me lying unsupported in the air, she uttered a sharp cry which frightened me so that I fell heavily to the floor. This gave rise to much talk among the Sisters, and one of the old religious tormented me for a long time with questions as to how I could lie thus in the air, but I could give her no explanation. I paid no attention to such things, they all seemed perfectly natural to me." We see by the above that whatever was requisite for her support was supplied by her Spouse from the Garden of Eden, whose products possess the power of dissipating pain and sorrow. Anne Catherine communicated these secrets before her death, either by order of her guide or her confessor. They are, doubtless, short and incomplete, though quite sufficient to prove that she received divine favors similar to those of Lidwina.

"The only remedies that afforded me any relief," she said, "were supernatural. The physician's only increased my languor, yet I had to take them and pay dear for them too. But God always gave me the money, as well as all that I needed in the convent, and I also received much for the house. After I left it the same things often happened to me, and once I was given quite a large sum of which I made use. I mentioned it to Dean Rensing, who told me that the next time this happened I must show him the money; but from that day I got no more.

"During the second investigation, I gave the nurse two thalers to go on a pilgrimage to Telgten for my intention and to get two Masses for the same. The servant-girl of the house lent me the money, and shortly after I found two thalers lying on my bed. I wondered what it meant and I made the nurse show me the money I had given her. I recognized it at once, and felt convinced that God had repeated the favor I had often received in the past in order that I might pay off my debt to the girl.

"Supernatural remedies were often given me by my angel, by Mary, or the dear saints and even by my Affianced Himself. Sometimes they were in the form of liquids in brilliant phials, or flowers, herbs, or little morsels of food. At the head of my bed was a wooden shelf on which I used to find these marvellous remedies during my visions, or even in my waking moments. Sometimes I found tiny bunches of herbs of exquisite beauty and delicious fragrance laid on my bed or placed in my hand when I awoke from vision;

and by pinching the tender young leaves I knew what use to make of them. Their fragrance at times was sufficient to strengthen me; and sometimes I ate them or drank the water in which they were steeped. After such nourishment I was again ready for my task.

" I also received pictures, statues, and stones from apparitions with directions how to use them; they were either put into my hand or laid on' my breast, and they always relieved me. Some I kept a long time and made use of to cure others, either applying them myself or giving them to those in need; but I never said where I got them. They were all real, but I cannot explain how it was. These incidents did actually take place, and I used the remedies in honor of Him whose goodness had sent them to me.

" Whilst in the novitiate, I was one day kneeling before the Blessed Sacrament, my arms extended, when I felt something slipped into my hand. It was a beautiful little picture of St. Catherine painted on parchment. I kept it a long time and then gave it to a good girl who asked me for a souvenir. She had a great desire to become a religious, but she died before accomplishing her design. The little picture was placed at her own request on the poor child's breast as she lay in her coffin.

" Once my Heavenly Affianced gave me a polished transparent stone shaped like a heart and larger than a thaler, in which there was, as if formed there by nature, a picture of Mary with the Infant Jesus in red, blue, and gold. The picture was exquisitely beautiful; the mere sight of it cured me, for I was ill at the time. I made a little leathern bag for it and wore it a long time when, at last, it was taken from me by the same power that had bestowed it. Again, my Betrothed placed on my finger a ring in which was a precious stone with a picture of His

Blessed Mother engraven on it. I kept that also for a time, when He Himself withdrew it from my finger.

"I received a similar gift from the holy patron of my Order. It was near the hour for Holy Communion. No one dreamed of my being able to rise, but I thought I heard them calling me. I dragged myself to the choir and received the Most Holy Sacrament with the others. Returned to my cell, I fell on the floor fainting. I know not how or by whom, but I was laid just as I was in my habit on the bed. Then St. Augustine appeared and gave me a sparkling stone shaped like a bean, from which arose a crimson heart surmounted by a little cross. I was told that the heart would become as transparent as the stone. When I awoke to consciousness, I found it in my hand. I put it into my tumbler, drank the water off it, and was cured. After awhile it was taken from me.

"There was another gift which I was permitted to retain for seven months during a severe illness. The infirmarian brought me food every day, but I could not touch it. I could take no kind of nourishment and the Sisters wondered how I lived. I had, however, received another sort of aliment from the Mother of God. She appeared to me in vision and when I awoke I found in my hand a large host of dazzling whiteness, thicker and softer than those of the altar, with a picture of Mary and some written characters impressed upon it. I was seized with profound respect, as if before relics or holy things. It was fragrant and, at night, luminous. I kept it by me, hidden in my bed, and every day for seven months I ate a little particle of it, which gave me strength. Then it disappeared to my great disquietude, for I feared I had lost this heavenly manna through my own fault. It had a sweet taste, but not like the Blessed Sacrament.

"One night, I was kneeling before the table in my cell, praying to the Blessed Virgin, when a female resplendent with light entered through the closed door, advanced to the other side of the table, and knelt down opposite to me as if to pray. I was frightened, but I went on praying. Then she placed before me a statue of the Mother of God, about a hand high and dazzlingly white, and laid her open hand on the table for a moment behind the statue. I drew back in fear, when she gently pushed the statue toward me. I venerated it interiorly and the apparition vanished leaving the little image, a mother standing with her child in her arms. It was exquisitely beautiful and, I think, made of ivory. I carried it about with me most respectfully for a long time, when I was interiorly instructed to give it to a strange priest from whom it was withdrawn at the hour of death.

" Once, Mary gave me a marvellous flower which expanded in water. When closed it resembled a rosebud, but when open it displayed leaves of delicate colors which bore a relation to the different spiritual effects it was to produce in me. Its scent was delicious. For more than a month I drank the water in which it was steeped. At last, I was wondering what I should do with this health-giving flower that it might not be profaned, when I was told in vision to have a new crown made for the Mother of God in our chapel and to put the bud into it. I told the confessor and Superioress, who ordered me to save up my money and wait awhile. But I was again commanded in a vision not to delay having the crown made, in consequence of which my confessor gave permission. It was made at the Clares, in Münster, and I myself put the flower in. As the Sisters were not very careful of the ornaments, I saw to the crown myself. The little flower was in it up to the suppression of the convent, when it disappeared and I was shown in a vision where it had been taken.

"My guide once gave me a little flask of whitish balm like thick oil. I used it on a hurt I had received from a basket of wet linen, and with it cured many sick. The flask was pear-shaped with a long narrow neck, about the size of a medicine phial, perfectly clear and transparent. I kept it for some time in my press. Again, some morsels of sweet food were given me which I used and also gave some to the poor to cure their maladies. The Superioress found it one day and reprimanded me for not saying how I had come by it."

In October, 1805, Sister Emmerich was appointed to assist one of the Sisters in carrying the linen from the wash up to the drying-loft. She stood above at the trap-door to receive the rising basket. The Sister below slackened the rope just as Sister Emmerich was about swinging the load over to the floor. The angel seized the rope and saved her from falling with the weight, too great for her strength, on the Sister below. The effort Sister Emmerich made dashed her to the floor, the basket of linen falling heavily on her left hip, crushing the bone in several places and inflicting other injuries which would certainly have been attended with fatal results, had not God miraculously preserved her life. It was soon evident that this accident was destined by God to play as important a part in Sister Emmerich's life as did Lidwina's fall on the ice in her painful career. It increased her expiatory sufferings and afforded her continual and painful humiliations. It now became very difficult for her to ring the convent-bell, her duty in quality of assist-ant-sacristan, and sometimes she was quite unable to do so, a circumstance which drew upon her the accusation of pride and laziness. But, in truth, it was a real privation to her not to be able to ring the bell; for she made of it so earnest a prayer that, whilst thus engaged, she seemed to forget her cruel pains.

" When ringing the blessed bell," she said, "I was full of joy, as if I were spreading around its benediction and calling on all who heard it to praise God. I united my prayers to each stroke to dispel all evil from their hearts and to excite them to glorify the dear God. I would have loved to ring out much longer than the prescribed time."

The furious unbelief of this epoch had proscribed the use of church-bells —and who does not see in this poor nun's tender devotion in the midst of her pains an atonement to God for violence so ignoble?

She could now only with great difficulty, and sometimes not at all, perform her accustomed duties of washing and ironing the church-linen and of working in the garden. God only knew the efforts she had to make; but the following fact shows how her zeal was recompensed. One day, a hot iron fell from her hand on one of the albs. With an invocation to God, she snatched it up and set it on the floor where it burned a hole, but neither the alb nor her hand was hurt. Those poor hands of hers were so emaciated by their constant sufferings that once she remarked :

"I suffered much from my hands whilst in the convent. If I held them up to the sun the rays pierced them like arrows, they were so thin."

The baking of the altar-bread was also very fatiguing for her, on account of the weight of the irons. She looked upon it as a sacred duty, to be performed prayerfully and respectfully. Once, fresh hosts were wanting, and Sister Emmerich lay on her poor bed ill and very sad at not being able to make them. She betook herself to prayer, arose from her bed, dragged herself to the chapel and there

implored strength from Our Lord to prepare the hosts.
Suddenly she was bathed in perspiration, and strength
was, indeed, given her for the work, in which her angel assisted her; but scarcely was it over when she became sick
as before, and only with difficulty regained her cell.

After the accident from the linen, she kept her bed till
January, 1806. In the spring she had violent pains in her
stomach which brought on frequent vomitings of blood.
Even whilst at work, her hemorrhages were so copious that
the Sisters feared they would prove fatal. But, at last,
having seen her quickly recover from such attacks and also
from her fainting-spells, so that she could soon return to
her duties, they came to the conclusion that they were not
very serious after all, and so she received very little attention in her sickness. They rarely thought of her when she
was too ill to be among them, and in winter it often happened that the straw of her poor bed froze to the damp wall
of her cell, or that, consumed with fever, she sighed in vain
for a mouthful of water. A kind-hearted person in Dülmen
heard of her distressing condition, and made it known to the
Duke von Croy, who immediately caused an infirmary to
be fitted up in the convent, furnished it with a stove, and
had Sister Emmerich removed to it.

In 1813, the physician made the following deposition:

" The care bestowed by the religious upon Sister Emmerich in her sickness was not always what it should have
been. I found her once after a profuse flow of perspiration,
trembling in her bed with cold. She had no change of
linen, her gown and bed-clothes were frozen stiff. The
Sisters complained of the expense of her frequent spells of
sickness, and by their murmuring they sometimes turned
the Reverend Mother, the infirmarian, and other Sisters

against her, although these latter were in general favorably
disposed toward her.

"In the beginning of March, 1810, she was seized with
a violent nervous fever. She suffered cruelly during this heavy
illness, more than two months of which she spent in a cold
cell. Profuse sweats, fainting-spells, convulsions, and violent pains succeeded one another more or less frequently
the whole time."

When Sister Emmerich was called upon by her Superiors
to give an account of how she had been cared for in the
convent, she spoke as follows :—

"What struck me on my entrance into the convent was
the little care bestowed upon the sick. There was not even
an infirmary to receive them. The Duke von Croy, hearing that the sick had to remain in their cell without a fire
in the winter season, interested himself in having a suitable
room prepared for them and gave a stove for it. In two
attacks I was nursed by Sister Soentgen when she was free
from her music lessons, and when these prevented, Sister
Neuhaus kindly attended to me. As long as these two
Sisters extended to me their charity, I had nothing of
which to complain ; but their attention to me drew upon
them the disapprobation of some others who were not so
kindly disposed toward me. Then Sister E— was named
infirmarian. She was full of caprice and neglected her
duty. When she might have attended to me, she preferred being in her cell. She used to leave me so long in the
morning without any regard to my wants that I trembled
with cold in my night-clothes soaked with perspiration ;
being unable to wait on myself, I endured thirst and many
other painful inconveniences. Sometimes I told Reverend
Mother not only of Sister E.'s conduct, but of the want of
even necessary things. My confessor told me to do so ;

but it did very little good, for Reverend Mother did not care much for me. At times she listened patiently, and again she would tell me the convent was too poor to procure what was necessary for the sick, and that I was never satisfied. I must say, however, in her justification, that she never thought me as ill as I really was. I will add, too, that she took more care of the sick than her predecessors did, as the aged religious testified ; and, on this account, she had to put up with the discontent of many."

The infirmarian mentioned above was the one to whom Sister Emmerich had rendered the most loving services when attacked by a disgusting disease and shunned by all, on account of her cross-grained temper. It was a welcome opportunity to Sister Emmerich to return kindness for neglect and to support fresh trials from the crabbed nun.

The only thing she craved when able to leave her bed, was a little tea or weak coffee. She says in her deposition before Dean Rensing :—

" I often passed several consecutive nights without sleep. Very rarely did I sleep soundly, my rest was usually a light doze often interrupted ; consequently, and especially when I had had heavy night-sweats, I was so weak and sick in the morning that I could not rise for Matins. But, as soon as I had taken a little coffee and had heard Mass, I could attend to my duties. The Sisters did not understand this ; they said my sickness was all put on, or at least greatly exaggerated."

It was customary for each religious to provide her own breakfast. But as poor Sister Emmerich had neither coffee nor money, she used to take her coffee-pot to the kitchen every morning and gather up the grounds thrown away by the other Sisters, from which she made her own little cup which she drank without sugar. Clara Soentgen, who gives

us these details, sometimes compassionately shared her breakfast with her, but not often; for as she ingenuously tells us, she
allowed herself to be too greatly influenced by the remarks of
the Sisters. Assistance, at last, came from another quarter.
One day, on Sister Emmerich's return from the choir to her
cell, which she had left locked, she found two thalers on the
window-sill. She took them at once to the Superioress, who
permitted her to buy a small quantity of coffee with them,
which lasted her a long time.

Clara Soentgen, in her deposition of 1813, gives the following instance of the same nature :—

"I always remarked in Anne Catherine Emmerich the
greatest satisfaction when she had it in her power to give
something to the poor. Both before and after her entrance
into the convent, she gave away all she had. I asked her
once why she did not supply her own needs. 'Ah ! ' she
answered, 'I always receive far more than I give !'—and
indeed I often saw to my astonishment that what she said
was true.

"One morning she had neither breakfast nor money.
She locked her cell door, as usual, and went to the choir ; on
her return, she found some money lying on the window-sill,
at which she was so astonished that she came running to tell
me and I had to go back with her to see it. This happened more than once. She had no greater joy than that of
rendering charitable service to her neighbor. One might
ask her for anything she had ; she gladly gave away even
the most necessary articles and, above all, was she kind
toward those who cared little for her."

One year, on her feast-day, a friend gave her two pounds
of coffee. During a whole year she used it for breakfast without diminishing the little stock, a circumstance which rejoiced her heart. But being attacked by a long illness

during which she received supernatural remedies, this earthly aliment was withdrawn.

"One day," she tells us, "the old Count von Galen insisted on my taking two gold pieces to give to the poor in his name. I got them changed and had clothes and shoes made which I distributed to those in need. God blessed the money, for as soon as all the small pieces were gone, I found the two large ones again in my pocket. I immediately had them changed and used them as before. This went on for a year, and I was thus enabled to help many poor people. The miraculous assistance ceased during an illness, two months of which I lay immovable and most of the time unconscious. This was commonly the case with such favors; for, as others had free access to my cell, God withdrew what might have proved a subject of scandal to them."

By a special dispensation of Divine Providence, all classes of people sought Sister Emmerich's assistance during her stay in the convent, the most abandoned receiving from her the greatest sympathy and relief. Although it was most frequently the poor who applied for help from the sick nun, yet her Sisters in religion also knew with what charity they would be received whenever they were willing to make known to her their wants. The excess of her own sufferings seemed but to increase her tender sympathy for others ; the prospect of doing a kind turn for her neighbor seemed to impart fresh vigor and energy to her wasted frame ; and she who received so little care and attention herself, could put no bounds to her zeal were there question of relieving another. She possessed a quick perception of what remedies to apply ; her prayers and the touch of her gentle hand attracted a blessing upon those for whom she prescribed. She was so patient, so serene,

so ingenious in providing relief even when treating with
the impatient and irritable, that they lost sight of the fact
that she herself was not an instant without intense suffering.
Her kindness was irresistible, and she knew so well how to
overcome the whims and prejudices of the sick that the
physician often sent for her when his own persuasion
proved ineffectual.

Among the boarders was a weak-minded girl named
K—, a native of M—, who had an abscess in the
back of her neck. When the doctor was about applying a
bandage, she escaped from his hands and refused to allow
him to do anything for her. The Superioress sent for Sister
Emmerich, whose presence wrought a magical effect upon
the child, who readily took from her hand the medicine
prescribed and allowed her wound to be dressed. When
the abscess broke, Sister Emmerich sucked it gently, and
it soon healed leaving no scar.

A servant-girl had an abscess under her arm. She
stole to Sister Emmerich's bedside one night, begging her
for the love of God to relieve her. The same charitable
service was rendered her and she was cured.

There was a young girl from Amsterdam in the house as
a boarder. She had an insupportable temper which burst
forth on all occasions. Sister Emmerich was the only one
who could calm her, she even won her affections, to the
amazement of all.

Speaking of a similar case, she says :—

"The physician of the convent was a little abrupt; one
day he scolded a poor woman soundly, because she had
neglected to show him her finger which was very sore.
The inflammation extended all the way up to the arm which
was perfectly black. When he said that he would have to
amputate it, the poor creature came running to me, pale with

fright, begging me to help her.   I began to pray when suddenly the proper way of treating it flashed upon my mind.   I spoke of it to Reverend Mother, who permitted me to dress the arm in Abbé Lambert's room.   I boiled sage, myrrh, and some of Our Lady's herb in wine and water; to this I added a few drops of holy water and made a poultice which I bound on the woman's arm.   It was surely God Himself who had inspired the remedy, for next morning the swelling had entirely disappeared, though the finger was very sore.   I made her bathe it in lye and oil. When it opened, I extracted from it a great thorn after which it soon healed."

Upon the nature of the compassion she felt for the sick and the poor, she says :—

" I can never grieve for a person who dies resignedly, nor for a child suffering patiently ; for patient suffering is the most enviable state of man.   Our compassion is rarely altogether pure ; it is most frequently mixed with a certain sentiment of softness and selfishness springing from the horror we ourselves feel for suffering, for all that can wound self.   Our Lord's compassion alone is pure, perfectly pure, and no human compassion possesses this quality unless it is united to His.   I only pity sinners, poor blind souls, or souls in despair.   But alas ! I often pity myself too much !"

The following facts will show the blessing attached to her prayers and exertions in behalf of the sick :

"A poor peasant-woman of my acquaintance," she said, "always had very painful and dangerous accouchements. She loved me and told me her trials. I prayed for her earnestly. A parchment band with written characters on it was given to me supernaturally, and I was told that the woman was to wear it on her person.   She did so and was delivered without pain.   When dying she requested the band to be buried

with her. Such requests are customary among our peasants.

"Once there was great mortality among the cattle. The
peasants had to take them to a certain place for treatment,
but numbers of them died. A poor mother of a family came
to me in tears, begging prayers for herself and the other
sufferers. Then I had a vision of the stables belonging to
these people. I saw both the healthy animals and those
affected by the distemper, as also the cause of the evil
and the effect of prayer upon it. I saw that many were attacked as a chastisement from God, on account of the pride
and false security of their owners who recognized not that
God can give and take away, and that their loss was a punishment for their sins. Then I begged Almighty God to take
some other means of bringing them into the right path.
Some of these animals were affected by the curse of en-
vious people; they belonged chiefly to men who failed to give
thanks to God for His benefits and to beg His blessing on
His own gifts. The cattle appeared to me to be shrouded
in darkness through which sinister-looking figures passed
to and fro. Blessings not only attract the grace of God,
but also dispel the evil influence of a malediction. The
cattle saved by prayer seemed separated from the others
by something luminous. I saw a black vapor escaping from
those that were cured and a faint light hovering over others
blessed from afar by prayer. The scourge was suddenly
arrested, and the cattle belonging to the mother of the family escaped untouched."

Anne Catherine's ill-health prevented her holding any
charge in the convent; she was always given as an aid first
to one, then to another Sister. She never held authority
over any one, but as Clara Soentgen says: "She was the
servant of all, but a servant who loved her lowly state. She

had the general good at heart, rendered great service to the community, and was always most laborious. Toward the servant-girls and laborers she was not only kind and discreet, but she gave them good advice and instruction."

The Reverend Mother, in 1813, also deposed :—

" In whatever obedience enjoined, Anne Catherine always gave satisfaction. When she had the care of the garden and out-buildings, she labored zealously, every one praised her. She was kind to the servants (as her Mistress testifies), although she exacted from them their duty. She was compassionate toward the poor and was accustomed to make caps for poor children out of the old church things."

CHAPTER XV.

SISTER EMMERICH'S ECSTASIES AND PRAYER.

Among all her privations, none was so painful to Sister Emmerich as the want of proper spiritual direction. She had no one with whom she could confer on her interior, no one to help her bear the burden that weighed her down. " Day and night," she says, " did I implore God to send me a priest to whom I might lay open my interior, for I was often in dread of being deluded by the evil spirit. This dread made me doubt everything, even what was before my eyes, my sufferings, my consolations, my very existence itself. The Abbé Lambert tried to quiet me ; but, as he knew little German, I was unable to make him understand clearly, and my trouble always returned. All that was going on in my interior and around me I found perfectly incomprehensible, ignorant peasant-girl that I was ! Though it was the experience of my life, it had never before disturbed me. The last four years in the convent were spent in almost uninterrupted contemplation and the incidents consequent upon this state were multiplied. I could not render an account of them to those that were ignorant of such things, they would have thought them simply impossible. Whilst in this state, as I was praying alone in the church one day, I distinctly heard this question: ' Am I not sufficient for thee ? ' The words made a profound impression on me."

It is not astonishing that Anne Catherine left thus to herself was tormented by doubt and anxiety. The gift of contemplation had been imparted to her for the furtherance of

her expiatory mission and, consequently, it entailed upon
her mental sufferings which, like her physical pains, corresponded to the state of the Church at the time. Her
soul gained strength and ripened in her childhood from the
rich contemplations presented to it,contemplations which embraced the whole history of Redemption ;. now, if we may so
express it, the dark side of her visions was to be placed before her, that is the unfolding of the mystery of iniquity,
the combat of the enemy against the Church. She must
now struggle against the malice and cunning of the
evil one who glides into the vineyard whilst the master
sleeps,and sows the bad seed ; she must destroy it before it
springs up and, clothed in the spiritual armor of purity,
humility, and confidence in God, she must wrestle with the
enemy in his attacks on the sacred priesthood. In such
encounters it is not the light of contemplation, but strong
and lively faith that insures the victory. The father of
lies may, indeed, cast her into mental agony, but he cannot shake her faith. Anne Catherine had never wished
for visions and extraordinary favors and, when she first received them, she knew not that they were extraordinary,
she dreamed not of their being peculiar to herself; but as
soon as the truth dawned upon her, her chief care was to
submit them to the decision of her director. Not her visions,
but her Faith formed the rule of her conduct ; rather would
she have endured a thousand deaths than violate its holy
teachings, and when the tempter cast her into doubt and
fear as to the origin of her supernatural favors, it was by acts
of this virtue that she put him to flight. In his rude and
oft-repeated assaults, Anne Catherine was deprived of spiritual assistance from the ministers of the Church. In this
she resembled the Church herself whose episcopal sees lay
vacant, whose flocks were wandering without pastors to

check the ever-increasing ravages of heresy, and whose
Doctors no longer raised a voice against the torrent of evils
pouring in upon her on all sides.

We cannot with indifference behold in the midst of this desolation the poor little nun of Dülmen, unfolding like a miraculous flower a beauty equal to any belonging to preceding ages. When Sts.Teresa and Magdalen di Pazzi adorned
the Church, the Order of St. Ignatius was in its first bloom.
It was rapidly spreading throughout the Church to which it
has given more saints and learned men than any religous
institute since the time of St. Francis and St. Dominic.
When Sts. Catherine of Sienna, Lidwina, and Colette embalmed her vineyard with the fragrance of their virtues,
the Church languished,it is true, in a most distressing state;
but beside these saints there arose in all countries holy and
learned souls.   But no period was more desolate than that in
which the Master of the vineyard poured out upon the little
shepherdess of Flamske the plenitude of His graces.
God gives His gifts only on condition of faithful co-operation;
if this be wanting, they are withdrawn and bestowed
upon others who will make a better use of them. Thus
does He act toward the mass of the faithful. At no period are the power and mercy of God lessened; but, when
vessels are wanting to receive the superabundant riches of
His gifts, He displays the wonders of His love in a few
faithful souls upon whom he bestows in addition to their own
share, the graces slighted by others. It is on this account
that Anne Catherine's privileges and sufferings have in them
something extraordinary and imposing. St. Magdalen di
Pazzi's ecstasies took place in a cloistered community where
such things were regarded with respect not unmingled with
fear. Being Novice-Mistress she was surrounded by her
young pupils, who delighted in speaking of God or His

saints, that they might behold their Mistress rapt in ecstasy.
But Sister Emmerich's raptures often seized her in the
midst of companions who regarded her with uneasiness on
that very account, and to whom she was as insupportable as
was the Church to the gross infidelity of the period, because she dared still to celebrate the grandeur and magnificence of God in His saints.

"I was frequently unable to resist the divine impulse,
and I fell unconscious before my companions. I was in
choir one day, though not singing with the rest, when I
became rigid, and the nuns happening to push against me,
I fell to the ground. Whilst they were carrying me out,
I saw a nun walking upon the highest point of the roof
where no one could go, and I was told that it was Magdalen
di Pazzi, who had borne the marks of Our Lord's wounds.
Again I saw her running along the choir-grate, mounting
upon the altar, or seizing the priest's hand. Her perilous
flights made me reflect on myself, and I took every precau-
tion not to yield to these states. My Sisters understood
nothing of the kind and they, at first, reproached me severely
for remaining in the chapel prostrate, my arms extended.
But as I could not prevent those raptures, I tried to hide
myself from them in a corner. Despite my efforts, however,
I was ravished out of myself, sometimes in one place,
sometimes in another. I lay prostrate, stiff, and immovable, or I knelt with outstretched arms. The chaplain
often found me in this state. I always longed to see St.
Teresa, because I had heard that she had suffered much
from her confessors. The favor was vouchsafed me. I
did see her several times, sick and weak, writing at a table
or in bed. I thought there was a close friendship between
her and Magdalen di Pazzi. It was revealed to me that
Magdalen from her infancy was pleasing to God, on account
of her simplicity and ardent love.

" In my duties as sacristan I was often lifted up suddenly, and I stood on the highest points of the church, on the windows, the carving, and the cornices, cleaning and dusting where humanly speaking no one could go. I was not frightened when I felt myself thus raised and held up in the air, for I had always been accustomed to my angel's assistance. Sometimes when I awoke, I found myself sitting in a large closet in which were kept things belonging to the sacristy ; sometimes I was in a corner near the altar where not a soul could see me, and I cannot understand how I squeezed into it without tearing my habit. But sometimes on awaking, I found myself seated on the highest rafter of the roof. This generally happened when I had hidden myself to weep. I often saw Magdalen di Pazzi mounting up in this way and running over the rafters, the scaffolding, and the altars."

Dean Overberg deposed :—

" Anne Catherine often had ecstasies in the convent, especially during the last four years of its existence. Everywhere, in the cloister, the garden, the church, and her cell, was she accustomed to sink down upon the ground. They came on chiefly when she was alone, though she had slight raptures in the refectory; but she used to beg God not to send them to her there. It seemed to her that the rapture lasted only a moment, though she afterward found that it was much longer.

" I asked her if she knew how to distinguish between ordinary fainting-spells and ecstasies. She answered : ' In fainting-spells from weakness, I am very, very sick as if about to die ; but in the other state, I know not that I have a body. I am often quite joyous, or again sad. I rejoice in God's mercy toward sinners, lovingly leading them back to Himself; or I mourn over the sins of mankind, I am sad at seeing God so horribly offended.

" ' In my meditation I looked up to heaven and there I saw God. When in desolation, I seemed to be walking in a path scarcely a finger in breath, on either side deep, dark abysses; above me all was blooming and beautiful, and a resplendent youth led me by the hand over the perilous path. I used to hear at this time the voice of God saying to me : " My grace is sufficient for thee !"—and the words were sweet to my soul.' "

Frequently during her ecstasies, Sister Emmerich received from her angel an order to bring the Sisters back to the strict observance of the Rule. Then, still in ecstasy and shedding abundant tears, she would appear in their midst and quote the Rules on silence, obedience, poverty, the Divine Office, enclosure, and others most often infringed; or again, she would cast herself at the feet of a Sister in whose heart she saw aversion or even downright hatred, and beg her to pardon, to be charitable, helping her to resist the temptation, and pointing out the guilt of entertaining such feelings. The religious generally yielded to her persuasions and opened to her their interior, begging her advice and prayers to correct. If, however, they found the former too difficult to follow, they indulged fits of pettishness and mistrust, and hence arose fresh suspicions in those weak souls. They imagined that Sister Emmerich had now ever before her mind their faults and imperfections whilst, in reality, she received such communications as those given her in vision. She guarded their confidence as a sacred deposit with the sole view of rendering glory to God and assistance to souls in need.

" It often happened," she said, " that whilst doing my work or, perhaps, lying in bed sick, I was in spirit among my Sisters. I saw and heard all they did and said, and sometimes I found myself in the church before the Blessed Sacrament, though without leaving my cell. I cannot explain how it was. The first time this happened I thought it was a dream. I was in my fifteenth year and absent from home. I had been urged to pray for a giddy young girl that she might not be led astray. One night I saw a snare laid for her. In an agony, I ran to her room and put to flight a servant-man of the house whom I found at her door. When I entered the chamber, she was in a state of consternation. Now, I really had not left my bed, and I thought it was all a dream. Next morning, however, the girl could not look me in the face and she afterwards told me the whole affair and thanked me repeatedly, saying that I had freed her from the tempter, that I had entered her room and saved her from sin. Then, indeed, I regarded the circumstance as something more than a dream. Such things often occurred at a later period. A woman, whom I had never seen, came to me in great excitement, thanked me with many tears, and recounted her fall and conversion. I recognized her as one for whom I had been told in vision to pray.

" It was not always in spirit only, as in the above cases, that I was sent to the assistance of poor tempted souls. I used to go really in body also. The servant-girls of the convent slept in the out-buildings. Once when I was very ill, I beheld at night two persons conversing together apparently on pious subjects, but their hearts were full of evil thoughts. I arose in the dark, but seeing my way clearly notwithstanding, I went through the cloister to separate them. When they saw me coming they fled in affright, and afterward they showed ill-humor toward me. As I returned I awoke. I was only half-way up the stairs that led to the convent, and I regained my cell with great difficulty as I was so weak.

" On another occasion, one of the Sisters thought she saw me at the kitchen fire taking something away in a vessel to eat in private, and again, gathering fruit in the garden for the same purpose. She ran instantly to tell the Superioress ; but, when they came to inquire into it, they found me in bed sick unto death. These incidents made my state a very embarrassing one, and the religious knew not what to think of me."

From Sister Emmerich's entrance into the convent, no suffering seemed to her sufficiently great to outweigh the supreme privilege of dwelling under the same roof with the Blessed Sacrament, of passing a greater part of her. day before It. When at work in her cell or elsewhere, she involuntarily turned toward the church, for the sentiment of the real and living presence of her Lord was never absent from her heart. Nothing could oppose a barrier to her loving communings. The very thought of the Blessed Eucharist threw her into ecstasy and, if untrammelled by the commands of obedience, she found herself prostrate on the altar-steps, although corporeally at a distance. In all that her Rule exacted of her, she discovered something bearing reference to the Blessed Sacrament and she was, consequently, as faithful to the least as to the greatest duty. Her charge of the sacristy she regarded as essentially sacred, to be attended to at any cost of physical suffering, since it was the service of the King of kings, a privilege the angels might well envy. Truly and at all times did she turn toward Jesus on the altar as a flower to the sun; all her thoughts and affections were His, all sent up to Him the sweet odor of love and sacrifice. Her sufferings for the Blessed Sacrament were great as her love, for no sins cried more loudly to heaven, none had greater need of expiation than those directed against faith in the Real Presence.

It was at this period, as we have before remarked, that Jansenism aimed at banishing the Unbloody Sacrifice of the altar and the veneration of Mary, the Mother of God. These abominations filled her soul with anguish as she knelt before the altar and shared with the Heart of Jesus the sorrow occasioned by such outrages. To none other could He turn, since His most cruel enemies were numbered among those whose sacerdotal character gave them unlimited power over this pledge of His love for man. Her ardor led her at night to the church to kneel in the cold before its closed doors, shedding tears of love and desire until daylight gave her admittance, for her only relief was found in the presence of her Saviour. Her sufferings were as varied as the sins of that period against the Blessed Sacrament, and she did penance for every affront offered It, from the tepidity and indifference of the faithful in receiving Holy Communion to the sacrilegious insults of Its greatest enemies. She would have sunk under the weight of this terrible mission, had not God effaced its impressions from her soul and inundated her, at times, with consolation. The more lively her intuition of the grandeur and magnificence of this great Sacrament, the more ardent became her devotion toward It, the greater her veneration. Her reverence for It, joined to the deep feeling of her own unworthiness, sometimes filled her with such fear that it was only obedience could make her approach the Holy Table. She believed herself responsible, on account of her own imperfections, for the numerous infractions of charity and the Rule committed by the Sisters, and this fear prevented her approaching Holy Communion as often as she might have done.

Dean Overberg says :—

" Her confessor wanted her to communicate oftener than

the other religious, and she obeyed for some time; but, from the Purification till Pentecost, she abstained through human respect, because she was accused of mock sanctity and all kinds of remarks were made on the subject. Besides, she looked upon herself as unfit to communicate so often and she fell into a state of sadness. At last, she recognized her fault, and resumed her custom of frequent Communion, though for two years she had to atone for her disobedience on this point, all consolation being withdrawn from her.

"At the end of this time, her peace of soul returned; and so great was her desire for the Holy Eucharist that she could not wait for the usual hour. Her confessor arranged for her to receive before the community arose on days not marked for all to communicate that, being less remarked, the circumstance might create less talk. Early in the morning she used to knock at the Abbé Lambert's door, who kindly went to the church and gave her Holy Communion. But sometimes she presented herself before the appointed hour, and on one occasion, even shortly after midnight, so great was her longing for the Holy Eucharist. Her whole soul was on fire, and so violently was she impelled toward the church that she felt as if her limbs were being torn from her body. The Abbé was not, as might be supposed, any too well pleased on hearing her knock at his door at such an hour; but on seeing the state in which she was, he went and gave her Holy Communion.

"She assisted at Mass with intense devotion. When the celebrant began: 'In nomine Patris,' etc., she contemplated Jesus on the Mount of Olives, and begged for the Faithful the grace of assisting devoutly at the Holy Sacrifice and for priests that of offering It in a manner pleasing to God; lastly, she implored Our Lord to cast upon all as gracious a look as He once cast on St. Peter.

" At the *Gloria,* she praised God in union with the Church Triumphant and the Church Militant, giving thanks for the daily renewal of the Holy Sacrifice, and imploring God to enlighten all men and console the poor souls in purgatory.

"'At the *Gospel,* she asked for all the Faithful the grace to practise fully the evangelical teachings.

" At the *Offertory,* she presented to God the bread and wine with the priest, praying that they might be changed into the Body and Blood of Jesus Christ, and she whispered to her heart that the moment was drawing near for the advent of the Saviour.

" At the *Sanctus,* she called upon the whole world to praise God with her.

" At the *Consecration,* she offered the Saviour to His Father for the whole world, chiefly for the conversion of sinners, for the relief of the souls in purgatory, for the dying, and for her Sisters in religion. She imagined the altar surrounded at this moment by crowds of adoring angels who dared not raise their eyes to the Sacred Host. She said to herself that, although it might be very bold in her, yet she could not deprive herself of the consolation of gazing upon her Lord.

" She often saw a brilliant light surrounding the Sacred Host and in the Host a cross of dark color, never white. Had it been white, she could not have distinguished it. It did not seem to be larger than the Host, but the latter was itself often larger than usual.

" From the *Elevation* to the *Agnus Dei,* she prayed for the souls in purgatory, presenting Jesus on the Cross to His Father that He might accomplish what she could not. At this moment, she was often rapt out of herself and, indeed, she sometimes fell into ecstasy even before the Consecration.

" At the *Communion*, she reflected on Christ laid in the tomb, and begged Almighty God to annihilate in us the old man and clothe us with the new.

" If at Mass or any other service, she listened to the music, she would exclaim : ' Ah, how sweet is harmony ! Inanimate crea'ures accord so perfectly, why should not men's hearts do the same ! How charming that would be !' —and the thought made her shéd tears.

" Once, during the Christmas Midnight-Mass, she saw the Infant Jesus above the chalice, and what appeared to her strange was that the celebrant seemed to hold the Infant by the feet, notwithstanding which, she saw the chalice too. She often saw an Infant in the Host, but He was very small.

" When she was sacristan, she occupied for a time a place in choir from which she could not see the altar, having given hers up to a Sister who was tormented with scruples when she heard Mass without enjoying that consolation. One day as she was watching to ring the bell for the Elevation, she saw the Infant Jesus above the chalice,—O how beautiful ! She thought herself in heaven. She was about to leap through the grate to get at the Child when suddenly recollecting herself, she exclaimed : ' My God ! what am I going to do !'—She succeeded in restraining herself, but forgot to sound the bell, a frequent omission of hers which drew upon her many a reprimand."

Clara Soentgen says : " When Sister Emmerich received Holy Communion her bodily strength increased. She loved, above all, to communicate on Thursday in honor of the Blessed Sacrament ; but, as this gave rise to remark, she obtained permission from her confessor to communicate in secret. Sometimes she went to receive a little after midnight, sometimes at three or four o'clock in the morning, her ardent desire rendering it impossible for her to wait longer.

"Once I asked her why she wore her best habit on Thursdays, and she answered that it was in honor of the Blessed Sacrament. She rarely made use of a book before or after Communion."

Sister Emmerich herself speaks as follows :—"I very often saw blood flowing from the cross on the Sacred Host; I saw it distinctly. Sometimes Our Lord, in the form of an Infant, appeared like a lightning-flash in the Sacred Host. At the moment of communicating, I used to see my Saviour like a bridegroom standing by me and, when I had received He disappeared, leaving me filled with the sweet sense of His presence. He pervades the whole soul of the communicant just as sugar is dissolved in water, and the union between the soul and Jesus is always in proportion to the soul's desire to receive Him."

Dean Overberg gives the following account of her prayer :—" Before she entered religion, Anne Catherine prayed for sinners and the souls in purgatory. In the convent she prayed also for her companions, rarely for her own wants. Save those prescribed by Rule, she said few vocal prayers, but made use of frequent ejaculations. She spoke to God as a child to its father and generally obtained what she asked.

" Her communing with God ceased neither day nor night, even at table it was not interrupted. She was often unconscious of what was said there, and if the Sisters made remarks about her at such times, she rarely perceived it.

" Abbé Lambert asked her one day at the end of one of the meals :—' How could you listen so quietly to what passed at table ?'— when she answered that she had heard nothing of what was said.

" She had, at one time, the habit of disputing with God on two points : that He did not convert all the big sinners, and that He punished the impenitent with everlasting pains. She told Him that she could not understand how He could act thus, so contrary to His nature, which is goodness itself, as it would be easy for Him to convert sinners since all are in His hand. She reminded Him of all that He and His Son had done for them ; of the latter's having shed His Blood and given His life for them upon the cross; of His own words and promises of mercy contained in the Scriptures. She asked Him with holy boldness, how could He expect men to keep their word, if He did not keep His ?"

" The Abbé Lambert, to whom she recounted this dispute, said to her : ' Softly ! you go too far !' and she soon saw that God is right ; for, if He did convert all sinners or if the pains of hell were not to last forever, man would forget that there is a God.

" She had great confidence in the Mother of God to whom she turned whenever she had committed a fault, saying : ' O Mother of my Saviour, thou art doubly my Mother ! Thy Son gave thee to me for mother when He said to John : ' *Behold thy Mother !*' and then again, I am the spouse of thy Son. I have been disobedient to Him, I am ashamed to appear before Him. O do thou pity me ! A mother's heart is always so good ! Ask Him to forgive me, He cannot refuse thee."

" One day just before the suppression of the convent, when she had sought in vain for consolation among her Sisters, she ran weeping to the church and prostrated in agony before the Blessed Sacrament crying for pardon, for she was overwhelmed by the thought that she alone was the cause of all the evil in the house. 'O God, I am the prodigal child !' she cried ; ' I have squandered my inherit-

ance, I am not worthy to be called Thy child! Have pity
on me! I ask it through my sweetest Mother, who is Thy
Mother, too!'—then the voice of God sounded in her soul
bidding her be at peace, that His grace would suffice for
her, and that she should no more seek consolation from
creatures.

" Often, when begging some favor most earnestly and
making great promises to Our Lord, she heard these words:
—' How canst thou promise great things, when little ones are
so difficult to thee!' "

The following is Dean Rensing's deposition :—

" Sister Emmerich said the prescribed prayers with the
religious, and some other vocal prayers ; but when she prayed interiorly she laid her request before God and in the depths
of her heart begged to be favorably heard. She added an
Our Father or some other short prayer, often going so
far as to dispute the point with the Almighty.

" She loved mental better than vocal prayer. She asked
herself : ' What ought you to be, and what are you ?'—
and then she went on until her meditation had been greatly
prolonged, not knowing herself how she had passed from
point to point."

Clara Soentgen says :—" Sister Emmerich told me that
from the Ascension to Pentecost, her state of contemplation
was uninterrupted. She saw the disciples assembled together praying for the coming of the Holy Ghost, and she
herself was present with them. This had happened to her
even before her entrance into religion. During the ten days
of preparation, she used to receive Holy Communion several
times. I sat by her at table in the convent, and she
was so absorbed at this time that I used to have to remind
her to eat."

Anne Catherine tells us :—

" I cannot use the prayers of the Church translated into German. I find them insipid and tiresome, though in Latin they are full and intelligible; however, I can confine myself to no set form of speech. I was always glad when we had to sing hymns and responses in Latin ; the feast was then more real to me, I saw all that I sang. When we sang the Litany of the Blessed Virgin in Latin, I used to see one after another in a most wonderful manner all the symbolical figures of Mary. It seemed as if I uttered the pictures. At first, it frightened me, but soon I found what a great favor it was, as it excited my devotion. I saw the most wonderful pictures !"

CHAPTER XVI.

SUPPRESSION OF THE CONVENT.—SISTER EMMERICH RECEIVES THE STIGMATA.

On December 3, 1811, Agnetenberg was suppressed and the church closed. Although Sister Emmerich had long foreseen this most painful event to avert which she had offered herself to God to suffer everything, yet she was so affected by it that she thought she would never be able to quit scenes so dear to her. The separation of her soul from her body would have been less agonizing than leaving the hallowed spot in which she had made her sacred vows.

"I became so ill," she says, "that they thought I should surely die. Then the Mother of God appeared to me and said: 'Thou wilt not die! There will yet be much talk about thee, but fear not! Whatever may happen, thou wilt receive help!'—Later I heard in all my sicknesses a voice whispering to me: 'Thy task is not yet finished!'"

The religious quitted the convent one by one, but Sister Emmerich remained till the following spring, so ill as not to be able to leave her bed. Into her cold, damp cell the painful scenes arising from the Sisters' aversion toward her never found their way. She lay alone, abandoned to herself and her sufferings. But the doves and sparrows hopped on her window-sill and the mice scampered familiarly over the coverlet of her bed, playing fearlessly by her and listening to her reproaches when she scolded them for destroying the doves' eggs. If the Abbé Lambert and an old servant-woman had not in pity rendered her the most necessary services, sad enough would have been her condition. The Sisters were too much occupied with their own affairs to think of her; and yet they had scarcely lost sight of her when they forgot their prejudice against her, as well as its cause. To the question put by ecclesiastical authority: "How was it that Sister Emmerich was not loved in the convent and why was she so persecuted?"—they had no other answer than that of the Novice-Mistress: "It is true, she was not much beloved, but I know not why." The Reverend Mother alone tried to assign a reason: "It seems to me that this was the cause: many of the Sisters were jealous of the particular interest the Abbé Lambert took in her, and some thought her ill-health made her a burden on the community."

The Abbé Lambert, an invalid himself and an exile, without a soul upon earth from whom to hope for sympathy in his old age, remained true to Sister Emmerich in her distress. What he had seen in her for the last ten years he had faithfully kept concealed in his own breast. He was the only one to whom she had revealed the wonderful way by which it pleased Heaven to lead her, the only one who had the least idea of her high mission. He felt himself called to guard to the best of his power her person as well as the mystery of her life, regarding her as a chosen instrument, a precious treasure, for which he was to account to God, since to him alone it had been given to know its value. When she could no longer remain in the convent, he accompanied her to the house of a widow named Roters, at Dülmen. She was still so sick that, after dragging painfully through the streets with the assistance of the old servant, she could hardly gain the little front room on the ground-floor which now took the place of the quiet cell whose religious poverty had transformed it into a heaven upon earth.

"I was so nervous and frightened," she said, "when I had to leave the convent, that I thought every stone in the street was about to rise up against me."

She had scarcely reached her miserable lodging, through which the footsteps of the passers-by resounded and into which the curious m ght freely gaze, as it was almost on a level with the sidewalk, when she fell into a deep swoon. Like a flower dragged from its home on the mountain-top and trodden under foot on a dusty highway, she seemed about to fade. Although the strict observance of Rule had fallen into decay, yet the cloister had been for Anne Catherine a consecrated spot, a place sanctified by the prayer and penance of its first occupants in the days of fervor and religious discipline, and where she herself had aimed at the perfect accomplishment of every duty. She had, as it were, identified herself with the conventual exercises still kept up in spite of the inroads of decay. The Divine Office and other religious duties were almost essential to her life, an aliment whose want nothing else could supply ; but, above all, the vicinity of the Blessed Sacrament, the house of God open to her at all times, appeared a necessary condition to her stay upon earth, to the accomplishment of her expiatory task. All this was now snatched from her grasp. From the holy asylum in which her life had passed for the last nine years in perfect seclusion, she was cast, so to speak, helpless and friendless, upon the public road there to begin the last and most painful stage of her mission.

That just before the Lent of 1812, a poor sick nun was led through the streets of the obscure town of Dülmen, was an event of little importance, doubtless, in the eyes of the world. And yet, this apparently insignificant circumstance was in strict accordance with the designs of Divine Providence.

On this poor religious woman, worn out by suffering and penance, despised and persecuted on account of her profession, were heaped all the tribulations of the Church at this time scorned and maltreated as never since her foundation. But as the Man-God Himself, "A root out of a thirsty ground" (1), " despised and the most abject of men," "the man of sorrows, wounded for our iniquities, bruised for our sins," willed to work out our Redemption, and would not prevent the word of the Cross from becoming "to the Jews a stumbling-block, to the Gentiles foolishness;" so at all times has He delivered His Church by choosing "the foolish things of the world to confound the wise, the weak to confound the strong, the mean things of the world and the things that are contemptible, and the things that are not, to destroy the things that are" (2). To accomplish this end, incomprehensible to men, sublime in the sight of the blessed, to procure by her means the deliverance of his Church, God now draws His spouse from the hidden retreat in which she had acquired that strength which surpasses all the strength and wisdom of man.

Many religious of either sex had left their cloister without regret to return to that world from which their sacred vows had never wholly detached them; everywhere unworthy monks and priests were met employed by the great ones of the world to spread in the hearts of aspirants to the priesthood the poison of error and revolt against the hierarchy and sacred traditions of the Church. The sanctity and dignity of the sacerdotal character, the graces and privileges attached thereto, were despised and denied even by those that were clothed with it; and the open enemies of the Christian name were not the only ones who confidently looked forward to the speedy destruction of the Church.

(1) Isaias liii. 2-5.　　　　(2) I. Cor. i. 27.

This explains the state to which the poor victim of expiation is now reduced, why she is thrown out, unprotected and proscribed. It is the Church and her Heavenly Bridegroom that suffer and mourn in the person of the helpless little nun of Dülmen.

Sister Emmerich became rapidly worse. All thought her end near, and her former Novice-Mistress sent for Father Limberg, a Dominican priest who, since the suppression of his convent in Münster had resided in Dülmen, to hear the invalid's confession. We shall give his own words on the impressions then received :—

"During the Lent of 1812, my aunt, who had been Sister Emmerich's Novice-Mistress, sent for me to hear her confession. At first I refused, since a special permission is necessary to hear a religious ; but, when I was assured that this restriction was no longer in force, I went. She was so weak as to be unable to speak, and I had to question her on her conscience. I thought her dying and delayed not to give her all the Last Rites ; but she rallied, and I became from that time her confessor instead of Father Chrysanthe, an Augustinian, lately deceased. She wore a cincture of brass wire and a hair-shirt in the form of a scapular, which I made her lay aside.

" I knew very little of Sister Emmerich before this, having seen her only occasionally. I often said Mass in the convent chapel, and I liked to do so ; everything there was so neat. I thus became acquainted with the chaplain, the Abbé Lambert. Sister Emmerich was sacristan, and I used to see her coming and going. Her health seemed to be so miserable that I thought she would soon die. I often said to myself on seeing her : ' What ! that poor soul still alive ! ' "

Sister Emmerich kept her bed the whole of Lent, her

soul the greater part of the time in a state of abstraction which was ascribed to excessive debility.

On the Feast of Easter she went, though not without great effort, to the parish church to receive Holy Communion, and she continued to do so until Nov. 2, 1812, after which she never rose from her bed of pain. In September she made a pilgrimage to a place called the "Hermitage," just outside Dülmen, where an Augustinian had formerly dwelt and near which was a small chapel. She went in the hope of receiving some alleviation to her fearful sufferings. She had hardly reached the spot when she fell into an ecstasy, becoming rigid and immovable as a statue. The young girl who accompanied her was seized with fright, and called out to a woman for help; they thought she had fainted and treated her accordingly. In doing so they discovered upon her breast a bloody cross which she had received on the preceding Feast of St. Augustine, August 28, but which she herself had never seen. When she awoke from her ecstasy, she was so weak that the two women had to help her home.

On December 29, 18.12, the daughter of the widow Roters found Anne Catherine again in ecstasy, her arms extended, and blood gushing from the palms of her hands. The girl thought it the effect of an accident and drew her attention to it when she had returned to consciousness, but Sister Emmerich earnestly requested her not to speak of it. On December 31st, when Father Limberg took her Holy Communion, he saw for the first time the bloody marks on the back of her hands.

"I made it known," he writes in his report, "to the Abbé Lambert who resided in the same house. He went immediately to Sister Emmerich's room and, seeing the blood still flowing, he thus addressed her: 'Sister, you must not think yourself a Catherine of Sienna!' But as the wounds bled until evening, he said to me next day: 'Father, no one must know this! Let it rest between ourselves, otherwise it will give rise to talk and annoyance!'"

Father Limberg was fully persuaded of the necessity of such a course. He thought more of treating the affair as of small importance than of seeking any relationship between it and other wonderful things he knew concerning the invalid, nor did he question her on the subject. Sister Emmerich herself rejoiced that the two priests did not pursue the affair and she sought to conceal from all eyes her new and cruel sufferings. Father Limberg did not at the time reduce his observations to writing; but in his ordo he made the following short entries :—

"Jan. 6th, Feast of the Kings, I saw for the first time the stigmata on the palms of her hands."

"Jan. 11th—She sat up in an arm-chair about six o'clock. She was in ecstasy an hour and a half."

"Jan. 15th—She communicated to-day. From seven till nine, stiff and immovable in ecstasy."

"Jan. 28th—Since the 15th, she has been in ecstasy more or less prolonged. To-day, I saw the marks of the wounds on the soles of her feet.

"Her hands and feet bleed every Friday and the double cross upon her breast on Wednesdays. Since the existence of these wounds has come to my knowledge, she has eaten nothing.

"Her state remained secret till February 28, 1813, when Clara Soentgen perceived it and spoke to me of it."

As Sister Emmerich never mentioned her stigmata but, on the contrary, anxiously hid them, we can glean further details on the subject only from the official inquiry to which she was subjected and in consequence of which her state soon became noised abroad.

CHAPTER XVII.

ECCLESIASTICAL INVESTIGATIONS.—DEAN RENSING'S REPORT.

Once Clara Soentgen had penetrated Sister Emmerich's secret, the news spread far and wide. Toward the middle of March, 1813, it was the talk of the town. Her case was freely discussed even in the public ale-house and, as might be expected, it soon reached the ears of Ecclesiastical Superiors at Münster (1).

Among those that took part in the discussion mentioned above was Dr. William Wesener of Dülmen, who now for the first time heard such things spoken of, and who saw in the whole affair but the grossest superstition; however, he resolved to visit the invalid that he might be better qualified to judge. He had lost his faith whilst studying at the University; but he was a man of so upright and benevolent a disposition that the mere sight of the patient produced a deep impression upon him. He knew not how to account for the singular facts he witnessed but, trusting to her rare artlessness, he hoped soon to discover their true cause. After a few visits, he offered his professional services, which were willingly accepted (2). Upon close observation he arrived at the conclusion that all suspicion of fraud ought to be discarded though there were, indeed, some facts beyond his comprehension which could neither

(1) The conversation in the public-house had not escaped Sr. Emmerich. After Dr. Wesener's visit to her, her confessor asked her how he knew of her, when she answered: "He was among the gentlemen assembled at the ale-house. He was incredulous, and so he came to see me."

(2) Dr. Wesener kept a journal from his first visit up to 1819, in which he noted down not only his observations and experience with regard to Anne Catherine, but also her exhortations for his return to the faith and the practice of his religious duties.

be denied nor concealed. He consulted with Dean Rensing, the parish - priest, with Father Limberg, and a physician named Krauthausen, upon the measures to be taken
for instituting a proces-verbal respecting the phenomena.
Whilst these gentlemen were discussing at the pastor's
residence the best means to adopt, Almighty God turned
Sister Emmerich's attention toward them, in order to prepare
her for what was to follow. The Abbé Lambert was talking with her when suddenly interrupting him she exclaimed : " What is going to happen to me ? They are holding a council at the Dean's upon subjecting me to an examination. If I mistake not I see my confessor there."

Shortly after these words Dean Rensing entered her
room, and announced that they had decided upon an investigation. It actually took place on the 22d of March,
1813. A report was drawn up of which we shall give one
passage : " On the back of both hands are crusts of
dried blood under each of which is a sore, and in the palms
are similar smaller crusts. The same thing may be seen
on the upper part of her feet and in the middle of the soles.
The wounds are sensitive to the touch, those of the right foot
had just bled. On the right side, over the fourth rib from
below, is a wound about three inches long which, it is said,
bleeds occasionally, and on the breast-bone are round
marks forming a forked cross. A little lower is an ordinary cross formed of lines, half an inch in length which
look like scratches. On the upper part of the forehead
are numerous marks like the pricks of a needle which
run along the temple back to the hair. On her linen binder we saw blood stains."

After this examination, Sister Emmerich said to Dean
Rensing :—" It is not yet over. Some gentlemen are coming from Münster to examine my case. One is a distin-

guished personage, who looks like the Bishop that confirmed me at Coesfeld, and there is another rather older man with a few gray hairs."

Her words were verified, for on the 28th of March (the Fourth Sunday of Lent) the Vicar-General of Münster, Clement Auguste von Droste-Vischering, so celebrated afterward as Archbishop of Cologne, arrived in Dülmen accompanied by the venerable Dean Overberg and a medical adviser, Dr. von Druffel. They had come with the intention of rigorously examining into Sister Emmerich's case. On March 25th, Dean Rensing had addressed to the Vicar-General an official report upon the invalid's case and forwarded the statement of the physician. It ran as follows :—

" Most Noble Baron,
    " Very Reverend Vicar-General :

" With a heart deeply touched and full of religious sentiments, I announce to you, as to my Ecclesiastical Superior, a fact well calculated to prove that God, at all times admirable in His saints, still operates in them even in our own days of infidelity, wonders which clearly exhibit the power of our holy religion, which lead the most frivolous to reflect, the most incredulous to turn from their errors. The Lord still chooses the weak to confound the strong, still reveals to His little ones secrets hidden from the great. I have up to the present kept the case secret, being so requested, and also through the deference I believed due to the favored soul. I feared, too, the annoyances attendant on its being divulged. But now that God has permitted the affair to be, so to say, proclaimed from the house-tops, I deem it my duty to make an official report of it to you. I shall not longer conceal the secret of the King.

" Anne Catherine Emmerich, Choir-Sister of the Augustinian convent called Agnetenberg, now suppressed, is the chosen of God of whom there is question, and Clara Soentgen is the school-mistress of this place. She took the religious habit on the same day as Sister Emmerich and with her parents the latter resided just before entering the convent. Sister Soentgen testifies that from her early youth Anne Catherine was extremely pious, practising conformity to the will of God in imitation of our Crucified Saviour. She was sick almost the whole of the ten years of her conventual life, in bed for weeks at a time, and she suffered much from the contempt of the other religious who regarded her as a visionary. Their treatment was not, indeed, very charitable. They disliked her because she received Holy Communion several times a week, spoke enthusiastically of the happiness there is in suffering, performed many good works of supererogation, and thus distinguished herself too much from them. At times, also, they had reason to suspect her of visions and revelations. Her state of debility has continued since the suppression of her convent. She has now been confined to bed for some months and for the last two she has taken no medicine and no other nourishment than a little cold water with which for a time a few drops of wine were mingled; but for the last three or four weeks she has dispensed with the wine. If she takes a third or even a fourth part of wine in water, in order to conceal the fact that she lives exclusively upon the latter, she instantly rejects it. Her night-sweats are so heavy that her bed linen is perfectly saturated. She is a living witness to the truth of Holy Scriptures: ' Not by bread alone doth man live, but by every word that cometh forth from the mouth of the Lord.' Every evening she falls into a swoon, or rather a holy ecstasy, which lasts ten hours and more, at which times she lies stiff and immovable in whatever position she may chance to have been, her face fresh and rosy like a little child's. If the coverlet or even a pillow be held up before her and by stealth, if I may use the expression, and a priest gives her his blessing, she instantly raises her hand which until then had lain immovable as that of a statue, and makes the sign of the Cross. She has revealed to her confessor, Father Limberg, and also to me after these ecstasies, secrets which she could have known only supernaturally. But what distinguishes her still more as the special favorite of Heaven is the bloody crown around her brow, the stigmata of her hands, feet, and side, and the crosses on her breast. These wounds often bleed, some on Wednesdays, others on Fridays, and so copiously that heavy drops of blood fall to the ground. This phenomenon creates much talk and criticism ; therefore, I engaged the physicians of this place to make a preliminary examination that I might be able to draw up a report. These gentlemen were greatly affected by what they saw. The result of their investigation is contained in a statement signed by them, by Father Limberg, by the Abbé Lambert, a French priest, who resides in the same house with the invalid, and by myself.

"I discharge this duty as one I owe to my Ecclesiastical Superior to furnish proper information in so singular an occurrence, and I beg to be informed as to what course to pursue, especially in the event of the decease of this remarkable person. She greatly dreads publicity and particularly the intervention of civil authority. I hope your influence will be able to avert such an annoyance. Should Your Excellency desire to convince yourself of the truth of this statement and of the supernatural character of certain attendant circumstances, which I deem prudent not to com-

mit to paper, I beg you to come to Dülmen with Dean
Overberg and to honor my house by your august presence.

" I should much prefer making this report in person ; but
the sickness of some of my parishioners, catechetical instructions for First Communion, and other affairs prevent my doing so at present. Your Excellency will certainly hold me
excused.

" With profound respect,

" RENSING.

"DÜLMEN, *March* 25, 1813."

CHAPTER XVIII.

The report given in the preceding chapter was coldly received by the Vicar-General on March 27th.

"When I read Dean Rensing's report with the official statement of the physicians," he says, "I was very far from regarding the affair as represented by them. As is usual in such cases, I suspected fraud or delusion. I had heard nothing of it before. As it was beginning to be noised about in Dülmen and thinking the truth might be easily tested since it was a question of things falling under the senses, I went the next day to Dülmen. I took them by surprise, as they did not expect me so soon. Dean Overberg and Dr. von Druffel accompanied me, for I was desirous of the latter's opinion; I know him to be clear-sighted and not at all credulous."

Their arrival was not, however, so great a surprise to Sister Emmerich as the Vicar-General supposed. Shortly after, the Vicar Hilgenberg deposed on oath that he had visited Sister Emmerich Saturday evening after the Litanies and, on inquiring how she was, had received for answer: "I have spent a miserable week on account of the medical examination of my wounds; but *to-morrow* and next week I shall suffer still more from new inquiries."

"We arrived about four o'clock in Dülmen," continues the Vicar-General in his notes. "On Sunday, we saw Anne Catherine Emmerich twice and conversed with her in presence of her confessor and the Dean. On Monday morning, the 29th, we had another conversation with her and I spoke also with her friend, Clara Soentgen of Coesfeld.

We left Dülmen about ten o'clock. The case seems to be more remarkable than we expected to find it. "

The 28th of March, 1813, was the Fourth Sunday of Lent and in the diocese of Münster, the Feast of St. Joseph. The Vicar-General caused a special report to be drawn up of the observations made on this day and the following, and Dean Overberg also made notes of what seemed most remarkable in the case   The report runs as follows :—

" We visited Sister Emmerich about five o'clock P. M., to assure ourselves of the phenomena said to be displayed in her person.   We remarked nothing striking in her countenance, nothing that indicated expectancy, no sign of pleasure or surprise.   When notified that her Superiors desired to examine into her state, she consented unreservedly, and unhesitatingly showed her hands, her feet, and her right side, remarking only that, although such proceedings were painful, yet she desired but to conform to the will of God.

" The lightest touch on her wounds is, as she says, exquisitely painful.   Her whole arm quivered whenever the wound of her hand was touched, or the middle finger moved.

" Toward nine o'clock that same evening we paid her another visit.   Soon after our arrival, she fell into ecstasy, her members becoming rigid, the fingers only remaining flexible. A touch on the wounds or the middle finger excited trembling.   Her head could now be raised only with difficulty and then the breast, as if following the movement of the head, rose also.   The questions put to her by the physicians remained unanswered.   She gave no sign of life (1). Then the Vicar-General said: ' In virtue of holy obedience, I command you to answer !'—Scarcely were the words pro-

(1) From Dean Overberg's Report.

nounced when, quick as thought, she turned her head, regarded us with a singularly touching expression, and answered every question put to her. Later, she was asked how it was that, although unconscious, she had so quickly turned her head on the Vicar-General's command, and had she heard his voice. She answered : 'No ! but when anything is commanded me in obedience whilst in this state, I seem to hear a loud voice calling me.'

" She has begged Our Lord to deprive her of the external signs of His Wounds ; but she has always received the answer : 'My grace is sufficient for thee !'— The Vicar-General bade her renew this petition forthwith."

Next morning the visitors returned for the third time and the Vicar-General decided that the surgeon, Dr. Krauthausen, of Dülmen, should wash the wounds in tepid water to remove the crusts of dried blood, apply linen bandages to the hands and feet in such a way that neither the fingers nor toes could move freely, and see that they so remained for eight consecutive days. Sister Emmerich readily submitted to the experiment. She repeated more than once that she would freely consent to any others they might desire to make, only begging them to avoid publicity.

The gentlemen were fully satisfied with her whole comportment especially her acquiescence in the orders of Superiors, although they greatly increased her sufferings. The favorable impression she produced on them appears from the following lines of the report :

" The countenance of the patient during the different interviews was remarkably serene, and one could not help being struck with the frank and benevolent expression of her eye."

"Lastly, the Vicar-General conversed with her in private, telling her that, although it was lawful for us to desire to share in the sufferings of our Divine Redeemer, yet we should not seek external marks of them. To which she replied: ' Those exterior marks form, indeed, my cross !'"

CHAPTER XIX.

Measures Adopted by the Vicar-General.

On returning to Münster, the Vicar-General adopted such measures for the prosecution of the inquiry as clearly proved that the impression made on him personally by Sister Emmerich's demeanor yielded to higher considerations.

"I could not," he remarks in his official report, "conclude from a single investigation that imposture or delusion was impossible. Supposing no deceit whatever in the case, the question as to whether those phenomena can be explained by natural causes, is not my affair. The stigmata are visible to whomsoever looks upon them, the facts themselves cannot deceive. The only question is: Has Sister Emmerich produced them herself, or not? or has some one made them for her? As she has solemnly declared that such is not the case, it remains to be determined whether she is practising deceit or is herself deluded. If the investigation leads to the conclusion that the slightest imposition may reasonably be suspected, there will be no need to push matters further; but to arrive at such a conclusion, we have only to make use of such means as will wound neither justice nor charity."

Clement Auguste von Droste-Vischering united to determination of character so tender a heart that he was often known to purchase birds merely to restore them their liberty. Now, when such a man resolved to regulate his mode of action by principles like those expressed above, we may readily conclude that the sufferings inevitably resulting to the subject of such an examination, would be alleviated as much as possible; yet such alleviation in Sister Emmerich's case

was not in accordance with the designs of God. As substitute for the Church, she must endure those pains and
trials which alone could draw down pardon on an ob-
durate world; consequently, in all the Vicar-General's
proceedings, his compassion was less consulted than the
necessity of satisfying public opinion. The spirit of the
times, his own embarrassing position as Administrator of a
see long orphaned and exposed to political vicissitudes,
imposed obligations to which all other motives stood
secondary.

In 1802, Münster had lost its last ecclesiastical ruler, the
Prince-Bishop Maximilian Xavier, brother to the Emperor
Joseph II., and Prussia had seized on the vacant see. The
States-Assembly of 1803 put Prussia in definitive possession of the episcopal city of Münster and the southern portion of the country, the other sections being divided
among seven petty sovereigns. Dülmen fell into the hands
of the Catholic Duke von Croy, who, at a later period,
caused the ancient church and convent of Agnetenberg,
the scenes of Anne Catherine's religious life, to be entirely
destroyed. Coesfeld and Flamske fell to the Count von
Salm. After the battle of Jena, these territories were again
wrested from their possessors and united to the Grand-Duchy
of Berg, which Napoleon had erected in favor of a child
still in the cradle, the eldest son of his sister-in-law, Hor-
tense, Queen of Holland. The year 1810 put an end to
this union; and Münster, Coesfeld, and Dülmen were incorporated with the great French Empire until the Congress
of Vienna, when the whole province passed into the hands
of Prussia.

The Vicar-General's difficult position may now be
appreciated. The secular powers were incessantly changing, and the people worn out with the same, daily regretted

the peace and happiness they had formerly enjoyed under their Prince-Bishops. Besides, Clement Auguste von Droste belonged to one of the oldest and noblest families of Münster, a sufficient reason for his being looked upon with a distrustful eye by the strangers then in power. In 1807, he had been appointed by the Cathedral-Chapter, Administrator of the diocese vacant since 1802; but, April 14, 1813, the Dean of the Chapter, Count von Spiegel, was named Bishop by a decree of Napoleon, and the Chapter was forced to deliver over to him the government of the diocese. Clement Auguste thus became the Vicar-General of Count von Spiegel, a proceeding which Rome refused to tolerate. He resumed, therefore, the Administratorship of the diocese until 1821, when Münster was provided with a pastor in the person of Baron von Lüning, formerly Prince-Bishop of Corvey, who soon, however, fell into a state of mental weakness which ended in death, 1825.

The Vicar-General von Droste bitterly mourned over the Church whose servant he gloried in being. He grieved to see her insulted and despised by the so-called lights of the age, treated as an institution which no longer had a right to exist, which was destined soon to fall to pieces; and he knew with what a torrent of outrages any sign of life in her would be pursued, anything which contradicted the opinion entertained by her enemies, that the extinction of Catholicism was already an accomplished fact. Nor was this all — in the ranks of those enemies were her own priests who, by word and writing, dared to wage open war against her ancient practices of faith and piety. Let us not, then, be surprised if, in such a situation, a man of his prudence and foresight should be greatly annoyed at finding himself connected with an affair so extraordinary, so foreign to the ideas of the times as was that of Sister Emmerich. He

had hoped promptly to unveil the imposture and prevent reports detrimental to the Church; but now that he
could not look upon the case as such, he felt himself obliged
to pursue inquiries into it as diligently as possible. He was
bound not to expose his authority to a shadow of suspicion,
nor to leave the least room for the charge of censurable
indulgence or carelessness in what might possibly turn out
to be fraud, and which, at all events, could not fail to
exasperate the enemies of the Church.

The Vicar-General's choice of Dean Overberg and Dr.
von Druffel to assist in the examination, was the happiest
that could have been made. Dean Overberg's name is
everywhere pronounced with respect. He was one of the
noblest characters of his time, esteemed throughout Münster as the most enlightened and experienced director of
souls. The Vicar-General fully appreciated his worth;
therefore, he commissioned him to inquire scrupulously into
Sister Emmerich's whole interior and exterior life, prescrib-
ing also to the latter, in virtue of obedience, to give an
exact account of herself to the Dean. The holy old man
found it no difficult matter to gain the invalid's confidence,
and on his very first interview he made the following note :—

" In spirit, she saw me coming and she told me so, though
as she declared to others, she had never seen me in her life
with her bodily eyes. 'I saw you interiorly,' she said to
me, and this made her as confiding as if we had long known
each other."

The childlike candor with which she opened her heart to
the venerable priest enabled him to gaze deep down into
her pious soul, and her interior life soon lay unveiled before
him. Every interview offered him fresh proofs of her extraordinary vocation ; and though multitudes constantly claimed
his advice and assistance, occupying his time and attention

continually, yet he deemed it his duty to undertake the additional task of noting down all he observed in her, even the words that fell from her lips. One might suppose that the Dean's rare kindness would invent some means of mitigating the sufferings attendant on the investigation; but God willed that from no quarter should any hindrance arise to the measures judged necessary to dissipate doubt as to the reality of the phenomena.

Prof. von Druffel, a learned and highly respectable physi - cian, was a man of unbiassed mind who examined the wonders displayed in his patient with the practised eye of an experienced scientist. When he first heard of them, he felt inclined to regard them as fraud; but his very first visit greatly modified these sentiments. Not only did the con- dition of the wounds and their manner of bleeding convince him that they could not possibly be produced artificially, but Sister Emmerich's whole demeanor forced him to reject ab- solutely all suspicion of imposture. We may here remark that Dr. von Druffel, as also Drs. Wesener and Kraut- hausen, had a lively appreciation of the sufferings that would result to the patient from such treatment as the Vicar- General prescribed, and personally they needed no such proof as to the reality of the facts witnessed. The publicity attendant on such an investigation and the interest it aroused, induced Dr. von Druffel to insert a long article signed by him- self in the Salzbourg "Journal of Medicine and Surgery," in which he gave a detailed account of his own observations respecting Sister Emmerich. He begins by declaring that he has no intention of trying to explain the phenomena and ends with the bold words:

"As to those that regard the phenomena in question as imposture let them remember that the ecclesiastical inves- tigation was made most strictly. If it be a fraud, it is of a very peculiar nature and very difficult to prove."

Dr. von Druffel, like all who fell under Sister Emmerich's influence, received a great grace from God through her intervention, for she perceived the state of his soul and the danger he was in of losing his faith. After her first interview with him, she confided her discovery to Dean Overberg, allowing him to make use of the information if he thought it advisable. The doctor entertained the highest respect for the holy priest by whom in return he was greatly esteemed. The Dean was amazed, indeed he could scarcely credit what he heard until the doctor himself confirmed Sister Emmerich's statement and gave unequivocal proofs of the benefit he derived from her acquaintance.

The Vicar-General dispatched to Dülmen on the 31st of March, a summary of the rules to be observed in the coming examination. They are a notable proof of this distinguished man's rare firmness, prudence, and foresight. His first step was to nominate Dean Rensing (1) Sister Emmerich's extraordinary director during the process, imposing upon him the obligation of carefully observing the patient's conduct, and of rendering a faithful account to him of the same. The following detailed instructions were also sent to the Dean :—

" It is our duty to investigate these phenomena as strictly as possible, in order to discover their origin : whether produced by sickness, or supernaturally, or in fine by artificial means. There is here no question of private opinion, but only that of verifying what may be possible ; which being premised, it is absolutely necessary not only that all that transpires in the soul and with regard to the soul (without encroaching, in the least, on the secrecy of the confessional) and all that takes place in the person and with regard to the person of Sister Emmerich, should be

(1) " Dean Rensing," he observed, " is a man of sense. It is to him, and to him alone that I venture to confide the direction of this affair."

reported simply and truthfully in writing; besides this, from the day on which Dean Rensing enters upon his charge every physical or mental phenomenon, every bodily change must be recorded in a journal and forwarded to me every eight days. What concerns the soul is confided to Dean Rensing. Dr. Krauthausen has charge of the body. The Dean will say to Sister Emmerich that in obedience to ecclesiastical authority, she will allow Dr. Krauthausen to do all he may judge proper to effect a cure. The patient must, in general, be allowed to perceive as little as possible that the examination has any other end in view than that of her cure. Let no importance be attached to her wounds, let them not be regarded as extraordinary favors. The less the whole affair is spoken of the better. "

The surgeon, Dr. Krauthausen, was charged to make notes of all that he observed respecting the physical phenomena.

" For Dr. Wesener," writes the Vicar-General, " who drew up the report of March 25th, sympathizes too deeply with the sufferer; he must not be engaged for the present. Dr. von Druffel is of opinion that we may unhesitatingly confide to Dr. Krauthausen the treatment of Sister Emmerich's wounds. Under no circumstances must the bandages be removed or even changed, by any other than himself. If he thinks proper, he may remove them at the end of four days provided he replaces them immediately."

The points upon which the weekly report was to turn were also named by the Vicar-General.

Dean Rensing was deputed, on the part of the Vicar-General, to prescribe the following rules to Father Limberg, Sister Emmerich's ordinary confessor:—1. To avoid as much as possible in his conversation with her any allusion to her sufferings; 2. Not to address to her, either during or after her ecstasies, any question upon her interior ; that was, for the present, the exclusive affair of Dean Rensing ; 3. To communicate to the latter all that Sister Emmerich, without any questioning on his part, might tell him either before or after her ecstasies.

Lastly, Clara Soentgen was commissioned to make private reports, " For," says the Vicar-General, " she is known to be a sensible person, absolutely incapable of deceiving. I have asked her to communicate what she observes unknown to the Dean, that by such independent reports I may arrive more surely at the truth."

The order addressed to Sister Soentgen contained the following lines : " In this affair I wish *to know* all—*no thinking, no guessing, but knowing !* What I *know* for certain alone has any weight with me."

The following instructions were given with regard to Sister Emmerich's sister :—" We have no objection to her staying with the invalid ; but if she should attempt to contravene the orders prescribed, let her be instantly dismissed. I may here remark that other measures, infinitely more painful for Sister Emmerich, may be avoided by a scrupulous adherence to those now laid down."

Dean Rensing was authorized to take the depositions of all persons, priests, religious, or laics, who at Dülmen, Coesfeld, and Flamske, had been most nearly connected with the invalid and who could communicate details upon her character, her disposition, and her whole former mode of life.

CHAPTER XX.

Sister Emmerich's Wounds are Bandaged.

On April 1, 1813, Dr. Krauthausen applied the bandages to Sister Emmerich's hands and feet. In his report to the Vicar-General he says :—

"In fulfilment of the charge intrusted to me, on Thursday before Passion Sunday, at 8 A. M., I bathed in warm water the spots covered with dried blood in the hands, feet, and head of Anne Catherine Emmerich, formerly an Augustinian religious. I then applied bandages in such a way that neither the fingers nor toes could be moved freely, nor could the said bandages be disarranged, much less removed without my knowledge. The bathing, though performed gently with a fine sponge, and the process of bandaging caused keen suffering for about twenty-four hours. When I had finished the bathing, I perceived on the back of the hands and the insteps an oval wound about half an inch long, which was smaller in the palms of the hands and soles of the feet. They were healthy looking and had no pus."

Some hours after the bandaging Dean Rensing visited the invalid whom he found " weeping from pain produced by the burning heat in her bandaged wounds." He comforted her, and she said : " Gladly, gladly shall I endure it all, if only the dear God gives me strength to bear it without impatience !"

But, when at Vesper-time she began to unite with the Saviour's Passion, her pains became more violent and she was seized with the fear " of not being able to endure them and of failing in obedience to her Superiors."

The Dean calmed her by promising that he and another priest would offer Holy Mass for her next morning to beg God to give her strength to suffer. She replied :—

"I sigh only for that grace, and God will not refuse it if the priests ask it with me."

The night of April 1-2 was so painful that she fainted three times ; it was only in the morning when Mass was said for her that she experienced any relief, though the twitching and smarting of her wounds still continued. On the evening of the 2d, in a hardly audible voice, she said to the Dean :

" There are some others who want to see my wounds; it frightens me! Can you not prevent it ? "

Her words were verified on April 4th. The French Commissary-General, M. Garnier, came officially from Münster to collect information respecting her. He asked her many questions, Abbé Lambert acting as interpreter. M. Garnier, appeared particularly anxious to know if she spoke on politics or uttered predictions. He made Dr. Krauthausen remove the bandages from the right hand that he might see the wound for himself. Sister Emmerich's demeanor produced so deep an impression upon him that, fourteen years after, at Paris, he mentioned this visit to Clement Brentano in the most feeling and respectful terms.

Dr. Krauthausen thus records this removal of the bandages :—" To-day, April 4th, upon an order from M. Garnier, Commissary of Police, of the department of Lippe, I was obliged to unbandage the right hand and, in the afternoon about half-past four, I unbound the left and both feet. The linen was steeped in blood and adhered so tightly to the wounds that it required some time to soften it with warm water before it could be drawn off, and even then the operation caused her acute pain. The wounds were in the same condition as on the 1st of April. That the bandages might not again adhere so tightly, and also to relieve the pain, I put a plaster on the wounds."

The plaster, however, only increased Sister Emmerich's sufferings and did not hinder the flow of blood. Next day, April 5th, the bandages were again soaked and the doctor, at the patient's request, took them off and applied fresh ones. In removing the plaster, he saw no sign of suppuration.

The following morning the bandages were again wet with blood, and the sufferings of the patient on the increase. This went on until the 7th, when she implored the doctor to unbind her hands and feet, as she could no longer endure the pain. The doctor dared not yield without an express leave from Münster. He was about applying for it by letter, when the Vicar-General and his companions arrived that same evening in Dülmen.

Upon the doctor's refusal to yield to her entreaties, Sister Emmerich proposed to herself to be patient one day more, when she was told in vision to represent to her Superiors that she desired nothing in this world, neither money, nor fame, but only solitude and peace, and that they ought not to subject her patience to so great a trial, since to increase her sufferings to such a degree was nothing short of tempting God. When, in pursuance of this order, she made her representations to Dean Overberg, he was, at first, greatly surprised; for, from what he had seen on his first visit, he thought he might count upon her ready obedience. But when she added that she had been ordered to make this representation, as well as to endure all that obedience might prescribe, he was satisfied. Later on, we shall see how perfectly she complied with the injunction received in vision, in spite of the intense sufferings it entailed.

CHAPTER XXI.

SECOND VISIT OF THE VICAR-GENERAL TO DÜLMEN.

The official statement relative to this visit runs thus:—
" On Wednesday, April 7th, about six P. M., the undersigned visited Sister Emmerich. The patient's countenance
appeared the same as on the first visit. The bandages had
been removed from her hands and feet by Dr. Krauthausen,
each fold of the linen over the wounds having to be mois-
tened that it might be drawn off with less pain, so saturated
was it with dark red blood. After their removal, the patient was somewhat relieved, and, with the exception of an
expression of pain from time to time, her countenance was
sweet and serene as on our first visit. The wounds were
healthy, no suppuration nor inflammation." At the last interview that the Vicar-General von Droste had with Sister
Emmerich in Dean Overberg's presence, she begged him
" to reflect upon what all this must cost her whose life had
hitherto been so secluded." She said also :

" These sufferings distract me in prayer. I have had
during the past days but very little consolation. I have
had to struggle not only with impatience, but also against a
feeling of resentment toward those who have made known
my state ; however, I am resigned to God's will."

She expressed to the Dean her fear " that her aged
mother would hear to what she was being subjected, and
that, on account of her age, she would not be able to bear
the grief it would cause her." And when the Dean asked
her how often she lost the presence of God, she reflected
a moment and then answered: " In these eight days (1),

(1) The days of the bandaging. (Dean Overberg's notes.)

oftener than in a whole year !"—A little before his departure she said : " Ah ! how I long to die !" To the question : "Can you, then, no longer bear your pains ?"—she answered : " O yes ! that is not the reason "—and " Her look told me plainly enough," writes the Dean, " why she so longed for death."

The impression Sister Emmerich made on her Superiors at this second visit was as favorable as at the first, and her request that the curious should not be allowed access to her pleased the Vicar-General. He wrote to Dean Rens-ing, April 9th :—" Sister Emmerich has expressed her gratitude to me for having prohibited useless visits. She has so earnestly begged their discontinuance that, had I no other motives, this alone would decide me to do so. You are at liberty to show this order to both ecclesiastics and laics who may be so indiscreet as to insist on seeing her. Let them understand also that she will receive, in obedience, visits authorized by you ; yet it would be unjust to inflict them upon her unnecessarily."

He expressed also his satisfaction with the Dean's pro-ceedings: " I am convinced that I could not have made choice of any one who would have acquitted himself better of the duty confided to you."

The Vicar-General and his party quitted Dülmen at noon, April 8th. Scarcely had they gone when Sister Emmerich, worn out by the prolonged conversations of the last two days, fell into a state of contemplation on the Passion of Our Lord and the Dolors of His Blessed Mother whose feast it happened to be. At Vesper-time the wounds of her head bled so freely that the blood soaked the bandages and flow-ed down her face. Whilst in this state, she sent for Dean Rensing to warn him that a visit from the Prefect of the Department had been announced to her which, under the circumstances, could not fail to be very annoying. The Dean asked whether she feared the gentleman would put questions which she could not answer. She said : "No. As to any questions that may be proposed, I feel no uneasiness. I trust in Our Lord's promises to His disciples that He would Himself suggest what they should say."

The Dean noticed that her countenance wore an expression of pain whenever the back of her head touched the pillow upon which she generally allowed only her shoulders to rest. Between it and her head, there was space sufficient for a person's hand. Dr. Krauthausen reported on the same day :

" For about three hours, Sister Emmerich complained of smarting and pains in her head. At a quarter before two, I found the linen which bound her neck and head soaked with blood in several places; it had also run down upon her face. After I had bathed her forehead carefully, I noticed a number of punctures, through several of which the blood again began to ooze.

" On the night of the 8th, her hands and feet bled freely and continued to do so the whole of the 9th. About 8 o'clock P. M. her pulse was so weak that I feared she would die."

Dean Rensing's journal contains a similar report :—

" When I visited her, Friday, 9th, half-past eleven, I was terrified to see her lying pale and disfigured like one in her last agony. When I addressed her, she held out her hand to me complaining in a scarcely audible voice of the frightful pains in her wounds, and I noticed that those of her feet were bleeding so profusely that the bed-clothes were tinged with blood. She told me also that her sick sister had been so ill during the night that she feared she should have to send for her confessor.

" This grieved me so,' she said, ' that I complained

earnestly to the dear God of the distress I was in, and I begged Him to help my sister.   Soon after she was relieved, and rested a little which gave me such satisfaction that I forgot my own sufferings.'" Her sister was soon able to resume her duties.

CHAPTER XXII.

VISITS.—A PROTESTANT PHYSICIAN'S TESTIMONY.

Although the Vicar-General, as we have seen in the preceding chapter, had forbidden visits of mere curiosity and had, at different times, renewed the prohibition, yet the poor sufferer was not secure from intrusion. The Dean found it hard to argue against the reasons of many who insisted on an entrance to her sick room, and some, especially physicians and people of rank, asserted their right to examine the invalid's stigmata.

Such entries as the following were frequently made in his journal:—

"Be not disquieted," she said to me, "even if they are vexed with you on that account. God will reward you for the charity you show me."

The inspection of her wounds was far more painful to Sister Emmerich than the wounds themselves, and though Dean Rensing repeatedly assured her that this mortification would be a source of increased merit, yet such visits never ceased to fill her with dread; even in her visions she was tormented by the thought of them. She told the Dean that three times already when begging for patience, she had received this reply: "My grace is sufficient for thee!" She added: "I am becoming more and more disgusted at the excitement on my account, though I console myself with the thought that I have given no cause for it."

Dean Rensing writes, April 3d:—

"A visitor presented himself to-day who would take no refusal, a Dr. Ruhfus, of Gildhaus, Bentheim. He was so determined on being admitted that only on my promising to ask the invalid's consent would he withdraw for a time. She, at first, objected, but ended by leaving it to my decision and I allowed the doctor to enter. He behaved with remarkable discretion, examined the wounds carefully, and asked for such information as he deemed necessary. On taking leave, he thanked the invalid for her condescension and expressed himself on the wonders he had just witnessed in a manner that did honor to his candor. As we left the room, he said to me : ' What I have seen is truly wonderful. There can be no question of imposture in this case. The religious sentiments of the patient testify to her truth, as does, likewise, her countenance, which expresses naught but piety, innocence, and submission to the Divine Will. The wounds speak for themselves, at least to a man of science. To ascribe them to natural causes such as imagination, induction, analogy, or similar causes, is simply impossible. The whole affair is, in my opinion, supernatural.'—I have thought it my duty to enter the opinion of a man so competent and whose impartiality cannot be doubted. I have given, as far as I remember, the doctor's own words, since before seeing the phenomena in question, he dropped some jests on the subject at the alehouse."

As Sister Emmerich's state was a mystery to all around her, and as she had no one at times to protect her from the curious, it often happened that they plied her with silly, indiscreet questions to which she neither could nor would respond. This prudent silence did not, however, prevent every word that escaped her lips in contemplation from being eagerly seized upon and construed into an answer, which when repeated from one to another often gave rise to all sorts of absurd tales throughout the little town. One day Dean Rensing mentioned this circumstance to the invalid, when she begged him to give her an infallible means of defence against inquisitive questioners.

"I beg you," she said, " to order me in obedience to reply to no question dictated by idle curiosity, were it even my confessor, or one of my Sisters in religion who put it. Then I will keep silence during my swoons. Then they cannot say that I have said, 'such or such a one is in purgatory, such a one is in heaven,' when God knows I have said nothing of the kind."

With respect to her confessor no such safeguard was necessary, as he himself was bound by a strict prohibition from Superiors to put no question to her during her ecstasies. Dean Rensing testifies to the fidelity with which he observed the command.

"Sister Emmerich told me one morning that she had fallen into *a swoon* (an ecstasy) the night before and that she had mentioned it to her confessor, Father Limberg, but that he had replied she must not say any more about it, as it was contrary to the will of Superiors; that, if she had anything to communicate on the subject, she must apply to me. 'This,' she added, 'gave me true satisfaction. If he had questioned me, I should no longer have full confidence in him as my confessor, because he would by so doing have disobeyed his Superiors.'"

CHAPTER XXIII.

LAST DAYS OF HOLY WEEK:—FEAST OF EASTER.

Sister Emmerich prepared to make her Paschal Communion on Holy Thursday, an ardent desire for the Holy Eucharist being enkindled in her breast as was ordinarily the case some days previously. Since the reception of the stigmata, she was incapable of taking any nourishment; but, in preparing for Holy Communion, she experienced a real bodily hunger for the Bread of Life. Wholly absorbed in Its contemplation, she cried out repeatedly: "I am hungry! I am hungry!" And her sister, taking her words literally, gave her two spoonfuls of broth which her stomach instantly rejected. She was so ill after it that the doctor sent for the Abbé Lambert to relieve her by his blessing. All knew well that this result was produced whenever she was forced to eat; but neither the doctor, her confessor, nor her sister desisted from their attempts at making her take nourishment.

Dr. Krauthausen reports, April 11th:—

"Twice I persuaded her to take a spoonful of soup, but she vomited instantly both times, as she had done the day before when by my order a few drops of wine had been given her."

April 14th, eve of Holy Thursday, another trial was made with fish soup. "But," says Dr. Krauthausen, "she could not retain it, vomiting immediately ensued." After she had received Holy Communion, her strength returned for a while and all were struck at the change in her appearance. When the Dean visited her at noon, she was again very weak, as the cross on her breast had been bleed-

ing since the preceding evening; but she was able to make
him understand that the consolation she had derived from
Holy Communion rendered her sufferings more endurable.
She had, during the night, prayed for Clara Soentgen who
was very ill.

Although her sufferings by virtue of the Holy Eucharist
had become less insupportable, they were by no means
diminished; on the contrary, they steadily increased until
evening, when their intensity was such as to force from her
the avowal that, if it were not otherwise ordained, she should
now die of pain.

" On Holy Thursday night, about eleven o'clock," reports
Dean Rensing, " all her wounds began to bleed and they
were still bleeding when I saw her at eight o'clock next
morning.   That of her side especially had bled so copiously
that I shuddered when I beheld the cloths dyed in blood.
I asked her how she had passed the night, to which she
answered : ' It did not seem long to me, for I thought at
every hour of what Our Saviour had suffered on this night.
That gave me consolation, O what sweet consolation !   I
had also a short swoon in which I thought that I ought to
pray for the marks to be taken from me, but their
pains left."

This meditation on the Passion was for Sister Emmerich a
real participation in the Saviour's sufferings; therefore, during
the days sacred to their commemoration, she endured without
intermission the most cruel torments.   Every nerve of her
body even to her finger ends, was racked with pain, and a
burning fever consumed her till midnight between Holy
Saturday and Easter-Sunday, April 18th, when relief came
about three o'clock in the morning.   Her wounds did not
bleed on Holy Saturday though the Dean found her very
weak.   His pious words strengthened her a little, and she

was able to answer the questions he asked her. To his question for whom had she prayed particularly during the last days, she answered :—

" For those who recommend themselves to my prayers and, above all, for sinners who know not their own misery. For myself, I pray : Lord, Thy will be done ! Do with me as is pleasing to Thee ! Give me Thy grace to suffer everything and never to sin. Once I could go to church in Holy Week and on the Easter feasts. O what happiness to see there all that recalled the death and resurrection of Our Saviour ! Now I must lie here, but it is the will of God. It is well, I rejoice that it is so ! "

On Easter-Monday the Dean found her brighter than usual, and Dr. Krauthausen remarks on the same day :—

" On the 19th, she was better and more cheerful all day than for the last month. Still, she took no nourishment with the exception of two mouthfuls of water and the juice of half a roasted apple."

When the Dean inquired into the cause of her gayety, she replied :

" It is from my meditation on the Resurrection. I feel now neither hunger nor thirst, but I know not what God has in store for me. It has seemed to me for several days that some gentlemen are consulting about me at the Vicar-General's. There is one in particular who spoke of me, and I think he is coming to see my marks."

After communicating on Holy Thursday, she said: " After Easter I shall have fresh trouble, they will surely try new experiments on me." These words show that she saw as clearly this time as on March 27th and April 15th, when she remarked to the Dean :—"My heart is very heavy, for I still have much to suffer from these gentlemen on account of my wounds."

April 13th, the Vicar-General wrote to Dean Rensing to engage a respectable and intelligent nurse to attend Sister Emmerich day and night for two weeks, observe all that happened and report the same conscientiously.

' When you find one whom you think suitable," added the Vicar-General, " ask Sister Emmerich before proceeding further, if she is satisfied with her. Assure her also that when I order anything disagreeable, it is through a motive of duty and only because I believe it absolutely necessary, and a means of shielding her from greater annoyances. I have to do violence to my own feelings in acting thus."

April 20, Easter-Tuesday, the Vicar-General came again to Dülmen with Dean Overberg. We give an account of this third visit as we find it in the Vicar-General's own notes :—

THIRD VISIT OF THE VICAR-GENERAL AND DEAN OVERBERG.

(From the Official Report of the Vicar-General von Droste.) " April 20, 1813, Dean Overberg and I set out again for Dülmen and arrived about two P. M.

" We had not yet finished dining, when a physician of Stadtlohn, whose name I do not know, came to beg me to allow him to examine Sister Emmerich's case. I think the Dean had refused him some time before ; but as I judge it proper that physicians should examine the phenomena exhibited in her person and as I intended to have all her wounds exposed to me, I promised to take him with me. We were about starting, when a very skilful surgeon of Gescher, whose name also I have forgotten, was announced. He, too, wanted to see for himself. I thought one more or less mattered little since the examination had to be made, so I consented to his being present. The Dean and Dr.

Krauthausen had, likewise, come and I begged the latter
to inform the invalid of our visit, as I knew well the presence of strangers would be very disagreeable to her. He
went on before to prepare her whilst Dean Overberg, the
two physicians and I followed soon after and reached the
house about four o'clock. Sister Emmerich was lying in
bed as usual.

"The examination began. No blood appeared on the
head but only punctures, and her wounds, both the backs
and palms of the hands, the insteps and soles of the feet,
were as usual, though I think the blood-crust of the right
hand had been broken by the bleeding. As I frequently
visited the patient during my stay at Dülmen, I cannot say
whether I noticed this on my first or on a subsequent visit.
I examined the blood-crust of the left hand with a magni-
fying glass and found it very thin and a little rugose, or
plaited like the epidermis when seen under a lens. On one
of my visits I examined, if I am not mistaken, the wound
in the palm of the left hand through the lens, and under the
dried blood I discovered a round hole. (*See plate, fig.* 1.)

"The cross on the breast did not bleed this time, but
appeared of a pale red color caused by the blood under the
epidermis. I examined also the lines forming a cross, as
well as the skin around them, and I could distinctly see that
they did not break the skin. The epidermis over the lines
and the skin surrounding them to some distance was un-
broken and, through the glass, appeared as if peeling off a
little.

"I examined also with the lens the grayish speck below
the cross, but I could not distinguish it sufficiently well to
describe it. Higher up it paled away and disappeared entirely at the centre ; the lower part was longer and a little
broader. It was something like this. (*See plate, fig.* 2).

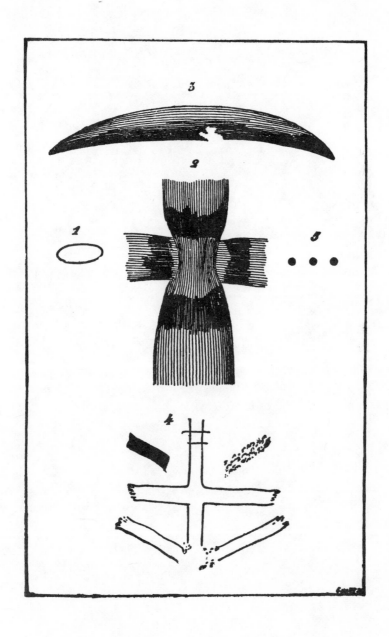

"The wound on the right side was not bleeding, but the upper part of it was encrusted with dried blood of a darker hue, as might be produced by extravasated blood just below the epidermis. It was a little like this. (*See plate, fig.* 3.)

"I used the lens over the parts where there was no blood, but the skin showed no signs of scratches whatever; it may, however, have been of a slightly deeper hue. I cannot remember that distinctly.

"Sister Emmerich consenting (1), Dr. Krauthausen laid on the wound of the left hand a salve of althea and other ingredients spread on lint, and over this he placed sticking-plaster. This was, perhaps, about six P. M. If I do not mistake, she complained that evening when I again visited her that this wound caused her more suffering than the others.

"April 21, Dr. Krauthausen called for me and we went together to see Sister Emmerich. He removed the plaster from the wound, as she complained of intense pain in it which had caused her to pass a sleepless night. The crust that had formed came off with the plaster. I think, however, that a little dried blood remained around it. The wound was clean and bore no trace of suppuration, though a little blood was to be seen and what appeared to be a watery fluid. We prevailed upon her to endure the plaster a little longer upon the same wound, promising to take it off in the evening if she suffered as before.

"I requested Dr. Krauthausen to turn the invalid more to the left that I might see the wound of the right side in a better light than on the preceding day. I examined it again with the glass, but I observed nothing now excepting that the place where a darker shade seemed to betoken extrav-

(1) Dean Overberg says: "After the physicians had examined the wounds, they asked the invalid if she were willing for them to try to cure one of them. She said she was, whereupon a piece of sticking-plaster was applied to the left hand."

asated blood, was less red. At the right of the upper wound, I noticed a few scratches some distance apart, which looked, I shall not say like the scratches of a needle, but rather like the spontaneous cracking of the skin itself.

" The crosses on the breast were red with blood. I washed the upper part and examined it again. Had the skin been broken I should certainly have remarked it. I think there was near the cross a short streak which seemed to be a depression filled with blood. (*See plate, fig.* 4.) Above the left arm of the upper cross and a little to the right, I noticed some scratches like those which I had observed above the wound of the side (1). I asked if the pin in her kerchief had made them, as it might easily have done; but the invalid answered that she always put the pin in so that the point turned out, and she showed me, at the same time, how she did it.

" Another plaster is now on the same wound. I visited the invalid several times to-day and found her in exactly the same state. I find upon examination of one or more of the wounds in the hands and feet that they are, particularly on the upper part, surrounded by a slightly inflamed appearance. Dr. Krauthausen says it is always so.

"Toward noon, I took Mr. Schwelling, of Münster, at his earnest request, to see Sister Emmerich. She consented to receive him on my telling her that he was a very honorable man who asked not to see the wound of her side, the crosses on her breast, nor even, I thought, the wounds of her feet.

" Dr. Krauthausen and I returned about six P. M. I think the invalid slept a little that afternoon. The plaster was removed and found to be saturated with blood. The

---

(1) "I must hear remark that these things are often as fresh in my memory as if I were really beholding them: then I say, ' It was so and so.' Again, I have but a faint remembrance of them, I cannot speak of them positively, and I express myself as above."--Clem. Droste.

wound evidently had bled again, for even supposing the
crust and dried blood had not all come off with the plaster of the morning, so small a quantity could not possibly
have produced such an effect on the second one. I think
the wound on the back of the right hand also had bled. As
she complained of the pain, we did not replace the plaster,
for it would be unjust to torture the innocent.

"Had I commanded it, she would, without doubt, have
submitted; but she feared yielding to impatience, and I
did not feel that I had any right to impose such a command.
She complained of pain in her head and felt sure that it
was going to bleed.

"About eight o'clock A. M. on the 22d, Dr. Krauthausen called at my request. He had just been to see Sister
Emmerich who told him she was under the impression
that her head had been bleeding, or that it would soon do so.
The doctor removed the linen, but saw no signs of blood.
We went together to see her. I think she had slept a little the night before. We found that her forehead had, indeed, been bleeding, the blood having run down as far as
her nose where it now lay clotted and dry. Her cap and the
linen binders being removed, we found large stains in the
back of the former and another large one on the right side
near the temple.

"Her hair being very thick, it was impossible to examine the punctures around the head. She consented to have
it cut close, though not so close, however, as to allow the
blood instantaneously to soak her head-dress and the pillow.
She requested this for the sake of neatness.

"The blood being washed away, a number of fine bloody
marks could be seen with the naked eye scattered irregu-
larly over the forehead and extending from the middle of
it almost to the top of the head. (See plate, fig.5)

"I examined them with the lens and I could see, especially in one of them, some liquid blood. These marks have not the appearance of having been made by a sharp point; they look like little holes. I think I saw distinctly that the one in which there was blood, was indeed a hole.

"Before leaving her, she told me that some one had come from Münster to see her, saying that the Dean had given permission for it. She seemed satisfied when I told her that it was so, and thanked me gratefully for lessening the number of visitors, begging me to remain firm on this point. I reminded her of the prohibition I had given against showing the wounds of her side, breast, and feet; but when I wished to prepare her to allow Drs. Stadtlohn and Gescher to examine them at the end of fourteen days, as they proposed, she answered decidedly: 'No! they shall not see them again!'

"I was obliged to examine the wounds and other phenomena as closely as I did, since Dr. Krauthausen could see nothing through the glass.

"On taking leave of her, I said pleasantly : 'Be sure to let me know when you are going to die'—to which she replied : 'I will!'"

Thus ends the Vicar-General's report.

The poor invalid had no heart for jesting. The preceding days had well-nigh exhausted her; but her patience and fortitude were proof against every trial, so that Clement von Droste, seeing her peace and calm, seemed to forget for the moment her cruel state.

After this third visit, the Vicar-General addressed the following official communication to the Commissary-General of French Police :—

"Sister Emmerich desires only to be forgotten by the

world that she may be free for spiritual things which alone interest her. She asks nothing, she accepts nothing, she desires not to be spoken of, and I trust the public will soon forget her. I cannot discover the slightest shadow of imposture in her case, yet I shall continue to observe her closely."

CHAPTER XXIV.

Dean Rensing and Dr. Krauthausen Grow Impatient.

As the result of the Vicar-General's observations accorded with the conviction already established among the physicians that the stigmata could neither have been produced nor preserved by artificial means, Dean Rensing confidently hoped that the inquiry would be declared at an end. Dr. Krauthausen thinking the same had discontinued his visits. He had been the attendant physician of the convent and had become so thoroughly acquainted with Sister Emmerich that the thought of imposture never entered his mind. Through respect for the Vicar-General, he had undertaken the medical examination and a daily report of the same. He regarded the stigmata as certain, incontestible facts which, however, baffled his experience and skill, as they could not be healed, and as they daily presented symptoms unknown in natural maladies. Day after day had he witnessed the sufferings they caused the invalid, and it was contrary to his conviction of her innocence, as well as repugnant to his sympathy for her, to behold her longer subjected to such tortures. He had also, like Dr. Wesener, to endure the taunts of his incredulous colleagues who affected pity for his inability to discover the fraud. He heartily wished that Sister Emmerich had known better how to conceal the wonders wrought in her person and so had escaped an examination which resulted, as far as he was concerned, only in fatigue and vexation.

As the Vicar-General had left Dülmen without giving any precise directions, Dr. Krauthausen waited no further orders, but declared in his last report, April 26th, that he considered himself discharged from the duty confided to him. But the speedy termination of the affair, no less desired by Dean Rensing than by the doctor himself, could not yet be effected, for the Vicar-General could come to no decision until Dean Overberg should have finished his notes on the invalid's interior life. Although impressed by what he saw and convinced that extraordinary supernatural favors had been granted, yet he was too prudent, too judicious a man to venture a judgment on the patient before having maturely weighed the reports and conclusions of all engaged in the investigation. Dean Overberg remained in Dülmen some days longer to complete his inquiries as the patient's strength would permit ; and, whilst waiting for the report, the Vicar-General resolved that the project formed on April 13th of placing Sister Emmerich under the surveillance of a confidential nurse should be put into execution. Such a measure he regarded as necessary to avert from himself the reproach of having failed to make use of every means that prudence and foresight could suggest.

Dean Rensing, unable to secure a suitable nurse as speedily as he desired, made a new proposition to the Vicar-General on April 27th, which, he felt assured, would be agreeable to the invalid. It ran as follows— :

"Dr. Krauthausen is beginning to tire of his frequent visits to Sister Emmerich. He informed me yesterday that he would continue his observations and reports till the end of the month only. The patient, too, perceives his weariness of her case and consequently dreads his coming. That she may have some repose of which, in truth, she will enjoy but little whilst in life, and at the same time to satisfy the censorious whom we must consider, the best

way would be to engage two or three physicians to remain
with her day and night by turns for a week and to observe
her closely. This is also the opinion of the Protestant physician, Dr. Ruhfus, who was here this morning and again
declared to me that the phenomena appeared to him supernatural. Sister Emmerich will freely assent to such an
arrangement."

The Dean renewed his proposition two days later, petitioning also for full powers of action. The Vicar-General
replied in very few words : " I still incline to the surveillance of fourteen days by a person of her own sex. Our
duty demands not that we should place the case so far be_
yond doubt that they who fear the truth may no longer object to it—such a task would, indeed, be fruitless and
thankless. What is there really in the body and in the soul ?
Whence has it originated ? How has Sister Emmerich been
reduced to her present state ?—such are the questions to
be answered to the satisfaction of all reasonable people, not
by isolated facts, but by a combination of circumstances ;
yet in the means employed to such an end, we must not
violate justice and charity. A mere suspicion founded on
possibility deserves not consideration."

We cannot marvel that Dean Rensing earnestly desired
an end to the affair. It was daily becoming more painful
to him to witness the cruel martyrdom of the poor victim,
without his being able to offer any other assistance or consolation than the bare mention of obedience ; besides, the
visitors to the little town were more numerous now at the
Paschal time and all desired to gratify their curiosity with
regard to the wonderful nun. Their indiscreet importunities were the occasion not only of vexatious interruptions,
but even of irritating disputes which, to so courteous a man
as the Dean, to one so systematic in his habits, were cer-

tainly most annoying and quite incompatible with his pastoral duties. In his daily visits he scrupulously exacted of
Sister Emmerich an account of all that happened to her interiorly and exteriorly, of which he sent a detailed report to
the Vicar-General with a multitude of facts which, he was
convinced, ought to remove every shadow of doubt regarding the phenomena under consideration. He could consequently see no reason to justify prolonging an inquiry so
painful to its object, so wearying to himself. Before
pursuing this subject, we shall glance at the Dean's notes,
since they contain many facts which throw light on Sister
Emmerich and the designs of God over her.

CHAPTER XXV.

Dean Rensing's Testimony.

Dean Rensing had long known Sister Emmerich's sincere piety and her ardent desire of living unknown and hidden from the world. From his very first visit to her he had regarded the truth of the wonders wrought in her as indubitable; but he was timid and cautious, and the objections raised by strangers or enemies failed not to influence him. A specious argument, a suspicion cast upon the freedom of his judgment or the firmness of his character, sufficed to torment him keenly and fill him with distrust. The wisdom and good sense which ordinarily characterized his conduct were not proof against the absurd suspicions raised on all sides as soon as the case was publicly known. Nothing, therefore, was wanting on his part to aggravate the invalid's sufferings ; her patience, her confidence in God were subjected to such trials as are imposed only upon chosen souls.

The Dean's favorable opinion of the invalid was first shaken by the idle talk of one of her former Sisters in religion who, about a month before the inquiry began, pretended to have seen her through the key-hole leave her bed and search in her closet for eatables. Two others declared that they had seen the same thing in the same way and that they had once found her lying on the floor with a slice of buttered bread in her hand. Dean Rensing, who had never doubted the invalid's inability to eat, took these words very much to heart. He sent for the persons in question and instituted a proces-verbal upon their reports ; but on trying to make observations himself in the same way, he became convinced of the impossibility of commanding from the point indicated a sight of either the invalid's bed or the closet. At last, his informants avowed that they knew for certain Sister Emmerich's inability to leave her bed without assistance; but even then the Dean desisted not from interrogating Sister Emmerich herself, for the bread-and-butter story disquieted him not a little.

"I asked her," he says in his journal, "if she remembered having been found at any time out of bed. 'Yes, certainly,' she answered. 'I lay on the floor by the bed out of which I once fell when I had no one to help me. It may be that I did have a piece of bread in my hand, though I think it more likely that it was on the floor. I had a piece by me for a poor woman whose child I was expecting, and it is probable that it fell to the floor with the coverlet.'"

This quieted the Dean somewhat, but he was not fully reassured till Dean Overberg took upon himself Sister Emmerich's defence. Again was he troubled by a fresh report circulated throughout Dülmen and Münster. It was said that even though Sister Emmerich's sincere piety could not be questioned, yet her stigmata would always be open to suspicion, inasmuch as there could be no certitude that they were not artificially maintained by the Abbé Lambert. Might not this foreign priest be fanatic enough to regard as a good work the assistance given to the simple-minded nun to bear constantly on her person the marks of the Saviour's Passion?

A priest from Münster on a visit to the Dean informed him of the conjecture. It made all the more impression upon the latter as he had just heard something similar in Dülmen. "This remark has been made here also," he wrote, "not only by judicious Christians, but even by a well-meaning Jew who was struck by the phenomena exhibited in Sister Emmerich's person.

Although Dean Rensing felt morally certain on hearing the formal asseverations of the Abbé and Sister Emmerich, that they were incapable of such a fraud, yet the report gave rise to doubts which haunted him until the invalid herself came to his aid and delivered him from his mental agony. Her penetration discovered his secret uneasiness and, as she knew that he would not explain himself freely, she asked his permission to speak to him of what was on his mind, and she set before him his disquietude and its cause.

"I was," he says, "exceedingly surprised. It was just as she said. I told her it would be better for her to declare her stigmata the result of pious enthusiasm, for then I should be freed from many annoyances and she from much suffering—'How could I make such a statement?' she said quietly. 'That would be a lie! Even the smallest lie is a venial sin and so displeasing to God that I would rather suffer any pain than be guilty of it.'"

Dean Rensing's silent reserve was now over. He spoke long of the danger of indiscreet religious zeal; and he conjured the sufferer, for the honor of God and the good of souls, to say whether her wounds were the result of exaggerated piety or not. "But," says his journal, "she protested in the name of all things sacred, that she could truthfully say nothing else about them than what she had already said, that she should be only too well pleased if God would hear her prayer and grant to the physicians the power of effacing them, adding: 'To obtain such a result, I would be willing to be punished as an impostor and despised and mocked by the whole world.'"

Sister Emmerich relieved the Dean in his doubts on another occasion when he had been commissioned by the Vicar-General to interrogate her former Superioress and companions respecting her life in the convent. She clearly

foresaw that these women would say many things calculated to perplex his mind and arouse fresh misgivings ; and
fearing that he would again hesitate to make known his
suspicions to her, she herself prepared him for it. " The
inquiry you are about to make of my former companions
will necessitate your appealing to my conscience in terms
the most severe. It will cost you much ; but I
beg you not to fear. Subject me, as well as those Sisters, to
the most rigorous examination. I shall pray God to give
you grace and courage to do so."

Sister Emmerich's uprightness and candor rendered the
Dean's position toward her less embarrassing. The
more he examined, the more convincing became the proofs
of the supernatural origin of the favors bestowed upon her,
the sublime perfection of her virtue. Her obedience and respect for ecclesiastical authority were unlimited, and her
fear of disobeying orders through excessive pain gave her
more uneasiness than the sufferings caused by the attempts
made to cure her wounds. Sometimes the Dean found her
in tears, or a word from him would call forth this touching
question : " Have I sinned by my sadness ?"—His as-
surances to the contrary quickly restored her to the innocent light-heartedness of a child, and she would say
through her tears :—

" Willingly shall I bear still more, if only the dear God
will give me strength to endure my sufferings and not to
fail in obedience."

Never did Dean Rensing hear her complain of anything
else than of the crowd that flocked to see her. When he
prohibited their entrance, she thanked him gratefully.
Her tearful pleadings often encouraged him to defend her boldly from the inquisitive throng. Never did he behold in
her a sign of impatience or discontent ; on the contrary,

the serenity of her countenance testified to her resignation and
union with God.   He says in his journal :—" I found her
extremely weak ; but as soon as she saw me, she assumed
the air of serenity usual to her."   And :   " Whilst I chat-
ted with her, her countenance was full of peace ; but I
noticed that as often as the back of her head chanced to
touch the pillow, her features contracted with pain."

If he reproached her with her stigmata, she took it quietly as if she herself entertained the same sentiments.

" If you had not those singular marks on you," he said
to her one day, "you would be free from the pains you now
endure from them (1)."

" I have prayed the dear God with all my heart," she
replied, " to take them from me, and I am willing to be
treated as a hypocrite and impostor, but my prayer has not
been heard."

He was often quite overcome at the sight of her sufferings
and, not being able to afford her any relief, he desired to
withdraw ; but she tried to compose herself and begged him
not to deprive her of the solace his presence and benediction
afforded.   Once he noted the following words in his journal :
—" I stayed with her a while longer, deeply affected at
seeing the grace of Our Lord so strong in the weak."

Such experience proved to him that the gift of longanim-
ity was attached to the fidelity of her obedience to Ecclesiastical Superiors, the representatives of God ; consequently,
though not at all enthusiastic, he acquired in spite of himself

(1)   When the reality of the stigmata had been unquestionably proved, Dean Rensing changed his tactics and reproached the invalid for having prayed for their disappearance. Dr. Wesener's journal contains the following notes on this subject, Jan. 10,
1815 :—
    " To-day, Tuesday, the wounds seemed larger than usual and, on examining them
closely, I came to the conclusion that they had bled both on the upper and lower surface.   I inquired why this had happened on a *Tuesday* ?   The invalid could not say,
but she told me the following :—' Dean Rensing was here yesterday.   He reproached
me for wishing and praying for the removal of these marks.   I do not think I did
wrong in this, for it was not from any bad intention.   I am resolved to conform to the
will of God, to abandon myself entirely to it.   Gladly would I suffer until the Day of
Judgment to please God and serve my neighbor !' "

a daily assurance of the power and plenitude of the benediction attached to the sacerdotal character. Whenever she spoke such words as these : "I am not so weak, I am stronger when you stay. What I say to you comes from God, it is for God, and it never tires me," etc.—he always saw them verified by effects.

The Vicar-General had enjoined on her to render to Dean Rensing an exact account of her contemplations and whatever happened to her exteriorly ; therefore, she answered all his questions most carefully. We are thus informed of the fact of her offering all her sufferings for the souls in purgatory and the conversion of sinners. Even during the examination, she spent her nights in prayer and contemplation, often " going out of herself," as she expressed it. On the Dean's first visit, she said in answer to his interrogatories : " Last night I was in purgatory. It seemed to me that I was taken into a deep abyss, a vast region, where I saw, and the sight filled me with sorrow, the poor souls so sad, so silent, yet with something in their countenance which tells that the thought of God's mercy gives joy to their heart. Enthroned in their midst was the Mother of God, more beautiful than I had ever seen her before."— Then she said to him : "Instruct your penitents to pray fervently for the poor souls in purgatory, for they in gratitude will pray for them in return. Prayer for these poor souls is most agreeable to God, as it admits them to His presence sooner."

Some days later she again said : " I had no rest all last night, on account of the sharp pains in my wounds, but I was consoled by an apparition of Our Divine Saviour. I saw how He recalls repentant sinners, how He acts toward them. He was so good, so sweet that I have no words to express it."

She was often strengthened and consoled by this vision at the approach of the Easter solemnities.

"My sufferings have become more endurable," she said one day, "for I have seen in vision that many great sinners will soon return to God. Some have already done so. This gave me strength and filled me with joy."

The week after Easter she again said to the Dean :—

"I have had a short but consoling ecstasy in which I saw how many sinners have returned to God this Easter and how many souls have been released from purgatory. I saw, too, the place of purification, and I noticed on the countenances of the prisoners an air of inexpressible joy which I took as a sign of their approaching deliverance. How glad I was to see them freed from their torments! I knew the souls of two priests who have gone to heaven. They had suffered for years; one for his neglect of little duties, the other for his inclination to jesting."

She saw also the conversion of certain sinners who had relapsed into their evil habits.

"Jesus stood before my eyes. He was maltreated in many ways; but during it all, He was so gentle and loving that His sufferings brought to me a sweet kind of sadness. 'Ah!' thought I, 'every sinner has in this suffering a share, and he would be saved if he only had a little good will!'—I saw also some persons known to me who recognized their faults and corrected them. It was all as clear before me as if I saw it with open eyes. Among them was one who is very pious, who speaks in humble terms of herself; but she knows not at the same time that she thinks too much of herself. It would cost her something to acknowledge her faults. It is not true humility for one to depreciate himself, and yet be unable to endure that another should speak ill of him or be preferred to him."

Again she said: " I was present when God passed sentence upon some notorious sinners. Great is His justice, but still more inconceivable is His mercy. He damns only those who are determined not to be converted; they who have a spark of good will are saved. Some there are who grieve for their sins, confess them sincerely, and trust confidently in the merits of their Saviour ; they are saved and their sins will no more be remembered. It is true they go to purgatory, but not to remain long. On the other hand, many stay a long time in purgatory who, although not great sinners, have lived tepidly. Through pride they would take no admonition or instruction from their confessor. The time was when the thought of only one poor sinner's condemnation grieved me so that I could not get over it; but on the present occasion, though many were condemned, I was perfectly calm, for I saw that God's justice called for it. All was as clear to me as if God himself had spoken.

" I saw Jesus on a throne, shining like the sun ; by Him were Mary, Joseph, and John, and before Him knelt poor repentant sinners, supplicating Mary to intercede for them. I saw then that Mary is the true refuge of sinners. All that fly to her find favor, if they have only a little faith."

The following vision on the value of prayer was afterward vouchsafed to the invalid :

" I was in a great, bright place which extended on every side as far as the eye could reach, and there it was shown me how it is with men's prayers before God. They seemed to be inscribed on large white tablets which were divided into four classes : some were written in magnificent golden letters; others in shining silver ; some in darker characters ; and others, again, in black streaked lines. I gazed with delight; but, as I thought myself unworthy of such a favor,

I hardly dared ask my guide what it all meant. He told me : ' What is written in gold is the prayer of those who have united their good works to the merits of Jesus Christ and who often renew this union; they aim at observing His precepts and imitating His example.

" ' What is written in silver is the prayer of those who think not of union with the merits of Jesus Christ; but who are, notwithstanding, pious and who pray in the simplicity of their hearts.

" ' What is written in darker colors is the prayer of those who have no peace unless they frequently confess and communicate and daily say certain prayers ; but who are, however, tepid and perform their good works through habit.

" ' Lastly, what is written in black, streaked characters is the prayer of such as place all their confidence in vocal prayers and pretended good works, but who do not keep God's Commandments nor curb their evil desires. Such prayer has no merit before God, therefore it is streaked. So also would the good works of a man be streaked who indeed gives himself much trouble to help on some charity, but with a view to the honor or temporal advantage attached to it.' "

Dean Rensing found her one day reciting the Litany of the Saints from a book. He wished not to interrupt her, but she said: "I am not anxious about it. I can take it up again where I left off. I do not think God is so strict. He does not mind where I begin," intimating thereby that she interrupted her prayer, not from carelessness, but as a mark of respect toward her director.

She relates another symbolical vision on prayer:—

"I was kneeling in my accustomed place in church, and I saw by the brilliant light that shone around two beautifully dressed ladies in prayer at the foot of the High Altar. With heartfelt emotion I watched them praying so devoutly, when two dazzling crowns of gold were let down as if by a cord over their heads. I drew near and saw that one crown rested on the head of one of the ladies, whilst the other remained suspended in the air a little above the head of the second. At last, they both arose and I remarked to them that they had been praying earnestly. ' Yes,' replied the second, ' it is a long time since I prayed as devoutly and with as much consolation as I have done to-day.' But the first on whose head the crown had rested, complained that, although she had wanted to pray fervently, yet all kinds of thoughts and distractions had assailed her against which she had to fight the whole time. Now I saw clearly by this that the dear God looks only at the heart in time of prayer."

This vision had been vouchsafed to Sister Emmerich to teach her that her own prayer, so often disturbed and interrupted by the presence of visitors and other annoyances, was now no less agreeable to God than the tranquil devotion formerly hers in the cloister. We may recognize a similar intention in a later vision, simple apparently and of no great significance, but which is a striking proof of God's constant care over His chosen one:—

"I had to cross a narrow bridge. In terror I gazed on the deep waters flowing below, but my angel led me over in safety. On the bank was a mouse-trap around which a little mouse kept running, and running, and at last it slipped in to get the bait. ' Foolish little animal!' I cried, ' you are sacrificing your liberty, your life for a mouthful!'— ' Are men more reasonable ?' asked my angel, ' when for a momentary gratification they endanger their soul's salvation ?' "

Her compassion for the poor little mouse was turned by her angel to men blindly rushing to their own destruction,

that she might help them from afar by her prayers and
supplications.   The vision appeared to imply what seemed
to her impossible, that the hidden, peaceful life of former
years was never to return, and so God willed.   That happiness so longed-for was never again to be hers.   The time
had arrived for the last and most painful part of her mission.
As the Church was bereft of her asylums of peace in which
piety could be practised unmolested and contemplation
sheltered from the vulgar gaze, so was Sister Emmerich
torn from that sacred abode in which she had hoped to end
her days, a trial which she shared with Holy Church up
to the last instant of her life.   What it cost her the following pages will tell.

CHAPTER XXVI.

FROM EASTER TO PENTECOST, 1813.

After the Vicar-General's third visit, Dean Rensing had commissioned Sister Emmerich to pray for a certain intention which he did not designate. On May 2d, he found her greatly consoled by an apparition of Mary and the Infant Jesus the preceding night. She said: "I invoked Mary for the intention prescribed; but I have not been heard. I prayed for it three times. I said to Mary: 'I must pray for it, because it has been given to me in obedience;' but I received no answer, and I was so full of joy on seeing the Infant Jesus that I forgot to ask again. I still hope, however, to be heard. I do not pray for myself. I am so often heard when I pray for others, but for myself never, excepting when I ask for sufferings."

Without knowing it, she had this time prayed for herself, Dean Rensing's intention being that the investigation might be speedily concluded. Every one connected with it had almost a greater desire for it than the poor sufferer herself. She often had to tranquillize those from whom she should have received comfort and support. But the suspicions cast upon the good old Abbé Lambert afflicted her more sensibly than her own pains (1). Father Limberg, her confessor, had known her too short a time to be exposed to unjust remarks ; yet he knew the exact state of her soul and, in spite of his naturally distrustful disposition, he

(1) Dr. Wesener's journal, Jan. 26, 1815 :—"I was bandaging to-day, in Sister Emmerich's room, an ulcer on the arm of Mrs. Roter's little boy, a child of ten years. The Abbé Lambert, who was present, was so overcome at the sight that he turned his eyes away and began to moan over the little fellow. I expressed my surprise to Sister Emmerich at the old priest's extreme sensibility. She replied : ' You see now what he is ! tender-hearted as a child. And yet they say he made my wounds!' "

doubted not the truth of her stigmata. He was a very
timid man and easily disconcerted. He trembled in the presence of an illustrious personage such as the Vicar-General;
consequently, it is not surprising that he frequently drew
upon himself the reproach " of imprudence." Had it been
in his power or that of the Abbé Lambert, the wounds
would have disappeared as soon as produced, particularly
as such a result would have been most conformable to Sister
Emmerich's own desires. Both he and the Abbe regarded them as an unavoidable misfortune to be borne as best
it could. They utterly rejected the idea that it was the
work of God, a distinction granted to few, and the ecclesiastical inquiry with the publicity attending it was annoying
in the extreme. All this combined to make the poor sufferer dread losing patience if not soon allowed to return to
that life of seclusion and recollection to which she had been
accustomed. It was this hope that led her to accede so
willingly to Dean Rensing's proposal of a medical surveillance of eight days, and the same hope of freeing herself
from further annoyance made her look forward to it with
ever-increasing desire.

May 9th, Dean Overberg came for the fourth time to
Dülmen on the part of the Vicar-General.

" I went over what she had before recounted to me,"
he says, "to assure myself that I had understood and
noted it down correctly. She gave me to understand that
this examination into her past life not a little increased her
sufferings ; for it might be thought that she was something,
but she herself knew better. I found her cheerful, although
she had suffered much the night before and her wounds
had bled profusely."

On the second day of his visit, Dean Overberg writes :—

" Sister Emmerich was again very prostrate this morn-

ing and her sister informed me that she had passed an agonizing night, often starting from sleep in dread of a
new examination.   She shed tears through her fear of yielding to impatience if not allowed a little rest, and complained
that the investigation had almost entirely deprived her of
recollection.   I was not able, nor did I desire to converse
long with her as she was so weak ; however, she again confirmed her former statements to me.   She was a little better
in the afternoon.   She insists upon the eight days' surveillance by physicians and other responsible persons, that her
annoyances may come to an end."

Dean Overberg, Dean Rensing, and Dr. Wesener united
with Sister Emmerich in asking for the surveillance. " She
told me with tears, " writes Dr. Wesener, " how ardently
she sighs for peace. ' Ah !' she said, ' I am willing to do
anything to serve my neighbor.   I would allow myself to be
cut to pieces and put together again to save one soul ; but
I cannot exhibit myself as a spectacle to the curious.   I
think if they watch me for eight days, they will be satisfied
about me.   It is not for my own sake that I want the truth
to be known, but for that of my friends, that they may not
on my account be wrongfully accused.' "

After Dean Overberg's departure, Dr. von Druffel came
to Dülmen.   Of his visit he writes : " Nothing new dis-
closes itself.   The impression produced on me by the invalid is the same.   The state of her wounds, the mark in her
side, and the cross on her breast presented no change."

Dean Overberg promised on leaving to gain the Vicar-General's consent to the proposed surveillance and to interest himself in its prompt execution.   He succeeded in
the first part of his mission, but failed in the second, as we may
glean from his communication to Dean Rensing :—

" ' Man proposes and God disposes ! ' Behold a fresh

proof! We cannot find suitable persons to guard our dear
Sister Emmerich. The physicians will not be free before
the Pentecost holidays, on account of the lectures, and they
are desirous that she be removed as soon as possible to a
more convenient lodging. Be so good as to console her on
the news of this delay, as distasteful to us as to her, and
remember me to her." A few days after this letter, there
arrived for her bed a leather covering which the good Dean
had had made, and with it the following lines : " Dr. Krauthausen told me that our poor sufferer ought to have a
leather cover on her mattress, as it is cool and prevents bed-
sores. I looked for something of the kind and I have been
so fortunate as to find one of chamois. I waited several
days for an opportunity to send it ; but as none presented itself, I express it to-day that she may have it as soon as possible. Have the kindness to see that it is placed on her
bed."

The delay of the surveillance was more grievous to Sister Emmerich than anything she had hitherto endured.
She read therein the withering assurance that her hopes
were vain, that there was no probability of her ever being
able to hide from the public gaze, and escape the manifold
annoyances of her present position. She had dared to count
on the Feast of the Ascension as the day on which she
would recover the only earthly goods she craved, peace and
solitude—but now, alas ! her expectations were blighted.
The Abbé Lambert often heard her sighing : " I am the
Lord's instrument ! I know not what is in store for me, I
only long for rest ! " She could not hide from herself the fact that this longed-for rest would never more be
hers on earth. Almighty God exacted of her this great
sacrifice and she made it unreservedly, but at the cost of
complete prostration and great increase of pain.

Dean Rensing's notes, May 17th—" She complained of
having had the night before pains so acute that she was forced
to beg God to lessen them. She was heard, and strength
was given her to suffer patiently. She added : 'Then I
said the *Te Deum laudamus* all through. I had begun it
several times but had never been able to finish on account
of my pain.' The next night she suffered still more. She
said to Dean Rensing :—' I have often begged God for pain
and suffering, but now I am tempted to say : " Lord, enough !
no more, no more ! " The pain in my head was so violent
that I feared I should lose patience. At daybreak, I laid on
it the particle of the True Cross which Dean Overberg had
given me and I begged God to help me. I was instantly relieved. Still greater than my bodily pains are those of my
soul, dryness, bitterness, and anguish ; but I have twice been
restored to peace and sweet consolation after receiving
Holy Communion.' "

As her interior was so little understood by those around
her, no attention was paid to her mental sufferings, and
they often complained before her of her vain expectations.
This made her feel more keenly her want of spiritual assistance, and she fell into such a state of anguish that she
seemed to lose all strength and fortitude. On May 19th,
Dean Rensing found her so prostrate and dejected that he
had not the courage to address her. When he returned in
the evening, he saw that the cross on her breast had been
bleeding profusely ; her garments were saturated with blood.
Strength had returned sufficiently for her to tell him that
the evil one, taking advantage of her helplessness, had
troubled her with frightful apparitions on the preceding
night:—

" I endured an agony. My sister was sound asleep, the
lamp was burning, and I was lying awake in bed, when I

heard a slight noise in the room. I looked and saw a hideous figure covered with filthy rags slowly approaching. It stood at the foot of my bed. It drew aside the curtain, and I saw it was a frightful-looking woman with an enormously large head. The longer she looked at me, the more horrible she grew. Then she leaned over me, opening her huge mouth as if to swallow me. At first I was calm, but soon I became greatly alarmed and began to invoke the holy names of Jesus and Mary, when the horrible apparition disappeared."

Father Limberg delivered her at last from her state of desolation. He reproved her a little sharply for complaining, telling her she must calmly await a decision and meditate more attentively on the words: "Lord, may Thy will be done!" Dr. Wesener, who was present at this little scene, made a note of it as follows:—"Sister Emmerich instantly submitted with the best grace in the world, and no more complaints were heard. Father Limberg told me that he thought it his duty to speak to her a little severely, as he knew from experience that the least imperfection was highly prejudicial to her."

Dean Rensing's journal of the following day runs thus:— "I asked her if she had had a vision or apparition the preceding night. 'No,' she answered, 'I was too much afflicted for having been impatient and discontented on account of so many annoyances. I ought to be like clay in the potter's hand, no self-will, no complaints, patiently receiving whatever God sends. That is hard for me, because I still think more of my own peace than of God's will, which tries me; but He knows what is best for me.' In the same way she accused herself before Dr. Wesener of her impatience. 'My attempt to disabuse her of this idea,' he remarked, 'was without effect.'"

God rewarded her humble obedience by sending her fresh consolation. On May 21st, Dean Rensing found her exhausted from suffering and loss of blood. Her wounds had bled so copiously that her head dress and chemise were stiff; but she had tasted great consolation in the midst of her pains, and particularly after Holy Communion.

" One thing gave me great joy," she said. " After Holy Communion, I saw two angels holding a beautiful garland of white roses with long sharp thorns which pricked me when I tried to detach a rose. 'O that these thorns were not here!'—I thought. And then came the answer: 'If you want to have roses, you must suffer the pricks of the thorns.' I shall have to endure much before I attain to joy unmingled with pain."

A short time after she had a similar vision:

" I was taken into a beautiful garden in which I beheld roses of extraordinary size and beauty, but their thorns were so long and sharp that one could not pluck a rose without being scratched by them. 'I don't like that,' I said. My angel replied: 'He who will not suffer shall not enjoy !'."

Joys without suffering were also shown her, but she was given to understand that they were to be hers only at death:

"I saw myself lying in the tomb, and no words can express my joy. It seemed as if I were told at the same time that I should have much to suffer before my death, but that I must abandon myself to God and remain firm. Then I saw Mary with the Child, and it was unspeakable joy for me when that good Mother placed Him in my arms. When I gave Him back, I asked Mary for three gifts which would render me pleasing to her and her Son: charity, humility, and patience."

Her fortitude began to increase from that day, and on May 26th, eve of the Ascension, she said to the Dean : "O how I should love to go to heaven with the dear Saviour ! but my time has not yet come. My sufferings increase, I must still be tried, purified more and more. God's will be done ! May He grant me the grace to persevere to the end in patience and abandonment to His good pleasure ! "

On the Feast of the Ascension when she received Holy Communion, she heard these words :—" Wouldst thou rather die than suffer longer ?" to which she answered : "I will still suffer longer, O Lord, if such be Thy good pleasure." She added, when repeating this incident to Dean Rensing : "My desire is fulfilled, but in the sense that I now suffer more intensely than before."

Dr. Wesener declares how numerous and varied were her pains and how much they were increased by all around her. On May 25th, he writes :

" I found her this evening very restless and quite beside herself with pain. Her back is covered with sores. Her sister had bathed it with brandy, and she had fainted from pain. She writhed on her bed, moaning : ' Why did you do that ? I am willing to suffer, but you ought not to do such things thoughtlessly.' Her face was inflamed, her eyes full of tears, and her pulse had not varied ; but when Father Limberg ordered her to be quiet, she lay still instantly and said no more."

Soon again she had to undergo a similar, though much greater torment : " I found," says Dr. Wesener, " her sister by her bedside with a plate of salad swimming in vinegar-sauce. I asked if the patient had tasted it, and was told that she had taken a little of the sauce and a piece of cheese. She lay in a stupor and quite unconscious. I soon discovered the cause. Her sister had wanted

to bathe her back again with brandy ; and, as the invalid
refused, she had left the vessel of liquor by the bed. Its
fumes stupefied her and when that stupid, self-willed sister
of hers presented the food, she had not the strength to resist. She fell into a pitiable state of nausea, convulsive
vomiting, and choking. I feared she would strangle. It
was not until nine o'clock that evening that she threw off
the food and got some relief. She regretted having taken
it, though at the time she knew not what she was doing."

Experience like the above did not, however, disabuse
Sister Emmerich's friends nor prevent their ill-advised
efforts to relieve her. They still had recourse to brandy as a
remedy. Some years after, Mr. Clement Brentano had an
opportunity of testing this fact. " I often saw Sister Emmerich,"he says, " reduced to a frightful state by the absurd
mania for bathing her bed-sores with brandy. She groaned
at the thought of such an operation and refused to submit to
it, for the mere smell of the abominable stuff was sufficient
to deprive her of consciousness ; but she had not the strength
to resist. The use of brandy as a curative is a fixed idea
among the lower classes of Münster, and poor Sister Emmerich was forced to endure it. Ah ! the poor thing was
often treated more like an inanimate object than a human
being !"

One of the chief reasons that awoke Sister Emmerich's
longing for a retired life was the crowd of visitors that
now began to press around her bed of pain. The disorder
it caused afflicted her less than the mental sufferings resulting from it. " She complains," says Dr. Wesener, " of
so many visitors. They annoy her exceedingly. She has
also other sufferings that she cannot indicate."

What these sufferings were, we may judge from the past.
They sprang from her gift of reading hearts and her keen

sense of the moral state of her neighbor. She saw with grief the sins of those who visited her ; their passions, the intentions that actuated them pierced her like arrows. This truly terrible gift had been one of her greatest sufferings. But now that she lay unprotected, as it were, on the public highway, for the ecclesiastical prohibitions were daily losing force, it was her greatest torment. She was overwhelmed by crowds of the curious, who gazed upon her and her priestly guardians with injurious suspicions and haughty contempt. Of what grace, then, had she not need to insure her against despair, when before her arose the certitude : " It will ever be thus till the hour of my death !"

CHAPTER XXVII.

The Vicar General's Fourth Visit to Dülmen.

Dean Rensing had informed Dean Overberg of the painful impression produced by his letter of May 18th upon Sister Emmerich, and of her dissatisfaction with the gentlemen of Münster chosen for the surveillance.

"I hoped," she said, "that the affair would be over by the Feast of the Ascension and that I should then have leisure to prepare for the coming of the Holy Ghost. The time between these two feasts has ever been to me so sacred; but now that consoling hope is gone. If physicians from Münster cannot come, those of our own city could be engaged, especially as they can see all that goes on and are more worthy of confidence than young men still pursuing their studies. Dr. von Druffel assured me that only such persons would be sent as I should approve, but that young men, like R. R., not twenty years old, should sit day and night at my bedside, is what I cannot permit."

Dean Overberg laid this objection before the Vicar-General. He took it into serious consideration, for Sister Emmerich's manner of expressing herself seemed to him little in accordance with the idea entertained of her obedience. He thought it his duty, therefore, to repair at once to Dülmen and have an explanation with her. He wrote to Dean Rensing, reproving him for having mentioned to her the names of the gentlemen chosen for the surveillance, and closed with the following remarks :—" It ought to have sufficed for Sister Emmerich and others concerned to know that the persons in question had the approval of ecclesiastical authority. I should not expect so much of every one. But of those whom God appears to have so highly favored, I make extraordinary demands; and when I weigh those graces in the scale of obedience, I am but imitating the example of the wisest and holiest men."

On June 3d, he arrived in Dülmen. "My intention," he says in his report, "was chiefly to examine Sister Emmerich's interior dispositions; the inspection of her wounds, which had recently bled, was but a secondary object. I wished to talk to her on her manner of expressing herself upon the surveillance and the persons chosen for it. I found things as usual."

The Vicar-General had scarcely seen the invalid and demanded an explanation of her apparent complaints than he noted down the following :

" As to the gentlemen from Münster engaged for the surveillance, Sister Emmerich brought forward but one objection, and that was touching their youth. She was also afraid that they might hear from her lips words which they would perhaps misunderstand. Such a fear is not unreasonable, for she sometimes dreams aloud, and she knows that she has already been reported to have said: 'Such a one is in heaven, such a one is in purgatory.' However, she was well-disposed, there was no need of reasoning with her."

As to her impatience at the delay, the Vicar-General was equally satisfied. He says : "Sister Emmerich alleged the following on this point : ' I have at this season always been in the cenacle with the disciples, awaiting the coming of the Holy Spirit.' (Clara Soentgen deposed that at this time she was always more recollected than usual.) ' This year I desired the same, and I took it into my head that I ought not to be prevented; but now I see that I made a great mistake. I have also been too presumptuous in praying for sufferings. "To suffer or die," I exclaimed. God has punished me for it. He said to me: 'Dost thou wish to suffer? thou shouldst be willing then, to suffer what I will that thou shouldst suffer.'"

The Vicar-General recalled to her St. Teresa's device, "To suffer or to die," and that of St. Francis de Sales, "To love or to die," remarking that the former was good for the saints, but the latter suited all. She readily understood the application and expressed her satisfaction.

A few days after the Vicar-General's arrival, Sister Emmerich's mother came to see her. The poor old woman was anxious about her child. We can easily conceive how sad for the good mother was the news that her best loved daughter had been subjected to an ecclesiastical inquiry. The pastor of St. James, Coesfeld, had made a trip to Dülmen for the sole purpose of gaining some information to relieve her mind on the subject; but on his report of what he had witnessed, she could not longer restrain her desire to see for herself. Clara Soentgen wrote to the Vicar-General:

"The day before yesterday, Sister Emmerich's old mother arrived. Sister Emmerich wished me to be present during the visit, as she felt a little timid before her mother. She had prayed God not to let her mother ask to see her stigmata or make any inquiries on her condition, and her petition was granted; the old woman's behavior was admirable. She said not a word on the subject of the wounds, but only exhorted her daughter to good. When strangers told her that she ought to rejoice in such a child, that they had never heard of the like before, etc., she replied that such things were not to be spoken of, and that, during the person's lifetime, no importance should be attached to them. Sister Emmerich told me that, having

heard such remarks as those given above, she had prayed
that if they were addressed to her mother she might
answer as she did. Truly her petition was heard."

After the old lady's departure, Sister Emmerich was disturbed by the thought that, although she showed her stigmata
to so many strangers, she had concealed them from her own
mother. She feared she had been wanting in filial respect. She spoke of it to the Vicar-General, asking him if
she should have shown her wounds although her mother
had not asked to see them. "I answered her," he wrote
in the report, "that if her mother had asked it, she
should have obeyed; but that as it was, she had done well
in concealing them."

The Vicar-General was highly pleased with this, his
fourth visit to the invalid, as his letter on the following
day to Dean Rensing proves. The Dean had keenly felt
the reproach of having mentioned before Sister Emmerich
the names of her custodians, and in this frame of mind,
had turned to her disadvantage some trifling remarks that
had escaped the Vicar-General. The latter took up her
defence as follows :—

"As to her visions, I have never entertained a thought
of imposture, but only of the possibility of delusion for
which, however, I hold no one responsible. Since my
conversation with· her, I can conclude but one thing concerning her expressions regarding the surveillance, and that
is, that perhaps she has not yet reached the degree of perfection to which she is called." He then gave in writing
the following injunctions :

"The project relative to Sister Emmerich must not long
be deferred. I should like it begun as soon as possible.
As to the choice of persons, I await your advice. Aged
men are to be preferred. I approve of Mr. N. N., but his

son is too young; neither to him nor to any other of his age must the duty be intrusted."

" When the custodians converse together, it must not be on a subject calculated to aggravate a measure already so painful. I hope you will visit her often and see if she desires a modification of any of the regulations. "

Dean Rensing was soon able to propose twenty gentlemen of Dülmen, all worthy of confidence, who were willing to watch in turn by the invalid under the direction of a strange physician. The Vicar-General approved all, and the surveillance began on the 10th of June. Before proceeding further, we shall notice the reports of the two Deans, Overberg and Rensing, to the Vicar-General on Sister Emmerich's stigmata, since they contribute powerfully toward establishing their truth.

CHAPTER XXVIII.

DEAN OVERBERG'S, DEAN RENSING'S, AND DR. WESENER'S TESTIMONY REGARDING THE STIGMATA.

Though from his very first visit the Vicar-General was convinced of the impossibility of imposture with regard to the stigmata, yet he commissioned Dean Overberg to submit the invalid to circumstantial interrogations as to their nature and origin. The Dean began the examination April 8, 1813, and continued it until May 12th. His manner of proceeding consisted in demanding of Sister Emmerich new and detailed explanations upon points already settled, whilst Dean Rensing's and Dr. Krauthausen's daily reports furnished matter for fresh interrogatories to which he insisted on answers. When the report of one of these questionings was forwarded to the Vicar-General, he in turn demanded yet further explanations from the invalid, being satisfied only when by various means he had arrived at conclusions similar to those of the Dean. We find, in his own writing, notes on the report, never contradictory but rather confirmatory of Dean Overberg's conclusions, since they present them in a clearer and more exact style.

The following are faithful extracts of the several reports :—

" I was commissioned," writes Dean Overberg, April 8th, " to inquire of Sister Emmerich if she had made the wounds herself, or allowed others to do so. I represented to her as forcibly as possible that she owed obedience to ecclesiastical authority, and that she was obliged to speak the truth even supposing she had sworn secrecy to the person instrumental in producing the wounds. I impressed upon her

that an oath which militates against obedience - to the
Church is invalid, and I asked her how she could stand before God's tribunal if she concealed the truth that obedience commanded her to reveal. Being assured that she
comprehended the above, I asked :

" 1—' Have you—perhaps, with a good intention—
pinched your hands or forced a nail, or something of the
kind into them, that you might feel more sensibly the
sufferings of Jesus Christ ?'

" Answer.—' No, never !'

" 2—' Have you not applied to those parts nitric acid or
lunar caustic ?' Ans.—' I know not what they are.'

" 3—' Has any one, who takes an interest in your spiritual progress and that you may be a lover of Christ's sufferings, made these wounds by pressing, by sticking, by putting
something on them, or in any other way ?' Ans.—' Ah,
no !'

" During the above questions and answers, her countenance maintained unalterable serenity. She then related
what follows :—

" ' I knew not of the wounds at first, it was another who
remarked them.' (I think she named the Abbé Lambert.)
' He drew my attention to them, saying : " Do not think
that you are now a St. Catherine of Sienna. You have not
yet come to that !" '

" When I objected that another could not have remarked
the wounds before herself, since we are generally sensible
of a wound received, she said : ' That is true ; but having felt
the pain three or four years before the wounds appeared,
I suspected not the change. When I received the external
marks, I had only a little girl to wait on me, and she did
not think of washing off the blood. I did not remark it, and
so it happened that the Abbé Lambert saw the wounds in

my hands before I did myself. The pain could not attract my attention to them, for I had long been accustomed to it and the external signs made no change in it.' (Sister Emmerich used to call the pain she felt for many years in the places where, at a later period, the wounds were formed, *marks*, and the wounds themselves she generally denominated *external signs*)

" ' The pains in my head I felt for four years before entering the convent. It is, as it were, encircled by thorns, or rather, as if all my hair were thorns ; I can never rest on the pillow without pain. The pains of the other wounds are not like ordinary pains, they go to my heart. A touch or light pressure upon the cross on my breast is not so painful outwardly, but inwardly it is as if the whole breast were on fire. As to the sign above my stomach, it feels like a flame of fire.'

" 4—' When did these signs appear on your person ? Ans.—' The sign on my stomach appeared on the Feast of St. Augustine ; the lower cross on my breast about six weeks after; the upper one on the Feast of St. Catherine ; the wounds of my hands and feet on the last Feast of Christmas ; and that of my side between Christmas and New Year.'

" 5—' When you first felt these pains and later when the wounds in your head, hands, and feet appeared, did you see anything like an apparition, or did you receive special light on any subject ?' Ans —' No, I was at the time in unusual suffering.'

" 6—' Do you not know what the crosses on your breast signify ?' Ans.—' No. But when the first appeared on my stomach, I felt that it was a sign that I should have much to suffer for Christ. When, on St. Catherine's Feast, the second appeared, I felt that my cross would be two-fold; and the same when the third became visible.'

" She told me again," remarks the Dean, " that she had prayed much to suffer the pains of Jesus, but never for the marks of His Wounds" (1).

" 7—' How must your first declaration (report, March 25th) be understood : " My wounds have not been made by man, but I believe and hope they are from God." ' Ans.—'I said: *I believe,* and not: *I am sure,* because the Dean and the physicians, as well as their rigorous examination, made me fear that they came, perhaps, from the demon. But the crosses on my breast reassured me, for I said to myself: They certainly cannot have been made by the devil. For the same reason, too, I said, *I hope,* because I do hope that these signs are the work of God and not a delusion of the devil!'

" 8—' And supposing your wounds were healed as Dr. von Druffel thinks possible ? ' Ans.—' I have been permitted to ask for their disappearance, but nothing has been said of their healing. I never thought of that. I understood it this way : that God would not be displeased at my praying for their disappearance, and that their pains would rather increase than diminish. The latter have already much increased.'

The Dean said: " I shall not believe that you have revelations if you cannot prove to me that you know how to distinguish a revelation from a mere remembrance." She replied : "Yes, but how can I prove that ? " He answered : " That I do not know." Then she said : " It may be that I have heard, or seen, or experienced something and that, when I spoke of it, it was misunderstood for a revelation." (' Here she cited an example," says the Dean.) " What we have heard remains in the mind ; but when we suddenly receive the knowledge of something of which we

(1) See Dean Overberg's first visit, March 28, 29.

had never before heard or seen, that cannot be a remembrance ! "

"9—'Do you not know at what time you felt the pains in your hands and feet ?'   Ans.—'Four years before the suppression of the convent, I went to Coesfeld to visit my parents.   Whilst there, I prayed for two hours at the foot of the cross behind the altar in St. Lambert's Church.   I was very much distressed at the state of our convent, so I prayed that we might see our faults and live in peace. I also asked Jesus to make me experience all that He suffered.   From that time I have always had these pains and this burning.   I used to think it fever and that the pains arose from it.   Sometimes I fancied it might be an answer to my petition ; but I rejected the thought, deeming myself unworthy of such a favor.   I was often unable to walk on account of the pains in my feet, and my hands were so painful that at times I could not perform certain work, such as digging.   I could not bend the middle finger, it often felt as if dead.

" 'After I began to feel these pains, I was one day earnestly praying that my Sisters in religion and I might see our faults, that peace might reign, and that my sufferings would cease, when I received this answer : 'Thy sufferings will not decrease. Let the grace of God suffice for thee ! Not one of thy Sisters will die before recognizing her faults !"— After this response, when I felt the *signs,* I consoled myself with the thought that my state would be known only to the Sisters, for it was frightful to think that the world would become cognizant of it.'

10—"To my questions concerning the crosses on her breast, she answered : 'I begged God from my childhood to imprint the cross upon my heart, but I never thought of an external sign.'

" She told me, besides, that the detailed inquiry into her past life was not the least of her sufferings, for reasons stated in a preceding chapter.

11—" On Thursday, May 13th, four P. M., the blood spurted from her head and her forehead. In less than a minute her kerchief was saturated. She became exceedingly pale and weak, and soon after her hands began to bleed. A short time previously she had had violent pains in her forehead and temples as if from the piercing of thorns which she felt even in her eyes. I told her that, if I could, I would draw the thorns out of her head and leave only one, to which she replied : ' I do not want them drawn out, I love their pains.' "

" I asked her what she meant by saying to Dean Rensing that they who believed not would feel ? Did she think that they who did not believe in her stigmata would be punished ?—She answered with a smile : ' Ah, no ! My wounds are not articles of faith. I only meant that they who believe not what the Catholic faith teaches, find no peace ; even on earth they will always feel miserable.' "

Dean Overberg gives an account of a subsequent visit made on Friday, September 15, 1814 : "In the morning, about nine o'clock, I saw the marks on her hands red and swollen, a sure sign of their going to bleed. I expressed surprise that there was no swelling in the palms, upon which Sister Emmerich explained that the wounds in the palms of her hands never swelled before bleeding ; on the contrary, they seemed to contract as if to puff out more on the upper surface.

" The cross on her breast did not bleed, though it was very red, as it invariably is on certain days, even when there is no effusion of blood."

From the first Sister Emmerich carefully sought to conceal her hands from every one. She hid them under the coverlet or, when much inflamed she laid a white cloth over them. This desire possessed her to such a degree that even in ecstasy she perceived any attempt to remove the covering.

Dr. Wesener says : "One day, I took my eldest sister to see Sister Emmerich and found her lying, as was often the case, unconscious. Father Limberg attempted to uncover her hands, but she showed signs of dissatisfaction. He said to her : ' What is the matter ? '—She answered in a low voice and without opening her eyes : ' They want something of me that I must not grant.'—I was wishing in my heart that my sister might be strengthened in her faith by this wonderful sight. Sister Emmerich again said : ' Some one wants signs from me that I must not give.' Then Father Limberg gave her his blessing, when instantly she began, still in ecstasy, to sign herself with her trembling hand, anxiously endeavoring all the time not to let the cloth fall from it."

Something similar occurred to Dean Overberg, Sept. 10, 1813, when he accompanied the Princess Galitzin to Dülmen. He wrote : "I found the invalid very weak. As I sat by her in the evening about six o'clock, she fell into one of her deep swoons (ecstasies). I extended the first fingers of my right hand toward her face. Instantly inclining her head she kissed them respectfully. Then I leaned over to kiss her left hand which lay before me stiff and immovable, but she drew it back frightened. I approached the other, but succeeded no better, so quickly was it withdrawn, although in these swoons her whole body lies stiff as a log."

The Dean had made these attempts through respect for the stigmata, but the patient's humility had become like second nature ; she shrank from such homage even when unconscious. She could not endure a glance animated by such a feeling, as the Pilgrim experienced at a later period. " I was sitting by her bed praying. She was in ecstasy and in intense suffering. I offered to God in union with the Sacred Wounds of Our Saviour, the sufferings of all the martyrs and the pains of all the saints who had had the stigmata and at the same moment I glanced reverently at Sister Emmerich's hands, when quick as lightning she drew them away. The movement surprised me and I asked what was was the matter. From her deep swoon she answered : 'Many things ! ' "

Dean Rensing was with her once just before the wounds began to bleed, and she complained of the sharp pains that always preceded it. He asked her why she did not uncover her hands, saying that she need not scruple doing so in his presence. " Ah ! " she answered, " I cannot myself bear the sight of my signs. They cry out to me of the special favors of which I am not worthy." The Dean adds : " Then she thanked me for having denied admittance to a party of visitors. She wept that these good people gave themselves so much trouble and esteemed her so highly, although before God they were much better than she. She said : ' I must also thank God that He does not hide from me my faults ; by them He strengthens me in humility. ' "

She spoke of the pain and anxiety such visits gave her and earnestly begged the Dean not to allow her to be seen any more, especially by strange doctors who often inconsiderately wounded delicacy. " It is very hard for me," she said, " to be forced to show my signs so often ; but still harder is it when I see that these people seek not the honor of God, but only something to talk about.

" From bodily sufferings I desire not to be free, God will leave them to me. But of what use are these inspections, these investigations ? Our Lord Himself did not satisfy all in such a way that they believed and were converted. Some pity me too much. Let them pray for me that I may humbly submit to whatever God ordains through my spiritual Superiors and that I may not lose His grace. God leads every one by a separate way. But what matters it whether we go to heaven by this or that road? Let us only do all that God demands of us according to our state!"

Once Dean Rensing told her that Veronica Giuliani had for a long time around her head the marks of the Crown of Thorns. When it became known, the physicians tried to cure her, which proceeding cost her frightful sufferings. The invalid sighed and said: "I have not yet suffered so much; yet when Ecclesiastical Superiors decided that my wounds should be cured, I felt it very much because I was undergoing such pain. I had the pains of the crown around my head even before my entrance into the convent. I felt them first in the Jesuit church at Coesfeld."

During the first Vespers of St. Catherine of Sienna, Dean Rensing found her wounds bleeding; but on the day itself, April 30th, the flow was much more profuse. He reports as follows: "I visited her at three o'clock. As I entered the room the blood was streaming from her head and hands. I was quite unnerved at the sight, and an expression of admiration at the extraordinary favors bestowed upon her escaped me. She noticed it and said: 'Yes, God grants me more than I deserve. I thank Him for them, but I would rather He would hide these graces from the eyes of men, for I fear they will think me better than I am.' Then we had a conversation which gave me an insight into her pure and humble soul. She related some incidents of her youth which convinced me that the Hand of God had ever conducted her, shielding her from all danger. I was astonished to find one with so little education yet with ideas of God and divine

things so clear, so just, so elevated. She told me that Almighty God had asked her the night before : 'Wouldst thou
rather be with Me soon, or still suffer more for Me ?'—She
answered : ' If thou dost desire it, I will gladly suffer more,
if only Thou givest me the grace to do as Thou willest !—
God promised me this grace,' she added, ' and now I am
right joyful. He also reminded me that, whilst in the convent, I had committed many faults against the perfection
to which my vows engaged me. I repented anew of these
faults and received the assurance that I had not lost His
grace by them, since I had humbled myself before Him and
men. I was also reminded that when in the convent,
despised by all, I had often prayed that the Sisters might recognize the faults they committed on my account. Often,
when thus praying and particularly during the last summer
I was among them, I received the consoling promise that all
would see their faults before my death. And all have entered into themselves since God has given me these extraordinary signs. This is a joy for which I thank Him in
the midst of the intense pains my signs cause me.'

" I asked her once," continues the Dean, " if she had not
also a wound upon her shoulder, for I think the Saviour
surely had His Sacred Shoulder wounded by the heavy cross.
' Yes, indeed !' she answered, ' the Divine Saviour had a
painful wound on His Shoulder from the cross ; but I have
not the wound, although I have long felt its pain. I have
venerated this wound from my childhood, because it is especially pleasing to Our Saviour. He revealed to me in
the convent that this Wound of which so little is thought
caused Him the greatest pain, and that when one
honors it, He is as much pleased thereby as if that person
had borne the cross for Him up to Calvary. At six or seven
years old, when alone and meditating on the Lord's Passion,

I used to put a log of wood or some other weight on my shoulder and drag it along as far I was able."

During the whole of May, 1813, Dean Rensing noted almost daily the bleeding of the wounds and their increasing pains. Up to the 8th of May, she was forced to lie on her back which was covered with sores. She suffered intensely from it, but she said : " It is nothing compared with my other wounds. Still 1 am ready to suffer any pain, provided the dear God withdraws not His interior consolation. But I often feel great bitterness of soul now. It is hard, but God's will be done !"

During the octave of the Invention of the Holy Cross her wounds bled daily, her sufferings proportionately increasing. When the Dean saw blood flowing on the morning of the 3d, he did not at once recall the connection between it and the feast of the day. He expressed some surprise, upon which Sister Emmerich replied : " It must be because the Feast of the Invention is kept to-day." She had communicated, but with spiritual dryness, a keener suffering to her than any physical evil. The pains of the Crown of Thorns were simply intense in her forehead, eyes, and temples, and they extended even to her mouth and throat. This state lasted for several days, no consolation being vouchsafed her. The Dean, unable to endure the sight, remained by her side as little as possible.

On May 6th, she exclaimed : " I feel the pains from my feet up to my breast. It seems as if all my wounds communicate their pains one to the other." Her back, as we have said, was raw in several places, and her linen adhered to it; but she declared this nothing when compared with each separate wound. The Dean remarked that she must have had a very bad night. She replied : " No ! my pains are my joy ! I rejoice when I have something to suffer and I thank

God that I am not lying idle in my bed." Once she said
to Dean Overberg that her greatest trial was to have
nothing to suffer ; she was never so happy as in suffering
something for the love of God.

On May 9th, her state remained the same, but she had
been consoled and strengthened from on high. She told
the Dean that she felt as if a hair rope were being drawn
through her head, and that she sometimes feared she would
lose her mind. "My suffering is, however, not too great.
God sweetens it by His consolations, although I do
not deserve them. Especially in the convent did I render
myself unworthy of such favors, for I often thought too
much over the faults of my Sisters and what they ought to
do, and too little of what I ought to be myself. That was imperfect and ungrateful; therefore, I am satisfied that God now
lets me suffer. If I knew that by it I could contribute ever
so little to His glory and the conversion of sinners, I would
gladly suffer more and more. God grant me patience !"
Her pains decreased toward evening when the Dean found
her unusually bright.

These effusions of blood were attended by so copious a
flow of perspiration that the bed-clothes were saturated as
if dipped in water. The wounds on her back resulted from
this and prevented her lying down. The wound of her right
side made it impossible to lie upon it, and her left hip-bone
was completely stripped of flesh; consequently she was forced
to remain in a most painful sitting posture. Mr. Clement
Brentano says : "For four years I was in daily communication with Sister Emmerich, and saw the blood flowing
from her head. I never saw her head uncovered or the
blood gushing directly from her forehead, but I saw it running down under her cap in such quantities that it lay in
the folds of her kerchief before being absorbed. Her head,

surrounded by an invisible crown of thorns, could not be rested on her pillow; she balanced it for hours in a sitting posture like a weight of untold pain. Often did I support it for a longer or shorter time on my two fingers placed against the bridge of the nose, the sweat of agony bathing her pallid face. I could not endure the pitiful sight without doing something to relieve her. Whole nights were often passed in this state, helpless and alone."

The absolute impossibility of taking nourishment of any kind coincided with the appearance of the stigmata. Dean Overberg writes, May 12, 1813: "For about five months, Sister Emmerich has taken no solid food, not even the size of half a pea. She can retain nothing, neither chocolate, coffee, wine, nor soup. The only thing she takes occasionally is a tea-spoonful of beef-tea. She endeavors to conceal the fact of her abstinence from food by having a baked apple or some stewed prunes placed by her; but of these she only tastes the juice.

"A little very weak coffee was what she could best take in the convent, but from the early part of last winter she could retain not even this. She then tried weak chocolate, but only for a few days; wine, pure or watered, she could not endure, and, at last, she confined herself to water alone."

We have seen that, in spite of her total inability to eat, she was at times suspected of doing so, a suspicion that was frequently renewed. Dean Overberg reports, Sept. 17, 1814:—" Dean Rensing told me that the widow with whom Sister Emmerich lodges, was very ill for about two months before her death. She had herself carried into Sister Emmerich's room, thinking that she could endure her sufferings more patiently there and better prepare for death. A day or so before she died, she acknowledged that she had once had doubts as to Sister Emmerich's not eating, but now she was convinced that she took absolutely nothing."

Dr. Wesener reports, Oct. 29, 1814, that he was often obliged to defend his patient against such suspicions :—" I had a visit from the Dean von Notteln, who came to find out for himself, as he said, the origin of the report circulating in Münster that Sister Emmerich had been seen out of bed eating some meat. I took him to see the invalid, telling him to watch her closely whilst I repeated the report to her in the plainest terms. She smiled as I told her, saying that such things only made her pity those who invented and propagated them. To render homage to truth, I must here say that I took a great deal of trouble to discover something she could eat without vomiting, but in vain. If I am deceived in her, I must refuse credence to my own senses. She is, moreover, surrounded by people who would be only too well pleased could they find the least thing against her, how equivocal soever it might be. Her own sister, who ought to wait on her, is a perverse, ill-tempered creature, constantly doing something to deserve reprimand both from Sister Emmerich and from me. She has no love for the poor sufferer; she often leaves her the whole day long without even a drink of water. Surely, such a pers n would not keep a fraud secret !"

Father Limberg himself was alive to such suspicions. Fifteen months after the investigation, he was tormented for several days by a stain on the coverlet of Sister Emmerich's bed, which he concluded could have been made only by food eaten in secret. Dr. Wesener and Clara Soentgen reassured him, explaining that it was made by a plaster which the latter had applied to the invalid's hip. Sister Emmerich could not restrain a smile at her confessor's unreasonable doubts. She remarked : " If I could eat, I

know not why I should do it in private!"—She begged
him to communicate to her any suspicions that arose in
his mind and not keep them to himself for entire days.
Later we shall see her suffering greatly from the doctor's
attempts to make her take food.

With regard to her manner of prayer when she received
Holy Communion, Dean Overberg says:—

"Sister Emmerich's immediate preparation for receiving
the Holy Eucharist consisted in begging God, her Saviour,
to give her His own Heart that she might worthily receive
and entertain Him. She represented to Him that it was only
through and with His Heart that she could love and praise
Him as He deserved. Then she offered Him her own,
begging Him to make it pleasing to Himself. After
this she called together all the powers of her soul and
body that she might offer to Him all she possessed —
her eyes, her ears, her members, supplicating Him to
make use of them in His own service and to accomplish by them what she herself could not. Then she
made a contract with Almighty God to praise and thank
Him with her whole being: every thought, every sigh,
every movement of her eyes and hands, every instant
of her sufferings, was to be an act of praise. She begged Mary for some gift from her superabundant treasures, supplicating her to place the Divine Infant in her
arms as she had done to the Eastern Kings. Then turning to the saints she went from one to another, begging for
something of their beauty, their virtues, their ornaments,
that she might prepare better for Holy Communion and
make a more fervent thanksgiving. 'You are so rich,'
did she say to them, 'and I am so poor! Ah, pity me!
I ask for only a mite from your abundance!'

"After Holy Communion, she fell into ecstasy as she
had always done in the convent."

CHAPTER XXIX.

The Surveillance of Ten Days.—End of the Ecclesiastical Investigation.

"On the 9th of June," says Dean Rensing's report, "I informed the invalid that the surveillance would begin the next day. She expressed her satisfaction and readiness to submit to the will of her Superiors. The cross on her breast was bleeding profusely, her garments were quite soaked with blood.

"When I visited her next day to prepare for the coming of the custodians in the evening, she said: 'Would it not be better for the Abbé Lambert to absent himself for the next ten days? He is willing to do so, if you think well of it.' The proposition pleased me, and I spoke of it to the Abbé who set out that very afternoon for the old Chartreuse, three and a half miles from Dülmen. That evening, about eight o'clock, the custodians began their watch."

Not only the Dean, but the Vicar-General also, was pleased with Sister Emmerich's proposal. The latter had earnestly desired the Abbé's absence during the coming days, but he felt a delicacy in proposing it. As late as June 8th, he had written to the Dean: "I beg you, if you can possibly do so, to arrange the Abbé Lambert's absence during the surveillance; at least, do not allow him to visit her. If you cannot effect this, we must commit the affair to God; and if you cannot broach it as coming from the Sister herself, we must give it up. Recommend to Sister Emmerich's prayers an intention which I forgot to mention to her myself."

The Dean replied to the above : " It would certainly be very desirable for the Abbé to go away for some time, but I see no way of effecting it."

The Vicar-General's directions for the surveillance are as follows :

" Her custodians are not to leave Sister Emmerich alone for a single instant. Her sister may be present and render her all necessary services, but under no circumstances must the custodians leave her; even when she makes her confession, they must be present. Father Limberg will speak to her in a low tone and carefully avoid everything calculated to arouse suspicion that he is in any way accessory to the existence of her wounds. Two custodians must be present at a time and I think it proper that one should, if possible, be an elderly man. They have nothing to do but *to watch*, anything else would overstep the limits of their charge."

On the fifth day the Dean sent the following report to the Vicar-General :

" The custodians have faithfully followed directions, and the invalid is so pleased at their comportment that she has already repeatedly thanked me for having chosen men so discreet for the discharge of a duty necessarily most painful to her.

" N... N.. .has withdrawn. He was unwilling to undertake so delicate an affair without the concurrence of his colleagues. Is it not sad to see men, who so often expose their life in contagious diseases, so fearful of the lash of public criticism when there is question of testifying to the truth ?"

The physician alluded to did, however, arrive on the 15th. He spent several nights by the invalid, but his hesitation very nearly frustrated the end proposed. The surveillance

had not been undertaken to confirm the opinion of Superiors,
but only to avert from them the suspicion of not having investigated the case as rigorously as they should have done ;
consequently this physician's withdrawal was a most unpleasant surprise for the Vicar-General.   He wrote to the
Dean :—

" That we may attain our end in this surveillance, it is
necessary for Dr. N. N — to go to Dülmen, direct the affair,
and certify to its having been conducted according to prescribed forms.   This is an indispensable condition, without
which any surveillance over Sister Emmerich will be useless."

The invalid herself was annoyed by the physician's conduct.   She prevailed on Father Limberg to go to Münster
and make known to the Vicar-General her fears that the
present surveillance would be declared defective ; that a
new one would be instituted ; and that she would, perhaps,
be removed to Münster, from which last proceeding she implored his protection.   The Vicar-General, with the severity arising from his upright intentions, sternly reproved
her for such a petition which, however, was most justifiable
in itself and supported on motives which, as we shall see,
were far from groundless.   His penetrating, we might even
say his mistrustful eye, had never been able to detect in
the invalid the least thing not in accordance with her sublime gifts, and what he knew of her past life and present
state confirmed his opinion that she was under the special
direction of Almighty God ; therefore, he met everything
that accorded not with the high idea he had formed of her
with rigor as implacable, as he would have shown had
a shadow of suspicion attached itself to her wounds.   He
was impatient at finding her not yet entirely " dead to self-
will," still disquieted about her future.

" Say to Sister Emmerich," he wrote to Clara Soentgen,

" with my kind regards, that the proverb runs thus :*Do not worry over unlaid eggs!*—I generally add : *Nor over spoiled ones.* The past is past, the future has not yet come; it may, perhaps, never arrive. To worry about the future is as useless as to grieve over the past; not only useless, but even pernicious, for such anxiety prevents the fulfilment of present duty and ordinarily proceeds from self-will. Tell her from me that all such expressions as these: 'I fear I shall become impatient,' 'We must not tempt God,' etc., appear to me the result of self-love."

If Sister Emmerich's fears called forth such a rebuke from her Superior, what would she not have received had he beheld in her a real fault ? The truth is, he had little need of being convinced of the poor sufferer's sincerity, he needed not the ten days' surveillance to establish the fact of her miraculous state; for, before the prescribed time had expired, he wrote to Dean Rensing as follows:—

" Send me as soon as possible the result of the interrogatories put to Sister Emmerich's companions, that I may close the inquiry without delay."—And some days later, he wrote for the journal of the custodians :—" I am desirous of receiving it by Monday, as it will close the investigation. I beg you, however, to keep me informed on the invalid's condition and to aid her, as far as you can, in the perfect acquisition of the virtue of indifference. St. Francis de Sales says: ' Fear nothing, ask for nothing, complain of nothing.' "

Dean Rensing added the following remarks to the report demanded of him:—

" As Your Eminence is about terminating the inquiry, I should like to know if the duty I have hitherto discharged with regard to visitors is likewise to cease. I greatly desire to be freed from the daily annoyances resulting from it; but, on the other hand, the poor sufferer will then have not one hour's rest from morning till night, she will be constantly assailed by the curious. She told me twice lately that Dr. Krauthausen has spread the report, both here and in Coesfeld, that if she herself gives permission there will be no necessity to apply to me ; and his wife confirmed this recently by her own example. She was sick, and on last Thursday, during the afternoon service, she had herself carried in a chair by two servants to Sister Emmerich's lodgings, without previous permission from me. I believe it my duty to inform you of this circumstance, as it has created much talk and it may be followed by unpleasant consequences. Several have already asked permission to visit the invalid to consult her on their bodily infirmities and other affairs."

The report of the twenty custodians accompanied this letter. It runs as follows :—

" We, the undersigned, having been invited by Dean Rensing to keep guard over the invalid, Sister Emmerich, and having been informed orally and by writing of the motives for the same and the points to be observed in it, went two by two to her lodgings, June 10, 1813, eight o'clock P. M., and entered upon our duty according to the order prescribed, which we continued day and night till Saturday, the 19th. No one approached the invalid during the aforesaid time, excepting her sister who waited on her, one of her former companions in the convent, and some visitors who entered with the Dean, or by written permit from the Vicar-General. No one could speak to her, much less concert anything with her, without our knowledge. The Abbé Lambert, who resides in the same house, had removed of his own accord before the surveillance began, in order to forestall objections to his presence ; he returned only at its

close. During these ten days, the patient took nothing
but clear water ; this she rarely asked for, but drank it
when offered either by her sister, the physicians, or the
custodians.   Once she sucked a cherry, but rejected the
pulp.   She took also some drops of laudanum from Dr.
Wesener one day when she had unusually keen and continued pains.

"Neither she herself nor any one else touched her
wounds even slightly.   The double cross on her breast began to bleed on the night of the 15th, after she had experienced sharp, shooting pains in it ; the effusion lasted till
seven A. M.   The other wounds bled early on Friday
morning, the 18th, and continued to do so more or less copiously the whole day.   Her head bled again for awhile on
Saturday morning.   Before and during these effusions, she
complains of shooting pains in her wounds.   We remarked
that in the morning until about ten o'clock, she seems
brighter and complains less ; before and after this time the
blood flows.   During the rest of the day, she complains of
weakness, fever, and shooting pains in her wounds, head,
and eyes.   She rarely sleeps soundly.   The state which
appears to resemble sleep is, as she says, of little benefit to
her, and she is generally weaker after it than before.   Between ten o'clock and midnight, she falls into ecstasy,
speaks aloud, shudders with terror, etc. ; though occasionally she lies as if in deep sleep.

"The foregoing deposition we are willing to repeat before
either ecclesiastical or civil authority, and if necessary, attest its truth on oath.

"DÜLMEN, *June* 23, 1813."

The Vicar-General expressed his satisfaction in the following letter to the Dean : "I cannot refrain from expressing to you my gratitude for having conducted the investi-

gation in a manner so entirely conformable to my desires and instructions. I can give Sister Emmerich no better advice than to encourage her to the practice of holy indifference with the help of God's grace, which is never wanting to those who ask it. I also advise her to make use of the means in every citizen's power to rid herself of importunate visitors. I pity Sister Emmerich from my heart, *but I dare not render her further assistance."*

These last words refer to an incident which took place before the close of the examination and which was attended by ulterior consequences. We shall not pass it over in silence since, four years after, it was made a pretext for attacks upon her through the press.

On June 16th, Dean Rensing received the following directions in writing from the Vicar-General:

" If the wife of the Prefect of the Rhenish Department of R— with her sister and Professor B— of Münster, should ask to see Sister Emmerich, do not fail to introduce them to her and tell her, in virtue of obedience, to allow them to see all her wounds. It is necessary that the Professor should see them; he is very incredulous as to their origin."

The above-named visitors arrived that evening. They first called on Dr. Krauthausen to receive from him an account of his observations. The Professor declared the whole thing ignorance and illusion and, even before seeing the invalid, condemned her as an impostor and pronounced the investigation valueless. On the morning of the 18th of June, Dean Rensing introduced them to Sister Emmerich who, in obedience to orders, consented to the inspection of her wounds, a proceeding highly repugnant to her feelings. The Professor saw in them only the veriest cheatery. " The crusts of dried blood were (as he repeated four years after in a pamphlet) nothing but starch, the cross on her breast was

put on so lightly that it crumbled under his touch, the
wounds had been made with pins and a penknife, and the
blood flowing from them was *paint*." The learned gentleman was, above all, disgusted by the blood oozing from
under her head-dress and trickling down her face. " It
was," he said, "far too gross an attempt to deceive a person of his experience." The invalid herself was, in his
eyes, " a healthy, robust person, wondrously well considering her pretended abstinence from food." So much for
this lynx-eyed Professor, who could see nothing in the invalid's case but sharp instruments, albumen, starch, paint,
and gum water, which important discoveries he imparted
some years later to the astonished public. The Prefect's
lady thought that similar wounds might easily be produced
with a penknife; the ecstasies she described to animal magnetism. She tormented the poor sufferer with innumerable
questions on war, peace, hidden things, and future events,
to all which, however, she received but the short answer :
"Interior peace is all I think about."

The Dean and Dr. Krauthausen were both highly offended, and the former refused them a second visit. This
displeased the Vicar-General, and he expressed his dissatisfaction in the following terms :—

" Under other circumstances it would have been wrong
to permit the repetition of a visit so painful to Sister Emmerich ; but, in this instance, when dealing with people disposed to believe that a pious fraud or, to speak more correctly, that gross ignorance or diabolical charlatanry had
been employed to produce, I know not what effect, the
slightest cause for suspicion should be avoided. Now
to refuse a second visit evidently furnishes such a pretext."

In his pamphlet, some years later the Professor did,
indeed, allude to his having been refused a second visit,

because as he said, " the cross on her breast had not yet been renewed."

The Prefect's wife protested to Dr. Wesener that her only desire was to ascertain the truth for her own and others' satisfaction, begging him, at the same time, to appeal to Sister Emmerich herself for a confirmation of her words. When questioned on the subject, the invalid answered : " The Prefect's lady was the most sincere of the party, yet she did not come with a pure intention. She is too haughty and very far from being a true Christian. I have suffered much from this visit, and I feel that I ought not to be so tormented."

On returning to Münster, the Professor boldly gave out as his opinion that Sister Emmerich was an impostor ; consequently the Vicar-General, though attaching but small importance to the Professor's private opinion, concluded to grant him full powers with regard to the invalid, hoping that prolonged observations would force from him a testimony to the truth, and thus place such an enemy in the impossibility of contesting or denying the real state of affairs. With characteristic boldness, the Professor declared that he could soon cure the wounds, and the Vicar-General took him at his word. In an appendix to the official report the latter expresses himself thus :—

" I stipulated for the experiment's being tried only on one hand, for I knew that it would subject poor Sister Emmerich to much suffering. But as the project would entail his perfect seclusion for some time, the Professor did not even attempt it, although he seemed to be convinced of the reasonableness of trying the experiment on one hand only, for he said : ' If one wound is a fraud, all the others are frauds also.' He declared her abstinence no less an imposture than her stigmata, and that it would all be brought

to light were she removed to Münster and placed under the
care of six physicians. To this I refused my consent. I
would not, by such measures, confirm the suspicions already
entertained of the invalid and which I believed utterly
destitute of foundation. Such a proceeding would seem to
me contrary to justice and charity."

Later, however, Professor B—'s plan was modified : two
trusty female nurses were to be chosen by him in Münster and commissioned to watch the invalid as closely as
possible ; she was to be removed to other lodgings, receive no visits save those of Dean Rensing, and the Vicar-
General was to go himself to Dülmen to make the arrangements.

But the French Prefect opposed the project and ordered
the Mayor of Dülmen to forbid a new surveillance. " The
civil power," he declared, "ought to protect a subject who had
already been subjected to a rigorous examination and of whom
so satisfactory a testimony had been rendered to the Commissary of Imperial Police." This declaration was accompanied by the threat to hand over any future inquiry regarding Sister Emmerich to the civil authorities, if it were proved
that the ecclesiastical investigation had been insufficient.
This threat determined the Vicar-General to abandon the
project and leave the Professor to his learned vagaries. It
seems a little strange at first sight that the Vicar-General
should have paid so much attention to the professor's unworthy proceedings ; but his own words afford the explanation : " I was myself most anxious for him to heal the
wounds."

From the beginning, he would willingly have got rid of
the stigmata and their bloody effusions even at the cost
of great sufferings to the invalid, for they attracted too
much attention toward a person whose whole existence was

so far removed from the ideas of the age in which she lived. He desired that everything calculated to become for the Church's enemies an occasion of attack should be shunned or ignored; therefore, the publicity given to the invalid's case which appeared to awaken the rage of unbelievers, was in his eyes a most vexatious affair. He himself regarded her stigmata as the work of God alone; but, sympathizing little with any sort of mysticism, he shrank with a sort of fear from further investigation of the mystery and made use of the following argument to dispense himself from it:

"I have aimed at discovering but one thing: *Is Sister Emmerich herself deceived, or does she deceive?* The result of the investigation has convinced me that imposture cannot reasonably be suspected; consequently, I seek nothing further. The stigmata are either natural phenomena of a very rare kind on which I pass no judgment, or they have a supernatural origin difficult to demonstrate."

Viewing it in this light, we can understand how the Vicar-General could entertain the greatest respect for the invalid, could ask her prayers for his own needs and those of the Church, could send to her humble abode the most distinguished personages of his widely-extended circle of acquaintances, and yet at the same time be so anxious to conceal her as much as possible from the eyes of the world.

He wrote to Dean Rensing, July 16th:—"I beg you to present my compliments to Sister Emmerich, and ask her prayers for a special intention. Tell her if the Count and Countess von Stolberg go to Dülmen, to show them all her wounds."

Count von Stolberg arrived in Dülmen with his wife and Dean Overberg, July 22d, one month after Prof. B.'s visit,

and remained two days. The following is from the pen of
the Count himself, published some time after with a few
additions :—

"Dean Overberg announced our coming to Sister Emmerich, and at nine A. M., accompanied us to her lodging.
Her little room opens directly on the street, the passers-by
can see into it ; in fact, all that goes on in it may be seen
outside. It is exceedingly neat, without the slightest disagreeable odor. Though a great trial to the invalid to be seen
by strangers, yet she received us most graciously. Dean
Overberg asked her, in our name, to uncover her hands.
It was a Friday, and the wounds of the crown of thorns
had bled profusely. She removed her head-dress, and we
saw her forehead and head pierced as if with great thorns.
We could distinctly see the fresh wounds partly filled with
blood, and all around her head was bloody. Never has
the painter's brush rendered so real the Saviour's wounds
from the Thorny Crown. The wounds on the back of the
hands and the upper part of the feet are much larger than
those on the palms and soles, and those of the feet larger
than those of the hands. All were bleeding.

"The physicians have been more unreserved than
ecclesiastics in pronouncing the case miraculous, as the
rules of science furnish more certain data for their judgments. They say that such wounds could not be naturally
maintained without suppuration or inflammation; that it is
incomprehensible how the invalid, suffering constantly and
cruelly, does not sink under the pressure of pain. She is,
on the contrary, full of life, intelligence, and benignity ; she
does not even grow pale.

"For sometime it has been optional with her either to
refuse or admit visitors, so she declines whenever she can
even those from a distance, as she finds such visits very

painful. It is only on the recommendation of ecclesiastics or the physician that she consents to make some exceptions. She has enough to do, she says, to beg God for patience in her pains. It is tempting Him to risk it for people who are, for the most part, actuated only by curiosity. 'They who believe not in Jesus Christ,' she says, 'will not believe on account of my wounds.' It must truly be very distressing for a poor, timid, sick religious to be gazed at by a crowd of curious, indiscreet people !

"Anne Catherine, whose childhood passed in labor and the care of flocks, speaks gently, and in an elevated style when touching on religious subjects. This she could not possibly have acquired in the convent. She expresses herself not only with propriety and discretion, but also with superior intelligence. Her glance is full of benevolence, her words kind and affable. Her voice is low, clear, and sweet, and there is nothing forced in her conversation or manners, for love knows no effort. She is a sublime spectacle. The love of God is breathed in her sentiments, words, and actions. She bears with everything, and is charitable toward her neighbor.

"' How happy we are,' she said to Sophie, 'In knowing Jesus Christ ! How difficult it was for our pagan forefathers to find God !'—Far from glorying in the external signs of the divine favor, she esteems herself wholly unworthy of them, and carries with humble care the treasure of heaven in a frail earthly vessel."

Mr. Kellermann was the first who took a copy of the foregoing letter for Rev. Michael Sailer,(1) afterward Bishop

(1) John Michael Sailer (1751-1832), Bishop of Ratisbon. Born of humble parents, he was by the providence of God raised to one of the highest dignities in the Church. As a student, he united to rare talents an *iron* industry and zeal together with a spirit of humility and kindliness toward all around. In 1770 he entered among the Jesuits. At their suppression in 1773, he continued his studies at Ingolstadt and was ordained in 1775. He held the professorial chair in pastoral and moral theology in different seminaries for many years. In 1821, he became Bishop of Ratisbon, in which position he accomplished a great amount of good.

For ten years he bore the accusations of his enemies in silence. That he should have of Ratisbon, who made known its contents to many of his friends. It fell into Clement Brentano's hands and inspired him with a desire of knowing more of Sister Emmerich. Count Stolberg regarded her with deep veneration and through Dean Overberg maintained a spiritual union with her till death. She on her side never forgot the Count before God ; he was one of those for whom she constantly prayed and lovingly suffered, the beauty of his great soul having been shown her.

It was not by an effect of pure chance that, just after the examination to which she had been subjected, one of the most eminent men of his day visited the poor stigmatisée to render open testimony to the wonders of divine power manifested in her. His visit was followed by several from the Princess Gallitzen accompanied by Dean Overberg.

---

endured his grievous wrongs in the spirit of Christ when he might have defended himself, must excite our admiration. Bishop Sailer was of a noble character without self-love or self-interest. He united piety with cheerfulness and was loved by all that knew him. He refused many splendid positions offered him in Wirtemberg, Prussia, etc., and counted numerous friends among the highest families.—(Taken from Herder's Kirchen-lexicon.)

CHAPTER XXX.

The Vicar-General's Last Visit to Dülmen.—He Desires to Remove Sister Emmerich to Darfeld.

The Vicar-General was always ready to encourage the visits of men eminent by their position and learning to the stigmatisée of Dülmen. He hoped through their testimony to silence the voice of calumny in her regard. He was accustomed to notify her of such visits and express his desire that she would allow them to see her stigmata. Animated by this laudable design, and intending to make observations as detailed as those of April 21st, he repaired to Dülmen some months after the investigation with a numerous party of friends from among the nobility. Dr. Wesener's journal gives us the following remarks on this visit:

"Thursday evening, August 26th, I met the Vicar-General von Droste and Professor von Druffel by the invalid's bedside. She was very dejected and the Professor inquired of me what her state had been up to this time. He saw no change in her wounds, her countenance and demeanor were about the same as on his last visit. On Friday evening, I found her in a miserable condition, her pulse so weak that we all looked for her speedy dissolution. Father Limberg and her Sister Gertrude accounted for it by telling me that the Vicar-General and his party had wearied her the whole day, repeatedly inspecting the cross on her breast and bathing her wounds in order to examine them better." She had passively yielded to her Superior and uncomplainingly borne these painful inspections; but it was too much for her. She fell into a state of prostration from which she rallied but slowly.

Dr. Wesener deeply compassionated the poor, defenceless invalid, and in a spirited letter complained of the injury done his patient by so protracted an examination:—

"Your Grace desires," he wrote, "to probe this affair to the bottom, and such, indeed, is your duty. So far, so good!—but the investigation should not have been made thus! The poor creature has been persecuted to death! Your Grace came with a party of eight or ten and remained by the invalid from eight a. m. till six p. m. I regret that my absence prevented my warning you of the result of such a proceeding. Had I been present she would not have had to endure such an infliction, nor would I have had the grief of finding her in so sad a state. She thought, and she thanked God for it, that her last hour had come. I could not account for your imposing such suffering on her, did I not recall having heard Dr. von Druffel's opinion that such treatment could not harm her; but I affirm, on my honor, that yesterday's proceedings would without a miracle have cost the invalid her life. If Your Grace continue your examination, the patient will offer no opposition. But, in God's name! let it be done more leisurely and not at the cost of her already feeble health!"

Poor Sister Emmerich rallied but slowly. When able to pronounce a few words, she said: "I feel that I ought not to receive such visits or show my signs. I was told so in vision. I was kneeling in spirit in a beautiful chapel before a statue of Mary with the Infant Jesus in her arms. When I invoked her, she descended, embraced me, and said: 'My child, be careful! Go no further! Shun visits and remain in thy humility!'"

The Vicar-General's motives excuse his seeming want of consideration for Sister Emmerich. He was seeking to provide her a secure retreat where, hidden from the eyes

of the world, she might accomplish in peace the mission assigned her. After mature reflection, he had decided to prepare for her an asylum on one of the estates belonging to
his family, where her wants would be generously provided
for. But before concluding his arrangements, he thought
that some members of his family ought to see the invalid
and convince themselves of the reality of her extraordinary
state. It was this that had led him to visit her with so
large a party and to subject her to so prolonged an examination. He thought it would be the last inspection of the
kind and that he would amply indemnify her by the advantages he had in store for her. No one at Dülmen was to
know of the project excepting Dean Rensing, who was to
advise her in the matter and, if she accepted the invitation,
accompany her to Darfeld Castle in the Vicar-General's
own carriage.

When the Vicar-General made this offer to Sister Emmerich, he imposed absolute silence on her, even with respect to her confessor, Father Limberg. He was to be informed only at the moment of departure by a sealed letter
which was also to contain a peremptory prohibition to take
any part whatever in the affair. The proposition threw the
invalid into great perplexity which told on her little remaining strength. The greatest, the only earthly advantages to which she aspired, solitude and repose, were now
held out to her, her acceptance seemed almost a duty of
deference and gratitude to her Ecclesiastical Superior, and
Dean Rensing represented to her that the retired asylum of
Darfeld alone could insure her against any attempt at a new
investigation. But, on the other hand, what assurance had
she that, in accepting so generous an offer, she would not
render herself unfaithful to God; that, in seeking a more
tranquil life, she would not pursue a course incompatible

with her mission ? Who would assure her that she did
not contravene her holy religious vows by giving the
preference to a position that would secure her from the
trials consequent on poverty ? Would she then have the
opportunities for works of mercy as she now had ? Would
her door stand ever open to the needy and distressed ?
Again, would not her non-acceptance of so generous an
offer offend her Superior ? Would she not appear ungrateful and capricious ? Her embarrassment was so much the
greater as she had ever been accustomed to absolute dependence on the words of her confessor; now, she was
forbidden to confer with Father Limberg on the subject,
and both the Vicar-General and Dean Rensing carefully
forebore saying a word that could influence her decision.
The acceptance or rejection of the offer was left entirely to
herself. She asked for time to consult God in prayer. After a few days, she dictated the following lines to Dean Rensing to be forwarded to the Vicar-General at Darfeld:—
" Sister Emmerich cannot resolve on a journey to Darfeld.
She is too weak to undertake it without risking her life.
The journey not being *ordered* by Superiors, she fears to
make it, lest by so doing she should tempt God and expose
herself to presumption. She is, moreover, of the opinion
that her sojourn at Darfeld among the Droste family, so
esteemed for their piety throughout Münster, would instead
of putting an end to calumnious accusations, only excite
fresh ones and she is unwilling to expose that noble family
to so disagreeable a result. Prof. B— and others of his
way of thinking would hardly be silenced by such a step;
on the contrary, they, would demand all the more loudly
that she should be removed to Münster and subjected to a
new examination."

Her weakness was indeed so great that she was sup-

posed to be dying several times between September 1st
and 10th. On the 2d, Father Limberg thought her soul
had actually departed and recited by her the prayers for the
dead ; but, when he sprinkled her with holy water, a sweet
expression passed over her face and she slowly returned to
consciousness.

The Vicar-General saw the solidity of her reasoning.
Though pained at the failure of his plan, by which he had
hoped to silence unjust suspicions and crush the calumnies
of unbelievers, yet he read in her non-acceptance of so
advantageous an offer a new proof of her virtue and purity
of intention. Neither his sympathy nor esteem for her diminished; he kept up constant communication with her
through Deans Rensing and Overberg, and visited her as
often as he could find leisure. A year after the investigation, learning through Clara Soentgen that the invalid's
death was at hand, he wrote as follows to Dean Rensing :—

"I wish to know whether you regard Sister Emmerich's
death as near as some suppose. If you do, let me know,
and tell me also whether you think it will be sudden. I
should be happy to receive a summary of whatever has happened extraordinary since August, 1813. Be so kind as to
present my respects to her."

The Dean replied :—

"I do not, as yet, see anything indicative of speedy
death ; but she herself seems to think her end not far off.
If God reveals anything to her concerning it and she says
anything definite to me on the subject, I shall inform Your
Grace forthwith. The same phenomena are still visible in
her person as were seen a year ago. The blood flows on
Fridays as it did then, but since August nothing new has
appeared. As regards her spiritual life, she has gained in
many points. She has overcome various little imperfections ;

she is more united to the will of God. What she relates of
her ecstasies is frequently of so elevated a character as to
excite my admiration ; it is, at the same time, accompanied by so much simplicity that one can never suspect deceit.
Supposing even that it does not belong to a superior order
of things, there is in it, at least, the most beautiful manifestation of a soul pure as the angels, wholly absorbed in God,
sighing only for His glory, and the salvation of mankind."

Two months after, the Dean made the following report:—

"Sister Emmerich is a little better; perhaps she will
again be well for awhile. As her existence has so long
been at variance with nature, we need not fear that
she will die because the symptoms of death appear.
Yesterday, in a moment of exhaustion, she told me that
she hoped God would give her strength before her death to
reveal certain things for the benefit of her neighbors. She
spoke very low, and it was only by an effort that I could
understand what she said."

On receipt of the above, the Vicar-General drew up
the following ordinance in the event of her death :—

"If the Augustinian religious, Anne Catherine Emmerich, sleeps in the Lord, Dean Rensing shall as soon as
possible :—

"1. Send me word by express wherever I may happen to
be, and even come himself if he can do so. If not, let him
take the following steps :

"2. Until my arrival, or until further orders from me, let
him see that :—

"(a) One or more females, of whose trustworthiness he is
assured, watch night and day by the remains. (I
shall defray the expense.)

"(b) Let none other remain near the body, and let permission to see it be given to as few as possible. If such visits

are too numerous, it would be well for the Mayor to interpose his authority for their discontinuance.

" (c) Until my arrival, or further instructions, let the body
remain absolutely untouched. Let no one examine it or
the stigmata in any way whatever.

" 3. Let the Dean take measures for having the death announced to him as soon as possible after its occurrence, and
let him at once invite the Mayor to accompany him to Sister Emmerich's lodgings, not officially, but as a friend. Let
him extend a similar invitation to Fathers Limberg and
Lambert and to Drs. Wesener and Krauthausen. Then, in
presence of all these gentlemen, an official report shall be
drawn up which all shall sign, and which shall consist of the
following points briefly stated :—

" (a) The manner and time of death with any remarkable
circumstances attending it.

" (b) The state of the body ; the different marks on the
hands, feet, side, head, and breast.

" N.B. Between the invitation to the above-named personages and their acceptance of the same, no time must inter-
vene. Let them not go all together to Sister Emmerich's
lodgings, that publicity may be avoided; and only those
mentioned ought to be admitted.

" 4. Lastly : Let the Dean request Fathers Limberg and
Lambert, as also the two physicians, to await my arrival in
Dülmen, if they possibly can, that I may have an inter-
view with them.

" 5. I shall provide for all subsequent steps in good time.

" Clement Auguste von Droste-Vischering,

" Vicar–General.

" Münster, *May* 26, 1814."

CHAPTER XXXI.

SISTER EMMERICH'S LIFE AFTER THE INVESTIGATION.—HER SURROUNDINGS. —THE ABBÉ LAMBERT.—HER SISTER GERTRUDE.

To appreciate the closing years of Sister Emmerich's life, her relations with the outer world must be understood; for without this it would be impossible to comprehend a life whose most insignificant incidents were disposed by Divine Providence for the highest ends. The smallest events in such a life, though in appearance the veriest trifles, are of the greatest importance. It was in the midst of the ordinary occurrences of daily life that Sister Emmerich was to accomplish her mission and thereby attain sanctity. Called to labor for the Church in tribulation, her outer life must be in conformity with her task. Her position had never yet been regulated by her own choice; it had ever been subject to direction from on high and, consequently, in itself a source of virtue and merit. They who influenced her outer life had not been chosen by her, they had been gathered around her by causes which sprang not from human foresight.

Let us first consider the effect produced on her life by the stigmata, whose supernatural origin had been undeniably established by the ecclesiastical investigation. Whilst in the cloister, she had been able to conceal the bloody effusions of the crown of thorns from the distrustful curiosity of her companions, for it did not enter into the divine economy to disclose at that time the mystery of God's wonderful ways over His servant. It had, therefore, been allowed her to feel the pains, but not to bear in her person the visible marks of her Saviour's Wounds. Without a miracle of divine power, she could not have endured those excruciating tortures a single instant; but, thanks to this assistance, she had become so incorporated with the nature of the vine that, like the branch around its support, she began to adapt herself to the form of the cross. Whether sitting or lying, her feet involuntarily crossed one over the other as closely as those of a crucifix. When recalled suddenly from ecstasy by her confessor and unable to rise as quickly as obedience prompted, she would exclaim beseechingly: "O I cannot! I cannot! Unbind me! I am nailed." The palms of her hands were pierced through and through, the middle fingers arose above the others in an unnatural position, and it cost her intense pain to make use of them. But scarcely had she left the obscurity of her humble cell to enter an unsympathizing world, than the exterior signs manifested themselves! Might she not, poor, sick, abandoned as she was, have hoped that her expulsion from the convent would, at least, have formed the culminating point of her sufferings? Not so! Now began a life compared with whose austerity and sublimity, all that she had hitherto endured sinks into insignificance.

There was still one desire cherished in that poor, suffering heart, and that was to serve the venerable priest, her benefactor and friend, the only human support ever vouchsafed her. He had remained with her at Agnetenberg until, forced to leave, they had both found a miserable lodging with a widow named Roters. In him she honored not only her friend and protector, but a confessor of the faith whose fidelity had condemned him to poverty and exile. The Abbé Lambert was the only one who treated her kindly during her life in the convent, the only one to whom she

could make known her sorrows. When at an early hour
he went to the sacristy to prepare for Mass, she used to
tell him of the directions received in vision the night before
for her mission of suffering during the coming day, beg his
prayers, and gratefully treasure up his words of encouragement and consolation. They were the most precious boon
she had ever received from any living creature; they were
what even her angel himself could not afford her. Her
heart beat and suffered as sensitively as other human hearts
and for it, as for others, the comforting words of a friend
were a sweet relief, an essential need. And still more—
this *poor nun* had even received alms from the *poor priest.*
He knew that what she earned by her sewing ordinarily
went to the Superioress, and that her trifling wants were
not provided for in return. Sometimes the kind old man
would bring her a little piece of white bread which she had
leave to take, pleased with the thought that from the hand
of him to whom she was indebted for a more frequent reception of the Holy Eucharist, she received likewise the
support of her natural life.

The hope of making some little return for his kindness
by her faithful service, was not to be realized. Her state
not only rendered her incapable of such duties, but even
exacted the charitable services of others, and her ecstasies
were frequent and irresistible. The Abbé had often found
her kneeling rigid and immovable, apparently lifeless. But
he had never dared to recall her by a command given by
virtue of his priestly authority; andconsequently, her raptures
had become day by day more frequent and prolonged. His
only anxiety had been to conceal them from all around and
keep this chosen soul in happy ignorance of her state. To
maintain her in humility and divert her thoughts from these
wonders, met but in the lives of the saints, he had absolutely

refused to receive any communication from her on the subject, saying shortly : " Sister, it's nothing ! it's nothing ! it's
only a dream !"—His infirmities made him long for repose,
and he earnestly hoped that his last days in a strange land
might not be troubled by fresh annoyances. The first sight
of her bleeding stigmata had afflicted him deeply, but he
consoled himself with the thought that they would disappear
in the evening, or at least that they might be kept secret.
Soon, however, was the good old man disabused. The
wounds did not disappear, and it added not a little to the
poor victim's sufferings to be obliged to sustain the courage
of her kind father and friend whilst struggling herself to
bear up against her own torrent of affliction.

No event of her life had cost her so much as the appearance of her marvellous signs. As Lidwina of Schiedam,
eaten up by worms and putrefaction, served Almighty God
for over thirty years as an instrument of expiation for the
Church, so now did the stigmatisée of Dülmen bear in her
person the marks of Redemption for the same end. Lidwina, too, had received their imprint ; but her other expiatory sufferings effaced, in a measure, from the mind of the
beholder the impression they would otherwise have produced.
Sister Emmerich's stigmata were precisely the cause of her
being drawn from her retirement and exposed to the public
gaze. At the time in which she lived, such wounds and
sufferings as those of Lidwina could not have been patiently endured by the scoffers at whatever bore a supernatural
character.

Sister Emmerich's miraculous wounds exerted an influence both internally and externally, in consequence of
which the circulation of blood seemed to be entirely changed
from the natural course, each wound being a centre to and
from which the currents flowed. Its very pulsations seemed

changed or, as it were, multiplied, being detected as sensibly at her finger ends as at her wrists. Her hands were pierced through and through, the wounds of her feet were formed on the instep and ran along the soles, and that of her side took an upward direction, as if made by a thrust from below. When they opened and the air blew on them, it cut through like a sharp knife or a scorching flame and caused unspeakable suffering to the poor invalid; for this reason she usually kept her hands wrapped in soft linen. After years of duration they were as fresh, as sharp, as free from purulent matter as on the first day of their appearance.

Dr. Wesener reports the following, Friday, Sept. 8, 1815 :—

" I found the invalid exceedingly weak but cheerful, her hands and feet bleeding. The wounds on the back of the hands are round and about as large as a small coin, the edges slightly puffed up, but without inflammation. One thing that seemed to me remarkable, though perhaps of little importance to any but a physician, was a slight excoriation at the lower joint of the right fore-finger. This excoriation was inflamed and a purulent liquid had collected under the epidermis in three different places. I asked if she had scratched it with a needle, and she told me that the day before, whilst wiping a tumbler, she had broken the rim and scratched her finger with it. Her skin is easily inflamed and inclined to suppuration. Let science bring this fact to bear on the unchanging condition of her wounds."

Dr. Wesener looked upon the above, as we may infer from his concluding remark, as an evident proof of the supernatural character of the invalid's stigmata; another very striking one is afforded by their bleeding only on certain days of the ecclesiastical year. Their effusions

were not confined to Fridays which would make them
fall on fixed and recurring intervals; they happened on all
movable feasts commemorative of the Sacred Passion, independently of the invalid's personal dispositions. Sometimes the only intimation she had of the approach of such
a feast was from the increased sufferings in her wounds.
One year, the annual fair-day held in Dülmen fell on a
Friday; consequently Sister Emmerich was importuned by
visitors, and seeing so many peasants in holiday dress, she
thought surely it must be Sunday. Toward three P. M. she
suddenly grew pale and the blood flowed in four streams from
under her cap, a circumstance for which she could not account
till some one remarked that it was Friday and not Sunday.

The blood always flowed in the same direction as did
that from the Sacred Wounds of Christ upon the cross.
From the palms of the hands it ran toward the inner part
of the forearm; down the feet toward the toes; and from
her forehead and temples it flowed down as far as the nose,
even when her head was not in an upright position. It was
on account of this unnatural course of the blood, that the
Professor of Chemistry hooted at the idea of its reality and
declared it only *paint.* Clement Brentano, some years
later, rendered the following testimony :—

" The flow of blood was visible at the upper part of her
high forehead just below the hair, where it oozed like drops
of perspiration, though no sign of a wound could be seen;
but when it dried up, small red specks like the pricks of a
needle might be distinguished, to which Drs. Wesener and
von Druffel gave a particular name. The quantity that
flowed from her head was, at times, greater or less, and the
same may be said of the other wounds; it seemed, however,
that the flow from some was greater in proportion as that
from the others was less."

Dr. Wesener confirms the last detail, Friday, June 3, 1814 :—

" The blood flowed to-day from noon till about four o'clock, streaming from her head so copiously that she grew frightfully pale and prostrate.   Her attendants in alarm tried to stop it by applications of cloths steeped in vinegar."

Friday, Sept. 29, 1815 :—"The Princess Galitzin came this afternoon from Münster to see the invalid, and they conversed together a long time, the Abbé Lambert and Clara Soentgen being present.   When the Princess withdrew, the invalid uttered a groan, and Clara Soentgen ran to her bedside to find a stream of clear blood gushing from three small punctures in her forehead ; she caught it in the folds of a linen cloth. Her other wounds began also to bleed, but not so copiously as her head.   I must not pass over the Abbé Lambert's exclamation.   When he saw the invalid bleeding so profusely, he shed tears and turning to Clara Soentgen, he said : ' *Ma sœur*, now you see *I* did not do it.' "

Six years after, Friday, Feb. 9, 1821, during the obsequies of the old Abbé, Clement Brentano witnessed an effusion of blood, which he noted down with the following remarks :—

" Sister Emmerich has a very high forehead, prominent temples and an abundance of dark brown hair, which, from constant cutting and the pressure of a tight head-dress, has, though naturally soft and fine, become rather coarse. Her headaches have rendered it sensitive to the touch, combing it causes sharp pain ; consequently, it is only when absolutely necessary that she consents to have it cut, though she was forced to submit to it during the first years of her stigmata. Ever watched and suspected, she could hardly keep her door closed long enough to arrange it ; for if any one had been kept waiting, suspicion would have been aroused. It was very difficult on this account to render her the most necessary services. When the attempt was made, it was often with so much hurry and anxiety that it gave her more suffering than relief. She herself experienced a kind of reverential fear at the sight of her person impressed with its marvellous signs. God, who in her early years had bestowed upon her such aptitude for manual labor, now gave her such facility and promptitude for whatever propriety and cleanliness demanded, both for herself and her surroundings, and this even in contemplation, that her poor couch of suffering was always as neat and well arranged as that of the most careful and best attended religious in a convent. And yet it must have been very difficult for her, notwithstanding her dexterity. For years she could take only a sitting posture in her bed, her head resting on her knees ; she was often scarcely able to move her wounded hands with their paralyzed middle fingers ; and her profuse perspiration made a change of linen necessary several times a day. But no one ever entered her room, no matter at what hour, without finding her carefully clothed and surrounded by such neatness as was pleasant to behold. I visited her daily and at all hours for four years, and I invariably saw a certain propriety in her and her surroundings which recalled those virtues of which she was truly the personification : innocence, chastity, and purity of heart."

We have one fact to prove how little she could expect from the attention of her friends. In summer, during her ecstatic prayer, swarms of flies sometimes settled on her wounds and stung them to blood. Dr. Wesener found her in this state once with none to relieve her. We are also indebted to him for the information that, chiefly during the octave of Corpus Christi, the wounds of the Flagellation, bearing an exact likeness to the cuts of a whip, appeared on her person. They were accompanied by signs of fever.

These marks of the Saviour's predilection were for Sister Emmerich sources of torture, fear, and anxiety, of the deepest and most painful humiliation. But God's grace was sufficient for her. She bore them not as something of her own, not as a mark of distinction, but as the seal of her expiatory mission. The mystery of Redemption had been effaced, so to say, from the memory of man ; for perhaps no age made so little account of the Saviour's sufferings as the one of which we write. Apart from the unbelieving, the open enemies of God's holy Church, we are shocked at the small number of those who then comprehended these words of St. Peter : " *Scientes quod non corruptibilibus auro vel argento redempti estis, sed pretioso sanguine quasi agni immaculati Christi.*" (1). It was a period in which perfect silence was kept, both in the pulpit and schools of theology, on the mystery of Redemption, sacrifice and satisfaction, merit and sin ; a period in which good works and miracles had to yield to hollow "theories of revelation ;" a period in which the Man-God, to be at all endurable, had to be presented as the " Friend of men, the Friend of sinners, the children's Friend." His life was, as they said, " *a lesson;*" His Passion, " *an example of fortitude;*" His death, " *fruitless love.*" The catechism was taken from the hands of the faithful and replaced by " Bible Histories," in which the absolute want of doctrine was veiled under " *simple language adapted to the understanding of all.*" The books of piety, the ancient formulas of prayer, the time-honored canticles of praise, were exchanged for modern productions as miserable and impious as were those

(1) Knowing that you were not redeemed with corruptible things as gold or silver, but with the Precious Blood of Christ, as of a lamb unspotted and undefiled.—I. Peter. i. 18. 19.

by which the Missal, the breviary, and the ritual were replaced.

This intellectual debasement might pass at first sight for a transient aberration, a false direction of the spirit of the age ; but before God it was a direct attack on the faith, imperilling the salvation of numberless souls, an expression of the deepest contempt for His love and justice. All this had to be expiated by an innocent victim who was to be treated not otherwise than Jesus Himself and His work of Redemption. The startling grandeur of His bloody sacrifice and His rigorous satisfaction for sin are a stumbling-block to many ; in like manner Sister Emmerich was a cause of offence by reason of her mysterious signs and, even for her nearest friends, she was an insupportable burden. The Abbé Lambert and her confessor ardently desired the disappearance of what deprived them of peace and repose ; the pastor of the parish withdrew from her with a feeling of irritation when he found his name associated with her singular case ; the Vicar-General, the highest functionary of the diocese, submitted her as an impostor to a most rigorous investigation, in order to spare the world the insupportable spectacle of her wounds ; and, finally, this end not being attained, she is abandoned, helpless and defenceless, to the importunate curiosity of a pitiless crowd, suspected and even most cruelly persecuted, as we shall see further on. Her own prayers are, as it were, unheeded by Almighty God. Those loving sighs which draw down torrents of blessings upon others, are powerless in her own cause when she cries to Him to deprive her of her stigmata. " My grace is sufficient for thee ! " does she hear, and the mysterious wounds remain. Clement Brentano's beautiful words may here be quoted :—

"Sealed with the Wounds of her Crucified Love, she was driven into the desert of unbelief to render testimony to the truth. What a mission to bear in her own person, to display to the eyes of the world, to the followers of its prince, the victorious insignia of Christ, the Son of the living God, Jesus of Nazareth, King of the Jews! Great courage, special grace were needed for it. To many she was to be an object of scandal and suspicion, to all an enigma. Where the roads of unbelief and superstition, of malice and wickedness, of intellectual pride and foolishness meet, there was she to hang upon the cross, exposed to the curious gaze of the passers-by, subjected to the absurd remarks and criticisms of the vulgar. To live poor and despised, a prey to mysterious maladies, slighted by her nearest friends, often ill-treated, utterly alone amidst the curious throng in which she sees not one who can understand or sympathize with her ; to be uniformly patient, affable, meek, discreet ; to edify the motley crowd, little considerate in their deportment toward her —this was the task of the outcast religious, the poor peasant-girl, whose only instruction was that found in her catechism."

Never did a word of complaint escape her lips. She saw herself suspected, she heard the absurd calumnies uttered against her, but she was silent ; only when looked upon with respect and admiration did she show signs of displeasure. For years she had suffered the pains of the stigmata before their outward marks were vouchsafed to her, regarding it merely as a favor granted to her petition for expiatory sufferings. When she received their visible impress, she still looked upon it as a symbolical vision, not as a real fact; and so, at all times, was she ready to see in them only what obedience bade her behold. She felt her own unworthiness so deeply, she feared the world's praises so greatly that, even in vision, she blushed at herself, she would have been willing to be punished as an impostor.

On Sunday in the octave of the Exaltation of the Holy Cross, 1815, she assisted in spirit at the solemn procession in Coesfeld of the miraculous crucifix; barefoot and adoring, she walked behind the holy cross. As they passed the church of St James, she felt that many of the assistants thought of her and spoke of her mysterious wounds, by which circumstance she was so confused that her efforts to hide them recalled her to consciousness. Sometimes the evil spirit reproached her, saying that she could rise and eat if she wished; that if she began with wine and water, she would soon see that it would be easy to take other nourishment, but that she was a hypocrite, etc. In her humility and forgetful of the tempter's malice, she would reply: " Yes, I am a miserable creature! I deserve to be despised as a hypocrite," and indignant against herself she would try to rise from her bed and call out to the passers-by : " Good people, good people, keep away from me! Be not scandalized at me! I am an unworthy creature!" but falling back exhausted by her efforts, she at last recognized the fiendish impostor.

Friday, August 9, 1816, Dr. Wesener records the following : " She complains of her innumerable visitors. ' I am sad unto death,' sighed she one day, ' on account of this concourse of people, and particularly because I see that many regard what God has done in me, His miserable instrument, with deeper veneration than they feel before the Blessed Sacrament. I could die of shame when good old priests, ten times better than I, ask to see me.' I tried to calm her, saying that God permitted these visits to try her patience, that people came not to see her, but the wonders of God manifested in her; that they did not admire her, but only the incomprehensible decrees of Almighty God. My words consoled and restored her to peace."

No precise knowledge would have been had on her reception of the wounds, if it were not for the visions relative to it which she had at various times during the last years of her life and which she related in obedience to her confessor's order. On Oct. 4, 1820, Feast of St. Francis of Assisi, she had the following vision :—

" I saw the saint among some bushes on a wild mountain in which were scattered grottos like little cells. Francis had opened the Gospel several times. Each time it chanced to be at the history of the Passion, and so he begged to feel his Lord's sufferings. He used to fast on this mountain, eating only a little bread and roots. He knelt, his bare knees on two sharp stones, and supported two others on his shoulders. It was after midnight and he was praying with arms extended, half-kneeling, half sitting, his back resting against the side of the mountain. I saw his angel near him holding his hands, his countenance all on fire with love. He was a slight man. He wore a brown mantle open in front with a hood like those worn at the time by shepherds, a cord bound his waist. At the moment in which I saw him he was as if paralyzed. A bright light shot from heaven and descended upon him. In it was an angel with six wings, two above his head, two over his feet, and two with which he seemed to fly. In his right hand he held a cross, about half the usual size, on which was a living body glowing with light, the feet crossed, the five wounds resplendent as so many suns. From each wound proceeded three rays of rosy light converging to a point. They shot first from the hands toward the palms of the saint's hands ; then from the wound in the right side toward the saint's right

side (these rays were larger than the others); and lastly,
from the feet toward the soles of the saint's feet. In his
left hand the angel held a blood-red tulip in whose centre
was a golden heart, which I think he gave to the saint.
When Francis returned from ecstasy, he could with difficulty stand, and I saw him going back to his monastery suffering cruelly, and supported by his angel-guardian. He
hid his wounds as well as he could. There were large
crusts of brownish blood on the back of his hands, for they
did not bleed regularly every Friday; but his side often
bled so profusely that the blood flowed down on the ground.
I saw him praying, the blood streaming down his arms. I
saw many other incidents of his life. Once even before he
knew him the Pope beheld him in vision supporting the
Lateran on his shoulders when it was ready to fall.

"Then I had a vision of myself receiving the wounds. I
never knew before how it was. Three days before the
new year, and about three o'clock in the afternoon I was
lying alone in the little room I used to have at Mrs. Roters',
my arms extended. I was contemplating the Passion of
Jesus Christ and asking to be allowed to feel His pains. I
said five Our Fathers in honor of the Five Wounds. I experienced great sweetness with an intense desire that my
prayer might be granted, when suddenly I beheld descending obliquely upon me a great light. It was a crucified
body, living and transparent, with extended arms but no
cross, the wounds more resplendent than the body, like five
circles of brilliant light.

"I was rapt out of myself, and I yearned with mingled
pain and sweetness to share my Saviour's sufferings. As
my desire grew still more vehement at the sight of His
Wounds, it shot, so to speak, from my breast, hands, feet,
and side toward them. At the same moment, triple

rays of red light, converging to a point, darted first from
the Hands, then from the Side and Feet of the Image upon my
hands, side, and feet.   I lay for a time unconscious, until
Mrs. Roters' little girl lowered my hands.   She told the
family that I had cut them and that they were bleeding, but
I implored them to say nothing about it.

"I had had the cross on my breast for some time, since
the Feast of St. Augustine when, as I was praying on my
knees, my arms extended, my Affianced signed me with
it.   After I received these wounds, I felt a great change
in my whole person ; my blood circulated toward these
points with a painful twitching sensation.   St. Francis appeared to me that night, consoled me, and spoke of the
violence of interior pains."

That the reader may understand the visions relative to herself, we must enter into some particulars upon their signification.   As an instrument of expiation, all her actions were to
be performed, her sufferings endured in a manner most pleasing to God.   To purify her soul from daily faults, she had
her confessor's direction and the Sacrament of Penance ;
but, when the imperfections committed in vision were to
be effaced, her angel stepped in to impose new efforts and
sufferings.   As her task increased, her visions on the same
became more comprehensive.   Her life was now drawing
toward its close, and it was fitting that every moment of it
should be employed in the accomplishment of its mission.
She had not only to discharge her duty in all that concerned
her personally and repair the faults arising from her own
poor nature, but she was also responsible for those whom
God had associated with her as aids in her work of expiation.   She knew the Vicar-General and Dean Overberg
long before they had heard of her ; and her prayers and
influence were around *the Pilgrim* whilst yet he wandered

far from the Church, careless of God and his own soul.

He had been shown her in vision as the one destined to record her contemplations, for which end she was to gain him to God. The following vision she related to the Abbe Lambert :—

" I was journeying toward the Heavenly Jerusalem with a crowd of people; but I had so weighty a burden to carry that I could hardly get along. I rested awhile under a crucifix around which lay numbers of small straw crosses and little dry branches bound together. I asked my guide what all these crosses meant. He answered : ' These are the little crosses you had in the convent, they were light. But now a real cross is laid on you, bear it !' Then the crowd dispersed and my confessor, whom I saw among them, slipped behind a bush and lay in wait for a hare. I begged him not to lag behind, to come with me ; but he would not listen to my persuasion, and I staggered on alone under my burden. But I feared that I ought not to leave him behind, that I ought to entreat and even force him on to our magnificent destination; so I went back and found him asleep and, to my horror, I heard the howling of wild beasts close by. I awoke him and begged him to continue his journey, but it took all my strength to make him come with me. At last we reached a deep, broad river spanned by a very narrow bridge which I should never have been able to cross without his assistance. We arrived, at last, at our journey's end."

We shall soon see the significance of this apparently simple vision. Father Limberg was a Dominican. The suppression of his monastery afflicted him deeply, and, on returning to the world, he had resolved to regulate his life as strictly as possible by his religious obligations. Sister

Emmerich thanked God for giving her this worthy priest,
who held toward her not only the office of confessor and
director, but also that of monastic Superiors ; and to him
she transferred the respect and obedience which, whilst in
the convent, she had paid to the Rule and lawful authority.
Almighty God willed that she should still continue the
practice of her holy vows ; and, although Father Limberg's
superior in intelligence and the spiritual life, she obeyed
him blindly, preserving toward him the attitude of a simple
child ready to be led and directed in all things.　His least
word was for her an order from God which admitted neither
question nor contradiction.　Though sometimes convinced
by experience or her angel's warnings that such or such a
prescription would be attended by injurious results, she made
not the least objection —no pain, no sacrifice counter-bal-
anced in her estimation the merit of obedience.　She often saw
that his direction aggravated her sufferings ; yet it was for
her the order of God who willed that she should accomplish
her mission, not by her angel's ministry but by that of His
priest.　There is one characteristic common to all souls
called to a sublime vocation —and that is the sacrifice, the
abandonment of their whole being, body and soul, to the
will of God, a characteristic which shone out most clearly in
Sister Emmerich's whole life, and in no part more than in her
relations with her confessor.　Obedience was the bond which
united her as a living representative to the body of the Church.
It was founded on faith which showed her in the person of
the priest God's vice-gerent on earth, a faith so much the
more meritorious as she saw more clearly in him the weakness of the man.　However extraordinary may be the gifts
of privileged souls, however elevated may be the task assigned them, they know no other law, no higher direction
than the rule of faith such as the Church, the pillar and

ground of truth, lays down.   True and pure mysticism flourishes in no other soil than that of ecclesiastical discipline, of divine worship, of the Sacraments, and of the devout practices and usages of Holy Church.   It admits no transgression, no dispensation with regard to the Commandments of God or of the Church, which are binding on all Christians without exception ; nor does it sanction the omission of duty under the specious pretext that high spirituality is not bound by ordinary laws and regulations.   They are the barriers erected by God for the safety of His chosen ones which the false mystic, the lying pretender to extraordinary favors, hesitates not to overturn.

When Father Limberg assumed Sister Emmerich's spiritual direction, he had adopted Abbé Lambert's opinion as to the necessity of concealing her state.   He qualified her visions as mere dreams.   He was of a timid turn of mind, easily disquieted. It was only after years of intercourse, that he justly appreciated his penitent's high gifts.   He himself relates the following incident :—

" The invalid lay one afternoon in ecstatic prayer, her eyes closed, whilst I sat near saying my breviary, which occupied about an hour.   When I had finished, Prof. B.'s doubts presented themselves to my mind, and I know not how I conceived the following idea : I remembered that the Abbé Lambert had that day consecrated two Hosts, reserving one for the invalid's Communion next morning. May I not, thought I, put her to the test, not through idle curiosity or any bad intention ?   Filled with this thought I went and got the Sacred Host, placed it in a corporal around which I folded a stole, and carried It back to the invalid's chamber.   She lay just as I had left her, buried in prayer ; but no sooner had I placed my foot upon the door-sill, than she arose hastily though with effort, stretched out her arms,

and fell upon her knees in adoration.   ' What do you want ?'
I said. 'Ah ! there comes my Lord Jesus to me with the
tabernacle ! '   I allowed her to adore the Blessed Sacrament
awhile and then carried It back."

The first time he had found her in ecstasy, he asked for
an explanation ; she was greatly confused and begged him
not to betray her secret.   It was the same with Maria
Bagnesi (1) between whom and Sister Emmerich there was
a striking resemblance.   Maria was once found in ecstasy
raised above the ground.   On returning to consciousness,
she was so affrighted that she hid her face with her hands
like a child taken in a fault, not daring to look upon those
who had witnessed her rapture.

Father Limberg understood so little of such things that
on finding Sister Emmerich absorbed in ecstasy, he would
try to arouse her by shaking her roughly, for he said: *"She's
raving."*   In August, 1814, she took upon herself the sufferings of a poor consumptive to obtain for her patience and a
happy death.   Father Limberg finding her one day moaning
in agony, shook her by the shoulders until she awoke, when
she said quietly : "I went to a poor sick woman.   On my
return, I was so weak that I had to mount the stone steps
on my knees (2).   It was hard work, my knees are paining
intensely."

Her knees were, indeed, blistered and the pain in them
continued for some days ; but Father Limberg treated it as
a dream until the consumptive, his own sister, begged to be
taken to Sister Emmerich, that helped by her prayers she
might die by her bedside.   He had her carried into Sister Emmerich's room, in whom all the symptoms of consump-

(1) The " Life of Maria Bagnesi," born at Florence, 1514, was written by her confessor,
Augustine Campi.   It may be found in the Acta S. S., Vol. VI. May.

(2) On Nov. 23, 1813, Sister Emmerich was removed to the house of Mr. Limberg,
master-baker and brewer, a brother of Father Limberg.   Her room was in the back
building looking out upon the garden and church of her loved convent.   The Abbé
Lambert had a room in the same house.

tion instantly appeared : burning fever, and pains in her
right side so violent that she fainted on being removed from
her bed, whilst the consumptive herself was relieved and
consoled. Dr. Wesener says :—" Sister Emmerich had a
very painful night; she was maltreated and mocked by some
children who fell upon and beat her. She had to use both
hands to defend herself without, however, being able to escape from them. Father Limberg, who was watching by his
sister, saw Sister Emmerich's gestures, and touched her on the
arm to restrain her. She awoke and, though seeing him by
her, lost not her dread of the children who continued to
ill-treat her. She complained of their having bruised her
and of having tried to make her eat by holding food to her
mouth. She was tormented all the morning with the taste
of it." This vision bore reference to the suspicions that the
dying woman had long nourished and communicated to
others respecting Sister Emmerich's perpetual fast, which
she had looked upon as imposture. The poor invalid expiated this fault by patiently enduring the ill-treatment mentioned above, and obtained for the consumptive the grace of
repentance and a happy death.

Father Limberg was, at last, forced to admit that his
penitent's raptures, etc., were something more than dreams;
still he remained in obscurity with regard to her state. On
the Vigil and Feast of the Assumption, Sister Emmerich
contemplated the Blessed Virgin's death with its attendant
circumstances. She spoke of her visions whilst still in ecstasy in so clear and animated a style, that even Father
Limberg was compelled to recognize the fact that there was
about her no trace of delirium. He held a little oil-paint-
ing of the Blessed Virgin's death a short distance before her
closed eyes, when her rigid form instantly inclined toward
it ; she bowed her head, took it into her hands, and said, in

allusion to St. Peter who was represented in it —" Ah! the
man with the white beard is a very good man ! "—Then she
fell back, and Father Limberg placed it on her hands which
lay crossed on her breast.   When returned to consciousness,
she said in answer to his inquiries : " I saw the Mother of
God dying surrounded by the Apostles and her friends.   I
gazed on the scene a long while, and then the whole room
with all it contained was laid on my hands.   O how glad I
was! But as I wondered how I could support such a weight,
I was told : ' It is pure virtue and that is light as a feather. '
All the night before I had visions of Mary's death.   I was
going to Jerusalem, and that in a strange way, for I was lying in bed neither sleeping nor dreaming, my eyes open.
I saw everything going on here in my room, as well as
upon the road."

Father Limberg was accustomed to treat her as an ordinary religious.   He spoke to her briefly and sternly, and
that was precisely what she most appreciated in him.   He
had been her confessor for two years when, one day Dr.
Wesener found her in tears.   On asking the cause, he received the following answer : " I fear losing confidence in
God, my only helper.   Now that I have to lie here, everything afflicts me.   I used to have such confidence that no
suffering, however violent, could shake it.   But lately all is
changed and I am now in distress because my confessor is
going to look for another position.   I value him and
prefer him to all others, on account of his severity."

Some years after, she again remarked in the doctor's
presence that she felt how beneficial Father Limberg's
sternness had been to her, and that nothing would grieve her
more than to see him relax in this point.   The following
characteristic trait is a good illustration of his conduct toward her :—

" One evening," says the doctor, " I found Sister Emmerich apparently dying; her pulse was almost gone, and
she could scarcely articulate a word. I knew not the cause
of her prostration, but I gave her ten drops of opium and
left her. The next morning, to my amazement, she was
bright as usual. I turned to her confessor for an
explanation, and he said : ' Early this morning she
was even weaker than yesterday and, fearing her death,
I gave her Holy Communion as quickly as possible.
Scarcely had she received the Sacred Host upon her tongue
than her face, before like that of a corpse, became rosy,
her pulse grew strong, and she remained over an hour in
adoration. Then I understood the cause of her extraordinary weakness. I had forbidden her Holy Communion for
two days for not allowing her back to be bathed in warm
brandy.' "

This incident affords a true and striking picture of the
invalid's position. The smell of liquor was intolerable to
her, its use as a wash a real torment; nevertheless, both
physician and confessor ordered it. If her weakness or the
stupor caused by its fumes prevented her rendering this service to herself, she had to commit herself to Gertrude's
hands, who made little account of her delicate sense of modesty ; so, to avoid her summary treatment, the poor sufferer
sometimes failed to make use of the remedy, and this was
the state of affairs in the present instance. The preceding Wednesday, Father Limberg discovered that she had
declined her sister's services. He punished her by de-
priving her of Holy Communion on Thursday and Friday,
and he would have prolonged the penance, if her state on
Saturday had not aroused fears for her life. The reader
will readily comprehend what benefit ten drops of opium
could be in such a case. But Sister Emmerich was accus-

tomed to receive all such events as punishments merited by her own failings, for which she never ventured an excuse.

Like Maria Bagnesi, her obedience to the priest's command was perfect. One day when Maria was writhing and groaning on her bed of pain, her friends sent for her confessor that his benediction might relieve her. He came consoled and encouraged her, and said on leaving: "Now, Sister Maria, be obedient and lie still!'—Instantly, she became immovable and stirred not from that position till the next day when her confessor came and revoked his command. Like Maria, Sister Emmerich also suffered more toward the close of every ecclesiastical year, because as a faithful servant, she had to correct the defects of slothful laborers in the Lord's vineyard. Dr. Wesener relates under date of Oct. 27, 1815 :—

" She was sick all day, her whole person quivering with pain. One remarkable feature in her case is her total deafness which has lasted for several days. Though not in ecstasy, she could hear nothing excepting what her confessor ordered her in obedience.

" In November she was taken with a severe cough. Intending to reserve the essence of musk for a last resource and fearing opium would attack the stomach, I tried rubbing with camphor which, however, only increased the evil. Fearing the worst, I begged the confessor to stay by her that night with her sister. Next day she was quite free from her cough, for which Father Limberg accounted in these words: 'I watched by her side with her sister until midnight. Her cough was so violent and incessant that, not being able to endure it longer, I had recourse to a spiritual remedy, and I commanded her in virtue of obedience to cough no more. At the sound of the word *obedience* she sank down unconscious and lay quiet till morning.'

Her cough came on again in the evening, but only slightly.

" On Friday, Nov. 10th, we were quite anxious about her as she had endured frightful pains in her stigmata all day. Her hands were clenched and death-like, every limb quivered, and she lay unconscious like one dead. Suddenly she sighed : ' Ah ! if I were only free ! if I could only pray before the Blessed Sacrament !'—Father Limberg replied : ' Do it, you are free !'—These rather indefinite words carried with them no strength to the invalid, and she said supplicatingly : ' May I ? Shall I ?'—I begged him to order her in virtue of obedience. He did so, when she sprang upon her knees and began to pray with extended arms. The sight of her kneeling and praying in such a state had in it something truly impressive. Fearing the consequences of such an effort, Father Limberg bade her lie down, and down she sank without a movement. When returned to consciousness, she said that she felt as if she were dead inside. A poultice steeped in hot brandy was laid on her breast, and at ten o'clock that evening I gave her eight drops of musk."

Her desires for Holy Communion were often most touchingly expressed. One day, her ardor was so intense that she was involuntarily transported in spirit to the church. Kneeling before the tabernacle, she was about to open it and communicate herself, when suddenly seized with terror at the thought of its being an unlawful act, she awoke to consciousness and implored Father Limberg's permission to confess. He dissuaded her, saying it was all a dream ; but it was not without difficulty that he succeeded in calming her.

During the octave of All-Saints, Father Limberg left Dülmen for a few days. Sister Emmerich dared not communicate in his absence, as she feared having yielded to impatience on her sister's account. In consequence of this privation, she became, to use Dr. Wesener's words, "so weak and miserable, her pulse so low, that we feared death." But when Father Limberg returned and she had confessed and communicated, she regained her strength and soon was bright as ever.

Not only in the spiritual life was Sister Emmerich passively obedient to her confessor. In everything without exception, she sought to regulate her conduct by his directions. Her longing for religious obedience had increased with her inability to practise it. To every creature she desired to submit for the love of God, and with this view she was ever perseveringly on the alert to sacrifice her own will in the daily incidents of life. Her perfect abandonment to God was not only a burning act of love, it was a fact, a reality in her existence, and every instant brought her fresh occasions for its heroic practice. Her humble forgetfulness of self led her friends to look upon her not as sick and requiring special care ; and, as in her early years her visions and sufferings were never a pretext for dispensing herself from labor, for rising above her lowly station, so now her actual condition wrought no change in her daily life. Simple, obliging, and industrious, never did she aspire to notice. As she could not without assistance superintend the Abbé Lambert's housekeeping, she had taken her younger sister Gertrude to help her ; but the latter was so inexperienced that the invalid had from her bed to teach her everything appertaining to domestic affairs. Sometimes even, in spite of her insuperable disgust, she was forced to prepare the food herself in the way that she knew the infirm old gentlemen could take it. Her skill in household affairs was intuitive, and she exercised it so well that all were accustomed to call on her for different services ; but no word ever fell from her lips expressive of desire for care or attention toward herself. Renunciation had become her second nature and the joy she felt in serving others was her sweet reward. Gertrud from the very first had accused her of keeping her bed through sloth, and of abstaining from food through fastidiousness. What she had to endure from such an attendant, one can readily imagine. To bear resignedly great sufferings and trials whose cause lies secret, to maintain patience and serenity in the midst of bodily pains, is easier than silently and meekly to endure marks of coldness, explosions of temper, the want of those trifling cares and attentions which cost so little, but whose value is priceless to a sufferer. Dr. Wesener gives us the following details of his first year's attendance on Sister Emmerich :—

" Gertrude Emmerich is weak-minded and hard-hearted, a great annoyance to the invalid and myself ; she has little love and still less respect for her sister, whom she leaves the whole day long without even a drink of water. If there were any fraud going on, Gertrude would surely denounce it. On one occasion, I made some remark to the invalid of her sister's want of feeling for her. She replied that Gertrude would, indeed, be the first to witness against her, did she discover the least hypocrisy, for that she treated her not as a sister but as an enemy. Gertrude cannot endure her sister's admonitions. I must say that I cannot put up with the girl's whimsical and contradictory humor. Sister Emmerich has to help her in every duty. I have often found her myself preparing on her bed dishes made up of milk, flour, and eggs. This gives rise to suspicion, and the poor Abbé Lambert cannot bear to see her attending to such things ; but if she does not do so, his wants would not be cared for. She cannot endure the odor of cooking, it is

one of her greatest torments. I found her once coughing
convulsively, because her sister had approached her im-
pregnated with the smell of warm bread just taken from
the oven. She was generally affected in the same way
when the door was left open and the fumes of the kitchen
reached her. One morning I found her perfectly exhausted from coughing all the preceding night, Gertrude
having blown out a wax candle by her bedside and left the
wick smoking."

Six years later, Clement Brentano wrote :—

" One of the invalid's greatest crosses was her sister Gertrude, whom she endured sorrowfully and compassionately.
Gertrude had a most unhappy disposition. Her sister strove
by suffering, patience, and prayer to obtain for her a
change of heart. Day and night was she at the mercy of
this creature, and owing to her terrible gift of reading hearts,
she saw her interior state, a sight which greatly added to
her torment. Not till after her death were Sister Emmerich's prayers answered, and Gertrude became a changed
person."

Gertrude had a perfect mania to make her sister eat.
Sister Emmerich often suffered for the dying, who had not
expiated their sins of intemperance in eating and drinking,
and her expiatory pains were then characterized by the
physical and moral consequences of this vice. She was
sometimes haunted by the savory odor of delicate dishes ;
again, she was assailed by an irresistible desire to eat ; and,
again, she experienced the irritation of an epicure whose craving for dainties cannot be satiated. These inclinations she
had to combat in the place of their miserable victims for
whom she obtained the grace of a happy death. Sometimes
she was consumed by thirst, and if she attempted to drink,
strangulation and retching followed which almost cost her her

life. Gertrude, in her stupid indifference, often forced her to eat when, absorbed in contemplation, the poor sufferer knew not what she was doing. It was more through obedience than ignorance that she accepted the food. Father Limberg's directions to her were that she should not reject her sister's attentions, and so she passively submitted to Gertrude's whims. Dr. Wesener gives several instances of this :—

"May 30, 1814—I found the invalid quite unconscious, in a pitiable state. I suspected that her obstinate sister had been worrying her, and I was right. Father Limberg told me that she had forced her to take some sour-krout. It was not till the following night that she was relieved.

"Sept. 2d—Again Sister Emmerich lay almost dead. Her pulse scarcely indicated life, and when at last she threw off some morsels of food, Gertrude explained : ' I made a ragout for the Abbé and gave her some to taste ; she must have swallowed a little.'

"Oct. 29th—She was this evening ill unto death— nauseated stomach, retching and convulsive coughing. This state came on about noon. On inquiring the cause, I found that during High Mass whilst she lay absorbed in ecstasy, Gertrude had made her taste a vinegar-salad. I sat up with her that night, but I could neither relieve the nausea nor stop the vomiting until some morsels of the salad came off mixed with mucus. Next morning she was alive and that was all. After Holy Communion she rallied a little, but at noon her sufferings recommenced. She was consumed by thirst, racked with terrible pains in stomach and throat, and a sip of water renewed her vomiting. I gave her six drops of musk but with no effect, and I repeated the dose in the evening. She reproached herself for having tasted the salad. I quieted her, telling her that it was not her fault, but Gertrude's want of judgment.

" May 9, 1815—I found the invalid exceedingly prostrate. Father Limberg and her sister were with her all
night, fully expecting to see her die in one of her violent
spells of vomiting. After Holy Communion next morning
she grew better, though I still noticed in her a convulsive
effort to swallow; at last she vomited a brownish liquid,
the cause of all the trouble. Her eldest brother had visited
her the day before and had offered her some beer of which
she had unconsciously swallowed a few drops."

Sister Emmerich never uttered a word of complaint
against her sister when she caused her such pain; on the
contrary, she blamed only her own imprudence. But when
she saw her turning a deaf ear to her sisterly admonitions;
fulfilling so carelessly the duty of her state; obstinately refusing to acknowledge or correct her faults; above all, when
she beheld her approaching the Sacraments in such dispositions, she became very, very sad. The doctor writes, Sept.
26, 1815 :—

"Sister Emmerich was very sad to-day. When I inquired into the cause, she answered : ' I am ready to endure patiently any pain, for I am in this world only to suffer, I even know why I have to do so ; but the thought, I
may say the conviction, that my poor sister grows worse
near me instead of better, makes me tremble.' I tried to
comfort her, saying that God would never allow her sister
to be lost, that she would surely change after awhile, that
perhaps just now she was the instrument He made use of
to advance her in perfection, etc. My words appeared to console her."

Sister Emmerich had no third person to whom she might
appeal when Gertrude became quite insupportable. The
Abbé was too kind and indulgent and, besides, he knew too
little German to interfere ; Father Limberg was naturally

too timid to assume any kind of authority over the head-
strong girl; and good Dean Overberg saw in her the
touchstone of her sister's humility, the instrument by which
Almighty God willed to purify her soul from every imperfection. So far as her reverend friends were concerned,
she could look to them for no redress, and yet an arbiter
was needed in the daily encounters that took place between
the poor invalid and the perverse Gertrude; so she begged
Dean Overberg to constitute Doctor Wesener judge, since
he knew her domestic affairs and could decide all differences.
The doctor very unwillingly and only in compliance with
her earnest entreaties consented to take upon himself the
thankless office.

"One day," so runs his journal, "I very gently and
cautiously made a few remarks to Gertrude on her ill-humor,
her want of obedience, etc., when she assumed an air of
surprise and wounded feeling, declared it her natural disposition, and that there was no harm in it. I reasoned with
her, recounting some instances of her perversity, but all in
vain. She even seemed to triumph in the fact of having
aroused her sister's indignation." Sister Emmerich regarded the office the doctor had accepted as a very serious one,
and she tearfully accused herself to him whenever she thought
she had yielded to impatience. He wrote as follows some
months later to Dean Overberg :—

"If it depended on me, I should long ago have banished
that evil spirit, Gertrude ; but whenever I proposed it, the
invalid would beg me to be patient. 'I alone am to blame !'
she would say. 'It is one of my trials, it is God's will.' I
think, however, that she should be sent away; an angel could
not put up with her. I shall give you, as an instance of her
difficult temper, something that happened lately. Gertrude
had shown ill-humor a whole morning, and the invalid had

meekly borne with her. In the afternoon Sister Emmerich set about mending something for the poor. She asked her sister to help her, showing her at the same time what she wanted done; but Gertrude saw fit to do just the opposite, and recklessly cut away the good part of the garment instead of what she was told. The invalid drew her attention to it and, taking up the scissors, she began to cut away the worn parts; whereupon Gertrude showed such obstinacy and insolence, that her sister took the work from her hands a little quickly, and the scissors fell to the floor. What a triumph for Gertrude! She picked them up and returned them with a taunting air, intimating that they had been thrown at her. This almost crushed the poor invalid. She became weak as death, and it was only after having confessed and communicated that she regained her strength. Such instances are by no means rare. Something must be done. The Abbé and FatherLimberg are too easy, they let things come and go."

Dean Overberg, on the reception of the above, was ready to consent to Gertrude's being sent away, but Sister Emmerich herself dared not separate from her sister without an express order from her angel. She bore with her daily and hourly annoyances until one year before her death when she was authorized by her guide to send her away. Almighty God generally places those whom He destines for high perfection in such situations as may be for them a school of spiritual renunciation and mortification, in which by constant struggling against their own weakness they acquire the virtues they need most. We see Maria Bagnesi in a situation parallel to that of Sister Emmerich. Her nurse exacted of her the most menial services. Having been for years a servant in her parents' house, she thought herself authorized to claim in her turn the services of their

daughter. When scarcely able to endure her pains,
Maria was ordered to bring wood and water, get ready the
meals, in short attend to all the domestic affairs, whilst
the servant herself went gossiping in the neighborhood.
Woe to Maria if on her return she found not things to suit
her! Then came explosions of rage to which the child opposed only gentle entreaties to be forgiven for the love of
Jesus! When forced to keep her bed by fever, or the excruciating pains of the stone, Maria could get not even a
glass of water from her hard-hearted nurse, and as she lay
parched and dying of thirst, the cats entering by the window brought her meat and cheese, as if compassionating
her state. One word from Maria would have rid her of the
insupportable woman. But she dared not utter it, knowing
well that she could not find a better opportunity for the
practice of meekness and patience. These daily trials were
for Maria and Anne Catherine what the meadow buds and
flowers are to the busy little bee. They drew thence that
ineffable spiritual unction by whose means they poured the
honey of consolation into the hearts of all that approached
them. Their exterior life was, without doubt, humble and
commonplace; but, in the sight of God, grand and magnificent, for it is He Himself who in His chosen instruments
labors, suffers, heals, and saves.

CHAPTER XXXII.

Dr. William Wesener.—Mesmerism.

Let us turn our attention to Dr. Wesener, a man who holds so prominent a place in Sister Emmerich's life, and to whom we owe the knowledge of many interesting facts. As we have seen, the first report of her extraordinary state had drawn him to her bedside, and a more intimate acquaintance with her had won him back to the faith and to the practice of his religious duties. Deeply grateful for the spiritual favors she had obtained for him, he made her case his careful study, noting down not only such facts as proved to him her rare perfection, but also those incidents and conversations which influenced his own progress in virtue. His simple memoranda, like those of Clement Brentano, five years later, show by what means Sister Emmerich gained souls to God. It would be difficult to imagine two individuals more dissimilar in talents and inclinations than the physician of Dülmen and the poet Brentano, so rich in natural gifts ; yet both aver that their connection with the stigmatisée, brought about by apparently fortuitous circumstances, was a most merciful dispensation of Divine Providence in their regard, one most fruitful in happy consequences.

The following are some of the doctor's own words :—

" It was in 1806 that I first heard of Sister Emmerich. I was then practising in Reklinghausen, where the attendant physician of Agnetenberg, Dr. Krauthausen, consulted me upon the inexplicable phenomena displayed in one of its inmates, Sister Emmerich. I had been reading an article on magnetism in " Reil's Archives," and I mentioned to him certain cataleptic cases to which, however, he paid but little attention. He was a stern old man and attended the convent gratuitously ; this was one of the reasons why Sister Emmerich felt obliged to accept his medicines, although at her own expense. He enumerated a long list of her maladies, each marked by its own special character. Scarcely was she cured of one, when she was seized by another. At the moment in which death seemed inevitable, they took a favorable turn, although medical skill seemed to exercise no appreciable influence upon them.

" On March 21, 1813, I visited her for the first time. I had heard her stigmata spoken of in a certain assembly. She lay in bed unconscious ; but on returning to herself, she regarded me with a frank expression, and when the Abbé Lambert introduced me she said smiling, that she knew me well. I thought her remark rather singular, and putting it down as a silly pleasantry, I assumed a grave demeanor. There was however no need for any such proceeding, and as I became better acquainted with her I was convinced of her candor and uprightness. She was a simple, truly Christian soul, at peace with herself and all around her, seeing in everything the will of God, and looking upon herself as inferior to every one. I shall never forget her kindness in calming my fears concerning the war. She often assured me most positively that Napoleon would soon fall and that Dülmen would be spared by the French. Her prediction was remarkably verified. In the French garrison at Minden were numbers of lawless bandits ; they committed many outrages at Dorsten, but passed by Dülmen without even entering the town.

"In our communications I always found Sister Em-

merich simple and natural, kind and gracious toward every
one, particularly the poor, the sick, and the unfortunate.
It is only lately that I have been able to understand her
ability to take upon herself the sufferings of others. She
possessed in a high degree the gift of imparting consolation
as I myself often experienced, for she reanimated my confidence in God, taught me how to pray, and thus lightened
in no small degree the heavy crosses which my natural inclination to sadness aggravated Her life was wholly
in God. The publicity given to her miraculous state
greatly annoyed her. She was constantly employed in
relieving the miseries, corporal and spiritual, of the crowds
that flocked to her. Her heart was free from creatures ;
consequently, it is not hard to divine the source whence
flowed the consolation she dispensed to her neighbor.

"In our first interview, she exhorted me to confidence.
Smiling sweetly, she said : ' God is infinitely merciful !
Whoever repents and has a good will finds favor in His
sight !' She begged me to help the poor, a work so pleasing
to God, saying with a. sigh : ' There never was so little love
of the neighbor as at present, although it is so beautiful a
virtue, whilst indifference or contempt is so great a vice.' She
protested that the Catholic faith alone is true, the only one
that leads to salvation, and she spoke warmly of the incom
parable happiness of belonging to the Catholic Church : 'Let us
trust in God !' she used to say. ' Let us hold to our holy
faith ! Is there anything more consoling upon earth ?
What religion or what philosophy could indemnify us for
its loss ? I pity the Jews above all others. They are
worse off, they are blinder than the pagans themselves ;
their religion is now only a fable of the rabbis, the curse of
God rests upon them. But how good is Our Lord to us !
He meets us half-way if we have a good will, the abund-

ance of His graces depends only upon our own desire.
Even a pagan may be saved if, sincerely desirous to serve
God, the Sovereign Lord and Creator, he follows the natural light infused by Him, and practises justice and charity
toward his neighbor.'

"Once I turned the conversation upon prayer. I remarked that, according to my ideas, true prayer consisted in
the accomplishment of duty and the exercise of charity
toward the neighbor, and that I felt curious to know how
she could spend entire hours in it, forgetful of all around,
lost, so to speak, in God. She replied. ' Think a moment !
May not a man become so absorbed in a beautiful book as
to be unconscious of aught else ? But if he converse with
God Himself, the Source of all beauty, how is it possible
for him not to be wholly lost in Him ? Begin by adoring
Him in all humility, the rest will come.' I then spoke of
the temptations man has to endure from the evil one, and
she replied :—' True, the enemy tries to hinder prayer ;
the more fervent it is, the more does he multiply his
attacks. Something of this was shown me one day. I was
in a beautiful church in which three females were kneeling
in prayer; behind them stood a horrible figure. It caressed
the first who immediately fell asleep ; it then tried the same
with the second, though not so successfully ; but the third it
struck and abused so cruelly that I was filled with pity. Surprised, I asked my guide what it all meant, and he answered
that it was symbolical of prayer. The first was neither
earnest nor fervent, and the devil easily put her to sleep ; the
second was not so bad, but still she was tepid ; the third
was fervent and therefore she was tempted the most
violently, but she conquered. The prayer most pleasing
to God is that made for others and particularly for the poor
souls. Pray for them, if you want your prayers to bring

high interest. As to myself personally, I offer myself to God, my Sovereign Master, saying: ' Lord, do with me what Thou wilt !' Then I remain in sweet security, for the best, the most loving of fathers can only seek my good. The poor souls suffer inexpressibly. The difference between the pains of purgatory and those of hell is this : in hell reigns only despair, whilst in purgatory the hope of deliverance sweetens all. The greatest torment of the damned is the anger of God. Some faint idea of His wrath may be formed from the terror of a defenceless person exposed to the attack of a furious man.'

"I spoke of man's destiny, and she said : ' Do you know why God created us ? For His own glory and our happiness. When the angels fell, God resolved to create man to fill their places. As soon as their number will be equalled by that of the just, the end of the world will come.' I asked her where she had learned that. She answered simply that, in truth, she did not know. In a little conference on indulgences, I remarked that I looked upon them merely as a remission of ancient ecclesiastical penances. She replied: ' They are more than that, for by them we obtain the remission of the punishments awaiting us in purgatory. To gain an indulgence, it is not enough to say some prayers, or perform some good work ; we must approach the Sacraments with true repentance and a firm purpose of amendment without which no indulgence can be gained. I believe that there is an indulgence attached to every good work. A person's good works are as diverse as their number ; and if upon the least of them there flows some little of the merits of Christ, it acquires great value. What we offer to God in union with these infinite merits, however insignificant it may be, is set down to our account and deducted from the punishment awaiting us. I cannot suffi-

ciently deplore the sad blindness of those for whom our holy
Faith has become a chimera. They live in sin, imagining
they can gain Indulgences by certain forms of prayer.
Many Christians will one day behold Turks and pagans who
have lived according to the law of nature, less rigorously
dealt with at God's tribunal than themselves. We possess
grace, and esteem it not; it is, in a certain sense, forced
upon us, and we cast it away. He who spies a little piece
of money in the dust, runs quickly, stoops, and picks it up;
but if the grace of eternal salvation were lying at his feet,
he would carefully shun it, in order to follow the vain
amusements of the world. Indulgences are of no avail for
such people and, indeed, the religious practices they perform through stupid routine will serve rather for their condemnation.'

"It is to this blind pursuit of worldly goods that the
following vision seems to refer:—' I found myself in a great,
broad field where I could see all around. It was crowded
with people, all striving in different ways to attain their
ends. In the centre of the field stood Our Lord full of
sweetness. He said to me: ' Behold how these people exert
and torment themselves after gain and happiness! They
pay no attention to Me, their Master and Benefactor,
although they see Me here before them. Only a few regard me with grateful feelings and even they thank me only
in passing, as if giving a paltry alms.' Then approached
some priests on whom Our Lord bestowed special attention;
but they threw him something, passed on quickly and mingled with the crowd. One alone went up to Him, but with
an indifferent air. Our Lord laid His hand on his shoulder,
and said: ' Why fly from me? Why slight me? I love
you so!'

"' Then the vision vanished. But I have had many such

on the life of the clergy of the present day which made me
very sad. Owing to the spirit of the world and tepidity,
if the Saviour returned to earth to-day to announce His
doctrine in person, He would find as many opponents as
He did among the Jews.'

" I once heard her relate the following vision upon the
teachings of our times : ' My guide led me to a stately edifice : " Enter, he said, and I shall show you the doctrines of
men." We entered a spacious hall filled with pupils and
professors. A warm dispute was going on; loud words,
contradictory statements resounded on all sides. I saw into
the hearts of the professors and, to my amazement. I discovered in each a little black casket. In the centre of the
hall stood a female of imposing appearance, who took a
foremost part in the discussion. I paused a few moments
with my guide to listen, when to my surprise I saw the
audience disappearing, one by one. The hall itself began
almost imperceptibly to fall to ruins, the floor was no longer safe. The professors mounted a story higher where
they continued their debate with renewed ardor ; but there,
too, the building began to crumble. I trembled on seeing
myself standing on a worm-eaten plank, and I begged my
guide to save me. He reassured me and led me to a place
of safety. Then I asked him the meaning of the little
black casket. " It signifies," he said, " presumption and the
spirit of contradiction. The female is philosophy or, as they
say *pure reason*, which seeks to regulate all things by its
own formulas. These professors follow her teachings and
not those of truth, the precious treasure handed down by
tradition." Then my guide conducted me into another hall
in which sat several professors in their chairs. All was
very different here ; the clearness and simplicity of their
words charmed me, order and charity reigned and many

who had left the ruined halls took refuge here. My guide
said : "Here is simple, unadulterated truth which springs
from humility and gives birth to love and all other blessings."'

"One day, I expressed regret at not having a fuller
knowledge of the life of Jesus before His public ministry.
Sister Emmerich replied : 'I know it, I have seen it
even in its smallest details. I know too the history of the
Mother of Jesus. I often wonder how I came by the
knowledge, since I never read it.' She promised to relate
all to me and, once when I got a chance, I reminded her
of it. She began by explaining that it had been made
known to St. Anne that the Messiah would be born of her
posterity. 'Anne had several children,' she said, ' but she
knew that the true child of benediction was not yet born ;
therefore, she prayed, fasted, and offered sacrifice to obtain
the promised blessing. She had no children for about
eighteen years, which circumstance rendered her very sad ;
but in humility she attributed the non-fulfilment of the
promise to her own sins. Joachim went to Jerusalem to
offer expiatory sacrifice in the Temple, but he was repulsed.
Overwhelmed with sadness, he prayed and received in a
dream the assurance that the promise would be fulfilled.
At the same time Anne received a similar assurance, and
afterward gave birth to the little Mary. Joachim and
Anne saw in the child a pure gift from God. They resolved
to consecrate her to the Lord in the Temple, which they did
in her third year. On reaching the Temple, they attempt
ed to take her little hands to help her to mount the high
steps ; but the child ran on alone. She wore a silk robe of
sky-blue. She was neither sad nor troubled on taking leave
of her parents, but gave herself up quietly to the priests.
She was instructed in everything in the Temple, and with
the other young girls she spent her time in working for it.

When she had reached her fourteenth year, the priests wrote to her parents to take their daughter home, for the Law did not allow any child to remain over that age. Mary would willingly have stayed in the Temple in a state of virginity, but it was not permitted. Her parents were anxious about choosing a spouse worthy of their admirable child; therefore, they repaired to the Temple to seek light from the Most High. Every youth aspiring to Mary's hand, was directed to bear his staff to the Holy of Holies ; but at first no change appeared in any one of them. Prayers and sacrifices were again offered, when a voice was heard saying that the staff of one was still wanting. Search was made and Joseph found. He was of a noble family, but not much thought of by his relatives, because of his simplicity and also on account of his remaining unmarried. His staff was placed in the Holy of Holies. That night it blossomed, and next morning it was surmounted by a white lily. Then Mary was espoused to Joseph, who was filled with joy when she made known to him her vow of perpetual virginity. Mary thought always of the promised Redeemer. In her humility, she prayed to be the handmaid of His chosen Mother. It was on this account that she was so frightened when the angel announced her sublime maternity. She said nothing to Joseph of her visions or of the angel's message.'

"In speaking of alms-giving and of the duties of one's state, Sister Emmerich sometimes alluded to her contemplations. Once she said : 'Use your strength and your means in the service of your patients without, however, wronging your own family ; not one only but many of the poor, call upon you for assistance. Their merit lies in their poverty. Faith teaches that it is an enviable condition, since the Son of God chose it for Himself and gave

to the poor the first title to the kingdom of heaven.'
Then she related some singularly beautiful incidents of
Christ's infancy, for instance that Mary' some days after the
Nativity, hid herself in an underground cave to escape the
gaze of the curious."

It soon became clear that God had placed the doctor
near the invalid, as later on He did Clement Brentano, to
aid her in the accomplishment of her mission. Under her
direction, he distributed not only his own alms among
his poor patients, but also money and clothing supplied by
her for that purpose. Sister Emmerich received an annual
pension of one hundred and eighty thalers which God so
abundantly multiplied that her alms far exceeded that sum.
Day and night was she occupied in works of some kind for
the needy and, when her own slender resources failed her,
she begged materials from others. Her skilful fingers soon
transformed pieces of old silk, etc., into beautiful little caps
for new-born infants. When in need, she used to invoke
with sweet familiarity the assistance of Lidwina, Magdalena von Hadamar, and other holy virgins who had been,
like herself, marked with the sacred stigmata. Addressing them as if really present, she would say : "Is that you,
little Magdalena ? See, it is almost Christmas and there
are still so many children without stockings and caps. You
must keep your promise and bring me some wool and
silk." Never did her petitions go unheeded.

The doctor, convinced by daily experience that she saw
and assisted in spirit every one whom he attended, used to
describe to her the sufferings of his patients. He followed
her advice with the most successful results. He was often
surprised to see unlooked-for recovery, or the alleviation
of maladies. These he ascribed not to his own prescriptions,
but to Sister Emmerich who had taken their sickness upon

herself, either to facilitate their cure or to prepare them for a happy death.

Up to the last he remained a faithful friend and support to the old Abbé Lambert, supplying the remedies his infirmities demanded with such care and charity as could spring only from his deep veneration for Sister Emmerich. This was to her a great consolation. The following incident will prove her interest in the good old priest's welfare, as also her wonderful foreknowledge of approaching danger.

Dr. Wesener's journal, Feb. 15, 1815 :—

"I tried to calm Sister Emmerich's fears for the Abbé, who is suffering from a chronic cough and oppression of the chest. Yesterday he had so severe an attack whilst in her room that he fainted. The confessor was present. He had yielded to her request and remained with her in the afternoon, as she dreaded some approaching danger, and it was fortunate that he did so."

Dr. Wesener's communications with Father Limberg bore very important consequences for the invalid. The timid religious would have abandoned his spiritual daughter at the first sound of the stupid calumnies spread against her, had it not been for the doctor whose experience rendered him deaf and incredulous to all such tales. Father Limberg could not reply coolly and unhesitatingly to the specious arguments and suspicions uttered on all sides. He grew nervous, gave shuffling explanations, and openly declared his desire to withdraw entirely from his connection with Sister Emmerich ; but the doctor's presence always lent him courage. He saw the change produced in the latter by Sister Emmerich's words. The earnestness and fidelity with which he now attended to his religious duties, and his indifference to the world's opinions and judgments greatly encouraged him. His confidence in the doctor

made him impose upon his penitent the obligation of simple
obedience to every prescription, thus placing her in exactly
the same position she had formerly held toward Dr. Krauthausen at Agnetenberg. Again she submitted to all the
remedies employed for her cure. Musk, opium, camphor,
and above all, hot brandy were, in the doctor's estimation
as well as in that of her confessor, the means most conducive to such an end. Truly, they lost sight of the fact that
her miraculous body contained not in itself the germ of
her singular maladies. They sprang only from the tribulations heaped upon the Church. She never complained even
when an aggravation of suffering proved the inefficiency of
their remedies. At such times she was even more grateful
and docile, so that years passed before the doctor and confessor recognized the uselessness of their prescriptions.
We find the following entry in the doctor's journal, May
16, 1814 :—

" The invalid suffers a martyrdom, terrible pains in her
breast and loss of hearing. We thought her at the point
of death several times. Her sufferings are so horrible,
spasms in the throat and stomach, that Father Limberg
wants to administer Extreme Unction, which, however, I
think not yet necessary; meanwhile, though convinced
that remedies are useless, I can no longer remain a passive
spectator of her struggles. She can retain nothing . . . . .
I gave her four drops of musk, but she rejected it even before
swallowing; then I diminished the dose but with no better
success. She suffered terribly all night, her stomach several
times rejected the musk administered ; it was only near
morning that she was able to retain five drops. I found
her in an alarming state of prostration, and I left expecting never again to see her alive. May 18th, she lay insensible almost all day, at intervals vomiting water with

violent retching. I determined to stay by her all night. She grew a little better about midnight, when I read to her from a pious book and spoke to her on religious subjects, which seemed to afford her great relief. On my expressing surprise at this she remarked : 'It is always so. However weak I may be, I am always relieved when God or holy things are spoken of; but if worldly subjects are mentioned, I grow worse.' "

Six years later Clement Brentano witnessed a similar trial of musk of which he highly disapproved. Sister Emmerich said to him : "True, it is particularly disgusting to me, it causes me great suffering. I am always worse after it, but I must take it in obedience to my confessor, although he has often seen what bad effects it has on me."

Shortly after she had a vision of her own past life, of which the following particulars relative to the remedies employed in her case will prove interesting :—"I have had a vision of the sorrowful side of my own life. All that certain persons had ever done to thwart my mission was shown me in pictures in which those persons themselves figured. I had never dared think of them for fear of temptations to aversion. Last night I had to struggle with that temptation, and I had the consolation of hearing it said that I had fought well. The pictures were shown me in various ways; sometimes as if a past trial had actually returned, sometimes people busy among themselves, and again it seemed to be a recital. I saw all I had lost thereby both in my life and spiritual work and what harm such or such a one had done me, although I was not aware of it at the time. What I had only suspected, I now saw for a certainty. It cost me much to endure again the agony of the past, the falsehood and wickedness of men. I had not only to crush every feeling of resentment, but to foster the most sincere affection for my cruel enemies.

" The vision began with my religious profession and all that my parents had done to prevent it. They had tried my patience and secretly hoped to hinder me. The nuns had made me suffer. I saw their great perversity. At first, they abused me ; and, when my state became known, they honored me immoderately, but without refraining from their gossiping. It made me so sad, for I loved them. I saw the physician of the convent, and how hurtful his prescriptions were to me. I saw the second physician and his medicines ruinous to my chest. My breast seemed to be quite hollow, and I felt that without care I could not last long. I would have been cured of all my maladies without medical treatment, if only the Church's remedies had been applied.

" I saw how wrong it was to expose me to the public gaze, to people who regarded only my wounds without taking other circumstances into consideration, and I saw how I had been forced to show them to curious visitors, a proceeding which had disturbed my recollection without benefiting any one. It would have been much better had they left me in peace. I saw the prayers and entreaties which I made not of myself, but in obedience to an interior warning. All was useless ; and, contrary to my better judgment, I was made a spectacle to the world. The greatest humiliations accrued to me from it. What I did sorrowfully and only in obedience was cast up to me as effrontery, and they who constrained me to show my signs uttered no word in my defence."

Such contemplations never affected Sister Emmerich's actual position. She endured the same absurd treatment as before, and the physician's remedies remained **unchanged.**

But her soul was enlightened. She recognized in persons
and events instruments and means destined by Almighty
God to advance her to her end, if she faithfully availed
herself of them. Her angel among other instructions
ordered her never to refuse remedies, a command
in strict accordance with the divine economy. The
representative of the Church, she was called upon to
expiate the sins of men who, by their principles, their
teachings, their baneful designs and measures, sought to
exercise over it an influence analogous to that produced
upon herself by the musk, the opium, and the brandy lo-
tions. She knew that her expiation would be so much
the more efficacious, the more simply and unhesitatingly
she submitted to every prescription ; therefore, we detect
in her neither resistance nor contradiction. When we reflect upon the waves of destruction that threatened the
Church at this period ; when we recall the ravages produced
by the unwholesome spirit of philosophy, the factitious exaltation of false mysticism, which generally ended in monstrous
depravity, we are involuntarily led to recognize in the opium
and disgusting liquor a striking symbol of these false doctrines.

To struggle against the dangers arising from mesmerism
formed also a part of Sister Emmerich's task, since both
her physician and confessor were the first to resort to it after
their vain use of opium and musk. Dr. Wesener tells us :—

"Father Limberg told me that, whilst the invalid lay apparently in a cataleptic state, he tried several mesmeric
experiments upon her, but without success. Then I determined to make some myself the first chance I should get.
I did so a few days later when she lay rigid in ecstasy. I
pronounced a few words on the pit of her stomach and the
extremities of her toes ; I laid the tips of the fingers of my

right hand upon the pit of her stomach and spoke some words upon the tips of the fingers of her left hand ; I called into her ear, but none of these actions produced the slightest impression upon her. At my request, her confessor made the same experiments, though with no better success; but, when he pronounced the word *obedience,* she trembled, sighed, and returned to consciousness. He asked what ailed her, and she answered : ' I have been called !' "

No further attempts of the kind were made until the following January, when the invalid fell into such a state of misery that neither the confessor nor physician could endure the sight. Daily for weeks she experienced suffocation and convulsive pains around her heart. Death seemed inevitable, and Communion alone enabled her to battle against her frightful pains. Not the poor invalid, but her confessor and physician at last began to lose patience. The doctor reports, January 26th :—

"I was with her this evening ; she was very ill, her pulse low. A kind of trance came on about five o'clock. Her eyes were open, but so void of sensation that I could touch the cornea with my finger without the eyelids closing. The day before she told me that her sight was so wonderfully piercing that, even with closed eyes, she could see. The trance lasted an hour, when she fell into ecstasy, arose on her knees, and prayed with extended arms. I prevailed upon Father Limberg once more to have recourse to mesmerism, to ask her the nature of her malady, and where it was principally seated. He did so several times and insisted upon an answer, but none came. I then begged him to command her in *obedience.* Scarcely had the word escaped his lips than she started and awoke with a sigh. To the question why she appeared frightened, she answered : 'I heard a loud voice calling me.' Again she relapsed into unconsciousness, and I administered twelve drops of musk. Next morning she said she had had vertigo all night from weakness."

There was no human remedy for Sister Emmerich's sufferings, since their origin lay not in physical evils, but in the sins of others. When her convulsions ceased, vomiting ensued and she threw off a watery liquid, although literally unable to swallow a drop of water to slack her burning thirst. Until February 9th, she daily lay for several hours in profound ecstasy which, on that day, was prolonged nine consecutive hours. She gave the following explanation to her confessor, as also to the doctor whose skill was completely baffled:—

"Thursday, Feb. 8th, as I was saying my Hours, my thoughts turned upon our utter unworthiness and God's infinite mercy and forbearance, and I was quite overwhelmed by the reflection that, in spite of His mercy, so many souls are lost forever. I began to beg grace for the unhappy creatures when, all at once, I saw my cross hanging there on the bed-post (1) surrounded by a bright light. I was wide awake, in my senses, and I said to myself: 'Is it not a mere fancy?' and I went on saying my Office, though the light dazzled me. At last, I knew it was not an illusion, and I began to pray fervently. I asked God, my Saviour, for grace and mercy for all mankind and above all, for poor, weak, straying souls. The cross grew brighter. I beheld a figure attached to it and blood streaming from the wounds, though not falling below the cross. I redoubled my prayers and acts of adoration, when the right arm of the figure stretched forth and described a circle as if to embrace the whole world. I was fully awake and conscious all the time. I noticed certain things around

(1) A little silver reliquary containing two small particles of the True Cross.

me, and I counted the hour every time the clock struck.
The last I heard was half-past eleven, after which I knew
no more, as I fell into contemplation on the Passion of
Christ. I saw it in a picture before my eyes, just as it
had really taken place. I saw the Saviour carrying His
Cross. I saw Veronica consoling, and Simon helping Him.
I saw Him extend His limbs and allow Himself to be nailed
to it. It pierced my inmost soul, though my grief was not
without a sentiment of joy. I saw Our Lord's Mother and
several of her relations. I adored my Lord Jesus, begging
pardon for myself and all mankind. Then He said to me :
' Behold here My love, it knows no bounds ! All, all, come
to My arms ! I will make all happy !' And then I saw
how most men turn rudely away from His embrace. At
the commencement of this apparition, I begged the Lord
to put an end to the horrors of war, to give us peace, and
again I implored His grace and mercy ; thereupon, a
voice said to me : ' The war is not yet over. Many countries will still groan under it ! But pray and have confidence !'—And now I firmly believe that Münster and Dülmen will not suffer from it."

The Abbé Lambert and Gertrude say that, during the
whole time the above apparition lasted, from ten a. m. till
about five p. m., she lay quite still. From ten till noon her
eyes were open, her face flushed ; but from noon till five
her eyes were closed, and tears flowed down her cheeks.

Feb. 8th was the Thursday before Septuagesima. On
this day she was accustomed to receive her task for the
holy time of Lent, which she accepted eagerly for the salvation of souls. The foregoing details, related to the doctor
on her confessor's command, determined the former to desist for the time being from further experiments in mesmerism. Neither he nor Father Limberg dared mention to her

their unsuccessful attempts which, it was evident, had not
in the least affected her ; so they allowed the affair to pass
unnoticed. A year later a medical friend of Neeff and
Passavant arrived in Dülmen with the express object of
making observations on the stigmatisee whom they believed
a suitable subject for mesmerism. This physician was something of a fanatic respecting Neeff's theory of somnambulism
and mesmerism in which he pretended to have found such
confirmation of Christianity as to compel his belief in its
doctrines. As he possessed the gift of persuasiveness in
no slight degree he found little difficulty in winning Father
Limberg and the doctor to his own way of thinking, and
both acknowledged that views so elevated had never before
been presented to them upon the subject. They were on the
point of adopting the mesmeric regime, when a higher
wisdom interposed to establish the unerring truth, which
facts we glean from Dr. Wesener's journal. He says:—

" Holy Saturday, April 5th, 1817, Dean Rensing announced a visit from a physician of Frankfort with an
introduction from the Vicar General. The invalid was so
afflicted that she implored me to represent to the Dean how
very painful such a visit would be to her. But he paid no
attention to her words and reiterated his orders through me.
She was distressed, but she soon regained her cheerfulness,
saying : ' Well, I submit in obedience ! '—and she begged
me to come with the stranger, as she could not talk to him.
Some hours after I introduced him to her. He was so struck
by her appearance that he fell on his knees to kiss her hand.
She withdrew it hurriedly and rebuked him gently for his enthusiasm, saying that she could not understand how a sensible
man could bestow marks of respect on one like her—' What
temptations I have to endure ! What trials of patience and
humility ! But now come others of a different kind.' "

A few days later, Dr. Wesener again records in his journal:—

"Dr. N. has convinced Father Limberg and myself that the science of mesmerism is nothing more than the flowing of certain vital spirits upon the sick. This spirit pervades all nature and the invalid receives it through a spiritual or even corporal communication. It acts upon the recipient according to the nature of the principle from which it springs, enkindling flame which belongs either to the earth or to the higher or lower regions, and operating accordingly either salutary or pernicious effects. This vital principle the Christian can and ought to kindle by religion and the love of God and the neighbor, in such a way as to render it salutary to soul and body."

The doctor knew, however, by repeated experience what possessed the power of inflaming his patient, for shortly before he had noted in his journal the following lines :— "I found Sister Emmerich to-day flushed as if on fire. I asked the cause and received the answer : ' Dean Overberg was here, we spoke only of God ! It excited me, but I do not feel sick.' " But now Dr. Wesener came supported by her confessor and, full of the new discovery, the mesmeric vital principle, explained it to her with so much warmth that she soon perceived the dangerous ground on which they were both standing. She maintained a prudent silence, listened patiently to their arguments in favor of the new science, and answered only when her angel ordered her to do so. It is again from the doctor's notes that we learn the following :—

"On a subsequent visit, the invalid asked me to remain awhile, as she had something to communicate. ' You have seen,' she began, ' how I received what you have all told me about mesmerism. I have not concealed my indifference, though I am pleased that you try to present it in its moral bearing. But now I shall communicate to you what I have been told in vision for the third time concerning it. The first vision presented it in an unfavorable light; the second filled me with terror; and in the third, last night, my angel showed me that almost everything connected with mesmerism is an illusion of the devil. I hope to have the strength to relate it in detail. For the present, I can only say that, if we desire to imitate the prophets and Apostles in their works, we must imitate them also in their life; then we would have no need of a mesmerizer's manipulations, the holy name of Jesus would be sufficient. There is no harm in trying to effect a cure by transmitting something from the healthy to the sick; but the juggling connected with such an attempt is both foolish and unlawful. The mesmeric sleep which affords a glimpse of distant and future things comes from the devil, who clothes it with the semblance of piety to gain adherents and, above all, to ensnare the good.'—She spoke in so impressive a style that I remarked that perhaps I ought to discontinue the mesmeric treatment I had begun on a young peasant-girl whose arm was paralyzed. She inquired how I conducted the operation. I told her that I made certain movements of my hands, described circles, and breathed upon the affected part; that the patient drank mesmerized water and wore on her lame arm a band of mesmerized flannel. She replied: ' The breathing upon the arm and warming it with the hands, I think strictly natural remedies; but the passes and circles I condemn as unreasonable and leading to superstition.'—When I asked her opinion of the strange physician's views, she answered: ' We must beware of intemperate, ill advised zeal in his regard; but I feel that he will return to the truth, that I shall be of use to him.''

The foregoing conversation made so deep an impression upon Dr. Wesener that he forgot his patient's admonition not to make known to Dr. N. her decision too bluntly. He communicated all she had said in the plainest terms, to the stranger's extreme surprise and vexation, as he entertained a high opinion of the piety of a certain somnambulist of Frankfort. Far from losing confidence in his favorite theory, he replied warmly that it could not be thought that men of such consideration as many of its most zealous supporters, had anything in common with the evil spirit. He declared that Sister Emmerich had looked only on the dark side of mesmerism, but that its bright side might be exhibited with her confessor's assistance by the imposition of hands and the sacerdotal benediction, which he denominated the " mesmeric healing process." Although Father Limberg had for years experienced his penitent's wonderful sensitiveness to the blessings and prayers of the Church, yet now, strange to say, he was tempted to ascribe their efficacy to the " mesmeric vital principle." He had been accustomed to use the power conferred on him by Holy Orders only when she was thought to be in extremity ; but now, blinded by novelty, he submitted her to the " healing mesmeric process " on every occasion. Sister Emmerich was not a little saddened by proceedings so extravagant and, at last, on a formal command from her angel to that effect, she warned her confessor to desist from such folly. It had been said to her in vision : " God wills that you patiently endure your sufferings. Your confessor must do nothing more than hitherto !" She related the following vision :—

" I was in a spacious hall, like a church, crowded with people. Some grave looking personages were going around and obliging others to leave the church. I was surprised, and on asking why they sent away people who looked so good and knew how to speak so beautifully, one of the grave-looking men answered: 'They have no right here, they are in delusion; and even if they spoke with the tongues of angels, yet their doctrines are false.' The stranger, Dr. N — was among those going to be turned out. I felt very sorry for him and I ran to his assistance. Some persons near tried to prevent me, saying it would not be proper, but I would not be restrained. I said: 'His soul's salvation is at stake'—and I kept him from being expelled."

This vision was very remarkably verified; for, in spite of their seeming inclination toward Catholicism, in spite of their plausible arguments, most of the members of the circle, bewitched by the mesmeric system, died out of the Church. Dr. N. alone, helped by Sister Emmerich's prayers, found another and more solid basis for his faith than mesmerism, to which he had heretofore ascribed the wonders wrought by God in His saints. Father Limberg never after tried any other experiment on his spiritual daughter than that of the Church's blessing, and the doctor also was cured of his enthusiasm for the new theory. His journal contains after this date only the following lines on the subject: "You may make use of the imposition of hands and insufflation when perfectly assured that it will be a cause of temptation neither to yourself nor your patient."

The following are the visions in which Sister Emmerich learned the real nature of animal magnetism, or mesmerism, the degradation into which it plunges the soul, and the dangers thereby incurred.

"The first I heard of mesmerism was from the strange doctor. Whenever he mentioned the clairvoyant and her friends, a feeling of repugnance arose in my soul, I knew not why. This clairvoyant was then shown me, I was en-

lightened with regard to her state. I saw that it was anything but pure or from God. I saw that sensuality
and vanity, though she would by no means acknowledge it,
had the greatest share in it and that without being aware of
it, she cherished too great an affection for her mesmerizer.
Scattered here and there in the distance, I saw as if
through a magnifying-glass other clairvoyants either
sitting or reclining, some having before them a glass with
a tube which they held in their hands. The impression
produced upon me was one of horror which arose, not so
much from the nature of the thing in itself, as from the
temptations it excited and to which its victims almost always yielded. The mesmerizer's jestures before his patient's eyes, his passes, the stroking of the hand, etc., were
so repulsive to me that I cannot express it. I saw the interior of both, the influence of one upon the other, the
communication of their nature and evil inclinations. I
always saw Satan directing the mesmerizer's manipulations
and making them with him.

"In vision these clairvoyants are very different from me.
If on entering into contemplation they have the least impure thought, they see only lies, for it is the demon who
presents their visions to them and glosses all over with a
fine appearance. If a clairvoyant has formed a desire of
saying something to render herself famous, or if she enter-
tains the least sensual feeling, she is instantly exposed to sin.
Some do, indeed, experience bodily relief; but the majority,
unknown to themselves, derive results pernicious to their
soul. The horror these things excite in me can only be compared to that which a certain secret society and its practices
inspire. I perceive the corruption, but I cannot describe it.

" Mesmerism is allied to magic ; the only difference between the two is this : in the latter the devil is invoked, in

the former he comes uninvited. Whoever delivers himself
up to mesmerism takes from nature that which can be lawfully acquired only in the Church of Jesus Christ, for the
power of healing and sanctifying is preserved only in her
bosom. Now, for all who are not in living union with Jesus
Christ by faith and grace, nature is full of Satan's influence.
Persons in the mesmeric state see nothing in its essence and
dependence on God ; what they see they behold in an
isolated, separated condition as if through a hole or a chink.
They perceive, as it were, a gleam of things, and God
grant that this light be pure, be holy ! It is one of God's
favors to have veiled us from one another, to have raised
walls of separation between us, since we incline to sin, are
so readily influenced by one another. It is well that we
have to act independently before communicating the con-
tagion of our evil inclinations. But in Jesus Christ, the
God-Man, we have our Head in whom purified and sanctified, we may all become one, one single body without our
sins and bad inclinations infecting the union. Whoever
tries to remove this barrier raised by God unites himself in
a most dangerous manner to fallen nature over which reigns
the author of its ruin, the devil with all his seductions.

" I see that the essence of mesmerism is true ; but there is
a thief unchained in its veiled light. All union between
sinners is dangerous, but the mutual penetration into one
another's interior is still more so. When this happens to
an upright soul, when one becomes a clairvoyant only
through simplicity and inexperience, a prey to artifice
and intrigue, then one of man's faculties possessed before
the fall, a faculty not entirely extinct, is in a certain measure resuscitated, and he lies helpless in a most mysterious
state, exposed to the attacks of the evil one. This state
really exists, but it is veiled, because it is a poisoned source

for all but the saints.   I feel that the state of these persons is, in certain particulars, parallel with my own, but springing from another source, tending toward a different end, and followed by very different consequences.   The sin of a man in his natural state is an act accomplished by the senses.   His interior light is not obscured by it.   It stings the conscience, it urges to other acts of the senses, repentance and penance; it leads to the supernatural remedies which the Church administers under sensible forms in the Sacraments.   The senses are the sinners, the interior light is the accuser.

" But in the mesmeric state, when the senses are for the time dead, when the interior light both receives and reflects impressions, then that which is holiest in man is exposed to the baneful influence of the evil spirit.   The soul cannot fall under such influence by means of the senses subjected as they are to the laws of time and space.   In such a state, the mesmeric, it cannot have recourse to the purifying remedies of the Church.   I do, indeed, see that a pure soul in God's grace cannot be hurt by the devil even in this state; but I also see that if, before entering it (and it may easily happen, especially to females) the individual has consented to the least temptation, Satan freely carries on his game in the soul, dazzling it with an appearance of sanctity.   Her visions are false and if, perchance, she discovers therein a means of healing the body, she purchases her knowledge at the price of her immortal soul; she is sullied by necromantic relations with her mesmerizer."

Females under the influence of mesmerism were often shown Sister Emmerich in vision that she might pray for them and labor to prevent the ulterior consequences of such practices.   She was always ready to help them, but never willing to be brought into contact with them either in the nat-

ural state or in vision. Once only when Dr. N. was boasting of his clairvoyant's *holy* visions, she said :—

"I wish she were here before me, her fine visions would
soon cease, and she would discover by whom she is deceived.
I have often seen her in my visions on this subject. I
see that, when in the mesmeric state, Satan cast his spells
over her whilst she takes him for an angel of light."

On one of his journeys Dr. Wesener met Dr. Neeff, the
mezmerizer of the clairvoyant mentioned above. He pointed out to him her danger and the latter resolved to go to
Dülmen himself to study the resemblance between Sister
Emmerich and his own patient. On his arrival he informed
the sister that his clairvoyant could discern remedies for
all diseases, that she was in communication with the blessed, that she was conducted by her own angel and the angel
of her mesmerizer through worlds of light, and that she received a species of sacrament from "The Holy Grail!"
Sister Emmerich shuddered. She tried sweetly and gently
to impress him with the immense danger both he and his patient ran (they were Protestants) but she did not succeed.
The doctor, completely infatuated by his mesmeric powers,
appealed to the good intentions which animated his patient
and himself, to the precautions they took before beginning
their operations, begging God to preserve them from the
snares of the evil one, etc. He declared that his clairvoyant
was led by a way that daily became more luminous, more
sublime, and he skilfully evaded a closer examination into the
nature of his practices. In vain did Sister Emmerich protest against the celestial nourishment and luminous worlds,
which she stigmatized as diabolical illusions ; the doctor
turned a deaf ear to her warnings and went his way.

"When such persons are shown me," said the invalid,
"I see the mesmerizer spinning from the clairvoyant a

thread which he knots and swallows. She holds him bound
by it and leads him around at will. I see this knot in him
like a dark cloud, weighing him down and stifling him.
Sometimes he tries to reject it, but without success."

Certain persons, actuated by curiosity and even by malice, had recourse to a clairvoyant to obtain information concerning Sister Emmerich's own state. During the second
investigation of which we shall speak later, they took her
head-dress to use as a bond between her and a certain clairvoyant of M——, hoping thereby to hear many interesting
things.

" This person," says Sister Emmerich, " was shown me
by my angel, but though she put herself to a great deal of
trouble, she could never find out anything about me. I
always saw the devil with her. When I was released from
imprisonment, I saw my confessor with her, the devil on
one side, another spirit on the other. The devil wanted
the woman to say all sorts of infamous things of me in my
confessor's presence; but, in spite of all her efforts, she
could see nothing. At last, she took Father Limberg by
the hand and said: 'Sister Emmerich is in prayer. She
is very sick. *She* is no impostor, but maybe some of her
friends are.'

" When my confessor returned from M—— and told me
this, I had another vision on this subject. I was seized
with fear at the thought of receiving Holy Communion from
him on the morrow, for I was afraid that he had gone to the
clairvoyant through curiosity; but I was satisfied when I
found that it was not by his own choice that he went. I saw
that she told falsehoods of other people, and that the devil
conjured up visions before her."

During the investigation referred to by Sister Emmerich
when she says, " I was released from imprisonment," an at

tempt was made to put her in communication with a mesmerizer, by making her wear around her neck a magnetic conductor in the form of a little phial covered with silk. So great was the disgust it excited in her that she dashed it from her, indignantly denouncing as a bare-faced lie the assertion that the horrible thing had been sent to her by her director, Dean Overberg.

A woman of Dülmen having allowed herself to be persuaded to consult a fortune-teller of Warendorf, thought she would try her skill by proposing some questions concerning Sister Emmerich. " What is going on near Sister Emmerich ? " she inquired. The fortune-teller shuffled her cards uneasily and answered : " Strange! All is exceedingly devout there ! There is an aged man quite stout ! There is a younger one ! There is an old woman dying ! " (Sister Emmerich's old mother who died by her). " The person herself is sick !"

The questioner had heard enough, she departed in fright. When Sister Emmerich heard of it, she remarked :

" Not the cards, but their faith in them, makes fortune-tellers see ! They say what they see, but not what the card shows. The card is the image of an idol, but it is the devil who is the idol. He is often *forced* to tell the truth, and then the fortune-teller announces it angrily."

In January, 1821, Sister Emmerich, whilst contemplating the public life of Our Lord, in a vision of the cure of one possessed, saw again the nature and moral effects of mesmerism. The relation between men and the powers of darkness were shown her in three spheres or worlds. The lowest and darkest comprised those that dealt in magic and openly worshipped the demon ; the second those that indulged superstition and sensual desires ; the third was the region of free-masonry and liberalism. These three worlds were bound together by innumerable interlacing threads which, like a ladder, led from the highest to the lowest. In the lowest sphere, as also in the middle one, she beheld mesmerism with its various states and bodily remedies. She understood that it was the most efficient means employed by the demon for the destruction of mankind.

" In the lowest sphere," she says, " I saw certain states and relations which in common life are not regarded as absolutely unlawful. Many individuals therein were under the influence of mesmerism. I saw something abominable between them and the mesmerizer, dark, shadowy figures passing from one to the other. I have rarely, if ever, seen persons mesmerized without discovering sensuality in them. Clairvoyance is produced by the agency of evil spirits. I beheld people falling from the upper and brighter sphere on account of their employing magic under the name of science in the treatment of diseases. Then I saw them mesmerizing and, blinded by their apparent success, they attracted many from the upper sphere. I saw them eager to palm off cures wrought by infernal agency, reflections of the mirrors of hell, as cures from heaven effected by God's favored souls. In this lowest story I beheld very distinguished men, laboring unknown to themselves in the sphere of the infernal church."

CHAPTER XXXIII.

ATTEMPTS TO REMOVE SISTER EMMERICH TO MÜNSTER. DEATH OF HER AGED MOTHER.

In June, 1815, Dean Overberg passed several days in Dülmen. "Not having seen Sister Emmerich for some-time," he wrote, "I visited her to-day, June 8th. She expressed her joy at seeing me, and we spoke almost an hour and a half on her affairs. I determined to remain with her as long as possible. Next morning, at half-past seven, I took her Holy Communion. I stayed by her from the end of her thanksgiving till noon, when I withdrew and again returned at four o'clock. She was weak and tremulous. I asked her the cause and she answered : 'It is from the pain in my wounds, but this pain is sweet.' She says that, even if she lies awake all night, it never seems long to her. She has received the last Sacraments twice since my visit in January. Her attendants thought her dying. She lay without pulse or respiration, her lips livid, her features drawn, her whole appearance more like a corpse than a living being ; but as soon as she had received Holy Communion, life and strength returned. It was her desire for the Eucharist that had reduced her on both occasions to such a state. If through obedience she abstains from communicating, though her desires may be just as ardent, she is able to support the privation ; but, if it is through her own fault, she falls into a death-like state.

"On Friday afternoon, I beheld her in ecstasy. When I stretched out my hand to her, she took the forefinger and thumb, the consecrated fingers, and held them firmly ; after a short time I withdrew them and presented the middle one, when she instantly drew back as if frightened. Then she clasped the thumb and forefinger again, saying : ' These are the fingers that feed me *!* ' "

The Dean made use of his stay in Dülmen to persuade her to allow herself to be removed to Münster for a time to undergo a new investigation by reliable persons, not to convince her Ecclesiastical Superiors of the truth of her case, but only for the silencing of infidel scoffers, for it was thought by many that the first investigation had been too easy, that another was absolutely necessary for the satisfaction of the public. Let her come to Münster, they said, let her submit to a careful medical examination to prove the reality of her stigmata and testify to the conclusions drawn from the first investigation. Dean Overberg was himself convinced that no one could look with an unprejudiced eye upon the invalid without being assured of the truth. On Friday, June 9th, when her wounds began to bleed, he involuntarily exclaimed . "No ! no one could produce such an effect artificially, and she less than any one ! " He hoped that a new investigation would be decisive. He could not understand why Sister Emmerich did not encourage the idea of her removal to Münster, a course so necessary, as he thought, to the general good. Very far from encouraging it, she declared that only on an *order* from Superiors would she undertake a journey physically impossible for her. But the Dean would not give such an order. Her removal must depend wholly upon herself ; consequently, he would not allow Father Limberg to interpose his authority. He did not, however, relinquish the hope of one day realizing the project, and he tried to win over Dr. Wesener to his way of thinking. The doctor, he thought could gain the Abbé Lambert, and all would turn out as he desired. We read in the doctor's journal:—

"Dean Overberg honored me with a visit for the purpose of explaining how necessary it was for the invalid to go to Münster and submit to a rigorous investigation. His arguments were so forcible that, at last, I began to share his opinion. That evening I spoke to the Abbé, who offered no objection. He only said: ' Well, so be it ! If she freely consents to the arrangement, let it be for the sake of the good that may result from it, but I fear my anxiety and her absence will cause my death ! If she does not consent, I shall defend her to my last breath against any violence that may be used to force her to do so. I am ready to make any sacrifice for the good cause, but why persecute her so cruelly in mind and body ? Take a shorter and easier way ! I will leave Dülmen for as long as may be deemed expedient, and then let them examine her as rigorously as possible.' The good old man was so overcome by emotion that the tears sprang to his eyes, and he could only add : 'I know not what good can come from it. It is a frightful thing thus to persecute the poor child !'

"Next day Dean Overberg and myself being together in her room, she herself turned the conversation upon the point in question, and I explained my reasons. After listening quietly for some time, to my great surprise she announced her firm determination never to consent to her removal from Dülmen. ' Dean Overberg,' she said, 'is so good and kind that he is often imposed upon. He is ready to sacrifice me, as he told me himself, to prove to some good people that the phenomena in my person are not the work of human hands. But how can they, his spiritual children, have so little faith in his word ? He is himself convinced of the truth, and he can at any moment bring

forward fresh proofs of the same.   Could they find a surer,
a more reliable witness ?'   When I remonstrated that something still more formal was necessary to prove her state she
replied : ' If five thousand people do not credit ten of acknowledged veracity, twenty millions will not believe the
words of hundreds.'   I asked if she would not be willing to
sacrifice her life for the salvation of one soul ?   She answered : ' Certainly !   But how am I to know whether such
can or will result from my removal, since it has not been
ordered by the interior voice which has always guided me,
and when, besides, my whole soul revolts from the step ?
I would like to say more, but it is not yet the time.   If, in
spite of my interior conviction, I undertook the journey
and died on the way, would it not be to the prejudice of my
soul, would it not be frustrating God's designs over me ?
And who can assure me that this would not happen, if the
interior voice does not ?   Truly, as soon as my guide says:
" You must go !"—I shall be ready to set out on the instant.
Dean Overberg says that I ought to go for Professor von
Druffel's sake, whose reputation has been attacked on my
account.   I would do anything in the world for him or any
one else unjustly attacked, provided I could do it lawfully.
I wish most heartily that he had published nothing relating
to me or my wounds.   How often have I not begged you
yourself not to publish anything during my lifetime !   But
why should I risk my life and even more than life to secure
to any man a little worldly honor ?   Where are his humility,
his patience, his Christian charity ?   And, after all, the
greater number would not be convinced ; for sloth, distrust,
self-love, incredulity, avarice, and with many the fear of
exchanging their own opinion for even a better one, render
men blind to truths as clear as day.   If so much importance
is attached to the verifying of what takes place in me,

those people who are in good health can come to me. I
cannot with impunity go to them. I consent to all
experiments not against my conscience. If others want
to be convinced, let them do what those who already
believe have done, let them take their place by my bedside and watch me. I cannot at the expense of my own
conscience spare the curious the cost and trouble of coming to me. Let those who are able to travel come to see
me. If I went to them they might attribute it to vanity,
presumption, or even something worse, since it is impossible for me to make the shortest journey without risk.
I surely cannot exhibit myself a spectacle to the curious!
Let them send prudent men whom the people esteem. I am
ready to obey their orders in all that is not prejudicial to
my soul; for the rest, I want nothing. I am nothing but a
poor, sinful creature, and I ask for nothing but a little
quiet, so that forgotten by all, I may pray in peace, suffer
for my own sins, and for the salvation of souls. The
Vicar-General has just returned from Rome. Did he
speak of me to the Holy Father? Thank God, he leaves
me now in peace! O be patient, all ye who are good and
faithful! The Lord will show forth His works to you. If
it be from Him, it will endure; if from man, it will van-
ish!"

"She uttered the above in a firm, animated voice. Her confessor entered at the moment, but took no part one way or
the other. When she made allusion to some words of the New
Testament, he remarked: 'She is thinking of what Gamaliel
said.'"

Dr. Wesener recounted the above to Dean Overberg
who could not but approve Sister Emmerich's reasoning;
consequently, he refrained from pushing the question further. However, eighteen months later, when Prof. B —

published his calumnies accusing her of imposture and
treating the ecclesiastical investigation as a lame affair,
the Dean again yielded to his friends' solicitations, and
expressed a desire for her removal, although he saw
that her weakness would render it impossible for her to go
to Münster. Meanwhile, regardless of her remonstrances
to the contrary, Dean Rensing publicly refuted the Professor's attacks, an attempt which ended as she had pre-
dicted. Prof. B —not only repeated his assertions, but even
multiplied them ; but with all who were not obstinately ob-
livious to the truth, they bore no weight. Dean Rensing felt
hurt that the invalid did not second his efforts in her defence,
and from that moment treated her with marked coldness. Although many were of opinion that she ought to submit to a
new investigation for the sake of establishing the truth of the
first, yet none of her Superiors undertook to give her a
formal command to that effect, as they feared the pain and
anxiety consequent on it would cause her death. Such was
the state of affairs when, in the fall of 1818, Bishop Michael Sailer arrived in Münster and expressed his desire to
visit Dülmen. The Dean was highly gratified, as he
looked upon the Bishop as a competent judge in such cases.
He procured a permit for him and suggested to Father
Limberg that his penitent should give a detailed account of
her conscience to him, which suggestion Sister Emmerich
most willingly obeyed. Bishop Sailer declared her right
in refusing to make the journey as it would endanger her
life, and he also thought a repetition of the investigation
unjustifiable since that of 1813 had been rigorous enough to
satisfy all reasonable minds. The poor invalid was grateful
for his decision, and clung to it all the rest of her life.
She often said that the Bishop's visit had been productive
of happy results for her, inasmuch as it had removed her

confessor's fears and given him courage to approve the course she pursued with regard to her removal. She was never after annoyed on this subject.

Sister Emmerich's mother had died by her child's bed-side, March 12, 1817, aged eighty years. After the suppression of Agnetenberg, she had visited her daughter only once, when the report of the ecclesiastical investigation reached Flamske ; but, when she felt death approaching, she wished to meet it near her favored child. She was taken to Dülmen, Jan. 3, 1817, and her bed of death placed near her daughter's couch of pain. Sister Emmerich had never forgotten her old mother's spiritual interests. She had asked to be allowed to render her in her last moments all that filial love suggests, her only anxiety being lest her own state of suffering would prove an obstacle to the accomplishment of her heart's desire. Almighty God gratified His servant. She had the consolation of her mother's presence and of doing all that lay in her power toward soothing her dying moments. On December 28, 1817, the doctor to his great surprise found his patient sitting up in bed. On asking for an explanation, he received from Father Limberg the following :—

" Last evening after an ecstasy of two hours, she returned to consciousness without a command and asked me, in an animated tone, if she might get up. I answered in the affirmative, when she sat up so briskly that I was frightened. She remained in that position without support until I ordered her to lie down again. She said : 'My guide took me to a place where I saw the massacre of the Holy Innocents and I beheld how magnificently God recompensed those youthful victims, although they did not and could not actively confess the holy name of Jesus. I admired their immense reward and asked for what I might hope, I who

had so long patiently suffered pains and opprobrium for the
love of my Saviour. My guide answered: "Much has
been dissipated in thy case, and thou hast allowed many
things to go to waste; but persevere, be vigilant, for
great will be thy reward."—This gave me courage, and I
inquired if I would recover the use of my limbs and be
able to take food again.—"Thy desires will be gratified,"
he answered, "thou wilt even be able to eat, but be patient!"—"How!" I exclaimed, "may I get up now?"—"Sit
up at the word of thy confessor," he replied, "and wait for
the rest. What thou sufferest is not for thyself, but for
many others and for Dülmen." Then I awoke and was
able to sit up.'"

She continued to improve for a week, as Dr. Wesener's
journal records :—

"She can sit up alone, she has even been able to leave
her bed once and dress without assistance. I am resolved
to make her take some nourishment. When I told her so,
I added : 'What will Prof. B—— say when he hears that
you can sit up and eat?' She answered: 'I know not
what is in store for me. I care not for the approbation of
men. I am indifferent to their opinion, although I pity their
blindness. Shall I suffer insults ? I am satisfied, provided
it glorify God. If, as His unworthy instrument, I am to
show forth something, the Lord will confirm it. May His
name be praised!'—She still refused to take food without
her confessor's order."

On January 16th, he again writes: "She takes daily without bad effects some spoonfuls of milk and water, equal parts.
I think she would now be still more improved, did she not
devote herself so exclusively to her sick mother. She rejoices that God in His mercy enables her to make some return for the tender care lavished upon her by that good

parent. On Friday, Jan. 17, her wounds not having bled, she began to hope that they would disappear entirely ; but her hope was not to be realized.—Toward the close of January, she was able to take at several different times a little thin broth.

" February 14th—She continues bright and cheerful, although she suffers day and night from the sight of her dying mother whose pains she shares.

" February 21st—She is not so well to-day. Her share in her mother's sufferings appears to be the cause of her languor.

" March 12th—Her mother died this evening. Sister Emmerich is much affected. The thought of not having done enough for her good mother distresses her.

" March 20th—She is in as weak and miserable a state as ever, but she expresses the most touching gratitude to God whose merciful hand supported her during her mother's last illness."

CHAPTER XXXIV.

CLEMENT BRENTANO--SISTER EMMERICH'S INFLUENCE ON HIS SPIRITUAL LIFE.

Dr. Wesener's journal contains a very significant conversation between Sister Emmerich and himself, Sept. 26, 1815. He had found her in a most deplorable condition from the effects of Gertrude's careless ministrations. He tried to console her by saying that God made use of her sister to purify her and that he felt certain Gertrude, with all her faults, would not be lost. Then followed a long conversation during which she expressed herself in these terms :—

"To serve the neighbor, I have always thought a virtue particularly pleasing to God. When a child, I used to beg for strength to be of use to others, and I now know that my prayer was heard. *But I have yet another task to accomplish before my death. I must reveal many things before I die!* I know that I have to do it, I feel it, but I cannot through the fear of drawing praise upon myself. I feel, too, that this very fear is in itself a fault. I ought to say what I have to say in all simplicity, because it is the will of God and for the sake of truth. But I have not yet looked at it in the right light, and *I must lie here until I have learned to overcome myself entirely.*"

The doctor suggested that the prolongation of her incomprehensible life could only be for the increase of her own personal merit ; otherwise it would be a true purgatory for her. She replied : "God grant it! Yet it is certain that not for myself do I lie here and suffer. I know why I suffer! Publish nothing about me before my death. What I have, I

have not for myself, I am only an instrument in the hand of
God. Just as I can put my little crucifix here or there by my
own will, so must I abandon myself to everything that God
does or wills in my regard, and I do it with joy. I know,
indeed, why I lie here, I know it well, and last night I was
again informed of it. I have always asked of God, as a
particular grace, to suffer and, if possible, satisfy for the err-
ing; but as this city once received me, a poor peasant-girl
whom other convents rejected, I have offered myself up
especially for Dülmen, and I have the consolation of
knowing that God has heard my prayer. I have already
averted a threatening danger, and I hope still to be useful
to it."

Three years passed, and no one with sufficient zeal or
leisure presented himself to take down Sister Emmerich's
contemplations. That task was reserved for Clement
Brentano, whom an apparently fortuitous circumstance led
to Dülmen. Professor Sailer, of Landshut, with whom
Brentano corresponded, informed him of his intention of
going during the autumn vacations of 1818 to Münster and
Sondermühlen, the residence of Count von Stolberg; he invited him to come from Berlin to Westphalia and accompany him. The Professor's other companion was Christian
Brentano. He had seen Sister Emmerich the year before
and had interested his brother in her singular case. Clement, therefore, embraced this opportunity of making a
short visit to Dülmen. The little city could have few attractions for a man like him, and nothing was further from
his thoughts than the idea of a prolonged stay. Sondermühlen had been named as the rendezvous; but Clement
having arrived before either the Professor or his brother,
resolved to proceed to Münster, see Dean Overberg, and
go on to Dülmen by himself.

He records in his journal: " Thursday, Sept. 24,
1818, I arrived in Dülmen, about ten o'clock, a. m ,
and Dr. Wesener announced my approaching visit
to the invalid. We had to pass through a barn and some
old store-rooms before reaching the stone steps leading
to her room. Her sister answered our knock at the door,
and we entered the little kitchen back of which is her
small apartment. She saluted me graciously, remarking
that she would recognize me from my resemblance to my
brother. Her countenance wears the imprint of purity and
innocence. It charmed me, as did also the vivacity of her
manner in whioh I could detect no trace of effort or excitement. She does not sermonize, there is none of that
mawkish sweetness about her which is so disgusting. She
speaks simply and to the point, but her words are full of
depth, charity, and life. She put me at my ease at once. I
understood everything, I *felt* everything."

The secret of Clement Brentano's gracious reception lay in
this—Sister Emmerich now beheld before her the one so
long desired, the promised amanuensis who was to note
down the communications she had been commanded to
make. But what the rough forest tree is to the master-
piece of art for which it is destined, was Clement Brentano
to the task in store for him. How will she retain by her
side one whose tastes and inclinations tend to a far different
sphere ? How will she engage this restless spirit, obedient
only to impulse and caprice ? this soul whose long and
dangerous wanderings have only within a few months led
him into the road of salvation ?—At the end of a few weeks,
she avowed to him her own surprise at the turn affairs had
taken : "I am amazed at myself," she exclaimed, " speaking to you with so much confidence, communicating so much
that I cannot disclose to others. From the first glance, you

were no stranger to me ; indeed, I knew you before seeing
you. In visions of my future, I often saw a man of very
dark complexion sitting by me writing, and when you first
entered the room I said to myself, ' Ah! there he is!' "

Clement Brentano's first idea was to weave her marvellous
life into a narrative more poetical than historical. "I shall
try," he wrote in his journal, " " to note down what I learn
from the invalid. I hope t) become her biographer." In
his poetical enthusiasm, he celebrates her praises in his
journal and letters to his friends during the first weeks of
his sojourn at Dülmen. "She is a flower of the field, a
bird of the forest whose inspired songs are wonderfully
significant, yes, even prophetic!"—Again, she is his
"wonderful, blessed, charming, lovely, unsophisticated,
simple, sprightly friend, sick unto death, living without
nourishment, altogether supernatural," etc. And again, "A
wise, pure, frank, chaste, tried, sensitive soul of good judgment, and yet perfectly naïve, who reminds him, at every
instant, in words, manners, and disposition of one most dear
to him." Finally, he indulges the hope of improving her
exterior situation;—" All might be rendered more endurable
for her were there some faithful creature, pious and intelligent, to relieve her of domestic cares and who, seated by
her bedside (the most delightful seat in the world!) might
ward off everything that could give her anxiety."

Sister Emmerich was kind and patient with Clement
Brentano whose whole life and aspirations formed such a
contrast to her own. Her confidence won his heart, and he
resolved to await the impatiently desired, but long-delayed
arrival of Prof. Sailer and his brother, Christian Brentano.
Dülmen possessed few charms for him apart from its miraculous "wild flower." He gives his impressions of the little
city in the following pleasing words :—

" This place may have attractions for simple souls. It is a little agricultural town without art, science, or literature; no poet's name is a household word here and, in the evenings, the cows are milked before their owner's doors. The people wear wooden shoes, and it is to be regretted that even the servers at Mass do the same. If a respectable looking person passes through the street, the children run in front of him, saluting with a kiss of their little hands. A beggar will promise for an alms bestowed to make the "Way of the Cross" with all his family that evening for his benefactor; indeed, on the the vigils of feasts, this road, with its pictures of Jesus bearing His Cross, is never without whole families thus united in prayer. The feminine employments of the gentler sex are carried on in the fields and gardens, preparing the flax, spinning the thread, bleaching the linen, etc. ; even the daughters of well-to-do citizens are dressed no better than servants. Not a romance is here to be found and, to a certain extent, fashion exists not ; clothes are worn, regardless of style, until no longer fit for use. The mail passes through the place, for it can boast of a post-office. The Duke von Croy resides here for six months in the year with a numerous household at least thirty persons. And yet, we hear of the wonderful progress of Dülmen in the last ten years and its consequent luxury and corruption ! "

Sister Emmerich's patience and kindness, the permission accorded by her confessor to visit her several times daily, the interest she manifested in the recital of his past life— all concurred to reconcile Brentano to the privations imposed by his stay in Dülmen. Accustomed to act on first impulses, he was unable to resist the interest shown in his spiritual welfare. But whilst his only thought was, in his own poetical words, to lend an ear to the " prophetic strains of the

wild forest bird," Sister Emmerich labored most earnestly
for his soul. She hid her own sufferings and sacrifices under
the veil of gentle sweetness and forbearance lest they
should intimidate this novice in the spiritual life. All her
desires in his behalf tended to one end—to reconcile him
perfectly with God, to renew his interior life by filial submission to the Church. She felt that her visions would be
realized in his regard, only when his lofty intellect should
bend to the yoke of Jesus Christ, when religion should
mould and vivify his every thought and action. Her words
fell like good seed on the soil of his heart. They
germinated unknown to himself. They began to produce their
fruit even whilst he indulged no higher hope than that of
gleaning fresh matter for his poems. The very novelty of
his position proved an attraction to his highly-gifted soul.
It was something new and strange, and it wove its magic
spell around his heart disgusted by indulgence in worldly
pleasures and pursuits. Brentano, or the "*Pilgrim*" (1),
as we shall often style him, seemed led to Dülmen by a
chain of merely fortuitous circumstances. But Sister Emmerich saw therein the direction of Divine Providence, and
it was not long before he was himself convinced that the
unforeseen prolongation of his stay might exercise a most
salutary influence over his life. It is always difficult for a
man to comprehend the call of God, to run counter to his
inclinations, and to free himself from old habits, in order to
respond to it; but for Clement Brentano, with his rich nature, his past life teeming with stirring events, there were
many things which, judging from a human point of
view, seemed to render him in spite of his rare gifts less
proper than another for carrying out the designs of God.
He had just completed his fortieth year on his arrival in

(1) Sister Emmerich used to designate him by this title.

Dülmen. But a very short time had elapsed since his reconciliation with Almighty God, his whole life having been spent far away from the Church of whose teachings he knew but little. A short time before his acquaintance with the invalid, he had written to one of his friends : " The forms of Catholic worship are to me as unintelligible, as repulsive as those of the synagogue. I feel that I am not happy ; but I feel, too, that if I seek peace in Catholicism, I shall find myself in such perplexity and embarrassment as to render my position worse than before. When I turn to the Catholic Church, I meet at every step a thousand things to disconcert me."—He was, on the contrary, so attracted by the pietism of a Protestant minister of Berlin that he said :

" The excellent Mr. H.'s church has, for the first time in my life, impressed me with the idea of a community. Nothing repulses, all attracts. Although the Catholic Church no longer has charms for me, yet through a certain reluctance to separate from her, I do not go to Mr. H.'s." This reluctance for which he could not account, prevented his taking the final step ; but the following fearful words show how broad was the abyss which existed between him and the fold of Christ : " The magical infusion of the spirit of God by the imposition of hands, has for me no more reality than the possibility of imposing poetical genius by the crowning of the poet-laureate ; "—and again : " What an abyss between the Lord's Supper and the Host in our ostensorium ! " (1) In these dispositions he set out on his quest for *truth.* He plunged into the writings of Jacob Böhme and Saint-Martin ; he expressed his enthusiasm over the pseudo-mystic sect of Boos and Gossner, in which he thought he saw " a faithful picture of apostolic times and a

(1) See Brentano's Correspondence, Vol. I., page 180, etc.

manifestation very formidable to the See of Rome; " and, whilst thus drifting away from the true source, he uttered the following unjust and bitter words against the Church: —" Among whom is the teaching of Jesus best seen? among the Papists, the Protestants, the Reformers, the Greeks, the Mennonites, the Moravians? Where?—Let each judge as best he can. If they tell me the Catholics are right, I answer : Why, then, must the Bible be taken from them that they may remain Catholic ? He that is right is Jesus! He alone is the Mediator, between Him and men there is no other. The only knowledge we can have of Him comes from His own teachings, from nature, and from man's own heart in relations the most intimate with Him It is my duty to shun whatever could disquiet me or remove me from Him. When an authoritative voice calls out to me : ' Here, here, this is the right way ! You must do so and so, the true Church commands it !'—I get perplexed, I undergo a species of torment !"—It is true that Brentano had, indeed, approached the Sacraments; but, at the time of his arrival in Dülmen, his ideas of faith were still very shadowy, and it was only when under the influence of Sister Emmerich's blessed presence that his soul found peace. In his wanderings he had involuntarily uttered a cry for deliverance: " I need a guide, one to introduce me into a region in which I may breathe a divine atmosphere of piety and innocence ; one to lead me like a blind man, for I cannot trust myself !"—Now, truly, did he experience the irresistible power of such an atmosphere. He saw the sufferings imposed upon this innocent victim, he saw the humble simplicity of her life in God ; in her he beheld the magnificence of the Church, the power and truth of the Catholic faith. Not her visions, not the communications she made to him, not the supernatural attraction he himself experienced, made the deepest impression upon him ; but her holiness, her faith whose principles regulated her every action, produced in him an emotion which found utterance in the following words :—" An entirely new world has here opened out before me! How thoroughly Christian is the sufferer! Now for the first time have I an idea of what the Church really is !"—The eighth day after his arrival he wrote in his journal :—

" I have left the post-house at which I first put up, and taken two small rooms in the same house with the invalid. Her apartment is in the rear. It is a tavern and a bakery belonging to her confessor's brother. I have made this arrangement to be able to observe her more closely, and I shall remain here at least two weeks.

" I shall soon be familiar with her exterior life, since it does not require much observation to understand the outer life of one so completely separated from the world. I shall note down my impressions without following any precise order, until I find some determinate point from which I can embrace all.

" The poor invalid's position is embarrassing, no careful female attendance. I see this with sorrow at every instant. Her sister is ignorant and awkward. The invalid has to help her in all the household arrangements, but she never complains, she bears all patiently. One day I found her lying helpless under a pile of damp linen which had been carelessly thrown on her bed. She could not stir under its weight. All this coarse, damp linen had to be examined with her wounded hands before being mangled, her fingers were blue and stiff with the cold. Half the day was often spent in such occupation. If in her life-like contemplations she made a gesture or spoke some word, her rude, ignorant sister treated her as a servant would a sick child in the delirium of fever, roughly bidding her be still.

" Her life, a perpetual martyrdom on account of her horrible bodily and mental sufferings, is besides worn out by indiscreet visitors ; but she is ever kind and gracious, seeing in it all the designs of God to try and humble her. She is most grateful to me for any little effort to relieve her and thanks warmly for it. She is carelessly and negligently attended by those around and even when they have a good will, they are awkward and unskilful ; for instance, in the wall by her bed is a crack which admits a strong current of air. No one thought of stopping it up, although it could easily have been done. I covered it with a piece of oil-cloth, for which she was very thankful.

" In spite of her pitiful situation, I always find her affable and cheerful. From her miserable bed she cannot cast a glance even upon the light of heaven or see the trees before her window in the garden below, she who grew up amid the rural scenes of the paternal cot, she whose relations with nature were so close and intimate !

" On Friday, Oct. 9th, I saw with fright and horror all her wounds. Her confessor wished me to see them that I might be able to testify to their truth. The mark of the lance in the right side produces a most affecting impression. I thought it about two and a half inches long. It reminded me of a pure and silent mouth whose lips are scarcely parted. Besides the double forked cross on her breastbone, there is a Latin one of an inch in breadth on her stomach, the discharge from which is not blood, but water. I saw to-day the wounds of the feet bleeding. It pierces one to the soul to see this poor body signed with so marvellous a seal, this body incapable of movement, saving the hands and feet, which can neither lie at full length nor sit up straight, which is surmounted by a head crowned with the pains of the thorny garland, whose countenance breathes benevolence and affection, and from whose pure lips escape only words of consolation and encouragement, words of fervent and humble prayer. By the couch of this holy soul, taught not by men but by the Lord, His angel, and the saints from her early youth, I learn a thousand things which throw new light on the Church and the Communion of saints. What wonderful, what soul-stirring experiments are daily made upon her by her confessor! What impresses me most is the power of the sacerdotal character over her. If she is in ecstasy and he presents to her the fingers that have received the holy unction, she raises her head and follows their every movement; when they are withdrawn, she sinks down heavily upon her bed. Any priest whatever may exercise the same power over her. Whoever, like myself, has had an opportunity of witnessing this, must feel convinced that the Church alone has priests and that sacerdotal ordination is certainly something more than an empty ceremony. Once I heard her say with tears : ' The consecrated fingers of priests will be recognizable in purgatory ; yes, even in hell they will be known and they will burn with a particular fire. Every one will discover the priestly character and load the owner with scorn.'

" How great and touching is her obedience to the priestly command ! When it is time for her sister to arrange her bed, her confessor exclaims: ' Sister Emmerich, arise in obedience !'—she awakes with a start, and makes an effort to rise. I asked him to give the command in Latin and in a low tone. He was seated at a little distance saying his breviary. He arose, drew near the bed, and in a tone so low that the words were indistinguishable, said : ' Tu debes obedire et surgere, veni !' (1). Instantly she sprang up, though with difficulty, as if about to throw herself from the

(1) " Arise in obedience, come !"

bed. Father Limberg asked in alarm : 'What are you doing?'—to which she answered : Some one calls me !'—At the order : 'Lie down again !'—she sank down at once.

" This sudden awaking at the priest's command always affects me deeply, and I pity the poor thing snatched without warning from her visions, from the world of light in which alone she truly lives, and cast into this dark, sad region in which everything shocks and wounds her. It fills me with such horror as I might feel on seeing a sick child, playing among the flowers, suddenly caught up on a pitch-fork and flung into a cold, dark dungeon. But suffering is her portion and, although it costs her a struggle, she thanks with a gracious smile for this very suffering. Her obedience is not involuntary and, though there be an irresistible force at work, yet her docile soul is always ready, like a submissive child, to obey. I have heard her say at the moment of awaking : 'I must go ! Yes, I am coming !'—or : 'I cannot ! my feet are nailed ! Loosen my feet !'—referring to the invariable position of her feet which cross one over the other like those of the Crucified. On returning to consciousness it costs an effort to separate them. Then she rubs her eyes, becomes fully awake when sprinkled with holy water, makes the sign of the cross, and takes up her chaplet if perchance it had fallen from her hand during her ecstasy.

" She acknowledged to me once that this sudden returning to consciousness is most painful to her. It is as if in some unexpected way she had fallen among strangers who could neither understand her nor she them. When her friends attempt to relieve her at such moments, their assistance only adds to her pain.

" Again I requested the confessor to give his order in writing, and he dashed off the words : 'Be obedient !

rise !'—She was absorbed in ecstasy, on her head a double head-dress and a linen covering. The paper was laid upon it, she sighed and sat up on the instant. ' What do you want ?' demanded Father Limberg. 'To get up ! Some one calls me,' she answered. But when he took the writing from her head and bade her ' Lie down !'—she again became immovable. I kept the paper, and I am going to try its effect on her in Father Limberg's absence."

The confessor having given permission for the trial, the Pilgrim made it some days later, as he himself tells us :—

" This evening as she lay in ecstasy, her confessor absent, I laid the written order upon her breast, and as usual she instantly awoke.

"To-day she swooned several times from pain. They gave her musk, which she invariably vomited, and then they rubbed her stomach with opium. Lying like a corpse she submitted to all. I was standing at some distance, distressed at her sufferings. At one time she inclined her head slightly to me. To all that her confessor said, she answered out of her deep swoon: ' Yes ! Yes !'—In the midst of this deathlike state, she displayed the most touching obedience and resignation. The other day she said to me : ' I had very much to suffer last night ; but when I can suffer in peace, it is sweet ! Then it is sweet to think of God. One thought of God is more to me than the whole world. Remedies do me no good, I cannot endure them. Sometimes I am left to languish, and then again all sorts of things are tried on me ; but this also must I bear !' "

It was only by degrees that the Pilgrim understood the deep humility which seemed to have become a part of her nature. His journal says :

" I expressed my desire of procuring an educated person possessed of simple piety and good judgment as a nurse for her. She began to cry like a child, saying that she herself had no education. I replied that she had mis-understood me, the qualifications I had mentioned were not wanting to her, and that it was for her own good I wished her to have such a companion. But she repeated the same words, until, at last, I grew a little impatient. I thought she misunderstood me. In a suppliant tone, she said : ' I do not wish to offend you, I have not those quali-fications ; but God is good to me !' "

As Brentano had tested the power of the priest's word, so now did he witness that of his blessing. He writes : "She said to me to-day : ' My bodily and spiritual sufferings and my frightful visions almost kill me. I am parched with thirst and I cannot move to get a drop of water.'— At these words I presented her a drink, having first wet the rim of the glass with holy water, and she exclaimed : ' It is wine ! Wine from the garden of the Church !'

"Once as I was sitting in her room whilst she lay in con-templation, she began to moan. I approached her with a glass that was standing near and which usually held holy water. I was alarmed at her livid paleness and I asked if she would have a drink. She shook her head and answer-ed in a weak voice : ' A little fresh water blessed by the hand of the priest. There are two priests near, they pos-sess the divine power, but they forget me whilst I languish. God wills that I should live upon blessed water. Ah ! will they let me die ?'—I ran to the Abbé Lambert's room close by and there, indeed, was her confessor whom we all thought absent. He blessed some fresh water which she drank saying: ' I feel better !'—Then he said jestingly : ' Come with me in obedience !'—She tried like a dying person to rise, but sank back swooning as the command had not been given seriously. The scene moved me deeply, yet I dared not say a word for fear of giving offence ; but the tears sprang to my eyes at the sight of her uncomplaining endurance of such trials.

" At another time, I heard her utter the following words : ' How sad that the priests of our day are so neglectful of their power, we might even say ignorant of what the sacerdotal benediction is ! Many of them hardly believe in it. They blush at a blessing as if it were a superstitious and antiquated ceremony, whilst some never reflect upon the power given them by Jesus Christ. When they neglect to give me a blessing, I receive it sometimes from God Himself ; but as Our Lord has instituted the priesthood and imparted to it the power to bless, I languish with desire for it. The whole Church is but one body. All must be deprived of what one member refuses to bestow. ' "

The pilgrim had daily evidence of the above, and he was sorely tried whenever she called for blessed water in her confessor's absence. One day as she lay in a burning fever, her throat parched and dry, he went for a glass of fresh water which, with the best intention in the world, he blessed himself before entering the room. The invalid took it with a smile and the words : " Ah ! why are you not a priest ! "—And, to his amazement, she told him that she had seen him blessing it through the closed door. This made upon him a deep impression which was increased when he suddenly became aware that his inmost thoughts were read by her. Once whilst conversing with her, the thought occurred to him that she would, perhaps, soon die ; and he remembered having read that a certain Pope had had one of the hands of a person favored with extraordinary graces cut off— just at this point, she smilingly interrupted the conversation with the words : " You are thinking of my death, and you want to cut off my hand!"—We find the following remarks in his journal: "Truly, this obviates the trouble of thinking! It is very easy to make one's self understood by a person who not only reads one's soul, but who even anticipates the undeveloped thought!"

Soon there arose in the Pilgrim a desire to profit by the great grace conferred upon him of communicating with this privileged soul. He says: "I have seen her in prayer. Her wounded hands, the middle fingers of which are always in pain, lay joined upon her breast and slightly curved inward. She seemed to smile, and her countenance wore the expression of one who both sees and speaks, although the lips and eyes were closed. The sight affected me. The blessed peace, the deep devotion of her childlike countenance awoke in me a keen sense of my own unworthiness, of my guilty life. In the silent solemnity of this spectacle, I stood as a beggar, and sighing I said in my heart: 'Thou pure soul, pray for me a poor, sinful child of earth who cannot help himself!'

"I feel that I must stay here, that I must not leave this admirable creature before her death. I feel that my mission is here, and that God has heard the prayer I made when I begged Him to give me something to do for His glory that would not be above my strength. I shall endeavor to gather and preserve the treasures of grace that I have here before my eyes."

This conviction becoming daily more profound, Brentano makes the following significant avowal:—

"The marvels that surround me, the childlike innocence, the peace, patience, and wonderful intuition of spiritual things I behold in this poor, illiterate peasant-girl, by whom a new world has been opened up to me, make me feel keenly the misery of my own life of sin and trouble, as

well as the folly of the generality of mankind. I see in another light the value of perishable goods, and I shed tears of
bitter repentance over my soul's lost beauty and innocence !. . . .

  "She went to confession to-day, fell into ecstasy as soon
as it was over, and recited her penance with extended arms.
I gazed in rapture on her holy expression. All that I have
ever beheld in art or in life representative of piety, peace,
and innocence, sinks into insignificance compared with her.
On the approach of my next confession, I was seized with
intense contrition and I commended myself to her prayers.
She consoled me and sent me to the dear Mother of God.
' Ah !' she exclaimed, ' the dear Mother of God ! she knows
us poor creatures well and she leads us to Jesus, her Child.
O what treasures of grace there are in the Church ! Be
comforted ! We have in this treasure wherewith to be encouraged !' . . . . I feel again that the Church is for her
something that I, in my blindness, cannot yet comprehend ;
and I ponder over all that I have here received, upon all
that I have learned for the first time. I compare with it
my past disorderly life, and a new longing for conversion
is aroused in my soul. In this frame of mind, I penned a
letter to her, telling her of my sadness and begging her
prayers for my conversion. She received it kindly. I did
not see her read it, but she knew well all it contained and,
perhaps, much more besides . . . . . .

  " The kindness and confidence shown me by this privileged
creature encourage me, do me the greatest good, for she is
so truly, so sincerely Christian. None ever knew as she
the misery of my soul, the enormity of my sins. I myself
know them not as they really are ; but she knows them,
she weighs and measures with a clear-sightedness unknown
to me. She consoles and helps me . . . . .

"Now I understand the Church. I see that she is infinitely more than an assemblage of individuals animated by the same sentiments. Yes, she is the body of Jesus Christ who, as her Head, is essentially united to her, and who maintains with her intimate and constant relations. And now, too, do I see what an immense treasure of gifts and graces the Church has received from God who communicates Himself to men only in and by her."

These last remarks refer to a conversation held with the invalid in which she had unquestionably established the purity and truth of the Catholic faith. Ruled by false mysticism, which made him look upon the Church "as a community of the children of God without distinction of outward profession," Brentano had one day shortly after his arrival expressed himself in glowing terms " of brethren separated in body but united in soul, since all belong to the universal Church." He was not a little surprised to receive the following grave and conclusive reply : " The *Church* is only one, the Roman Catholic ! And if there were left upon earth but one Catholic, he would be the one, universal Church, the Catholic Church, the Church of Jesus Christ against which the gates of hell shall never prevail."—When he objected that all that believe in Jesus Christ are sons of God, she replied ; " If Jesus Christ declares that the children of God should love and honor Him as their Father, they should also call the dear Mother of God their mother and love her as their mother. The *Our Father* is for him who does not understand this, who does not do it, simply a vain formula; he is far from being a child of God." — Then, returning to the subject of the Church, she continued : " The knowledge of the greatness and magnificence of this Church in which the Sacraments are preserved in all their virtue and inviolable sanctity is, unhappily, rare in these

our days, even among the clergy. It is because so many
priests are ignorant of their own dignity that so many of
the faithful forget theirs and comprehend not the expression
to belong to the Church! That no human power may ever
destroy it, Almighty God has attached an indelible character to Holy Orders. Were there but a single priest on earth
rightly ordained, Jesus Christ would live in His Church
as God and Man in the Most Holy Sacrament of the altar ;
and whoever would receive this Sacrament, after being ab-
solved by the priest, would alone be truly united to God.

" It is something grand but, at the same time, something
impossible without true interior light, without purity and
simplicity of heart, to live in accordance with the faith of
this Holy Church ; to celebrate with her the divine worship
and thereby participate in the infinite treasure of grace and
satisfaction she possesses in the merits of her Divine Head ;
and, through His merits, to share in the blood of her innumerable martyrs, in the penance and sufferings of her saints, in
the prayers and good works of the devout faithful. This treasure she communicates without diminishing to all in union
with her, to all her true children. It is from it that she
draws wherewith to satisfy the justice of God, to liquidate
for the living as well as for the souls in purgatory, the debts
which they themselves could never cancel. Every hour
has its own particular grace ; he who rejects it, languishes
and perishes. As there is an earthly year with its seasons,
an earthly nature with its creatures, its fruits and its peculiar properties ; so also does there exist an economy of a
higher order for the restoration of our fallen race. It has innumerable graces and means of salvation all linked together
in the course of the spiritual year which, too, has its different seasons. Each year, each day, each hour ripens these
fruits for our eternal salvation. The children of the Cath-

olic Church that piously celebrate the spiritual year with its feasts and ceremonies, that regulate their life according to its prescriptions, that recite the holy Canonical Hours, alone are faithful laborers in the vineyard, they alone will reap abundant benedictions. It is sad to behold in our times so few that understand this economy of divine grace and conform their life thereto. But a day will come on which, conscience-stricken, they will at last comprehend what the ecclesiastical year is, with its feasts and seasons and days consecrated to God, its public and private devotions, its Canonical Hours, its breviary recited by priests and religious. It is the Divine Saviour Himself who abides with us in this order of things, who gives Himself to us at all times as food and victim, that we may become *one* with Him. How strikingly do not His untiring mercy and solicitude for us shine forth in the thousands of Masses in which the propitiatory sacrifice, His bloody death upon the cross, is daily renewed in an unbloody manner and offered for us to the Heavenly Father! This sacrifice of the cross is an eternal sacrifice, a sacrifice of infinite efficacy, unalterable and ever new. But men must profit by it in time which is finite and during which all things are taken into account. In accordance with the precept of the Son of God made man, this thrice holy Sacrifice shall be daily renewed until the account is filled up and the temporal existence of the world shall reach its term; for it is Jesus Christ Himself who, by the hands of lawfully ordained priests (even were they otherwise unworthy) offers Himself to His Heavenly Father under the species of bread and wine for our reconciliation."

When Sister Emmerich held such conversations with the Pilgrim, she profited by the opportunity to exhort him to prayer, to the practice of penance, to Christian charity, to self-victory and renunciation, and all in so simple and natural a manner that her remarks penetrated his soul less as words of exhortation than of consolation, or as the necessary consequence of what she had previously said and which he had recognized to be true.

When unable to hold long conversations, she begged his prayers as a spiritual alms for herself or some intention recommended to her, or prescribed to him certain pious exercises, certain prayers, encouraging him to hope in God and thus unite himself more closely with the Church. She would use arguments like the following :—" We enjoy the goods left us by our parents and ancestors, but we forget what we owe them in return How they sigh for our gratitude! How much they need our help! They cry : 'Suffer, pray, give alms for us! Offer the Holy Mass for us!'" When he asked what he could do for his deceased parents, she advised him, besides prayers and alms-giving, to impose upon himself for a certain time determinate practices of self-renunciation, patience, sweetness, and interior mortification.

The Pilgrim could not, indeed, resist the force of Sister Emmerich's words. But there was one opinion dear to his heart and of which he scarcely wished to be disabused : viz., the possibility of practising piety, of being very agreeable to Almighty God even without actual and exterior union with the Church. He alleged as a proof of this that, numbers of non-Catholics are better than some Catholics living in communion with the Church, whose sad state in many countries he painted so eloquently that Sister Emmerich dared not reply. She saw plainly that her arguments would have no effect upon him at the time. One day she herself turned the conversation on this point:

" My spiritual guide has reproached me severely for having listened with too much complaisance to your eulogy of

pious heretics. He asked whether I had forgotten who I
am and to whom I belong. He says that I am a virgin of the
Catholic Church, consecrated to God and bound by holy
vows; I ought to praise God in the Church and pray with
sincere pity for heretics. I know better than others what
the Church really is, and I ought on that account to praise
the members of Jesus Christ in the Church, His Body ; as
to those who are separated from this Body and who inflict
cruel wounds upon It, I ought to commiserate them and
pray for their conversion. In praising the disobedient,
one participates in their faults ; such praises are not charitable, since true zeal for the salvation of souls is cooled by
them. It is well for me that I have been reproved on this
head, for we must not be too indulgent when there is question of things so holy. I, indeed, behold many good people among heretics who inspire me with great compassion ,
but I see, also, that they are children whose origin dates
back no further than their own times. They are drifting
about without helm or pilot, and they are incessantly split-
ting up into parties one against the other. A movement
toward piety which at times affects them, emanates
from the Catholic stock to which they formerly belonged ;
but it is soon counteracted by another in an opposite
direction, a spirit of ignorance and indocility which urges
them to rise in rebellion against their common Mother.
They are eager to practise piety, but not Catholicity.
Although they pretend that ceremonies and lifeless forms
are of no importance, and that Almighty God must be served
in spirit and in truth, yet do they obstinately hold to their
own forms which are in reality dead, to forms of their own invention, which are in consequence ever changing.
These forms are not the result of internal development, a
body animated by a soul ; they are mere skeletons. It

is for this reason that they who practise them are infected
with pride and cannot bend their necks to the yoke. How,
in truth, could they possess humility of heart, they who
are not taught from their infancy to humble themselves,
who confess not their sins and their miseries, who are not
accustomed, like the children of the Church, to accuse
themselves in the Sacrament of Penance before the representative of God? Behold, then, why I see even in the
best among such people only defects, presumption, obstinacy, and pride. The only heretics that are not in a
positively dangerous position, are they who, wholly ignorant of the Church out of which there is no salvation, practise piety as far as they know how ; but as soon as God
gives them the least doubt, they should regard it as a call
from Heaven and seek to know the truth. Heretics become members of the Church by holy Baptism, if validly
administered. They live only by the Church and have, in
point of spiritual nourishment, only what falls to them from
the Church ; but they do not sit at table with the children
of the house, they are outside insulting and boasting, or
dying of starvation. When in vision I behold baptized
heretics returning to the Church, they appear to come in
through the walls before the altar and the most Blessed
Sacrament ; whilst the non-baptized, Jews, Turks, and Pagans, are shown to me as entering by the door."

One day she expressed her thoughts by means of the
following symbolical picture.

"I beheld two cities, the one on the right, the other on
the left. A beautiful avenue of flowering trees led to the
city on the left ; but the flowers fell to the ground one after
another, no fruit was to be seen. My conductor said to me :
' Notice how much poorer this new city is than the old one
on the right.' The city itself was full of windings and

streets, but all within was dead. Then my conductor drew my attention to the old city on the right. In many parts it presented a more irregular and dilapidated appearance than the other; but all around arose magnificent trees covered with fruit. In it there were no poor, save those who neglected to gather the fruit or take care of the trees, which were of great age and rose majestically to heaven. The trees on the left appeared neglected, their branches broken, and the fruit fallen; but on the right, they were healthy, vigorous, and laden with fruit."

The Pilgrim was still more disconcerted when he saw how uncompromisingly Sister Emmerich condemned the false mysticism of Boos and Gossner, their secret practices and their adherents. As she herself had once been looked upon as a clairvoyant by the supporters of mesmerism, so now in the early stage of his acquaintance with her, the Pilgrim was tempted to see in her an illustration of his pet mysticism; but a closer study of her demeanor, her purity of faith, her respect for ecclesiastical authority soon led to a more just appreciation. One day he spoke warmly in praise of the sect. She replied: " Yes, I know Gossner. He is abominable to me! he is a dangerous man! The hard, obstinate Boos, too, is abhorrent to me! It would take a great deal to save him." The Pilgrim then spoke of Marie Oberdorfer, one of the foremost in the circle of false mystics, as of a woman highly favored by Heaven, and he supported his opinion upon that of an ecclesiastic whom he greatly esteemed. Sister Emmerich suddenly exclaimed: " Enlightened ! What is that?" and upon his explaining that it meant light for the understanding of the Holy Scriptures, she replied: " Such light as you speak of is of no account, but great is the grace of the true children of the Church ! They alone, by their sincere and obedient confession of the only true Catholic faith, by their living communion with the visible Church, are on the right road to the Heavenly Jerusalem. As to those who presume to revolt against the Church and her spiritual authority, who pretend that they alone possess understanding, who call themselves 'the communion of saints,' they have no real light, for they are not of the faithful; they wander, sepa₁ated from God and His Church. I behold even among the best of them, neither humility, simplicity, nor obedience, but only pride, frightful pride. They are terribly vain of the separation in which they live. They speak of faith, of light, of living Christianity, but they contemn and outrage the Holy Church in which alone light and life should be sought. They exalt themselves above the ecclesiastical power and hierarchy, paying neither submission nor respect to spiritual authority; they presumptuously pretend that they comprehend everything better than the heads of the Church, better than her holy Doctors; they reject good works but, at the same time, are eager to possess perfection, they who, with all their so-called light, deem neither obedience, nor mortification, nor penance, nor disciplinary rules necessary. I see them straying ever further and further from the Church, and I see of how much evil they are productive."

As the Pilgrim was shocked by her severe condemnation, which grated harshly upon his own opinions, she returned, again and again, to the same subject:—

"I always see these 'Illuminati' in a certain connection with the coming of Antichrist; for, by their secrets, by their injustice, they forward the accomplishment of that mystery of iniquity."

Brentano dared not contradict her words, but it was long before he fully understood that they attacked false mysticism in its very essence. No errors entail consequences so disastrous as that pride of intellect which impels men to aim at union with the Divinity apart from the painful road of penance, without the practice of Christain virtue, and with no other guide than that interior sentiment which they regard as an infallible sign of Christ's workings in the soul. "Christ for us! Christ in us!" such is the watchword of these sectaries. They reject the decisions of the Church, they shake off the yoke of faith and the Commandments, and they level every barrier between them and the baneful influence of their theories. Brentano had not, indeed, fully accepted these teachings, but he had looked upon them favorably, and their pet expressions, "Spirit, Love, Light, Way to God, Dwelling in God, Operations of God, the Word of God in us, etc.," held out to him the possibility of attaining their end in the sweetest and easiest way. But in the vicinity of this true servant of God, his delusions vanished. With all the energy of his soul, he now began to cultivate that pure, strong faith which he saw to be the fundamental principle, the essential element whence she herself drew the strength to accomplish the work assigned her.

On October 22d, Bishop Sailer and Christian Brentano arrived in Dülmen. Clement, at first, thought of returning with them to Berlin; but he yielded finally to Sister Emmerich's advice to remain a while longer to continue the work of his spiritual regeneration.

"God is good to me!" he exclaimed gratefully. "Sister Emmerich does wonderful things for me. I have become her disciple!" He truly desired to treat her as his spiritual teacher, to be most submissive to her; but we shall soon see how often his resolution was broken. As his position, attainments, and mental endowments were super-

ior to the invalid's surroundings, so also was his appreciation
of her and her extraordinary gifts clearer and more elevated. Eager not to lose a word that fell from her lips, particularly when in vision, he regarded as time lost every
moment not devoted to himself and such communications.
He aimed at deriving the greatest possible advantage both
for himself and others, and consequently the crowds of
sick and poor who claimed her aid, the time devoted to
the direction of the little household —all annoyed him, all
grieved his impulsive nature, little used to contradiction.
The doctor no longer dared ask advice about his patients,
the confessor speak of his spiritual duties, or the Abbé entertain her with his infirmities ; Gertrude must be removed,
the door must be closed to the few visitors from Flamske ;
and, above all, her old companions of Agnetenberg
must be denied admittance, in order that nothing might
divert her from the one great object—the Pilgrim and the
communication of her visions. His intention seemed to
him most laudable, his demands most just. He assured
her with tears that he would willingly employ his intellect,
spend his life itself in making known to the world the
wondrous favors Almighty God had bestowed upon her,
His chosen instrument of mercy. All Sister Emmerich's
tact was unavailing to restore harmony between her friends
and this impatient, requiring man, unaccustomed to self-
control. No other remedy could be devised than that of
his temporary withdrawal from Dülmen ; and, accordingly
at her earnest request and on the assurance of a gracious
reception at some future day, Brentano left the little city,
Jan., 1819, to be absent until the following May. It,
was long, however, before he attained that liberty of soul
necessary to fulfil the task allotted him by God.

CHAPTER XXXV.

The Pilgrim's Return.—Rumors of a New Investigation.

To leave Dülmen was very painful to the Pilgrim, but Sister Emmerich's kind words reconciled him. "We shall meet again," she said. "You will again taste many consolations and write many things here at my bedside. I would have died long ago, if I had not a special mission to fulfil through you." Father Limberg also had given him the assurance of a kindly reception on his return which, however, was not to be at too early a date and only to be countenanced on the condition that he would not impose his presence on the invalid in such a way as to exclude all others. The good Father, nevertheless, shared the sentiments of the old Abbé and Dr. Wesener. He would have been well satisfied never to have seen Mr. Brentano again, for all knew that, in spite of his protestations, a repetition of the last three months' scenes might lawfully be expected. Such considerations, however, weighed little against the invalid's own conviction that the Pilgrim was destined to the perfect accomplishment of her mission. He, on his side, suspected not how painful it was to her to authorize his return, or what she suffered on his account. On Dec. 21, 1818, he had written the following :—

"She was very much exhausted this morning from cutting out and making up clothes for poor children, but she bore my questioning with inexpressible patience. She was weak and feverish, and answered with an effort. She asked me

afterward if she had not repeated the same thing several
times. I did not, at first, remark her great exhaustion.
I begged pardon whenever I put a question, to which
she invariably replied, 'It is nothing!—'" The Pilgrim, unaccustomed to self-control, could pass from the most joyous
mood to one of profound melancholy at the slightest contradiction of his wishes or plans. At such moments the invalid
would try to calm him with words like the following :—
"Never yet have I confided so much to any one as to you.
I have never spoken so freely to any one before, but I have
been ordered to do so." Persuaded that no one understood
her as well as he did himself, he was too much inclined to attribute her confidence to his own personal influence, and on
that account he felt justified in wishing to remove from her
vicinity all that could annoy her. Scarcely had he returned
to Berlin than he began to take measures for re-establish-
ing himself by the invalid as soon as possible, and to
this effect he wrote to Dülmen. The impression produced
upon the Abbé Lambert by the news would be difficult
to describe. He implored Sister Emmerich with tears to
forbid the return of so importunate a guest. She could
hardly calm the old priest, usually so gentle and indulgent,
but now more persistent in his request as he was supported
by Dr. Wesener. Both thought her life drawing toward
its close, and wished not to be deprived of the consolation
they experienced in their intercourse with her by an intruder, for such they deemed the Pilgrim. His intellectual
superiority crushed them, they felt that he thought them
incapable of appreciating her high privileges. Various
circumstances combined to aggravate the Abbé's uneasiness :
the Pilgrim's stay at Dülmen had already attracted attention throughout Münster, and he had also aroused suspicion
by his inconsiderate freedom of speech ; in Dülmen itself

it was not understood how he, a perfect stranger, could gain so easy and continual access to the invalid; the most contradictory surmises were circulated on the subject, and it was only his charity to the poor, his piety, and his simplicity of life that disarmed the malevolent. The Abbé also dreaded a new investigation, and not without reason; for, by means of the Pilgrim, the report was spread in Münster that since Christmas, 1818, a change had taken place in the bleeding of her wounds. On Dec. 6th, Sister Emmerich said whilst in ecstasy: " My guide hast said to me : ' If thy wounds are withdrawn from thee, thou shalt suffer greater pains. Tell this to thy confessor, and do what he says.' I replied : ' Ah ! I would rather have the sufferings than the wounds ! I am so afraid, I am so ashamed !' "

On the 23d, Dr. Wesener records the following :—

" I have visited her every day since the end of October, but I find no change, nothing new in her physical condition. In the early part of November, we moved her into the little room next the one she was then occupying. This caused some confusion and bustle and gave us a fresh proof of her weakness and nervousness. She was quite overcome, began to vomit, and lay in this state for two weeks. Her hands and feet bled as usual on Fridays, her head all the time." From Friday, Dec. 25th, he made the following entries :—

" To-day, Christmas, her head, the cross on her breast, and the wounds in her side have bled more freely than for a long time; but the skin around the wounds of her hands and feet is white and dry, the crusts of a clear brown.

" Dec. 28th—The crusts fell from her hands and feet. There appeared on the upper part of both a long transparent mark; and on the opposite surface is a slight induration also of an oblong form. The pain has increased instead of diminishing.

"Friday, Jan. 1st—The wounds of her head and side bled as usual, but not those of her hands and feet.

"Good-Friday, April 9th—The invalid has lain for a week in a state of inexpressible suffering. To the tortures of her stigmata are added bronchial catarrh and cough, pains in the throat and breast. *The wounds of her hands and feet reopened to-day.* I found them bleeding this morning at ten o'clock. Sister Emmerich showed them to me sadly and begged me to say nothing about it. . . . . . The following Friday her hands and feet remained as they have been since Christmas, the wounds closed."

As soon as the report was spread in Münster that her hands and feet had ceased to bleed, the Prussian authorities thought it an opportune moment for executing a project of long standing : namely, that of taking the stigmatisée of Dülmen under their own immediate jurisdiction.

Dr. Wesener says : " Feb. 18th—Sister Emmerich sent for me to-day to advise her on the introduction of two persons : Dr. Rave, of Ramsdorf, and Vicar Roseri, who had arrived with an order from the Chief President von Vinke to inquire into her present state. I advised her to admit them. They called on me that afternoon to inquire about the effusions of blood and many other particulars. I saw that Dr. Rave suspects fraud and that he is resolved to discover it. I begged him to wait until next day when he might witness the bleeding of her wounds for himself.

" Friday, Feb. 19th—The two visitors wearied the invalid all the morning with questions on matters well-known to the public. Instead of waiting until her wounds bled, they left about noon. Toward three o'clock, the cross and her head bled, but not the wound of her side. I sent her head-dress stained with blood to Dean Overberg by Father Limberg, after having shown it to the burgomaster Mr.

Moellmann. Roseri belongs to the so-called *Illuminati* (1)
but he went away with changed sentiments. It seems as
if God touched his heart (2). Rave, the physician, is a
worldling, another Bodde; one could read in his eyes his
suspicion of imposture. He found fault with me for not
having kept the crusts from her hands and feet. ' When
one has the grain,' said I, ' he throws away the husk. Now
that I understand the most striking features of the case,
unimportant details do not interest me'—but Rave could
not comprehend my meaning. A few days before this
visit the Abbé Lambert had been called upon to present his
papers of nationality to the burgomaster. The order was
from the Chief-President and was couched in the following
terms : ' I have been apprised that there is now at Dülmen
a French emigré, a priest, whose position is rather doubt-
ful'—Fancy how such reports must affect the poor invalid
and the old Abbé ! Idle tales and calumnies are rife on
all sides ; but Sister Emmerich confides in God, and we,
her friends, rejoice to suffer for Christ and the truth !"

As Dr. Rave, besides his official statement, had circulated a (3) letter containing his own private opinion on the
subject very unfavorable to Sister Emmerich ; as he revived
the former attacks ot Bodde, and threatened to stir up fresh
storms, Dr. Wesener thought it high time to come forward in defence of the innocent, by a memorial addressed

(1) Letter of Dr. Wesener to the Pilgrim.

(2) The doctor was wofully deceived in Roseri, as the sequel will show. The invalid
received information in vision concerning him and his clique. "I saw Rave full of
malice, calumniating me, even against his own conviction, in order to please the followers of the *Eagle*" (the Prussian government.) "I thought Roseri changed, but he
is essentially false and he acts at random. I said to myself : ' How can such a priest help
souls ?—and I received the answer : ' He helps as few as the Good Book does among
the separated. He has no benediction in himself, but he can distribute the Church's
goods without possessing them himself.'—I saw the government of the *Eagle* badly
administered in this part of the country. The Chief-President has a noble heart, he
means well, but he has bad counsellors. If he came to see me himself, I doubt not that
I would be able to gain his good judgment to the truth."....

(3) The Landrath Bœnninghausen, of whom we shall hereafter speak more at length,
acknowledged that Dr. Rave, besides his protocol, had privately written to Dr. Borges,
at Münster, expressing his own views *with a little more freedom.*"

to the Chief-President of Münster. But Sister Emmerich was opposed to such a step. She asked Dean Overberg's advice. He replied as follows:—

" How much I have wished to visit my dear friends at Dülmen, among whom you hold not the last place! But such is not the will of God. Sickness and other obstacles prevent. I would like to lay before you my reasons against writing to the Chief-President, but not now, not till I can do so by word of mouth. Neither do I advise you to have the declaration forwarded to me inserted in the journals. Every response is specie payment. We must not buy lead, or what is even of less value, with pure gold. It is written: ' Cast not holy things to the dogs, nor pearls to swine.' I desire to compare no man to dogs or swine. But there must be some deserving of such comparison, else the Saviour, the infinitely wise Son of God, would never have given us this warning . . . . Nothing is so consoling and delightful as to suffer something with Christ! But why attach so much importance to Bodde's pamphlet? why see in it so formidable an attack? I have heard many persons declare that it betrays its spirit too openly to find supporters, it cannot do the least harm."

When Dr. Wesener declared later on that these public attacks ought to be met and refuted for the sake of those concerned, the invalid gravely replied: " Ah! ye good people, I thank you for the interest you take in me. But I must say that one thing in all of you, without exception, afflicts me : that is, that you treat the case with presumption and selfishness and, consequently, with bitterness. Whilst defending the truth, you wish also to defend *your own opinion, your own reputation!* You combat not the *lie* only, but also those who contradict you; in a word, you seek yourselves and not the glory of God alone ! "

The Vicar-General now thought it his duty again to visit
Dülmen, the reports that had reached him being far from
satisfactory. It was rumored that access to the invalid
was refused by the old Abbé, and that evening re-
unions were held around her couch.   Sister Emmerich soon
gave satisfactory explanations to his inquiries, her irresistible candor and simplicity again pleading in her favor. He
said to her, half in jest, half in earnest : "I have been a
little displeased with you, many things around you shock
me ! "—to which she replied : "That distresses me, but
you know not my position, and it is not possible to explain it
in words."—Then he enumerated certain points : the Abbé's
proximity, the Pilgrim's prolonged sojourn, the frequent
visits she received, the room in which she was (instead of
a more retired one at the back of the house), etc. But
when she begged him to point out the remedy for all this,
he confessed himself unable to do so. She explained to
him the Pilgrim's intentions, the command she had received
in vision to make use of him to record her revelations, and
begged him to decide, as her Superior, upon what course
she was to follow. Whereupon the Vicar-General concluded
that Brentano must not be forbidden to fulfil his task. He
was, at last, satisfied, or as Sister Emmerich herself expressed
it : "It passed off well.   We came to the same conclusion !
He went away satisfied and remained so !"

So stood affairs in Dülmen, when the announcement of
the Pilgrim's speady return threw the good people into great
agitation Father Limberg said nothing and left to the
invalid the care of lulling the storm ; but as this proved no
easy task, she had recourse to Dean Overberg for advice.
She knew from experience that his decisions were always
well received by her little circle, and it was on this account
that she had so earnestly desired a visit from him during

the Pilgrim's former stay ; she wished him to explain to her friends that it was not in her power to dismiss the object of their dislike, that his coming or going depended not on her choice. The Abbé and the doctor allowed themselves to be persuaded to appeal to the Dean, but at the same time, they wrote to Brentano to dissuade him from returning. Whilst these negotiations were pending, Sister Emmerich prayed that the glory of God and the salvation of souls might accrue from the whole affair.

The Abbé's letter ran thus : "Sir, be not offended with me, if I desire not your return. I feel that I have not the strength and courage to undergo a second time what I endured during your last visit to Dülmen. For many years have Sister Emmerich and I lived in peace, and so we wish to die. It was very hard for me whilst you were here, to be forced to see and speak to her, as it were, by stealth. I cannot consent to your return. No ! No! my dear sir, no! What I now write I should have said to you before by word of mouth, if you had listened to me. I often wanted to speak to you on this subject, but you would never permit me."

To the above written in French, the doctor added the following lines:—"My object in writing is to beg you not to return. You may smile at this, but your inflexible will cannot always be a safe guide for your actions. I have acquainted Dean Overberg with your manner of life here and your treatment of us all. *Follow his advice!* All Sister Emmerich's friends, both here and in Münster, are of one opinion —that your return will have most vexatious results. The fault lies in yourself. You have expressed yourself in Münster about the clergy of Dülmen, and principally of one, in terms so free and sarcastic that all declare against you, not one in your favor. No one is willing to write this

to you; therefore, I do it. I feel obliged to say that the
inconveniences resulting to Sister Emmerich from her relations with you infinitely outweigh the advantages derived ;
consequently, we are resolved, in the event of your return,
not to allow you the free access to her that you enjoyed
before. Sister Emmerich sympathizes with your sad fate
and solid conversion, but she sees, too, with anxiety your
distempered imagination, she dreads your ungovernable
will. If you return, she is resolved to admit you to her
room but one hour a day; and besides, you are not to interfere in her household affairs. Her sister is, in truth, a
miserable creature ; but Sister Emmerich is willing to bear
with her, persuaded that God makes use of this sister to help
her to practise virtue. The good old Abbé Lambert has suffered much from you though, of course, without your intending it. All has not gone so smoothly as you think.
Dean Overberg is of our opinion. Prevail upon him to say
what he thinks of your return."

Dr. Wesener had written, as follows, to Dean Overberg
respecting the Pilgrim :

" Our dear invalid has entreated me to write and give you
some explanation of the Abbé Lambert's letter, and my own
inclinations, as well as my affection for her, urge me to give
you news of her present condition. Mr. Clement Brentano
has visited you ; he has told you marvellous things of the invalid and has spoken to you of her progress in the interior
life. This gentleman, it is true, has been very generous
toward her. He has procured her a convenient lodging
where she can enjoy more quiet; and he has, perhaps, been
of great advantage to the public, furnishing many interesting details by his sagacious observations and researches,
but all at the price of the invalid's domestic peace ! What
do I say ? At the price of her health, her life ! He is in

himself good, his faith is firm, his works noble and Christian; but His poetical genius is out of place among the simple and unlettered. The invalid knows very well that her surroundings are not what they might be, she clearly sees the miseries by which her sister is enslaved, and the sight causes her inexpressible torment; but she is not less firmly persuaded that severity and constraint are not the means to correct and reclaim her. What she cannot cure by the way of charity and peace, she is willing to endure with humility and patience. The invalid has borne with Mr. Brentano and kept silence on all occasions, with the sole intention of being useful to him and to others. She wishes to forget past annoyances, to sacrifice them to God and her neighbor; but she dreads his return. He understands not the way of mildness, he wishes to overcome all obstacles by force. Sister Emmerich is determined not to receive him again unconditionally, not to regard all that he does as right. However, as there is a certain imposing air about him which intimidates some, and as her friends cannot always be near her, she feels unequal to the task of communicating with him directly and she seeks means for ameliorating the evil. He loves and esteems you highly and places in you unlimited confidence; consequently, the invalid entreats you most earnestly to write to him, to represent to him the state of affairs and authorize him to return only upon certain definite conditions."

To this letter, Dean Overberg replied as follows:—

" It is a great satisfaction to me to hear something of our dear invalid from a pen other than that of Mr. Clement Brentano. From his account, I should have conjectured that she was well pleased to have him by her, and perfectly satisfied with his manner of acting. On reading your account, the legal phrase, *Audiatur et altera pars*, recurred to my mind. He also assured me of his intention to return as soon as possible and continue his observations, which I hardly think we can prevent if Almighty God does not oppose some obstacle to his doing so, nor do I see any possibility of persuading him to take up his abode in Münster. That he may comport himself differently toward the invalid and her friends, she must herself assign some hour for his daily visit to her and, moreover, positively decline his interference in her domestic affairs. She must do this *herself*, for if any suggestion to this effect came from me, it would certainly not be adopted for the following reasons :—He is persuaded or wishes to be persuaded that Sister Emmerich is very well pleased to have him near her and that she is satisfied with his proceedings; he thinks that, at all events, it tends to her greater good. He knows that I cannot go to see her and converse with her upon these subjects; consequently, he would undoubtedly look upon what I might say of her sentiments concerning him and his manner of acting as suggested by those around her. Now, he might very reasonably suspect that they *wish to remove him from the invalid through motives of envy, jealousy, and the like.* He would then imagine it his duty to espouse her cause so much the more earnestly as he saw that some desired to deprive *her* of the consolation his presence affords her and *him* of the opportunity of securing to her a greater degree of repose by his zealous efforts to keep others at a distance. The arrangement to which I have referred should, as the case demands, be made in your own and Father Limberg's presence, and during the first days of its going into effect, you should watch closely to see if the prescribed time be observed. I foresee very plainly that in the beginning the invalid will have difficulty ; but I know no better means to adopt. I hope that if she is firm in the commencement,

Brentano will by degree become less exacting. I must, besides, beg you not to refer him to me for a decision. That would only render the case more confused and *strengthen him in the persuasion that the invalid would rather see things remain as they were heretofore, and that, if she expresses herself differently, it is only through the fear of offending either party. Her own free will and choice must decide this question.* Mr. Clement Brentano told me something, but only in a passing way, of the change that has taken place in her wounds. If you noted the time of this change, I beg you to send me your account in a day or so. I heard yesterday that she has begun to eat (1). Perhaps God will raise her up again. Salute her kindly from me. I presume she has received my letter."

The Pilgrim was stung to the quick by the Abbé Lambert and Dr. Wesener's letters and he complained bitterly of them to his friends (2). But when the first storm was over, he wrote an answer to the same which unfortunately has not been preserved. From the doctor's and Father Limberg's reply, however, it may easily be inferred that they were deeply touched by his humility and repentance. The doctor responded: "I have read your letter, and I thank God that I have done so! It has moved us to tears, it has satisfied all! . . . . . Your intentions were good, you meant well; but, under the influence of your impetuous spirit, you forgot that we are only poor, weak gnats unable to follow you in your rapid flight . . . . . Were you calm, gentle, patient, then would you be a sword, a flame in our Holy Church!"

Of Father Limberg's kind reply, the Pilgrim thus speaks :—

(1) This refers to Dr. Wesener's attempts to make her take some light nourishment, such as milk and water, barley soup, or sago. She tried to obey, but without success, and the doctor was forced to desist from such attempts.

(2) Clement Brentano's Gessammelte Briefe, vol. I., p. 334 and 340.

"From Father Limberg, too, I have received a very beautiful and consoling letter, singularly touching, affectionate, simple, and scriptural. A very elevated spirit, a truly sacerdotal spirit, pervades it. He rejoices at the prospect of my return. I submit, however, to Dean Overberg's decision" (1).

On arriving in Dülmen, May, 1819, Brentano received a most cordial welcome from all, and Sister Emmerich set herself to work to maintain peace on all sides. She exhausted herself in her efforts to keep Gertrude silent in presence of the stranger who seemed insupportable to her; she exacted from Dr. Wesener a renewal of his promise to treat the Pilgrim kindly; and she spared no efforts to make the Pilgrim himself less irritable, less alive to the little weaknesses of his neighbor. One day, after a conversation with her on this subject, he wrote, as follows, in his journal:—
"May the confessor, good and kind as he is, find in me some day a sincere friend! This I desire with all my heart, I really mean it. I have no after-thought in this—may it be so, too, with him! I have no concealments from him. How happy must two men be who trust and warn each other in Christ! God grant that my earnest efforts may earn His love and blessing!"

When he communicated his good resolutions to the invalid, she could scarcely conceal her fears for their constancy. "I saw the Pilgrim," she said, "under a flourishing, but short-lived gourd-vine—it reminded me of Jonas." He understood well the deep significance of her words, though he cared not to acknowledge it even to himself. He remarked in his notes:

"Her strange anxiety troubles me. She wept, and I was distressed, for she could not tell me the cause. May

(1) Letters of Clement Brentano, vol. I., p. 344.

God comfort her, give peace, confidence to all hearts, and
to me fortitude and unbounded charity toward all my brethren! The confessor is very good and kind. Does the
gourd of Jonas withering so suddenly signify a short-lived
peace ?"

Yes, without doubt, this vision was to be realized only
too soon. The order of the priesthood is, as it were, the
channel by which the gifts and graces of God's chosen ones
are distributed among the faithful in accordance with His
commands ; now, in their ranks not one was to be found to
secure the fruits of the visions granted Sister Emmerich
for the good of her fellow-men. By leading the Pilgrim
back to his faith, by preparing him for the duty imposed
upon him in the midst of such suffering as it entailed on
herself, she supplied for what was wanting in the priestly
co-operation and discharged the debt their negligence contracted. Still the accomplishment of her mission was to
depend wholly upon ecclesiastical authority. For the Pilgrim's return, she had to gain the consent of her chief Superior, the Vicar-General von Droste. Her director, Dean
Overberg not having come to Dülmen as soon as expected,
she sent her confessor to Münster to learn from him if it
were the will of God that she should communicate her visions to the Pilgrim ; and she reminded the Abbé Lambert
of the commands so often received to reduce to writing
what was shown her of Our Lord's Passion. Dean Overberg could, consequently, on June 6, 1819, unhesitatingly
assure her friends that the Pilgrim's employment near Sister
Emmerich was in accordance with the will of God. This declaration consoled her, as we glean from the Pilgrim :—

"Dean Overberg has gone. The invalid is so exhausted that she can relate nothing ; still she refers with
pleasure to her interview with the Dean." Now began a

new duty for Sister Emmerich, that of leading the Pilgrim to
comprehend that, not being a priest, he possessed neither the
sacerdotal power nor authority, and that it was only by his respect and submission to those by whom it was represented,
Dean Overberg and her confessor, that he would render
himself worthy to receive the communication of her visions.
She repeatedly and gravely made use of expressions to him
which, at first, seemed strange ; as, for instance, " You are
not a priest ! I sigh for Dean Overberg. He has the
priestly power that you have not ! You cannot help me,
you are not an ecclesiastic ! Were you a priest, you would
understand me, etc. !" It was long before he seized the
meaning of such words. Only two years before Sister Emmerich's death, he wrote : " Where, then, is the priest who
has understood her ? I am reproached in these words:
' Were you a priest, you would understand me and that
would spare me many torments'—but *no one* has understood her !" It was only by invincible patience that she
by degrees curbed his rebellious spirit, reduced him in
some measure to respect for spiritual authority, and enabled
him to fulfil his mission with a blessing to others as well as
to himself. Superior to good Father Limberg in learning
and experience, Brentano saw himself in a position in which
he could not approach the invalid for a single word without
express leave from the former, and day by day he received
convincing proof that strength to communicate her visions
was accorded her only by the priest's intervention. He failed
not to perceive that this simple and unlettered man, whom he
so vehemently accused of not understanding his spiritual
daughter, possessed by virtue of his lively faith an influence
over her immensely superior to his own ; he could not close
his eyes to the fact that he had yet to rid himself of many
faults, and acquire many virtues before arriving at a just ap-

preciation of Sister Emmerich and his own relations with her. Sister Emmerich's prudence in aiding him to acquire this knowledge was admirable. If charged by her angel to give him an admonition, she did it only after having adroitly prepared him to receive it well; and she generally clothed it in parables or striking comparisons which, appealing to his intellectual mind, charmed and attracted him, forced him, so to say, to accept them in spite of himself. If he expressed disgust at something wounding to his æsthetic tastes, she would say : " One may, indeed, be displeased by bad singing at Mass or an indifferent performance on the organ, whilst others are edified by the same. We ought to banish such sentiments by prayer. He who resists such a temptation in church acquires merit, gains new graces." This simplicity of faith she recalled in words such as these : " He who in his search after truth relies on his own efforts and not on the grace of God, may cling to his own opinion, but he will never dive into the truth."

Some weeks after his arrival, she laid open her soul to him :—

" Every evening I am told to make such or such a meditation. Last night I received an instruction upon myself, and a great deal was said to me about the Pilgrim. Much remains to be corrected in him. I was shown how we can render him better, more easy to deal with, and thereby more useful. As I thought over my manner of acting toward him, asking myself how I could perform his task as well as my own, and by what means we could have a larger and richer share of merits, I learned that we must be patient with each other in the sufferings that will come upon us, and that he must receive Holy Communion for my intention ; for spiritual union is thereby strengthened. 'Do what thou canst,' was said to me, ' but, for the rest, do not mind the Pilgrim. Many will come to speak with thee. When they present themselves, examine whether it be for their good or not. . . . . . Pray that the Pilgrim may resolve to be humble and patient, for he must overcome his wilfulness. Aim at making him more earnest. Through mistaken condescension, be not deceived by fair words. Do thou resist, be firm, that he may become resolute. Thou art too indulgent, this has always been thy fault. Do not allow thyself to be persuaded into seeing good where, in reality, there is a fault. . . . . . .' My guide told me again that I should have much to suffer, that I must not be frightened, but in the name of God calmly await what is in store for me. He reprimanded me for many faults. He says that I keep silence on many points through false humility which is, in the end, hidden pride; that I ought to receive and to communicate the divine favors as I did in my childhood when I received much more than I do now; that I ought to speak out boldly on suitable occasions; that I ought to tell my confessor whatever troubles me even if he seemed but little disposed to hear it, for in this way, I should receive his help more frequently. He reproached me for my too great condescension to some, which causes me often to fail in prayer and my duties toward others. He says that I am very unreasonable when I complain of lying in bed unable to act. He knows I would like to wrap in my mantle, go out in the evening, and distribute alms, because of the pleasure it would give me; but that what God imposes is not agreeable to me. He says that I ought to know that I am not lying here without an object. I must act by prayer and communicate all that I receive. I shall soon have something to impart that will cost me an effort, but I must say it. A great storm is near, the clouds are lowering fearfully;

there are few who pray, the distress is great, the clergy are sinking lower and lower. I must exhort the good to pray earnestly. He told me that I must be more calm, more collected to meet approaching sufferings, else I might suddenly die. My task is not yet completed. Were I to die now through my own negligence, I should have to undergo the rest of these sufferings in purgatory where it would be much harder for me than here."

Sometimes Sister Emmerich encouraged the Pilgrim by holding out to him the blessings she saw flowing from his labor. She related a vision in which, under the appearance of a garden, she had seen many things of his past life, his present work, and its fulfilment after her own death.

"I saw," she said, "the Pilgrim far away, sad and lonely in his room. He could interest himself in nothing, all was distasteful to him. I wanted to fly to him, to help him, but I could not.

"Then I saw a garden, a large garden divided into two parts by a hedge over which some people were looking, but who were unable to cross it. My guide took me where the vegetation was rich, beautiful, luxuriant, but all overrun with weeds. I saw beans and peas, and there were blossoms and flowers in abundance, but no fruit. Many people were walking about apparently well pleased with themselves.

"My guide said to me as we walked around : 'See, what it means :—beautiful flowers of rhetoric, brilliant but sterile ; abundant, but producing no harvest ; plentiful, but yielding nothing !'—'Ah !' I exclaimed, ' must all the labor be lost ?'—' No !' was the answer, ' nothing will be lost ! It will all be turned under to make manure,' at which I felt glad and yet sorry too.

"The second time we went around, we found standing

in the centre of the path a tent made of the branches of a stunted walnut-tree. It was covered with a cloth. The nuts on these branches were the only fruit in the whole garden. Further on we saw an apple-tree and a cherry-tree around which the bees were gathering honey. The place was desolate enough.

" My conductor said : ' See ! Thy confessor ought to imitate the bees and gather these nuts'—but my confessor feared being stung. I thought to myself his very fear would be the cause of his suffering what he dreaded. If he would go along coolly, the bees would not harm him ; but he ran from tree to tree, he did not even see the nuts.

" When my guide took me the third time, the growth was still luxuriant. I was charmed at seeing the Pilgrim gathering certain strange plants in the corners of the garden which, although partially hidden by others, yielded the most fruit.

" Again I went into the garden where the too luxuriant vegetation was beginning to decay, and at last it was all turned under. I saw the Pilgrim actively digging and tilling.

" When I came again, the garden was all ploughed up and the Pilgrim was setting out plants in beds. It was a pleasing sight. At last he left the garden, and some people entered whom I knew only by sight, I knew not their names. They fell upon me in a rage and abused me terribly, inveighing against my communications to the Pilgrim, complaining that a new sect would arise from it, and asking what they were to think of me ! I took it all in silence. Then they broke out against the Pilgrim who, I thought, was within hearing. I rejoiced at being able to bear it all patiently and I ceased not to exclaim : ' Thank

God! Thank God! I can bear it! another, perhaps, might not.'—Then I went and sat down on a stone in a neighboring grove.

"And now a priest came along, an active, energetic man, about as tall as the Prior, robust and florid. He expressed surprise at my not defending myself; but after a little reflection, he said : ' This person endures bad treatment very coolly, and yet she is both intelligent and sensitive! The Pilgrim's conduct is probably very different from what we imagine ; the confessor, too, is a good man who would not permit anything wrong.' As the unknown ecclesiastic continued thus speaking in favor of the Pilgrim, the brawlers began to slink away and I noticed how diligently the Pilgrim had worked and how much the plants had grown and flourished.

" My guide said: ' Make good use of this heavenly instruction. Thou shalt, in truth, endure these injuries and outrages. Be prepared! For awhile thou shalt live at peace with the Pilgrim ; but lose not time, squander not the graces given thee, for thy end will soon come. What the Pilgrim gathers he will bear far away, for here there is no desire to have it. But it will produce fruit where he goes, and that same fruit will one day return and make itself felt even here.' "

The Pilgrim understood the foregoing vision only little by little, as his oft-repeated complaints that the time of peace would never dawn, prove. He thought the words meant freedom from exterior annoyances, whereas they really signified peace of mind, which alone could fit him to receive the visions of *Our Divine Redeemer's Life.* Over a year elapsed before, upon the admonition of her angel, Sister Emmerich began the narration, July, 1820. The Pilgrim had, it is true, planted diligently, but many weeds yet re-

mained to be rooted out. His rich, lively imagination was
as yet too undisciplined for the reproduction of Sister Emmerich's visions in their native simplicity, and it cost him a
struggle not to embellish them with his own poetical ideas.
The interpretations he gave them were infallible in his eyes,
and he hesitated not to introduce them freely without
specifying their origin. This happened principally during
the first year when Sister Emmerich's labors for the Church
formed the greater part of her communications. He had
repeatedly been told that the invalid had asked Almighty
God as a special favor not to be informed for what individuals among the clergy she was called upon to pray and
suffer; yet it was not without difficuty that Brentano
could be dissuaded from introducing the names of persons
to whom he fancied certain visions particularly applicable,
instead of the terms Sister Emmerich herself used; such as
spouse, affianced, pastor, etc. Later on he erased
many of these early notes from his manuscripts, when he
recognized the incommensurable distance between the
highest flights of his own fancy and the pure light in which
this favored soul dwelt; and then it was that he began to
esteem no trouble too great to reproduce as conscientiously
as possible whatever was transmitted to him for the good
of the faithful.

When we cast a glance at this man of genius, this poet
so admired, the light of the cultivated and intellectual circle
in which he moved, we are forced to admit how slight are
the claims to superiority of all such natural qualities. The
atmosphere which he breathes by the suffering couch of
this poor peasant-girl is far purer, far more elevated than
any he had yet known; her detachment, her patient sufferings,
her voluntary mortifications rendered her inaccessible to any
influence of an inferior order and ever more susceptible of

the sacred light of prophecy. The Pilgrim could, indeed, annoy and afflict her, but to her interior, to her visions he had no access. Nothing could be more absurd than the supposition that his energetic nature had established between the invalid and himself a kind of magnetic communication owing to which he received from her only what he had himself previously dictated. This conjecture loses weight at once when we recall the fact that only one clothed with the priestly dignity could exercise any spiritual influence over her. She endured his presence as she would that of a poor, sick person sent her by Divine Providence to heal and save. He is the debtor, he is the favored one, he is the pupil; she is the dispenser of gifts, she is the teacher, or, in other words, the instrument under God to snatch one of the most brilliant minds of that period from the snares of the world, to win him over to the glorification of His Most Holy Name. No one possessed a more piercing eye with regard to his neighbor's weakness and foibles than did the Pilgrim, a gift he afterward bewailed with bitter tears of repentance. He was the most pitiless, the most acrimonious observer that the invalid and her little circle ever had to endure. When his enthusiasm vanished, and the charm of novelty wore off, woe to Sister Emmerich did he discover, or fancy he discovered the least thing to arouse suspicion or distrust! He was an inexorable judge! Up to the time of her death, his manuscripts teemed with bitter remarks: the words, the gestures, even the steps of her confessor were noted down with tiresome prolixity and interpreted with unsparing rigor. And yet, the only charge that could be brought against the reverend gentleman was that he made little account of the Pilgrim's notes, that he would gladly have dispensed with Sister Emmerich's visions altogether and thus been freed from the obligation of the aforesaid notes, and that he treated her communications with freezing indifference. Sister Emmerich herself met with no greater lenity at the Pilgrim's hands. Let her utter a word of consolation to the poor and afflicted who flocked to her for relief, or show the slightest sign of weariness in relating her visions, and she is instantly rebuked for unfaithfulness to her mission, for dissipating the graces she received, for injustice to himself. But soon, overcome by her angelic sweetness and forced to recognize his own unreasonable humor, he records the following words in his journal : " She is full of goodness and patience ! Yes, she is a most admirable vessel of divine grace !"

CHAPTER XXXVI.

SISTER EMMERICH IS PLACED UNDER ARREST.—HER PRE-
SENTIMENT OF THIS EVENT.—ITS RESULTS.

From the beginning of the ecclesiastical year, 1818-'19,
Almighty God prepared Sister Emmerich for the expiatory
sufferings in store for her. The events from which these
sufferings were to arise were still future, but the invisible
enemy of man had already his powerful engines at work
toward their furtherance. The mystery of iniquity which
"already worketh," according to St. Paul, was making at
that period new and vigorous exertions to sap the foundations of faith in many dioceses, and the weapons used were
precisely those which are now about to be turned against
the poor invalid herself. As in preceding ages, so was it
now: unworthy clerics in the service of anti-Catholic and
secret societies, were the inventors and executors of
measures which, under the name of " *Fundamental Rules,*"
" *Ecclesiastical Laws,*" " *Conventions,*" " *Acts' of Endow-
ment,*" etc., were destined to destroy secretly but surely
the Church of Jesus Christ. As the struggle drew near,
the invalid's visions became more comprehensive, more significant. They were not only prophetic pictures, but real,
personal combats, fruitful in results inasmuch as they were
a continued development of the great combat of the Church ;
she suffered and accomplished in very truth all that she
saw in vision. The sentiments and designs of the Church's
enemies were made known to her, that she might oppose
them by prayer. Her visions were not idle dreams, nor
her action in them vain and imaginary, rather was it the

confirmation of her own marvellous spiritual life. This life was *one*, having but *one and the same* operations although existing in two different worlds and following a two-fold law, the world of sensible things and that elevated above the senses. In contemplation, she prays, she struggles, she triumphs ; whilst, at the same moment, she suffers in the natural state, or accomplishes her duties of ordinary life. In both cases she is free, in the full possession of her faculties and of all that is requisite, in the natural and supernatural order, to produce meritorious acts. Her external life bears the same relation to her transcendent interior life as the symbol to the thing signified, the similitude to the reality, the shell to the kernel. Her persecutors are, though unconsciously, the representatives of the tendencies of the period. Of these prophetic visions, the invalid was able to recount but a very small part. It is, however, enough to awaken the surprise of the reader, when he beholds how exactly they were realized in all that referred to her own approaching trials.

Advent, 1818.—" I have been warned by my guide to prepare for a severe struggle. I must invoke the Holy Ghost to inspire me what to answer. I do it now all day, and I know what this struggle will be. Artful men will attack me and try to make me contradict myself by their perfidious questioning. It seemed as if my heart would break. But I turned to my Heavenly Spouse and said : ' Thou hast begun the work, Thou wilt also bring it to a close ! I abandon myself entirely to Thee !'—and then when I had put the case into His hands, I felt great strength and peace in God. I said : ' Joyfully will I be torn to pieces, if thereby I can help the world !'—Among my persecutors I saw a physician and some ecclesiastics who came, one after another, to take me away. They pretended to be very friendly, but I saw the deceit in their heart.

" May 19th—I have had a bad night. I was assailed on all sides and torn to pieces, but I remained calm, I rejoiced at what was done to me, and I recognized the instigators of the affair and the chief actors in it. They all talked at once, clamored around me, and ended by tearing me piecemeal. Not one of my friends was present, no one to help me, no priest. I became sad, and I thought of Peter's abandonment of his Lord.

" I saw a party of men assembled to deliberate and exult over their cunningly devised plans to carry me off. They resolved to make use of new means. My guide told me to be calm, that if they succeeded, it would end in their own confusion and be all for the best.

" May 28, 1819—I saw myself alone in my time of trial and, what was worse, my confessor dared not come to me. He seemed forced to go away without bidding good-by. I had a vision in which I found myself alone in a room with only Sister Neuhaus. Then some people came and fell upon me at the right side and foot of my bed, I was utterly defenceless.

" June 6th—I have had a very miserable night. I saw myself abused more than ever, I cannot think of it without shuddering. I was abandoned by all my friends. My bed stood in the middle of the room, and I was tended by strangers. I knew that I was in this miserable state on account of a quarrel between some ecclesiastics and laics, who tore me to pieces to show their mutual contempt. I saw Dean Overberg in the distance sitting sad and silent, and I thought all was over with me.

" July 17, 1819—Again I had visions of my approaching trials. I saw all my old convent companions visiting me, speaking of our past intercourse, and questioning me as to whether I had or had not said when in the convent such or such things of my state, etc. I could not understand what they were aiming at, and I said : 'God knows what they and I have done ! '--Then I saw them all going to confession and Communion, after which they came back to me. They were, however, no better than before, and they tried to find something out from me, I know not what. I asked them if they did not know that, long before my joining them, I had had unaccountable pains in my hands and feet; that when with them, I had often made them touch the palms of my hands which were burning hot; and that my fingers had been quite dead, without my understanding what it all meant ? Was I not unable for a long while to take food on account of the vomiting it brought on ? Was not this the case for seven months without my attaching any importance to it ? Did I not think it a sickness, although it never kept me from my duties, or from prayer, my only delight ? But I found them all hesitating and insincere in their declarations. All sought to clear themselves from blame, all excepting the Superioress and Sister Neuhaus —they alone were honest. After this came a great many of my acquaintances—they did as they always do, they spoke at random, not one willing to stand up for me. The Abbé Lambert could not help me, they would not listen to him. My confessor was not far off, but he was dejected and weary. Then six ecclesiastics and laics, among them two Protestants, came not all together but one by one, and some were false and malicious to the last degree. The sweetest and blandest among them treated me the worst. Then a man came in saying : 'Whatever is done to this person will also be done to me.' I knew him not, but he stayed by me a long time and was honest and true to me. He saw all that was done, but he could not help me. When the others surrounded me (my bed stood in the middle of the floor) they were

careful not to jostle him. Then they began to put all kinds
of questions, but I made no answer. I had already responded three different times, as recorded in the report, and
I had nothing more to say. The Vicar-General was
near by; there was some question of him. I saw that
the Dean (Rensing) was interested ; he gave instructions
but he was not for me. Dean Overberg was absent,
but praying for me. The two little nuns Frances and
Louisa comforted me. They repeated continually: 'Have
courage, only courage! all will be right!'—My persecutors
began to draw off the skin from my hands and feet. They found
the marks of a deeper red than those on the surface. They did
the same to my breast and discovered the cross more plainly
marked below than on the skin. They were amazed, they knew
not what to say ! In silence they slunk away one after another ; each told his own story, but all were confounded.
Whilst lying there awaiting the operation on my wounds,
I was seized with anguish ; but the two holy nuns encouraged me, promising that no evil would result from it.
Then a marvellously beautiful little Boy in a long robe
appeared to me ; His face shone like the sun. He took
my hand, saying: 'Come, we will thank our dear Father!'—
and raising me up lightly we went into a beautiful
chapel, open in front and only half-finished. It appeared to
be split down the middle. On the altar were the pictures
of St. Barbara and St. Catherine. I said to the little Boy :
' Why the chapel is split !'—and he replied : ' And it is only
half-finished.'—I felt that we were near a magnificent mansion
in which many persons were awaiting me. It was surrounded
by gardens and fields, paths and groves, it was like a
little village. Still it seemed as if it were afar off, and
there did not appear to be any place as yet destined for
me. I know only that I looked into the chapel with the

little Boy and saw the pictures. It was as if I had been
caught up in spirit whilst they drew the skin from my
wounds, for I felt nothing; I only saw, after it was over,
the shreds of red skin. I beheld the amazement of the
men when they found the marks penetrating the flesh,
and I saw them *scratching behind their ears!* In this
confusion of the chapel and the operation, I awoke. The
vision of the nuns and the people from the city was obscure. It seemed as if I were informed of an interrogatory to which I was to be subjected. I saw, too, something like a tumult in the city.

"The little Boy said: 'See, now all that troubled and
disquieted thee lasted so short a time, but eternity has no
end. Take courage! A rude trial is in store for thee,
but thou wilt bear it well, it will not be so hard as it
seems. Many evils can be averted by prayer, be comforted!' Then he told me to pray in my waking moments at
night, for many are in danger of perishing, a great storm
threatens. 'Fear not to say it out boldly and urge every
one to pray.'"

A few days later, Sister Emmerich had another vision,
that of a young virgin-martyr, and the sight strengthened
her for her own approaching struggle : — " I was in prayer.
Two unknown men came to me and invited me to go with
them to Rome to the place in which the martyrs were tortured.
There was to be a great combat that day, some of their
friends were to engage in it, and they wanted to see them
die for Jesus. I asked them why they exposed themselves.
They answered that they were Christians in secret, no one
would know them and, as they were relatives, a place was
reserved for them that the sight of the martyrs' torments
might affright them ; they desired also to strengthen themselves by the sight and to encourage their friends by their

presence. They took me to the amphitheatre. Above the inclosure, facing the entrance to the right of the judge's seat, was a gate between two windows through which we entered a large neat apartment in which were thirty good people, old and young, men and women, youths and maidens—all Christians in secret and assembled for the same purpose.

"The judge, a tyrannical old man, waved a staff right and left and at the signal, the subalterns down in the *circle* began their work. There were about twelve.—To the left before our windows, I saw something like an idol. I knew not what it was, but it made me shudder with horror. On the same side were the prisons. They brought out the martyrs, two by two, driving them forward with iron spears. They were led first before the judge and, after a few words, given over to martyrdom. The whole building was filled with spectators seated in tiers, raging and shouting.

"The first martyr seemed to be about twelve years old, a delicate little girl. The executioner threw her to the ground, crossed her left arm over her breast, and knelt upon it. With a sharp instrument, broad and short, he cut all around the wrist and peeled off the skin as high as the elbow; he did the same to the right arm and then to both feet. I was almost distracted by the horrible treatment of the tender child. I rushed out of the door, crying for mercy. I wanted to share her torments, but the slave pushed me back so violently that I felt it. The child's groans pierced my heart. I offered myself to suffer in her stead, and I had an impression that my turn would soon come. I cannot say what this sight cost me.

"Then the slave bound her hands across and it seemed to me that he was about to cut them off. When I went back into the room (it was semi-circular and there were square and also triangular stone seats around it) two good people comforted me. They were the little girl's parents. They said that their child's torments had pierced their soul, but that she had drawn it upon herself by her excessive zeal. It was very sad; she was their only daughter. She used to go openly to the catacombs to be instructed, and she always spoke out boldly and freely as if courting martyrdom.

"Now the two slaves wrapped her up and laid her on the round funeral-pile which stood in the middle of the place, her feet toward the centre; below was a quantity of little branches which quickly caught fire, and shot up their flames through the wood above. The good people, though resigned, appeared to me quite overcome with grief. A woman among them opened a roll of parchment as long as one's arm, fastened in the middle with a large clasp. They read in an undertone, three or four together, and passed it along from hand to hand. I understood perfectly what they read. They were short sentences, how strong and elevating no words can say. The sense of it was that they who suffer go straight to God out of this miserable world. I was sure that I could never forget the words. I still feel them, though I cannot repeat them. The reader often interrupted herself after a short sentence with the words : 'What think you now?' The petitions were addressed to God in most energetic language. I, too, looked at the parchment, but I could not read a letter; it was in red characters.

"During this martyrdom I was in indescribable anguish, never before had the spectacle affected me so. The little maiden with the skin hanging loose around her arms and lower limbs, was always before me and her groanings pierced my soul. I could not get away, they would not allow us to cross the arena. Many others were afterward martyred. They were pushed from side to side with iron points, struck with heavy clubs and their bones broken, the blood spouting around. At last, there arose wild cries from the spectators and shrieks from one of the tortured. He was the last, and they maltreated him so that he wavered in the Faith. He cursed and yelled at the executioners; despair, pain, and rage made him an object frightful to behold. The good people near me were very sorrowful on his account, for they knew that he had to die. When the others were thrown on the funeral-pile, I grieved over this one, I felt that his soul was not in glory. All was now over, and the good people left me. The bodies were not entirely consumed, and a ditch was dug to receive the bones. I saw coming down from the heavens a shining white pyramid of light into which the souls of the martyrs entered with indescribable joy, like happy children. I saw one fall back again into the fire which now disappeared and in its stead, arose a dark, gloomy place where the soul was received by others. It was the fallen martyr. He is not lost, he went to purgatory—this makes me rejoice. Ah! but, perhaps, he is still there! I always pray for such poor, abandoned souls.

"I have a feeling that this martyr was shown me to animate me to patience in my sufferings, and lately I have seen my own skin peeled from my feet and hands. These old Romans must have been of steel. The tormentors were like the spectators, the martyrs like their friends; but nowadays people are lukewarm, soft, and slothful, they pray to the true God as coldly as the pagans did to their false gods."

From the Feast of the Visitation till the end of July, Sister Emmerich suffered violent inflammation of the chest. A breath of air from the opening of a door, or even a person's approach provoked convulsive coughing; profuse perspiration flowed from her breast, and involuntary dread of coming events pursued her. On the 2d of August, the Pilgrim found her sad and nervous. The next day there arrived in Dülmen a Prussian "Commission of Inquiry," so-called, the Landrath Bœnninghausen at its head. The other members were Dr. Rave of Ramsdorf, Dr. Busch of Mün-ster, the Cure Niesert of Velen, Vicar Roseri of Leyden, and Prof. Roling of Münster. The Landrath went with the Vicar to announce to Sister Emmerich the " new investiga-tion." She replied that she knew not what they wanted with an *investigation* since she was ready to give them all the information they might desire, there was nothing which had not already been investigated.

" That is of no account," replied the Landrath. " The investigation has been resolved upon, it must be begun at once ; therefore Miss Emmerich must forthwith allow her-self to be removed to the residence of the Councillor Mers-mann."

" If such be the orders of my Ecclesiastical Superiors," she replied, " I willingly submit to all demanded of me. I shall look upon it as the will of God. But I am a religious and although my convent has been suppressed, I am still a religious, and I cannot act independently of my Superiors. The Vicar-General has already proposed a mixed investiga-tion, and if that is what you mean I am ready, for I cannot but desire to see the truth established !"

The Landrath replied: "Ecclesiastical Superiors are in this case of no account; but here are three Catholic priests." At these words Sister Emmerich turned to the Vicar Roseri and said : " How can you, a priest, appear here if ecclesiastical authority is of no account ? You took part in the last investigation in a manner little becoming a priest, and I am deeply grieved to see you here again. I have lost confidence in you." Roseri excused himself, saying that

his presence on the occasion alluded to was only accidental ; but that now it was not only permitted by the Vicar.
General but even desired, and that he regretted not having
with him the document to that effect (1). Sister Emmerich
again declared that she would not consent to her removal,
that her physician would not countenance such a step. The
Landrath withdrew, declaring that she should be conveyed
to Münster whether or not. Dr. Wesener's journal runs as
follows : " Aug. 3d —I found the invalid this evening excited, but not disconcerted. She feared only that the old
Abbé, who was sick, would be neglected.

"Wednesday, Aug. 4th—I found her to-day quite resigned. She saw in a vision last night that they would
make her fine promises, but that she would be reduced to a
most wretched state of weakness in which her confessor
would assist her."

The Pilgrim was indignant and tried to avert the persecution from the poor invalid. On Aug. 3d, he wrote her a
long letter, begging her to propose him to the Commission
as a witness possessed of the necessary qualifications for
assisting at the investigation. But when she presented his
petition to the Landrath, he declared the Pilgrim "*especially excluded.*" Mr Brentano then appealed to the Chief-
President von Vinke, at Münster, who wrote as follows :
" In reply to your letter of the 4th inst., which I had the
honor to receive, I regret my inability to gratify your desire to take part in the investigation instituted with regard
to Miss Emmerich, as I have been expressly enjoined to
remove her from her present surroundings. This is so
necessary for the attainment of the end in view that I cannot neglect the instructions given me on this point. All,

(1) A false statement, as will hereafter be seen in the official acts. Sister Emmerich saw the sad state of the young man's soul, but she could only say that she had no
confidence in him.

however, that you may wish to communicate to the Committee concerning your personal observations will be received with pleasure.

" I am also inclined to think that your presence would prove unpleasant to Miss Emmerich ; for last winter during a certain medical visit paid her, she showed uneasiness at the mention of your name. We have earnestly recommended to the commissioners to treat her with great consideration and all possible kindness, although the choice made of them is sufficient to assure us that such a suggestion was unnecessary.

" I shall be most happy to make the acquaintance of M. Savigny's (1) brother-in-law. My approaching visit to Dülmen will, I trust, procure me that pleasure."

The Pilgrim next applied verbally to the Landrath himself; but here, too, he met a refusal. Disappointed in his hopes of being placed on the commission, he went, in compliance with the invalid's desire, to the paternal mansion of Cardinal Diepenbrock, at Bockholt, to await the result of the investigation.

Aug. 4th, the Landrath again renewed his persuasions, but Sister Emmerich persisted in her refusal to consent to any change not authorized by her ghostly Superiors. " I demand," she said, " an order from the Vicar-General, officers delegated by him to execute it, and impartial witnesses; then I shall accept whatever happens as coming from God, then I shall have nothing to fear."—The Landrath did not as yet dare to attempt force. His visit was followed by one from Curé Niesert and the Vicar Roseri. The latter began :

" Now, tell us how would you like to be treated ?"

Sister Emmerich answered : " Why do you ask ? Have

(1) M. Savigny, a celebrated lawyer, professor at the Berlin University, who had married Mr. Brentano's sister.

you an order to treat me as I would like ? If so, I ask for
priests lawfully commissioned and for two witnesses to draw
up an official statement which they will read to me, that I
may know what is ascribed to me."

" You ought not to complain," said the Curé ; " you are
lying there comfortably, you seem to be very well."

" How I am," responded the invalid, " God knows !"
then turning to Roseri, she said : " I know now through
the Dean (Rensing) that you have no authorization from
the Vicar-General to be here."

On Friday, Aug. 6th, Dr. Borges of Münster, a Protestant, arrived in Dülmen accompained by a mesmerist.
As soon as they entered the inn, the former boasted that he
would " make short work of the girl, that there would be no
shuffling now !— He would have her removed to Berlin by
the police without its doing her the least harm." The news
of this incident soon spread, and the people became alarmed
lest, indeed, force might be used with the poor invalid.
The liveliest sympathy was manifested by all. An assembly
was held to protest against proceedings so opposed to law
and justice and Commissioner Keus selected to draw up resolutions. These were placed in the Landrath's hands, who
solemnly promised to present them at head-quarters. This
restored calm, and the good citizens hoped they had averted
the threatened blow. Dr. Borges and his companion went
with the Landrath to see Sister Emmerich and urge her once
more to consent to her removal. As the doctor held a high
position among the Freemasons, his presence was particularly
odious to her, and his flattery more disgusting than his abuse.

" How unreasonable in you," he said jeeringly, "to reject
the fine offer made you of being surrounded by the most
distinguished men, and of receiving their attentions in a
place far preferable to this ! "

"The good intentions of these gentlemen," replied Sister Emmerich, "I leave to God. I wish them every blessing, although I have not as yet profited by their good will. If you wish merely to discover the truth, you can examine me here in this room; but I know there is no question for you of the truth, which you could easily discover. If you want the truth, why not seek it *here* by me ? "— As both gentlemen asked what they could do for her during the investigation, she replied : "I demand, being seriously ill, the presence of my physician and confessor, a companion to attend to me, and two priests and two laics as witnesses; nevertheless, I again protest that I will leave this house only by force." Then she remonstrated against Dr. Rave's having any share in the matter, since, besides his official report in February, he had published another and very different account greatly prejudicial to her. The result of the remonstrance we shall see later on. The mesmerist's discreet and reserved behavior during the interview made it evident that he saw not in SisterEmmerich any marks by which to recognize a medium (1).

Dr. Wesener says: "In the morning I found the invalid tolerably strong, but still opposed to the idea of moving. Dr. Borges tried to persuade me to consent, but when I told him Sister Emmerich was not in a condition to be moved he grew angry, and threatened force. Toward midnight, they did, indeed, intend to remove her, but as there were some assemblies going on, the execution of their scheme was deferred."—

Mr. von Schilgen, an eye-witness, gives the following account of this nocturnal escapade : "Many of the citizens

(1) The Landrath himself declared: "There can be no question of mesmerism in Sister Emmerich's case. I may say once for all that I have remarked that she holds it and its adherents, individually and collectively, in abhorrence,"

and myself had made use of the Landrath's acceptance of
our protest to calm the people and persuade them that force
would not be resorted to. I was so fully convinced of the
truth of what I said that I went quietly to rest; but just
about midnight, I was aroused by one of the police who
came with orders to assemble his comrades, one of whom
lodged in my house. I was, of course, surprised. I ran to
the invalid's house where I found quite a number collected
awaiting the issue of the affair. The police were in motion.
At midnight, Dr. Borges, Landrath Bœnninghausen, and Dr.
Busch made their appearance. After rapping for some time
at the door leading to Sister Emmerich's lodgings and receiving no answer, they went around to the kitchen and
made Mr. Limberg show them the front room on the lower
floor; but this they did only to ward off suspicion. They declared it suited to their purpose and went away leaving the
owner, as well as the assembled crowd, under the impression that they would hold the investigation there. The
people, however, did not disperse till daylight called them
to their various occupations. It was rumored that at eight
o'clock the next day, the invalid would be carried off by
force. To be able to give an exact account of the affair,
if it really happened, I went half after seven o'clock to
Sister Emmerich's. After the usual salutations, I inquired
upon what she had resolved. She answered : ' I am extremely embarrassed. The Landrath has appealed to the
Dean to use his influence to gain my consent to being removed and to submit to a new investigation. He came to
see me for that purpose (1). I know not what I shall do !'
I remarked that something must be resolved upon, when she
cried : 'No! never will I consent to it! I persist in my
refusal!' and she implored me to stay and get the police to

(1) Dean Rensing told her that the Landrath had complained bitterly that he would
lose his position if she did not yield to their demands.—(Pilgrim's Notes).

protect her. Just at this moment the Landrath entered and renewed his entreaties. I interfered and reminded him of the protest of the preceding evening, but all to no purpose. He raised her by the shoulders himself, wrapped the bedclothes around her, and a nurse, whom he had brought with him, took her by the feet; thus they carried her down stairs, laid her upon a litter there in readiness, and four of the police bore her away to the house of the Councillor Mersmann, escorted by the Prefect and his men. There was no disturbance, the lookers-on expressing their sympathy only by sobs and tears. I noticed, to my satisfaction, that at the moment they wrapped her in the bed-coverings she fell into the cataleptic state and was, consequently, unconscious of what was being done to her (1)."

We shall now subjoin Sister Emmerich's own account:—

" The afternoon preceding my removal, being fully awake, I saw in vision all that was to take place the following day. The pain it caused deprived me of speech. Dean Rensing wanted me to submit freely, and the Landrath told me that he would lose his position if I did not; but I still refused. When he seized me by the shoulders, my spirit was caught up out of this miserable world into a vision of my youth which I had often had before my entrance into the cloister, and I remained perfectly absorbed until the next day. When I awoke and found myself in a strange house, I thought it all a dream. The whole time of my captivity, I was in a state of mental transport unaccountable to myself. I was frequently gay, and again full of pity for the blind investigators for whom I prayed. I offered all that I endured for the poor souls in purgatory, begging them to pray for my persecutors. I

(1) In Sept., 1859, the author visited the abode of Sister Emmerich at Dülmen, and found the marks of the government seals still visible on the doors of the house. Father Limberg's brother, the owner, was living. He told him that, when the poor Sister was carried off, the cows in the adjoining stable bellowed piteously.

often went down into purgatory and I saw that my sufferings
were like those of the holy souls. The more violent my
persecutors were, the calmer and even the more contented was I, which infuriated the Landrath. God kept me
from making any outward demonstration, my graces were
silent ones. Without the blessing of a priest or anything
holy, I received from God a strength hitherto unknown, as
well as every word that I had to say. I had nothing prepared. When my persecutors attacked me on one side,
questioning and abusing, I saw on the other a radiant form
pouring out strength and grace upon me. He dictated every
word that I should say, short, precise, and mild, and I was
full of pity. But if I spoke any words of my own, I perceived a
great difference; it was another voice, rough, hard, and shrill."

On the Feast of St. Lawrence, I saw his martyrdom. I
saw also the Assumption of Mary, and on St. Anne's day,
my mother's patroness (1), I was taken up to her in her
blessed abode. I wanted to stay with her, but she consoled me, saying : ' Although many evils are before thee, yet
terrible ones have been averted from thee by prayer.'
Then she pointed out many places in which they prayed
for me. 'The heaviest trials thou hast well sustained, but
thou hast still much to suffer and accomplish.'

" On the Feast of my Holy Founder, I had a clear view
of the position I should have been in, if my enemies' desires
had been fulfilled. Some of them were fully confident that,
in my person, they had all Catholics in their power, and were
about to disgrace them. I saw some ecclesiastics even
animated by very evil dispositions. I saw myself in a
deep, dark hole, and I thought I was never more to come
out ; but, day by day, I rose higher and higher and the light
increased. My persecutors, on the contrary, were buried

(1) The **Feast** of **St.** Anne falls on August 16th in the Calendar of Münster.

deeper and deeper in darkness; they grew uncertain as to how they should act, struck against one another, and finally, sank to the bottom. St. Augustine, whom I invoked, stood by my bed on his feast-day, and confounded my cruel tormentors. St. John also came to me on his feast and announced my speedy deliverance.

" When my persecutors came, I always saw the wicked enemy standing by. He looked like an assemblage of all the bad spirits : some laughing, weeping, cursing, playing the hypocrite ; some lying, intriguing, making mischief. It was the demon of secret societies.

" In this vision my guide led me by the hand like a child. He lifted me out of the window of my father's cottage, led me over the meadow, across the marsh, and through the grove. We went on a long, perilous journey over desert countries, till we reached a steep mountain up which he had to draw me after him. It was strange to think myself a child, although so old ! When we gained the summit, he said : ' See, if you had not been a child, I should never have been able to get you up here. Now, look back and see what dangers you have escaped, thanks to the providence of God !'—I did so and I saw the road behind us full of pictures of different kinds. They represented the various snares of sin, and I comprehended how wonderfully I had been preserved by the watchfulness of my angel. What on the way had appeared to me simply as difficulties, I now saw under human forms as temptations to sin. I saw all kinds of troubles which, thanks to the goodness of God ! I had escaped. I saw people blindfolded. This signified interior blindness. They walked safely on the edge of the abyss for a time, but at last they fell in. I saw many whose safety I had procured. The sight of these dangers filled me with alarm, and I knew not how I had escaped.

" When my angel had pointed all this out to me, he went on a few steps ahead, and I at once became so weak and feeble that I began to stagger like a child not yet able to walk alone, to cry and lament like a little infant. Then my guide came back and gave me his hand with the words : ' See, how weak thou art when I do not lead thee ! See what need thou hast of a guide in order to pass over such dangers ! '

" Then we went to the opposite side of the mountain and descended, crossing a beautiful meadow full of red, white, and yellow flowers, so thickly crowded that I was in dread of crushing them. There were, too, some rows of apple-trees in blossom and different other trees. Leaving the meadow, we came to a dark road with high hedges on either side. It was muddy and rough ; but I passed over gaily, holding my guide's hand. I did not even touch the muddy path, I only skimmed above it. Then we came to another mountain pleasant to look upon, tolerably high, and covered with shining pebbles. From the top I cast a glance back upon the perilous road, and my guide said that the last road, so pleasant with its flowers and fruits, was typical of spiritual consolations and the manifold action of grace in the soul of man after resisting temptation. My fear of walking on the flowers signified scruple and false conscience. A childlike spirit abandoned to God, walks over all the flowers in the world, without thinking whether it bruises them or not : and, indeed, it does them no harm. I said to him that we must have been a whole year on the journey, it seemed to me so long. But he replied: ' To make the journey thou seest, ten years would be needed ! '—

" Then I turned to the other side to look at the road that lay before me. It was very short. At the end of it, only a little distance from where I stood, I saw the Heavenly Jerusalem. The gloomy, perilous road of life lay behind me, and before me only a little way off was the magnificent city of God shining in the blue heavens. The plain I still had to cross was narrow and beyond it was a road from which, right and left, branched by-paths in different directions, but which finally returned to the main road. By following them the journey would be considerably lengthened. They did not seem so very dangerous, though one might easily stumble on them. I gazed with joy into the Heavenly Jerusalem, which appeared much larger and nearer than it had ever done before. Then my guide took me to a path that led down the mountain, and I felt that danger threatened. I saw the Pilgrim in the distance. He seemed to be carrying something away, and I was eager to go to him. But my guide took me into a little cottage where the two religious, whom I know, prepared a bed and put me into it. I was again a little nun and I slept peaceably in uninterrupted contemplation of the Heavenly Jerusalem until I awoke. On the journey, I gave my hand at several different times to people whom I met, and made them travel part of the way with me.

" The Heavenly Jerusalem I saw like a glittering, transparent, golden city in the blue sky, supported by no earthly foundations, with walls and gates through which I could see far, far beyond. The view was rather the instantaneous perception of a whole than of a succession of parts such as I have here been obliged to present. It had numerous streets, palaces, and squares, all peopled by human apparitions of different races, ranks, and hierarchies. I distinguished whole classes and bodies bound together by ties of mutual dependence. The more I gazed, the more glorious and magnificent did it become. The figures I saw were all

colorless and shining, but they were distinguished from one
another by the form of their raiment and by various other
signs, sceptres, crowns, garlands, croziers, crosses, instruments of martyrdom, etc. In the centre arose a tree, upon
whose branches, as if on seats, appeared figures still more resplendent. This tree extended its branches like the fibres
of a leaf, swelling out as it rose. The upper figures were
more magnificent than those below ; they were in an attitude of adoration. Highest of all were holy old men.
Crowning the summit was a globe representing the world
surmounted by a cross. The Mother of God was there,
more splendid than usual. It is all inexpressible ! During
this vision I slept in the little cottage, until I again awoke
in time."

CHAPTER XXXVII.

Measures Taken by the Vicar-General.

We shall here interrupt our narrative to say a few words of the ghostly Superiors to whose authority Sister Emmerich so often appealed.

The Vicar General von Droste wrote to Dean Rensing, August 3d—"I hear they are about to institute a new investigation with regard to Sister Emmerich. Inform her of it without delay. Tell her also that they have not consulted me and that I have not authorized any ecclesiastic to take part in it."

The Vicar Roseri received, at the same time, a severe reproof for going to Dülmen without orders. "No ecclesiastic ought to accept an order of the kind from secular authority," wrote the Vicar-General. "He dishonors and forswears his august calling when he allows himself to be employed in police affairs."—Mr. Roseri and Mr. Niesert were, consequently, obliged to quit Dülmen, and the same order was given to Prof. Roling. The latter delayed until the Chief-President and Landrath Bœnninghausen should use their influence for him to remain ; but Clement von Droste was not a man to act in contradiction to himself. A second order was despatched to Dean Rensing :

"The Chief-President von Vinke," he wrote, " asks that I should allow some ecclesiastics to take part in this investigation, but I cannot consent. . . . . . I will permit no priest, Prof. Roling no more than any other, to take part in it, especially as Baron von Vinke does not speak of a mixed commission. Once for all, then, until further orders, observe

the instructions I have given you. I trust Prof. Roling will
be not less obedient than Mr. Roseri and Mr. Niesert."

In answer to Sister Emmerich's appeal for assistance and
counsel, the Vicar-General wrote to Dean Rensing. "I
hasten to reply that I can give no particular advice for the
future, as I know nothing respecting the projected investigation. As for the rest, it seems to me that what Sister
Emmerich has done up to the present and what she intends
doing is very proper. Her saying that I ought not to abandon her entirely, shows that she has taken a wrong view of
the case."

When, later on, Sister Emmerich forwarded to the Vicar-
General through Dean Rensing a copy of the protest presented by her to the commission, he sent the following note
from Darfeld : "I have received your communications of
August 5th and 7th, with Sister Emmerich's protest. I shall
reply as briefly as possible. This investigation is *purely
secular*, ordered and directed exclusively by the civil authorities. If ecclesiastics were to take part in it, contrary to
established rules, that fact would not alter its nature ; it
would still remain secular. It is most important that it
should in no way, not even in appearance, assume the
character of a mixed investigation. Therefore, 1st—No
ecclesiastic (yourself included) must take the least share in
it, either for or against ; we must absolutely ignore it. If
Sister Emmerich asks advice of you, Canon Hackram,
or any other priest, it is only right that it should not be refused her ; but neither you nor any other priest must accede
to demands from a commission whose very existence should
be ignored. Act so that all other ecclesiastics may clearly
understand this.

"No. 2—I know not by what right some of Sister Emmerich's friends have laid a protest against the investigation

before the chief tribunals of the country. If such a course is resorted to, it is Sister Emmerich herself who should do it, or at least, her friends should have from her a formal request in writing authorizing them to make such a protest.

" No. 3—It would not be proper for any priest to remain alone with her under the present circumstances, either for counsel or spiritual assistance." This was the only decision to which the Vicar-General could possibly come, since about a year previously the Chief-President had, on some futile plea, positively rejected the proposed idea of a mixed investigation. "I have," he wrote, " proposed to Baron von Vinke, in accordance with his desire, a commission of investigation, partly secular, partly ecclesiastic, which, however, was not accepted. He assured me that four persons could not be found (I had expressed a wish that there should be some Protestants among them) who, alternately with four others named by me, would guard Sister Emmerich for eight days at least."

The Chief-President, however, pushed the matter on, designedly eluding the intervention of ecclesiastical authority. He named a commission, the choice of whose members made it plainly visible to the Vicar-General what were its tendencies ; therefore the latter deemed it obligatory upon himself to protect the Church's dignity by forbidding clerics to take part in it. He knew also that he could not hazard any step in favor of persecuted innocence under the then existing government without exposing it to worse treatment ; he looked upon the projected investigation as unworthy of notice, feeling confident (as the invalid had been shown in vision) that, " what was of God would be upheld by God."

Some time before, when Prof. Bodde had published his attacks upon the invalid and, through her, upon ecclesiastical authority, the Vicar-General, to prevent the intervention of the civil authorities, had again seriously thought of removing her from her surroundings and placing her in some peaceful retreat entirely secluded from the world. He was, however, forced to admit that Almighty God, in signing her with the stigmata, had willed to leave her in a position apparently little suited to such a distinction, although he could not be persuaded that the Abbé Lambert and Father Limberg were wholly free from blame in the unsuccessful project of removing her to Darfeld (1). Some years later, owing to the idle talk of one of her former Sisters in religion, it was rumored in Münster that the invalid was going to retire to a place near Dülmen called "The Hermitage." The Vicar-General immediately dispatched an order to Dean Rensing, couched in the following severe terms: "Having learned that Sister Emmerich proposes to go to the *Hermitage* with the Abbé Lambert, or Father

(1) As the venerable old Abbé suffered much in this affair, we think it proper to give here the following letters of Dean Overberg to Dr. Wesener. They testify to the charity and solicitude with which the Dean, the most venerated priest in the country of Münster, interested himself in Sister Emmerich and her little circle.

I.

"Sept. 6, 1818.

"Have the kindness to inform me at your earliest convenience : 1—How much the Abbé Lambert still owes the druggist ; 2—Whether our dear Sister or the Abbé has as yet paid anything, and how much ; 3—Whether our Sister herself still owes anything to the druggist, and how much. I shall try to help them discharge their debt, at least in part. Salute our dear Sister cordially for me, and assure her that I shall write soon, D. V., though I would rather go to see her, if it pleases God to grant me the use of my limbs. I should be much pleased, if you would kindly lend me again for some months your journal of the invalid. I do not write to the Abbé concerning the apothecary, but of the other affair. The position for writing suits not my limbs, it is very fatiguing ; therefore, I must be brief. May God be with us!"

II.

"Sept. 13, 1818.

"I have the honor to send you not only the 8 Thlr. 23 Gr. of the apothecary's bill, but also what is due for the Abbé's medicines, 25 Thlr. We can also count among the medicines, the wine still necessary or, at least, very desirable during convalescence. Let our Sister employ what remains after paying the apothecary in procuring wine or anything else of which she may have need, or wine for the Abbé until he is able to return to his beer. No sick or poor person has suffered by my sending her this sum, but let her remember the donor in her prayers. It is not I. I shall name him to her some time—and yet, there is no reason why you and she should not know him. It is the Prince-Bishop of Hildesheim to whom I wrote about the bill. I leave it to your and our Sister's discretion to let the Abbé know that there is something in reserve to procure him wine. If it please God to cure my limbs so that I can undertake a journey to Dülmen, I shall have the pleasure of seeing all my beloved friends. May God be with us !

"P. S. None of the money is to be returned, even though it should not be expended in wine for the Abbé."

Limberg, or with both, I charge you, Rev. Sir, to inform Sister Emmerich immediately, as well as the two aforesaid ecclesiastics, that, although I cannot forbid her residing at the place named, yet I formally forbid her to allow either one or other of these two priests to accompany her. I also prohibit the latter, under pain of reserved punishment, to lodge at this Hermitage, or even to pass a single night therein, in case Sister Emmerich makes it her abode."

Reports like the above succeeded one another, accusations and threats against the invalid and her friends were addressed to the Vicar-General which aroused in him the fear that it would turn to the prejudice of religion. He resolved therefore, upon an expedient which would insure her removal from Dülmen by placing it out of her own power or that of her friends to object; an expedient, however, to which spiritual authority ought not to resort. Oct 21, 1817, he wrote to Dean Rensing :—

"I thank you very much for your letter concerning Sister Emmerich. I should have replied the same morning had I not committed to writing and sealed what I propose in her regard, and I look forward to breaking the seal only in your presence. Say to her in my name that as her Superior, I command her to beg God to vouchsafe to her the knowledge in detail of the plan I have formed for her. Tell her also that she can never fail when in obedience. As soon as an opportunity offers, I shall take the liberty to send you a copy of my brother's book on the 'Church and State.' May God command the wind and waves!"

It was, then, upon the hope that his thought would be divined that the Vicar-General rested the execution of his project. He forgot that he was treading on the forbidden ground of divination when he gave such a command. He lost sight of the strict rules of Faith and the very principles that constitute authority in the ascetic life, which alone ought to dictate the measures and trace the limits of an ecclesiastical investigation. His purity of intention, however, was pleasing to God, who granted him the desired satisfaction of seeing the invalid separated for some time from her habitual surroundings. One feature in his project was directly opposed to the will of God, and that was his resolve to sequester her for the rest of her life in an asylum absolutely cut off from the world, for she still had a task to fulfil, that of *relating the Life of Jesus.* Scarcely had Dean Rensing informed her of the above-mentioned command, than she was enlightened by her angel on the Vicar-General's secret project. Next day, Dr. Wesener made the following report:—

"Oct. 25—I found her deathly weak. She had had a miserable night and had seen herself near death. She could not exactly designate the day, but she thought it not far distant.

"Oct. 26—Extreme debility. We resolved to sit up with her last night which she spent miserably. She had three spasmodic attacks in which the muscles of the abdomen were drawn back toward the spine. She announced each attack, saying she *should have to bear this suffering, but that God would give her patience.*"

Her sufferings increased until the first week in November, the doctor and confessor looking upon death as certain. On Nov. 6th, the doctor recorded in his journal: "I found her to-day weak indeed, but cheerful. 'During my last sufferings,' she said, 'I had constant visions. I had to climb a rough mountain with my guide. Right and left on the road, I saw paths leading to precipices and I beheld the distress of the wanderers for whom I had to pray. Half-way up the mountain, I came across a city with a magnificent church; but before I could enter, some holy

little nuns of my own Order received me, and clothed me
in a shining white habit.   I told them I was afraid of not
being able to keep it unstained.   They answered: 'Do
what thou canst.   Stains will, indeed, appear, but thou
wilt cleanse them with thy tears.' . . . . I had also a conversation with my guide about the secret the Vicar-General
had imposed upon me through Dean Rensing, and he told me
that I must observe the strictest silence on the subject.   I
was to tell no one whatever.   'If they push the affair
further,' he added, ' God will put an end to it.' "

This absolute silence of the invalid threw the Vicar-General into a state of incertitude.   He wrote to Dean Rensing,
April 5, 1818 :—

" I have not yet come to any decision, although I have done
what I could to fathom the case.   Herr von Vinke is responsible for the non-execution of a mixed investigation,
under the empty pretext that he could not find four individuals to engage in it.   *I think God will take the affair into His own hands !* " . . . And, as if to attest his belief in
the invalid's extraordinary vocation and perfect sincerity,
he added :—" This letter will be handed you by Prince
von Salm Reifferscheid, accompanied, perhaps, by his son
and Rev. Herr von Willi.   They wish to converse with
Sister Emmerich and look upon at least one of her hands.
As they are *God-fearing* people, I could not refuse them,
and I beg you to escort them to her lodgings.   I mention the
Prince's son and his venerable tutor merely for the sake of pre-
caution.   I know not for certain whether they will go or not."

When Bishop Sailer visited Dülmen in the fall and, conformably to Dean Overberg's wish, received an account of
conscience from Sister Emmerich, she revealed to him the
Vicar-General's secret and the order she had received in
vision.   He encouraged her to silence, and the Vicar-General allowed the affair to rest.

CHAPTER XXXVIII

The Captivity.

Sister Emmerich was conveyed to Councillor Mersmann's house and placed in a room on the second floor to which there was no access but by one door which opened into an ante-chamber. Her bed stood in the centre of the room, and from the ante-chamber the most minute observations could be made (1). Here two commissioners were to remain constantly six hours at a time, when they were to be relieved by two others; they were not to lose sight of the invalid a single instant. The bed-clothes and linen of the invalid were carefully examined that no sharp instruments or chemical preparations by whose aid, as they imagined, she procured the effusions of blood could be there concealed; her finger nails also underwent inspection lest they should be long enough to tear the skin.

The Chief-President sent from Münster an experienced nurse, a Mrs. Wiltner, on Prof. Bodde's recommendation. She had never seen Sister Emmerich and the commissioners did all they could to prejudice her against the patient, telling her that she was an impostor whose fraud she was to expose. The Chief-President's instructions were that the investigation was to continue until they arrived at a definitive decision. The first day was Sunday, 8th of August. On the preceding evening the invalid had regained consciousness. She perceived the change in her surroundings, but soon relapsed into contemplation which lasted until the

(1) For an account of this investigation, the author has referred to the details published at the time, to the Pilgrim's notes, and especially to Dr. Wesener's. In September, 1819, Sister Emmerich related the particulars of her captivity to the latter, who wrote everything down and daily submitted his notes for her approval.

next morning when she requested her confessor to give her Holy Communion. She offered herself in sacrifice to God, prayed for her persecutors, and drew such strength from the reception of the Holy Eucharist as to look with perfect peace and resignation upon all that might happen to her. The day passed calmly, the watchers often approaching her bed, but most politely. Prof. Roling, of Münster, expressed his amazement at her serenity : "I cannot understand how you can be so self-possessed and serene," he said to her. The nurse, too, testified her astonishment, and Sister Emmerich, noticing the marked attention she paid to her demeanor, to her every word, rejoiced with the thought : " Now the truth will appear !"

That night was a restless one. Her custodians frequently approached her one after another, holding the light in her face and calling her. She said in allusion to this : " Even then I was not left without help. When they came to me with the light, my angel was always present. I obeyed him, I heard him, I answered him. He called out to me, ' Awake !' and when they put insidious questions to me, he told me what to answer."

The following day the interrogatory began, Dr. Rave, to whom she had objected, opening the inquiry. She was obliged to allow him to examine her wounds, which he did in the roughest manner, a proceeding very wounding to her exquisite delicacy. He noted down her answers as she gave them. Perceiving the effort she was obliged to make, he frequently asked her if he should discontinue his questions ; but she begged him to go on. " For," she said, "I am here for that purpose ; I must go through it." From time to time, Dr. Borges and Landrath Bœnninghausen came in, seated themselves at the foot of her bed, and watched her closely. She tried to answer every question as precisely as possible in the hope of establishing her truth and innocence. The interrogatory lasted the whole day and even late in the evening, when completely exhausted she fainted away. Dr. Rave and the Landrath appeared to have concerted together to sound each other's praises; they attributed to each other the best intentions and tried to impress the invalid with the belief that they were her protectors. Dr. Borges's presence was most odious to her. She regarded him as the chief instigator of the injustice done her, and he, on his side, lost no opportunity of wounding her by his coarse and unfeeling remarks. On the third evening, she was informed that neither Father Limberg nor Sister Neuhaus should any longer have access to her, and that Dean Rensing would bring her Holy Communion every week. The night passed with the usual annoyances. She was almost overcome by fear, her custodians continually touching and examining the wounds in her hands; but she kept silence and allowed them to do what they pleased (1).

On Tuesday morning, the 10th, the examination was resumed. Dr. Rave had declared his task finished the preceding evening; yet he began again with Dr. Borges and the Landrath to put differently worded questions on the same points as before, trying to force her to contradict her former statements. He had reported, in February, that she had callosities or painless swellings on her feet, a proof that she really did walk in secret. After he had repeatedly inspected them the invalid said: "What think

(1) Her very patience and silence were for the Landrath a most convincing proof of imposture. "If she, indeed, suffered so much," he reasoned, "she could never have kept silence."—"One single trick," he wrote, "one single act of dissimulation, sufficed to betray the whole affair. We were enlightened sooner than we expected by a seeming trifle. Her friends had united with her in assuring us that the slightest touch on her wounds caused her acute pain, that she even cried out on such occasions; but we found that when engaged in a conversation that embarrassed her, the wounds of her hands might be tightly pressed or even rubbed without her giving any sign of uneasiness. I tested this myself, and so did others."—(Bœnninghausen's Report of the Investigation, 1819).

you, doctor ? Can I walk ? Do you judge by my feet that
I can walk ?"—To which he was forced to answer before
his companions : " There is no question of it. You are too
weak and suffering."

When these interrogatories had continued two hours, all
the commissioners were assembled by Dr. Borges for
the reading of the official report. This lasted four long
hours, from ten A. M. till two P. M. ; for each thought
himself obliged to test the accuracy of the statements by
repeated inspections of her wounds. She was treated with
as little consideration by them as if she had been a log of
wood. Their savage brutality would not even allow the
timid, consecrated virgin to veil her breast. Whenever she
tremblingly covered herself, they brutally tore away the
linen, answering her plaintive entreaties by cynical railleries. Toward two o'clock they left her, but only for an
hour. They all returned at the end of that time and recommenced torturing their victim, who happily fell into contemplation and beheld the martyrdom of St. Lawrence. She
remembered only one of the remarks made to her that
evening : " Now it is all right. You can go home again on
Saturday."

" This day," she said, " was the bitterest of my life. I
thought I should die of shame and confusion at what I had
to endure, and the words to which I had to listen. I said
to myself on the shameful treatment I underwent : ' My
soul is in the prison of the body ; now is the body itself in
prison, and the soul confined to a little space, must deliver
up the body of sin. Crucify it, outrage it ! It is but a
wretched log."

On Wednesday, Aug. 11th, they adopted a new plan of
action. After the preceding examination, the existence of
the stigmata could not possibly be denied ; therefore must

the invalid be adroitly led to confess that they had been artificially produced by French exiled priests. Dr. Rave undertook to extort from her the avowal. He made his appearance about nine o'clock A. M., assumed an air of extreme kindness, seated himself by her bedside, and expressed the desire "to speak to her heart to heart." The custodians withdrew, and the doctor began in emphatic terms to praise the intelligence, the virtue, the whole life of the poor invalid. With his hand on his heart, he exclaimed: "Yes, indeed! I feel the most heartfelt compassion for you, sick and suffering as you are! I wish to speak with you in perfect sincerity and assist you as far as I can. Landrath Bœnninghausen, also, esteems and pities you, like myself. He is disposed to serve you, and Chief-President von Vinke is of the same mind; he wrote to us last evening that he would like to take charge of you and all your family. Confide in us, be perfectly open and sincere with us."—At these words Sister Emmerich interrupted him and said :—

"I only wish that you and he could see into my heart, you would find nothing hidden there, nothing bad."

"Yes," he continued, "you may trust me as you do your confessor. I will keep all to myself—even the Landrath shall not know what you confide to me. I shall arrange everything for the best, you will soon see an end to this affair."

"I do not understand," she replied, "why you would hide from the commissioners anything concerning me. The commission must and shall know all that I have to say !"

Then he began to run over her life, from time to time putting captious questions to throw her off her guard, such as— "Did you not use the discipline in the convent ?"

"My chief discipline consisted in overcoming myself interiorly and in rooting out my faults and evil inclinations."

"You have always borne great veneration toward the Five Sacred Wounds. Now, it is not an unprecedented thing for pious persons in an excess of love to imprint them visibly upon their person."

"I know nothing of such things. I have already said all that I can of the origin of my wounds."

"Ah! believe not that I imagine you have made them with a bad intention or through hypocrisy. No, I know you too well. I heard of you from every one as a person given to virtue from your childhood. But there would surely be no harm in wishing to become like to the Redeemer. One might do such a thing out of piety."

"No, not in this way. It would be sinful and unlawful."

"Yes, I think so, too. I esteem you too pious and upright for such a fraud. But I regret that you are now so abandoned by your friends. Do you not wish me to bring your sister or the Abbé Lambert?"

"No! I wish no suspicion to rest on them!"

"But you have been visited by other French priests, and you could not know what they did when you were unconscious."

"Just after the suppression of the convent, I had, it is true, long fainting-spells; but I am certain that no one ever did anything to me. There was only one attendant by me, and she saw the blood flow for the first time."

"It is not possible that such a thing could happen of itself. French priests are very pious, they esteem this sort of thing very highly; they did it with a good intention, and you allowed it through piety."

"No! that would not be a good intention nor piety. It would be so great a crime that I would rather suffer death than consent to such a thing."

"Reflect well upon your position! Let it not come to this, that ecclesiastical authority demand an oath of you."

"What I say I can swear to at any time. Ecclesiastical Superiors may come."

"Then we are all in the dark, and you alone are in the light!"

"What do you mean by that?"

"You are so suffering, so full of pains, so tortured on all sides!—Can that be the calling of man?"

"Ah! you disquiet and torment yourself still more for the evil things of this world, you live in constant agitation, you perplex your brain over things you cannot understand; but my sufferings are not so grievous to me, because I know why I suffer."

"No! I tell you, the wounds come not as you say! It is impossible! If you have not made them, others have!"

"Now I see plainly what you mean, and what a double game you tried to play last winter!"

"Well, let us remain good friends."

"No! Friendship cannot exist on such terms. You shall not make me tell a lie!"

Dr. Rave retired and Herr Bœnninghausen entered. Sister Emmerich declared to him her readiness to confirm on oath all that she had stated, whereupon he replied: "O that is nothing! such an oath is of no value! We would not receive an oath!"—And when she objected that Dr. Rave's duplicity would oblige her to defend herself by sworn testimony, he responded:—

"Dr. Rave has written nothing bad of you, his statement was good. For the rest, he may say and write what and how he pleases, only what is official has weight or truth."

Thursday, Aug. 12th, she was less importuned. She

had violent vomitings all the morning, but they paid little
attention to her.   One or another made his appearance
from time to time, but immediately withdrew.   A young
man named Busch, hardly yet free from the school-room,
was the only one who frequently presented himself, tormenting her with his self-confidence and arrogance.—" Will
your wounds bleed to-morrow ?—What! you do not know?—
When the blood begins to flow, let me know immediately,
etc."—At first, she sought to silence him by her own gravity.   But failing in this, she at length addressed him:
" Young man, take care !   Do not allow yourself to be
drawn into acts of injustice and rash judgments !   It is not
so easy to decide upon things of this kind, on which older
men than you have suspended their judgment.   You are
young, and it is becoming in a young physician to be reserved, to judge leisurely."   He was moved by these
words and said before the nurse : " Sister Emmerich knows
how to touch one's conscience.   Were she innocent, I might
weep tears of blood !"   He, however, hardened his heart.
He was to the end more insulting than the older members.
The nurse could not conceal her sympathy and veneration
for the persecuted invalid.   That afternoon, Dr. Rave offered her some oatmeal porridge which she declined. He insisted, whereupon she tasted it, when vomiting immediately
came on.

August 13th, Friday.—This day had been impatiently
awaited by the commissioners.   Would there, or would
there not be an effusion of blood ?   In either case, they had
resolved to view it as imposture.   Herr von Bœnninghausen and Dr. Rave kept watch the night before and, to
give her confidence, as he imagined, the former expressed
to her his great desire that the following day would bring
an effusion of blood.   " Understand," said he,   "I do not

wish it on my own account, but for Dr. Borges's sake. Only
yesterday were we speaking about it, and he assured me
that, if he saw the blood flow, he would certainly become a
Catholic. He assured me of it."

Sister Emmerich replied indignantly : " On the Day of
Judgment, perhaps that man, if he remains what he is, will
be dealt with more leniently than they who know the Law,
but who do not live conformably to it. It may be that he
is not so guilty as you."

The entire night between Thursday and Friday she lay
in contemplation, and the dawn of day found her physically stronger. "I begged the nurse," she said, " to give me
water to wash. She did so, with these words : ' May
God and His holy Mother permit the wounds in your head
to bleed! then these gentlemen will be convinced of your
innocence.' I rebuked her for such a wish : ' I hope there
will be no blood,' I said. 'Of what use would it be ? These
gentlemen would not let themselves be convinced. Still
we must commit ourselves to the will of God !' I washed
and said in jest, ' My forehead especially I shall wash clean.'
Then I took off my cap and the nurse had just spread a
clean white linen towel over my head, when in came Dr.
Busch with his usual questions. He said : ' You must let
the blood flow '—In about a quarter of an hour, he made
me take off my binder, and behold it was stained with
blood ! It was a most unwelcome sight to me, I had hoped
there would be no blood. I did not dare to cover my head,
and all the commissioners were called in. They examined
my binder and head, and set to work to wash my forehead,
first with a warm, then with a cold liquid, which gave me
great pain."—The nurse deposed that the invalid's forehead
was rubbed first with saliva, then with strong vinegar, and
lastly with oil of vitriol. At this application she cried out

in pain. "It burns, it burns like fire!" and then, as the nurse said, some red streaks appeared.

"They spent the whole morning in examining, washing, and rubbing my forehead. I fainted from pain. The gentlemen-commissioners showed great embarrassment. The nurse was closely questioned as to how the blood came on my binder. She related all that we had said and how it had happened, but they declared that I had wounded myself. The nurse greatly excited came toward me, wringing her hands : 'O Miss Emmerich, you are betrayed and sold! They say you have put the blood on your bindder yourself! O unhappy woman that I am to be employed by such people! Yet do I rejoice that I now know you and can help you!'—I consoled the woman, telling her that I knew they would act thus, and I exhorted her to trust in God."

Mrs. Wiltner's honest testimony to the truth was exceedingly distasteful to the commissioners, who summoned her before them next day and interrogated her anew. They employed every artifice to make her say that, two minutes before Dr. Busch's arrival, she had left the invalid to empty the basin ; but she firmly refused to tell the falsehood. On the contrary, she declared herself ready to swear solemnly that she had not left the room and that the invalid, after the removal of her binder, had not once raised her hands to her head, but had kept them clasped on her breast the whole time. She forced Dr. Busch to acknowledge that, when he entered the room, the basin of water was still standing on a chair. But her protestations were of no avail. They entered into the report the following words as Mrs. Wiltner's deposition : "Mrs. Wiltner, the nurse, absented herself for two minutes to empty the basin."

Some time after the investigation, the nurse gave her testimony to the public through Dr. Theodore Lutterbeck, of Dülmen, and offered to repeat it under oath before any tribunal; upon which the Landrath Bœnninghausen had the audacity to publish the following : " If Dr. Lutterbeck contests the right of the commission to public confidence, he will find his words received as oracles by few. I claim it with much more reason for myself, as I have submitted every detail to a minute examination with perfect impartiality, and a mind free from prejudice. Should more credit be accorded to a nurse's deposition which, after all, proves nothing, than to my testimony ? This I leave to the judgment of the reader. I shall only observe that, from the first eight days, Mrs. Wiltner manifested a disposition to talkativeness and a veneration for Sister Emmerich which led the commission to deliberate whether it would not be well to supply her place by another, a less bigoted person. But as she seemed to get on well with the nun, and as it was very important that the latter should mistrust us as little as possible, she was retained (1)."

That afternoon the commissioners again met around the patient's bed, and Dr. Rave experimented on himself to prove that the effusion of blood had been artificially produced. The Landrath's report is as follows :—

" The circumstance (2) offering the most conclusive proof of the fraud and which shows that Anne Catherine Emmerich plays not only a passive rôle in it, but that she is also an active accomplice, happened in the following manner. The fact that the bleeding ceased not entirely in her head as in the other parts, formed the only basis upon which it was possible to experiment. The only difficulty was as to how she made her head bleed, not an easy matter in truth, since she was never alone and was, moreover, in a position

(1) History and Result of Investigation, 2, p: 46.
(2) History and Result of Investigation, 2, p. 34—39.

that exacted the greatest precautions; besides, a certain one of our members was so inconsiderate as to wish to treat with her candidly and openly, which manner of acting would not, as is evident, have led to the end in view, but would have put her still more on her guard. However, the trial had to be made, and it was announced to her that the commission would not separate until a positive decision had been reached. She informed us herself that her head bled at times, although the other parts had ceased to do so, and the appearance of this phenomenon being all that was required to end the investigation, so painful on both sides, we entreated her to beg God not to delay it. As these words seemed to be pretty well received and, moreover, as we saw that the need of more substantial nourishment began to be felt by our patient, they were again repeated to her with every imaginable mark of sincerity, and lo! that very evening was made the prophetic announcement that, *perhaps the next day, Friday, August* 13th, *a little blood might appear on her forehead!* Now, at last, we had grounds for hope. That she might not be disturbed by too rigorous a surveillance, I took that duty upon myself, and when all were asleep I threw myself gently on the lounge in the ante-room. Toward midnight, I heard a rustling. I arose quietly, peeped through the open door and saw that Sister Emmerich had changed her position. Her back was turned to me and she was in the act of removing the bed-clothes. She caught sight of me; but, as the light did not fall on her face, I could not say whether she was annoyed at being detected or not. Next morning, however, at six o'clock, nothing had as yet appeared on her forehead. I was on the point of giving up hope, when half an hour after, the nurse very much excited brought me the wished for information that Sister Emmerich's head seemed to be bleeding.

The phenomenon was carefully examined by all, and each member was invited to commit his observations to writing. I regard this circumstance as the most important and decisive in the course of the investigation; and I am of opinion, as are also the other members of the committee, that nothing was left undone on the occasion. Our unanimous conclusion is, that the red marks on the invalid's forehead perfectly resemble what might be produced by rubbing or scratching. There were two where the epidermis had evidently been scratched. From them flowed the ordinary lymph which adhered to the head-band, whilst a third had begun to form a crust. This opinion is that of men, unprejudiced, impartial, and of sound judgment; it alone should suffice to convince the most incredulous. Mark well what follows:—to arrive by comparison at still greater certainty, Dr. Rave that same morning scratched his forehead in two places until the epidermis broke and lymph flowed. The result was the same in both cases : the simple red marks made by the rubbing disappeared in two days ; in other places the crust formed by the lymph fell off in six days, when the epidermis was renewed, which in both cases took place on the seventh day.

" When we had thus acquired convincing proof that what we had seen was altogether different from the effusions of blood we had heard described —still more that they had been made by the hand of man, and that unskilfully enough, it remained only to be ascertained how far the invalid would carry her denial of the facts. It was easy to see, as is proved by the report that when she was in a state of consciousness, two or three minutes would have sufficed to do the work ; and this time she could have had when the nurse left the room with the basin. I exhorted her in presence of some of the members to depose to the report, but she declared that the scratches on her forehead were neither of her own making nor that of any one else, and she offered to take an oath to this effect. A feeling of grief came over me when I heard this declaration on oath of an evident lie, uttered coolly and smilingly by one whose pitiful condition I could not forbear compassionating. She appeared in my eyes as a hardened impostor deserving neither pity nor consideration, one with whom severe measures should be used to bring her to an avowal of her guilt. But the sight of suffering humanity regained its empire over me ; her desolate state effaced my first impression of horror and turned my indignation against the revolting malice of those who had perverted the poor creature."

As some stains had appeared on the invalid's linen, the wound in her side having bled also, an explanation must be found for that. The Landrath said they were merely the stains of the coffee she had vomited. But Mrs. Wiltner declared at the time and afterward to Dr. Lutterbeck that she was ready to swear to the fact that the very weak coffee taken and rejected by the invalid had been received in a blue cloth always at hand, and that not a single drop had fallen on the chemise which had been, besides, protected by a four-double covering. The article was then examined, the stains found to be the red color of blood. After washing it, Mrs. Wiltner showed the water tinged to the commissioners. Still Bœnninghausen clung to his opinion of the coffee stains, and forbade the nurse to show it or the water to Dr. Zumbrink who arrived from Münster the following day. She however disregarded the Landrath's injunction and informed Dr. Z— of all that had passed, offering to confirm what she said by oath (1).

----

(1) Mrs. Wiltner's deposition was published some time after by Dr. Theodore Lutterbeck, upon which Landrath von Bœnninghausen immediately made the following

In the afternoon they again assembled around her bed to renew the torture of the morning. But Sister Emmerich flatly refused to yield to their wishes; whereupon, the Landrath exhorted her to obedience and patience.

"We must all do our duty," he said. "We are all servants of the State and one must help the other. You, also, must give an account to the State of whatever there is extraordinary in you."

Sister Emmerich replied: "I respect civil authority and I am willing to fulfil my duty; but I do not recognize all here present as competent judges in this case!"

They answered by all kinds of persuasive reasoning, but to no purpose. The Landrath exclaimed: "For whom do you take us, then?"—Instantly in a solemn tone, she answered: "I look upon you all as the servants of the devil!" (1).

These words from the lips of a defenceless female made such an impression upon one of the gentlemen present, Mr. Nagelschmidt, the druggist, that he left the room, exclaiming: "No! I'll not be the devil's servant!"—and he refused to take any further part in the iniquitous affair. All were dumbfounded. The Landrath had no answer to make and, one by one, they slipped away, leaving Sister Emmerich in peace.

Dr. Busch came again late that evening, feigning compassion and offering his services. He made the nurse re-

explanation: "The numberless frauds already discovered and the others yet to be disclosed, lead me to suspect that the reddish stains on Sister Emmerich's linen were made by blood from her gums. This assertion is not quite so ridiculous as is the attempts to prove that by capillary attraction it must have flowed from her internal organs ; for the stains were darker outside than inside. I do not, however, affirm that her perspiration was wholly free from blood."

(1) When Sister Emmerich, in September, recounted this scene to the Pilgrim, she added : "The Landrath was sitting at the right of my bed smoking, near him stood the apothecary The former pretended to pity me because, as he said, my friends had reduced me to so pitiable a state. But, he said, I was not too old to be cured, and so on, and again began to flatter me. I saw the devil behind him. I was too frightened to speak, and the nurse, thinking I was going to faint, brought me some water. Then came the talk about authority, and I said, ' First comes God . . . .' "

move the invalid's head-dress, when he poured on the top
of her head some drops of a liquid which deprived her of
consciousness. "Those drops," she said afterward, "gave
me pain through my whole body and took away my senses.
The nurse thought me dead. I lay for a whole hour immovable."

On the morning of Saturday, the 14th, they began
again to rub and to bathe her head. The new physician
from Münster, Dr. Zumbrink, carefully examined everything, but behaved with so much propriety as to gain
Sister Emmerich's confidence. In the afternoon, she had
a chance of convincing herself in an interview with him
that her first impression was not false.

"Before he came," she related, "I had a vision in
which I beheld a tall, dark-complexioned man approach
me and hold out his hand. I thought he was sent from
God to save me and I told my nurse so. He did come, in reality. He was an upright, honorable man; the others were
afraid of him, concerted among themselves, and kept out
of his presence. The chief-officer ironically called him
my doctor ; he said that he was of *my* party and asked me
if I were not particularly fond of him. I answered that
I hoped each would do his duty. Dr. Zumbrink was no
flatterer; he was more attentive and more active than
any of the others. He said to me from the first: ' I shall
write whatever I discover, innocence or imposture. Be
not bewildered by anything, neither by fair words nor by
threats. Hold to the truth; with that a person cannot be
worsted (1).'

"The others I saw in vision in the black, filthy, four-

(1) Dr. Lutterbeck declared in his second pamphlet that he had read the opinion
Dr. Zumbrink had given in writing and in which he stated, " Not having seen Anne
Catherine Emmerich for seven years before, he had formed no opinion as to the origin
of her wounds ; but that, during the investigation, he had remarked no fraud.
From the impression made upon him at the time by the invalid, he esteemed her
incapable of imposture."

cornered, false church, with a high roof and no turrets ;
they were very intimate with the spirit that presided
therein. This church is full of impurity, vanity, sottishness,
and darkness, but scarcely one of those men knew in what
obscurity he labored. It is all proud presumption. The
walls are high, but they surround emptiness ; a stool is
the altar, and on the table is a death's head veiled, a light on
either side. In their worship they use naked swords, and
at certain parts of the ceremonies the death's head is unveiled. It is all bad, thoroughly bad, the communion of the
unholy. I cannot say how abominable, how pernicious and
empty are their ceremonies. Many of the members know
it not themselves. They wish to be one single body in
some other than the Lord, and if a member separates
from them, they become furious with me. When science
separated from Faith, this church was born without a Saviour, good works without faith, the communion of the unbelieving with the appearance but not the reality of virtue ;
in a word, the anti-Church whose centre is malice, error,
falsehood, hypocrisy, tepidity, and the cunning of all the
demons of the period. It forms a body, a community
outside the Body of Jesus, the Church. It is a false church
without a Redeemer. Its mysteries are to have no mysteries and, consequently, its action is temporal, finite, full
of pride and presumption, a teacher of evil clothed in
specious raiment. Its danger lies in its apparent innocence. It wills differently, acts differently everywhere. In
many places its action is harmless, in others it aims at corrupting a few of the learned. But all tends to one end, to
something bad in its origin, an action outside Jesus Christ,
through whom alone every life is sanctified, and outside of
whom every action, every work remains in death and in
the demon."

That evening Sister Emmerich reminded the Landrath of his promise to have her conveyed home on Saturday. "It cannot be," he replied. "The case is not closed, we have arrived at nothing definite." The next day, he jested among the other commissioners : " Miss Emmerich shall not escape, though we need not stay by her the whole day, or guard her so closely." Dr. Zumbrink expressed his indignation at such a speech—"What! is this not an investigation of a serious nature ? Every one eats, drinks, sleeps, walks, amuses himself. The affair is not conducted as it should be. I do not trust such men ! "

On the Feast of the Assumption and the two days following, Sister Emmerich was less tormented than usual. The committee could not agree upon what further experiments to make ; the Landrath went nervously in and out, and spoke of indifferent things. On the 17th, she demanded an end to the investigation, she recounted the torments she had undergone, and asked what they still exacted of her. The Landrath replied that so many new questions had been forwarded from Münster for herself, the Abbé Lambert, and her sister, that he could see no end to it. She responded sadly :

" They have put me off from day to day with vain promises, and the end is still far distant! "

The Landrath grew angry and began to threaten her : " You dare to reproach me, but things will soon be changed! Then you will find your man in me ! You yourself and your French priests are the cause of your not being released."

Dean Rensing's entrance at this moment interrupted his invectives. Sister Emmerich turned to him saying : "They exact of me confessions that I cannot make."

The Dean replied : " If there is question of your avowing anything, you can testify to it on oath,"

" Truly ! but they tell me that my oath is of no account."

" Who has told you that ? " inquired the Landrath.

" He who said it, ought to know," was her answer.

Thursday, Aug. 18th—This day was spent without special annoyance, excepting the Landrath's menaces and reproaches against her and her absent confessor, to all which
she listened in silence.

Drs. Borges and Busch were to watch that night. They
hoped that, as the next day would be Friday, they would
witness the bleeding of her wounds (1).

Fortunately, Dr. Zumbrink was also present which restrained their brutality. Frightful visions disturbed her
rest, and to her great joy the morning brought no effusion of
blood. " This circumstance," she says, " seemed to give
the Landrath satisfaction, as he looked upon it as a confirmation of his opinion that I am an impostor. Perhaps,
too, he hoped to hear something from me. It is only
in this way that I can explain his polite attentions, and the
flattery with which he loaded me on the following day, forgetful of past scenes. His kindness was more insupportable
than his threats."

Dr. Borges was in bad health. The night-watch had
greatly fatigued him, and he returned to Münster disgusted
at the whole affair.

On Friday evening, Dr. Rave appeared after an absence
of a week. He could not conceal the impression made upon him by the invalid's appearance.

" How miserable and suffering you are ! " he exclaimed,
and turning to the Landrath, he said : " She is unusually
weak, she has fever. I cannot answer for her life much

(1) " They gave me that night a small phial," she said "wrapped in a scrap of black
silk, saying that Dean Overberg had sent it to me, and that I must lay it awhile on
my breast. It inspired me with horror, especially the silk. I felt that it came from an
impure being. When they insisted on my putting it on my breast, my heart beat so
violently that, in an agony, I dashed it away."

longer ! "—When she reminded him that the next day
would be the third Saturday since they brought her there,
he said : " I can do nothing ! I, too, am worn out here.
If you cannot trust us longer, we cannot trust you, etc."

She represented to them their unworthy conduct, saying
sternly : " Which of you can accuse me of falsehood ?"—
but they returned no answer.

On Saturday several of the commission, scarcely knowing
what further course to pursue, assembled around her. They
spoke of their own weariness of the affair and proposed
bringing it to a close. The nurse ventured the remark:
" What expense this affair has entailed ! And where will
the money come from to pay these gentlemen ? "

" All will be defrayed by the king," answered one.

" The king is badly served by his subjects," rejoined
Sister Emmerich. " They deceive him to get his gold, which
is steeped in the sweat of the poor peasants ground down to
blood by taxation. Of what use is such an investigation ?
Of what value are all these reports made by men ignorant of
such things, who understand them not, who possess not the
key to them ? Better to distribute the money among the
poor and exact an account of secret prevaricators, of skilful
cheats, for that would do some good and draw down a blessing from God !"

She spoke many earnest words to which the commissioners replied not, though they seemed impressed. The Landrath felt his position as president growing more embarrassing every day ; Dr. Borges had withdrawn in anger at
not being able to persuade the invalid to acknowledge herself an impostor ; Dr. Rave saw all his artifices fall to the
ground, whilst Mr. Nagelschmidt and Dr. Zumbrink had
become her declared friends; the others were wavering. The
president had as yet discovered nothing to substantiate

his private suspicion of fraud, and what report should he make to Baron von Vinke to whom he had promised to bring the case to a definite conclusion? He began to cast around for some escape from his embarrassment, and for three days, from the 21st to the 23d of August, he sought to throw the invalid off her guard by insulting remarks and sudden attacks. He approached her only to irritate and perplex her; for example, he would address her as follows : " There you still lie ! A person in health ought not to lie in bed. You are only feigning. You pray not, you work not, and yet you are so weak and languid ! But you do not impose upon me. It does not escape me that you have strength enough when you wish ! You can speak as loud and as long as you want. I know that at home you were able to sew," etc.

Sister Emmerich full of compassion for the poor man, sel-dom answered a word. Hearing that his wife had a can-cer, she longed to suck the wound and heal her; the cer-tainty that her request would be refused alone restrained her from asking to do so. Sometimes Dr. Busch joined the Landrath in his railleries : " You are pretty well off in this investigation," he would say. " You suffer nothing, you lose nothing." One day as she was in the act of throw-ing off blood, he, without a word of explanation, suddenly wrenched open her mouth, thrust in the handle of a spoon, and examined her gums. Only from some remarks dropped by the Landrath did she discover what was meant by so violent an action : " Your case," said he, " is some-what similar to that of an impostor recently unmasked at Osnabruck. She, too, with lips dry and parched, vomited blood ; but it was discovered that she sucked her gums to produce the hemorrhage. You do the same"—then softening his manner a little, he continued: "I pity you though, I do not think you so very guilty. The French priests say you are a patient, good creature willing to do all they tell you. They think they will be able to revive the practices of the Catholic Church and faith in her legends, if they can reproduce in you things of this sort."

Dr. Zumbrink was indignant at the outrages offered the poor invalid, and the nurse wept. "The president," she says, "proclaims you an accomplished cheat."—But Sister Emmerich, consoled and strengthened by God, bore up courageously.

"One day," she afterward related, "an old man with a little Child took me by the arm, led me away, and hid me in a nettle-bush. I was satisfied even to be stung by the nettles; it was better than the talk of that man. It was St. Joseph and the Infant Jesus who had taken me away. One night the same little Boy that used to help me with the cows, came to me. He was very bright and gay and ran merrily around, a little stick in his hand. I said to Him: ' Ah! dear Child, it is not now as it used to be in the fields, now I am in prison!' and we talked together joyously and freely. At another time, I had a shining Child by me in a glittering cradle. I rocked Him and cared for Him. He carried a cross, and when I asked what it was, He answered: —' It is thy cross which thou wilt not carry!'

"One day in the third week when I was very sick and longing for the Most Holy Sacrament, I had a vision. I went by a narrow, level, shady path to an island surrounded by walls. And now came two spirits to me, I think they were females, and gave me, for I was very weak, two morsels on a little plate. I remember the nurse was lying near me asleep and, that she might not see them, for they approached from her side, I threw my towel over her head."

August 25th found her so full of courage that she said: "I have lost all fear, all dread. I shall now be strong and cheerful in proportion as my troubles increase." And she begged the Landrath to put to her the questions he had had on hand for several days. But he replied:

"You are too weak and sick! You cannot answer!"—"If I am ordered to answer," she replied, " I can do so. The Lord will give me strength."

After some hours, he returned with Dr. Rave to begin the interrogatory. They had about fifty points to investigate. Dr. Rave felt her pulse at intervals to see how far her strength might be taxed, as he told the nurse (1). Sister Emmerich, alluding to this interrogatory afterward, said: "Before it began I was weak and miserable, but as it went on I grew stronger. But the questions were so singular, so ridiculous that they amused me, sometimes I could not help laughing heartily; for instance, they asked what was done to my wounds when people were kept waiting at the door, etc. When I had responded to all their questions, the report was read to me and I signed it after they had made some changes in it. Then I became again quite prostrate."

On Friday, Aug. 27th, her annoyances recommenced on the part of Dr. Busch. "Your blood must flow," he said, "Yes, make it do so! We are here uselessly, nothing comes of it. What can we say? What have we seen? etc."—"I have not that power," Sister Emmerich replied. "You should have come sooner, if you wanted to see my blood flow. If I could help you in any way with my blood, I should willingly do it; but I have not now as much blood as would satisfy your desire."

(1) He made a note in the report in his own peculiar style: "When Sister Emmerich forgets herself, she can speak very distinctly and at length; otherwise, she speaks in almost a whisper—a proof of her great dissimulation."

Then came the Landrath, impatient at her wounds not bleeding and asking angrily : " What will be the end of all this ? We have as yet found out nothing !"—and he broke out into threats against the invalid for not confessing what he termed *the truth.* At three P. M., he returned, sent the nurse out of the room, and closed the door. His excited appearance alarmed the poor invalid for the moment, but she soon regained her self-possession. He began : " Every day, every hour discovers so many new things that this case becomes more and more serious and complicated. Those Frenchmen's intrigues are now unveiled. Lambert, the old fox, has betrayed himself, but I am more cunning than he ! We now know why he, the Abbé Channes and Father Limberg distributed rosaries. I am now upon Limberg's track. I know that he used to be the exorcist in the parish of Darup. Yes, yes, I tell you, the French made those wounds on you, or you yourself did it. Come now, confess!"

Sister Emmerich replied quietly : " What I have said I hold to. I neither can nor do I wish to say anything else. Father Limberg never was at Darup." In a solemn voice, the Landrath said : " Miss Emmerich, I state the truth to you. It is all a fraud, the work of the French !"

The invalid silently busied herself with her tea. Assuming a gentler tone, the Landrath addressed her : " You shall no longer be annoyed, all will be ended if you only confess. Fear nothing. You and yours will be well cared for ! We wish well to you and to them."

" What you ask I cannot do. It would be a scandalous falsehood !"

" Confess !" he cried in a rage. " If the French did not do it, the Germans did ! But no ! they are not so bad, they are not cheats. But confess, at least, that you made your head bleed the other day !"

" That also would be false. Ask the nurse who saw the blood, ask the commissioners," replied Sister Emmerich.

" The nurse is of no account! And your good Dr. Zumbrink ? Let him keep out of this affair !" retorted the Landrath.

" Give yourself no further trouble! I understand you. It is useless ! You gain nothing !" said Sister Emmerich quietly.

" Ah! you hypocrite ! Cunning woman! I know you! I have watched you closely, I have often felt your pulse ! You have strength enough when you wish, when it pleases you," said he in a rage.

She was silent—her innocent, peaceful expression only exasperated him, and he began again. " What! you will not answer me ?"

" I have nothing to say to you ! You do not want the truth. I fear you more than all hell. But God is with me and with all your threats and blasphemies you cannot hurt me !"—answered the Sister.

" It is a fraud, and it will remain a fraud ! Confess it ! (1) It cannot come from God, and a God, who does such things, I would not have ! I offer you *pure wine* (2). What kind of conscience have you ? I have something with which to reproach myself, but I would not exchange places with you !"

" It is not *pure wine*, it is gall that you offer me. You would drive me to perdition, but God will protect me. Truth will triumph ! I have nothing more to say to you !" and she turned away in silence. The Landrath withdrew, saying : " You shall regret this soon, very soon ! Still, I give

(1) Some weeks later, Von Bœnninghausen published the following: "Sister Emmerich must acknowledge that, when the investigation was over, I frankly made known to her my conviction founded upon evident reason." (The afore-named Work, p. 10.)

(2) " Pure wine"—that is the *truth*.

you till to-morrow for reflection. Be reasonable! Allow yourself to be persuaded!"

This scene, which lasted over two hours, the nurse wit: nessed from the ante-room. When the Landrath withdrew, she entered hastily, weeping and wringing her hands; but the invalid, cool and calm herself, soon restored her peace. When on Nov. 28th she related the affair to the Pilgrim, she said: "The two holy religious who had so often helped me, came and offered to deliver me. But I thought of St. Peter in prison and of his deliverance. I said: 'What am I compared with Peter? I will remain till the end.'"

On August 25th, Dr. Rave paid his last visit. "A curious case," said he, scornfully, "a curious case! I shall have nothing more to do with it! I am going home. I shall not be an obstacle to things turning out well for you!"

As Dr. Rave retired, the Landrath entered to announce a new scene for the evening: "Your affairs go ill," said he. "In the first place, you shall not soon, perhaps you will never return to your lodgings. Still, I leave you till this evening to reflect."

" This evening you shall receive no other answer than that already given," replied Sister Emmerich. Mr. Mœllman, the burgomaster, came to see her, assuring her of the generous intentions of the Landrath in her regard. He tried to draw from her expressions of satisfaction upon all that had been done in the investigation up to the present moment; but she indignantly repelled his insinuations. About six, the Landrath returned in great excitement, closed the door as on a former occasion, and began:—" Do you remember what I told you?"

"I have no other answer to make," said the invalid.

"Reflect upon what you are doing. Lambert has committed himself. I'll soon catch him," said the Landrath.

"Then hold him fast!" replied Sister Emmerich. "Only take me to my home until he has revealed all, for then I shall have a long rest."

"Will you also confess?" said he, unmindful of her last remark.

"To be sure," she answered; "but I can tell you nothing but what I have already told you."

"You are an impostor! You are not sick! You know how to appear so, but I am more cunning than you. I have watched you. I have noticed every pulsation, every breath. You will have to quit Dülmen. Never again shall you see your relations and your good friends, the French. Yes, those French are they who have perverted you, etc., etc.!"

Two hours were spent in such invectives, during the greater part of which the invalid observed strict silence. At last, her tormentor said: "My patience is worn out. We shall remove you this very evening."

"Have you really the power to do so?" asked Sister Emmerich. "You have repeatedly said that, as a servant of the State, you would follow your orders closely"—but he interrupted her, saying: "I am now going to write the report. I understand the whole case. You cannot confess your guilt, because you are bound by terrible oaths; but I'll bring all to light! You must leave Dülmen."

Sister Emmerich replied. "Do without fear or hesitation whatever you will. As for myself, I dread nothing. You call yourself a Catholic Christian, but what is your religion? You see me receive the Holy Sacrament! And yet I impress upon myself the signs of the Redeemer! I

am bound by oaths ! I am acting a lie, a horrible crime !
What is your religion ?"

He made no answer, and withdrew.   In about an hour he
returned with a written paper in his hand, and began :
''Must I send this report ?   You have yet some time.   Reflect seriously !"

"Yes, send it," was the answer.

" I warn you!   Think over it well !" said the Landrath
gravely.

" In God's name, take it away !" moaned the poor invalid.

In a solemn voice, he once more inquired : " Again, I
ask you, shall this report be sent ?   Think of the consequences !"

" In God's name, yes !" she again answered.

He left the room in a rage, returned, renewed the scene,
and left again angrily as before.   Sister Emmerich saw
through the farce got up for the occasion.   She quieted her
agitated nurse and, the first time since her removal, enjoyed for two hours a calm and refreshing sleep.

" I can say sincerely," she afterward remarked, " that
I was quite calm and more cheerful during this scene than
I had been the whole time previously."

Saturday night, the 29th, passed quietly.   At ten the
next morning the Landrath reappeared.

" Now, will you go ?" he began.

" O yes !   I will gladly go *home !*" answered Sister Emmerich.

"No ! not *home*, but out of the city !" repeated the
Landrath.

" I'll not consent to that," said Sister Emmerich firmly.

" How will you return to your home ? " inquired her persecutor.   " You are too weak !"

"Leave that to me!" answered Sister Emmerich. "You had the care of bringing me here, leave to me that of returning! The servant-girl will take me."

"But it is Sunday!" he retorted. "You will be seen."

"Let me go at once!" said she. "The people are still at High Mass, the streets are empty."

"Well, let it be so!" he replied. "But before you go, you must promise me something."

"If I can, I will," said the poor invalid.

"You can. Promise to let me know immediately if blood again flows."

She promised, but he was not yet satisfied. He presented a paper, saying: "Here I have written your promise. Sign it, that it may be a pledge of its fulfilment." In her desire to return home, the unsuspecting Sister signed the paper without reading it (1). When he held in his possession the desired signature, he said: "I shall conduct you home myself. As I brought you here, I shall also take you away"—with these words, he seized the coverlet, rolled it round her in spite of her struggles, and carried her down stairs. Here he confided her to a female servant who bore her to her home without attracting much attention, the Landrath following at a distance. She had lost consciousness from the moment he took her into his arms. When she recovered her senses, he said: "I still hold to my opinion, but we shall remain friends!"—She kept silence, and he withdrew.

Some weeks after, he returned and entered her room unannounced. She was so terrified at the sight of him that she almost swooned away.

(1) Oct. 14th, Von Bœnninghausen published the following:—
"Anne Catherine Emmerich has giving me in writing, signed by her own hand, a solemn promise to inform me immediately of any change that may occur in her physical state; she has, besides, *expressly authorized* me to contradict all that may be published about her without my knowledge, and to declare him guilty of falsehood who propagates such things."

" But" (she afterward said to the Pilgrim and Dr. Wesener, who both relate this scene), "I turned my thoughts to God and became calm and brave. This man is quite inexplicable to me. He pretends to be very kind, speaks to me with tears of his wife's sickness, makes protestations of friendship, mentions the goodness that he has shown to me, and then says : ' But your wounds have not bled since the investigation, else you would have let me know ?' Then he began to speak of the publications which might be issued. He thought that printed relations of the affair would entail very fatal consequences for me ; and he begged me earnestly, with tears in his eyes, to prevent my friends from publishing anything. I replied : ' Be assured, my nearest friends certainly write nothing for the public. As to what others may do, I know not ; and again, I know not how I could prevent them.' At this he appeared still more affected and said : ' But your position afflicts me greatly. I feel such a desire of befriending you !' ' No,' I replied, ' you mistake on that point, I cannot believe it.' ' I am speaking the truth,' he said.—' I cannot consider it such,' I replied .—' Well, we shall not speak of that,' he said ; ' I have formed my opinion, and I fear not to make it public. However, listen to me, be persuaded ! I will give you whatever you ask, your brother also ; but you must leave this place. Your surroundings are prejudicial to you. The French mislead you. You are so upright a person, you have ever been a good child, a virtuous young girl, and a perfect religious. I am acquainted with your whole life, I know it to be exemplary ; but even that excites my pity for the situation in which you now are.' I replied quietly : ' I can neither speak nor act otherwise than I have done. No one around me has had any part in making my wounds. But I am satisfied with my position, I neither wish to accept nor do I demand anything but repose. My brother has no more need than I of your money ; he is happy in his poverty for his heart is content.' Then he spoke to me with great earnestness and gravity. 'Miss Emmerich,' said he, 'you will repent of not having accepted my offer. Reflect seriously upon what you are doing.' 'My resolution,' I replied, 'is firmly taken. I trust in God,' whereupon he left me."

This visit was followed some weeks later by the public declaration of Von Bœnninghausen in which he said: " Anne Catherine Emmerich. as she has herself informed me, will leave this place where she has endured so many sufferings and miseries. She will retire to her brother's cottage in the neighborhood of Coesfeld, as soon as the mildness of spring will permit her to travel. A quiet room in which she may pass the rest of a life which has been rendered miserable by a set of impostors, has already been prepared for her. Who would not desire as I do to see her regain that peace and rest lost partly by her own fault ?" (1)

We may more easily form an opinion of this man with the numberless and strange contradictions manifested in his words and actions, if we consider the firm conviction under which he was even before the inquiry and which he had avowed in these terms : " The phenomena manifested in the person of Anne Catherine Emmerich being diametrically opposed to the best known laws of nature, cannot be natural. There is in the case either a miracle or a fraud." But his want of religion allowed him not to admit the existence of a miracle or of an immediate interposition of Almighty God, as he unhesitatingly declared : " I would not

(1) Work mentioned above, p. 43.

have a God who would do such things." Imposture it must be, and the only point to be investigated was how far the invalid was an active or a passive accomplice in it. He was inclined to decide upon her passive participation; for, even in his most violent attacks upon her, he felt that she was innocent and unjustly persecuted, he bowed to the mysterious power of her purity and elevation of soul. He could, in fact, truthfully say in his "History of the Investigation": "Who could be so hard-hearted as not to pity her? I feel for her, I shall make every effort to draw her from the snare that holds her captive, the snare of ignorant fanaticism or infernal malice." Had he presented to the Chief-President the faintest suspicion of Sister Emmerich's sincerity, he never would have been allowed to publish such a declaration as the following: "I was authorized by the Chief-President von Vinke to offer pardon and support to the unfortunate woman, if she would freely confess everything and make known the principal impostors that have led her astray (1)."

As to solving the question how in one and the same individual could be found diabolical imposition and incomparable purity, the Landrath gave himself no trouble. He left that to Dean Rensing, whom he had gained over to his own opinion, though both Dean Overberg and Dr. von Druffel were more and more strongly convinced of her truth. The year before Dean Rensing had defended her against Prof. Bodde's calumnies. "Up to the present," he says, "I have discovered no reason for supposing the phenomena in question. (the stigmata) were produced artificially. I cannot pride myself on having made the natural sciences a special study; but I do not subscribe to that love of the marvellous which sees the supernatural in what is merely

(1) " Report upon the Phenomena Observed in the Person of Anne Catherine Emmerich," by Rensing. Dorsten, 1818.

extraordinary. If I must say what I candidly think, Anne
Catherine Emmerich is not guilty of imposture, although I
refrain from honoring as miraculous the singular manifes-
tations I behold in her. As to explaining her case naturally,
my limited knowledge of nature's forces is inadequate to
such an undertaking, as is also what I have read and heard
on the subject from scientists. No report of any professor
has as yet thrown light upon the case ; consequently, I can
make nothing more out of it than thoughtful Christians do
of the explanations given by commentators on the miracles
mentioned in the Bible."

On May 29th, the Dean addressed a long letter to the
Vicar-General in which he expressed himself, as follows :
" I have been for the last three years and I am still of the
opinion that Miss Emmerich is not an impostor. Trifling
circumstances did, at times, shake my conviction a little ;
but after having submitted them to a severe investigation
by the surest rules of criticism, *the passing doubt ever served
to convince more strongly of the truth.*"

Landrath von Bœnninghausen, however, knew how to raise
a bridge by which the timid Dean might pass from the de-
fensive to the aggressive, and thus escape the dreaded blame
of the new authorities and the disagreeable reproach of cred-
ulity ; this bridge was that of flattery. He was lavish of his
praises. "I must here make honorable mention," he said,
" of Dean Rensing, a man in every way worthy of respect,
but who, on account of a former literary dispute with Prof.
Bodde, has sometimes appeared in a disadvantageous light.
From the first he endeavored to persuade Sister Emmerich
to submit to the investigation, and afterward he did all in his
power to further its ends." This public eulogium, which
classed him among the partisans of the commission, was at
first most disagreeable to the Dean ; he sought to justify

himself with the invalid personally. But this was the last
visit he paid her, and from that time he shunned even the
appearance of communication with her. Still more, in
March, 1821, some weeks after the Abbé Lambert's death,
he wrote a dissertation under the title, " *Critical Review of
the Singular History of A. C. Emmerich, Religious of
the Suppressed Convent of Augustinians, of Dülmen,*" in
which referring to the Landrath Bœnninghausen, he
actually sought to prove the stigmatisée an impostor (1).
All that he had witnessed seven years before, her
virtue displayed in the investigation directed by himself, the innumerable testimonies he had collected and
forwarded to his superiors together with his own observations—all were of little weight compared with the fear
of incurring disgrace with the new government officials.
" At present," he says, " the signs of a skilful fraud discovered by the director of the commission, strengthen the
suspicion that all may not be exactly as the Sister states ;
they have, also, shaken the Dean's faith in her sincerity
and truth. He can no longer resist the desire of diving into the mystery, bearing in his hand the torch of criticism."
And it was thus that he dicovered, "that at a very early
age she was inflamed with an extraordinary love of corporal
penance, self-inflicted torture, and voluntary suffering. Now,
this strong inclination for exterior penance and mortification affords room for the conjecture of many, who seek

(1) The author would have been silent on this much-to-be-regretted act of the Dean, if
after the publication of the first volume of this work, remonstrances had not been addressed to him from Westphalia. After the severe condemnation pronounced by Dean
Overberg and Mr. Katerkamp upon his " Critical Review," Dean Rensing kept itsbut
up in his secretary until his death, 1826. Ten years ago, Dean Krabbe sent the author
a literal transcription made under his own supervision. Dean Krabbe, who had known
Dean Rensing well, remarked several times to the author that he could not account for
the " Critical Review," excepting by attributing it to the influence of Mr. Bœnninghausen's persuasive powers which were very great. He was certain, however, that the
Dean had recognized his error and had, consequently, never made his writing public.
That this opinion is well-founded we may infer from the fact that three weeks after
the invalid's death, Sunday, Feb. 29, 1824, he made in the Pilgrim's presei ce and of his
own accord the following declaration: " *The deceased Sister Emmerich was truly
one of the most wonderful personages of this century !*"

the truth with impartial views, that the phenomena exhibited in her person owe their origin rather to a skilful hand
than to imagination. Although her piety, her uninterrupted efforts from childhood to lead a life agreeable in
the sight of God, and the fact that she has never been unfaithful to her principles, may indeed exonerate her from
the charge of a premeditated design to acquire fame, yet
we may believe that, either at the suggestion or with the
approbation of her French director, she may have allowed
those wounds to be made upon her, in order to render the
Passion of Our Saviour ever present by the sight of her
own bodily marks; and that, desiring to make these signs
efficacious for the good of devout souls, she added thereto
her abstinence from food, her mysterious cataleptic state,
and her imaginary revelations. Having satisfied her conscience by such specious reasons, she decided to play this
fanatical part. As she was convinced by her good intentions that she was doing a meritorious work, it was easy
to persuade her of the necessity of the most rigorous silence.
To this she bound herself by the most frightful oath not
to betray her accomplices or her own share in the affair
(1), and not to draw contempt upon the religion she aimed
at serving. In all this, of course, there would be a detest-
able abuse of so sacred a thing as an oath, but such an
abuse is not unprecedented among fanatics. We know
how far certain devout souls can be drawn. Fascinated
by their confidence in religious zeal and the superior intelligence of their counsellors, they come, at length, to despise
as vain scruples all reproaches of conscience when there is
question of co-operating in a work whose end appears to
them holy."

(1) Nevertheless, Dean Rensing, in this same dissertation, characterized her accomplice, the venerable Abbé Lambert, as a priest esteemed by all, on account of his great
piety.

Dean Rensing, however, had been a witness of Sister Emmerich's docility in submitting to the attempts made for her cure by order of the Vicar-General. He had often been deeply touched at the sight of her sufferings and those bloody effusions surpassing anything of the kind that could be produced in a purely natural manner. And yet, with "the torch of the critic," he went on to discover a new explanation, "the action of the demon."—"Let no one here ask," says he, "how Almighty God could permit a person endeavoring to please Him by a life of virtue from her very childhood, to be so frightfully deceived by the devil. 'God's thoughts are not our thoughts, nor our ways His.' If we refuse to accord to the devil such an agency over men, we subscribe (although unwillingly) to the unbelieving spirit of the age, we spread the reign of the world and of the prince of darkness even whilst protesting most warmly against his power." The "critic's torch" could not, however, preserve so clear-sighted a man from adopting the senseless and revolting opinion that a soul, upright, pious, and faithful to God from her very infancy, could be possessed by the devil and employed by him in his diabolical works. And the light of this *torch* failed to make him perceive that, in expressing himself thus, he blasphemed as much against God and wounded not less the integrity of the faith than did that spirit of the world against which he disclaimed.

We must not omit saying here that this persecution, although stifled in the germ, did not escape the divinely-illuminated intelligence of the invalid, nor must we fail to mention the means employed by an ever-watchful Providence to preserve her from the ulterior consequence of so outrageous a calumny. We read in the Pilgrim's journal, Jan. 24, 1822: "She thanks God for her great sufferings; she rejoices at the thought of the numerous labors she has performed (for the Church) and for what is marked out for her to do this new year, of which task she has already accomplished much. She undertook a new labor last night ; she had a vision of plums which, at first, tormented her greatly. 'I was sitting near a fountain,' she said, ' in the midst of a vast field of wheat where the ears shed their grains in abundance. My confessor ran into the field and saved much of the wheat, he reaped a large part of it. I held his hat, for there were yet many places for him to reap. At every moment, black clouds oharged with hail passed over me. I thought they would fall and crush me, but only some few drops fell on me. I saw also a sack full of small plums,which are here called *wichter*,and which I thought were intended for me. They had been gathered and put into the sack for me by people of consideration. They. were injurious fruits, beautiful in appearance but full of falsehood and deceit. There flowed from the tree that bore them a great quantity of gum well enough to look at, but which corroded the tree. The sack was above a ditch, lying half upon heretical ground. I beheld those who busied themselves with it. I knew them, but I do not want to know them (that is, I want to forget their names, to be silent about them). The sack signified the many wicked designs and calumnies that one of them had formed against me. This made me anxious, and I was ashamed of the plums. But I was reprimanded by the soul of a poor woman who had died long before ; she had been employed in the convent and she now came to me, because I had something to do for her. She told me that formerly I would not have paid so much attention to fine large plums as I now did to this miserable fruit that I was dying to eat ! Then the sack was covered with a white cloth by the priest that I might not see it any longer. I saw there

Dean Overberg, Mr. Katerkamp, Father Limberg, and others whom I knew; but I forgot who had prepared these suffer_ings for me, I felt no resentment toward them. The Father's labors in the field had relation to the care he had taken of souls at Fischbeck and of his spiritual children dispersed in other parishes who had come to consult him. I kept his hat as a pledge that he would not leave the field, for I always begged him not to refuse to hear the people even when he was fatigued. The season, the condition of the fields, all was as when Dean Overberg was here."

"Strange thing!" adds the Pilgrim in his recital, "the vision of the plums has reference to a fact which is, as yet, perfectly unknown to her. The Dean, when he went to Münster, circulated a pamphlet in which he declared that he had changed his opinion of her on reading Mr. Bœnninghausen's intelligent report and that he attributed all the blame of the affair to the deceased Abbé Lambert. But by this he, the Dean, only drew upon himself contempt. Dean Overberg, Mr. Katerkamp, and others have pronounced against him. Sister Emmerich knew nothing of all that.

"January 31, 1822. Her nephew has come from Münster where the report has spread that she is dangerously ill. He spoke of the Dean's pamphlet against her. She talked with him about it coolly and without bitterness, saying that the reports made by one of her old companions of the convent had given rise to something in it. Sister Soentgen reads to every one Dean Rensing's letters in defence of his pamphlet."

In this conversation with her nephew, Sister Emmerich related what follows of the time of her captivity: "When I sent word to the Dean to come and hear my confession, he came, but refused to allow me to confess. I fell into a

state of contemplation and, wishing to touch a priest's hand,
I begged him to give me his. In Landrath Bœnninghausen's presence he extended to me one finger. I took
the whole hand, saying to him : ' Do you refuse me your
hand ?' He answered : ' You have never yet had it !'
I let it go and said. ' I know what will be exacted
of this hand.' Then he spoke in a low voice with the
Landrath, as the nurse told me afterward."

Sister Soentgen was the chief cause of the susceptible
Dean's conceiving an aversion which culminated in the
most frightful suspicions of the good and pious Abbe Lambert and even of the invalid herself. After the investigation of 1813, she had repeated to him all that the Abbé,
Dr. Wesener, and later the Pilgrim had said, or were supposed to have said. She had laid before him with particular
care, "her anxiety and scruples on the invalid's imperfections and her surroundings," whenever she felt herself disposed to complain of either one or all of the above-mentioned personages. It is true the Abbé's welcome of Sister Soentgen to the invalid's bedside was not the most
cordial since her indiscreet circulation of the wonders
wrought in Sister Emmerich ; he looked upon her as the
primary cause of all their troubles, nor was he slow in expressing his sentiments. Sister Soentgen, on the other
hand, had become quite an important personage. The Vicar-
General had communicated with her during the first
investigation, and received from her, by his own orders,
secret reports. This and other circumstances of the kind
had placed her in a position which she was unwilling to relinquish when her services were no longer required.
After the investigation she wrote to the Vicar-General :
" I still have something to say in confidence to Your Grace,
but I am unwilling to commit it to writing," to which she

received the command to forward it by letter without more
ado. She replied: "I shall state my reason for wishing to
speak privately to Your Grace. For some time I have
remarked in Sister Emmerich little imperfections that give
me uneasiness, though it would not do to remind her of
them. I often thought that I was wrong in observing silence, above all when I heard various interpretations put
upon her surroundings. The idea haunts me, and I fear
that it may be an obstacle to her perfection. The Dean
has remarked the same; he says he would certainly call
her attention to it, *were he her confessor.*" Some months
later, she wrote again: "Your Grace will forgive me for
again intruding. It is too true that Sister Emmerich has
still her daily weaknesses like other people; but you know,
too, her *surroundings*....and who can say why God permits that she should not perceive the danger herself, or
have sufficient courage to free herself from it? The Dean,
I see, keeps aloof, he rarely visits her."

The Vicar-General wished not to understand these insinuations, or to remove the "*surroundings*," viz., the Abbé Lambert; so Sister Soentgen, six months later again renewed
her communications, though in a different strain: "For a
long time I have been urged to write to Your Grace. Truly
I am daily charmed by the sight of the sufferings of my
dear fellow-religious and at seeing her soul becoming perfect. What a pity she has not the strength to converse!"
And again: "The absence of self-will in Sister Emmerich
is now much more noticeable than in the past. Many interesting things took place after the Rev. Dean began to absent himself. I often regret his lack of interest in
the good cause; but, even in this circumstance, there may
be something which will one day contribute to the glory of
God. As I continue to visit her daily, I have a chance of

remarking many little things, particularly her interior peace, her progress in perfection. Dr. Wesener has been a little imprudent in reading to her a medical journal in which there was an article about herself. He should not have done it; it only embarrasses the interested party. The Rev. Dean is not aware of my writing." But the Vicar-General desired no further information, and so the matter ended.

Of not less interest to Sister Soentgen were the visits Sister Emmerich received from distinguished individuals. She failed not to be in attendance on such occasions; and, although as little mindful of the poor invalid as the other religious, yet she alway introduced herself as her intimate friend through whose intervention the convent doors had been opened to her. This gave her access to the most distinguished families. But the *"surroundings"* saw through it quite clearly, as the following incident proves : " Sister Soentgen," says Dr. Wesener, " received from different quarters some little presents for the invalid which she exhibited to her with all kinds of indirect remarks and objections, and ended by keeping them for herself. Sister Emmerich does not want to accept presents for fear of giving rise to remarks, so I told her to get them from Sister Soentgen and send them back to the donors.—' Ah, ' she said, ' I cannot be so hard on one who is so intimate with me !' ' Certainly,' chimed in the Abbé, ' she knows very well that Sister Soentgen has done wrong, but she will listen to nothing against her ! ' Then Sister Emmerich begged me to say nothing more about it."

The Abbé and Dr. Wesener always yielded to Sister Emmerich's entreaties not to disturb the peace by their remarks, but not so with the Pilgrim. He thought it an heroic act if, on meeting Sister Soentgen or some other nun in

the invalid's room, he managed to keep silence ; but the
displeasure depicted in his countenance, the angry glance of
his rolling eyes as speedily showed such visitors the door as
the plainest words or actions would have done, and this
to the deep annoyance of the invalid.

Soon after her deliverance from captivity, Sister Emmerich received the following consoling letter from Dean Overberg : " What personal evils have come upon you of which
you can complain ? I address this question to a soul that
longs for nothing so much as to become daily more like unto her Heavenly Spouse. Have you not been much better
treated than He ? Ought you not to rejoice in spirit that
they have helped you to become more comformable to and,
consequently, more agreeable to Him ? You have, indeed,
had much to suffer with Jesus Christ, but the opprobrium
was comparatively little. To the thorny crown were still
wanting the purple mantle and the white robe of derision,
nor did the cry, ' Let Him be crucified ! ' resound. I
doubt not that these are your sentiments."

As soon as his health permitted, he and Dr. von Druffel
came to Dülmen. The latter desired to assure himself of
the condition of her wounds. The day after their arrival,
Dean Overberg took her Holy Communion and spent the
morning with her.

" She opened to him her whole heart," wrote the Pilgrim,
" and received the consolation that a holy man can impart,
even though he says nothing more, nothing different from
others who are acquainted with all the details of her life."
The Pilgrim did not yet comprehend that the priestly character lent secret unction to the old Dean's words.

" She confided to him all that troubled her, she spoke of
the Pilgrim and again received an injunction to tell him
everything ; she asked his advice with regard to her sister,

and although he gave no decided answer, yet she was consoled and encouraged. He spoke earnestly in her confessor's presence of her gift of recognizing relics and upon the importance he attached to the Pilgrim's recording everything.—Dr. Wesener gave the Dean a detailed account of her state just after the investigation. Before his departure, she related to him many details of her visions to which he listened with emotion and gave her three little sealed packages of relics which she gratefully received."

Dean Overberg sent to the Vicar-General an account of the ill-treatment to which the invalid had been subjected during her imprisonment; whereupon, the latter ordered her to " demand of Mr. Bœnninghausen a copy of the report of the commission, and in the event of a refusal to carry her case before the supreme court. But Mr. von Bœnninghausen knew how to forestall such a claim by declaring in the preface to his pamphlet : " *Geschichte und Vorläufige Resultate, &c.*" : " All acts reduced to writing during the investigation were sent to the Chief-President and by him forwarded to the Royal Minister " (1).

The inhabitants of Dülmen manifested in various ways their respect and sympathy for the poor sufferer. On the Feast of St. Lawrence they organized a pilgrimage to the Chapel of the Cross, to ask for her speedy deliverance, and on the day of her return home, Mr. von Schilgen announced it in the daily papers :

" This morning, August 29th, a little after ten o'clock,

(1) Mr. Krabbe, the Dean of the Chapter, and Mr. Aulike, the Director, put themselves to the greatest trouble to search up the documents relating to the commission, as well at Münster as at Berlin, but without success ; no trace of them could be found. On May 13, 1860, Mr. Aulike wrote to the author at Berlin : " I have searched in every place where there was a probability of finding such papers, for the documents relating to the official proceedings toward A. C. Emmerich. I have not only asked for them as a favor, but I have, as my duty authorized, demanded them officially. On all sides I am told that these acts are not to be found. The oldest archivist attached to the department to which such affairs belong, a respectable old man worthy of belief, remembers very well that these acts were once in existence. " But they assure me," says he, " that they were lost at the house of a high functionary now dead for thirty years." (he mentioned his name) " they could not be found among his papers."

the invalid was carried back to her own home by a servant of Mr. Mersmann. The joy of those that sympathize with her was unbounded. All feel that, if this long investigation of twenty-two days had resulted to Sister Emmerich's disadvantage, had proved her either an impostor or the victim of impostors, she never would have been set at liberty."

Not only in Dülmen, but throughout the whole country of Münster, was the publication of the so-called investigation eagerly awaited. Dr. Theodore Lutterbeck, of Münster, a man of great independence of character, boldly called for it, expressing at the same time the indignation of the community at large at the unheard-of treatment offered an irreproachable female. "It has been undeniably proved that Anne Catherine Emmerich, now forty-four years old, has led from her infancy a life pure, innocent, peaceable, and retired, nor has she ever drawn, or desired to draw the least emolument from her extraordinary state."

Rev. Mr. Cramer, Archpriest of Holland, says in his pamphlet: "Considerable sums have frequently been offered her which she has always refused. She never made a spectacle of herself; on the contrary, she withdrew as much as she could from the gaze of the curious. This being the case, it is incomprehensible that government officials could consider themselves authorized to declare this timid, suffering dove, who interfered not in public affairs, deprived of her lawful right to live in peace, and condemned to imprisonment and an investigation of three weeks such as might have been exacted of an open violator of the laws. We may remark here that all citizens, whether interested in the affair or not, feel their domiciliary rights attacked by such proceedings. According to the ancient laws of Münster, the courts of justice would have deemed such an imprisonment by order of police officials, an encroachment upon their rights, and would have inveighed against such a commission. When in our own times, some German Vicars wished to submit certain individuals under their jurisdiction to a far less rigorous inquiry (which they had every right to do) what denouncements were not uttered, what measures taken by civil authorities to oppose them! Much less then should secular tribunals busy themselves with a religious living in absolute retirement, asking and expecting nothing from the world; much less should they trouble themselves about the wonders wrought in her person, wonders whose truth had already been sufficiently proved by men of probity, such as Dean Rensing, Count von Stolberg, Dr. von Druffel, Dr. Wesener, and a host of others, some of them citizens of Dülmen, others strangers from a distance. But, as some persisted in suspecting Sister Emmerich's friends of a pious fraud and as suspicion fell principally on Father Limberg and the Abbé Lambert, two most worthy ecclesiastics, it was thought desirable to separate the invalid from her personal and local surroundings, and submit her to a legal investigation. Now, as there was question of inquiring into the culpability or innocence of ecclesiastics, it was, doubtless, in the right and power of the Vicar-General von Droste, by virtue of his high spiritual authority, to demand for such an undertaking representatives chosen and authorized by himself, and not by the head of the police; in a word, a mixed commission alone would have been in accordance with right and justice, whilst the one in question was but a commission of police, not a judicial one entitled to *fidem publicam :* i. e., to the credit of the public. Whatever it may be called, however, the public demand the results obtained; they hereby call upon it to publish its observations."

As the above was accompanied by Mrs. Wiltner's deposition to which she declared herself ready to attest on oath,
Landrath von Bœnninghausen could no longer maintain
silence. The Chief-President ordered him to reply. This
gave rise to the pamphlet, "written from memory," but
which was followed by no official report. The impression
produced by this pamphlet, entitled "*Preliminary Results,*"
may be gathered from the words of Dr. Lutterbeck, who
hesitated not to meet the Landrath's publication with the
following words : " He who openly accuses Sister Emmerich of imposture without supporting his assertion by proof,
may (and the enlightened public will agree with me) put
me in the same category with her. I appeal to the honest
opinion of the public at large."

The Pilgrim notes in his journal, Nov. 14, 1819 : " I
found the invalid to-day unusually cheerful. She had read
the Landrath's publication, she was perfectly reassured."

Dr. Wesener's journal furnishes an account of Sister
Emmerich's physical condition after her inprisonment. He
visited her August 29th, just after the Landrath's departure —" The sight of the invalid alarmed me. She looked
like a skeleton, her eyes dull, her face emaciated and deathly pale ; but her mind was calm and energetic. In speaking of what she had lately gone through, she alluded to
some things that astonished and distressed me."

" Sept. 2d—She is still surprisingly bright, but her pulse
is weak, her hands and feet cold as death ; she is very
much reduced."

" Sept. 3d—I was called to her last night, and I was
sure she was dying although Father Limberg, who arrived
fifteen minutes before me, said that she had rallied a little.
When he first saw her, he thought her dead. At intervals
she vomited a liquid of an offensive odor. I made a poul-

tice of wine and camomile flowers and applied it to her
stomach ; it seemed to relieve her.   Before leaving I asked
her if she forgave every one, and she answered by a sweet
smile.   I left her fully convinced that she would soon
breathe her last.   Father Limberg remained to administer
Extreme Unction."

" Sept. 4th—The invalid has rallied slightly, and the vomiting has ceased."

" Sept. 5th—She communicated to-day and regained her
strength wonderfully.   I began this morning to write an
account of her sufferings during the last investigation."

The vomiting mentioned in the doctor's journal was the
rejection of the decoctions the commissioners had forced
her to swallow in spite of the bad effects that always followed (1)."

(1) Von Bœnninghausen wrote on this subject, Oct. 14th : " The vomiting may have
arisen from Sister Emmerich's having given up the coarse diet to which she was accustomed.". .. . .

CHAPTER XXXIX.

CLOSE OF THE ECCLESIASTICAL YEAR.

Sister Emmerich now resumed her spiritual labors with unabated courage. " Thou art lying there persecuted," said her Divine Spouse to her, " that minds at variance may be united, that many may see their errors." The work begun had to be perfectly fulfilled, and for this end she received all that assistance which a true child of Holy Church derives from the communion of saints: the help of the blessed, the fruits of her own good works, and the prayers and protection of the souls in purgatory. Speaking once of her suffering life, she said : " I can see no end to my pains, they daily become greater ; they increase like the branches of a tree which multiply in proportion as they are pruned. I have often thought over them, as a child in the fields, a religious in the convent garden, and in my own interior ; they will keep on increasing to the end. I have left much behind me, but I grieve that many means of shunning evil have been neglected, many graces rendered useless. It has often been shown me that great harm comes from making small account of the gifts granted me, and from not recording my visions, which show the hidden links of many things. It has often distressed me ; but it is a consolation to think that it is not my own fault. I have also greatly relaxed through condescension."

Her visions now turned upon the views and plots of her enemies. She saw their underhand dealings and their sympathy with the tendencies of the period, tendencies hos-

tile to the Church and Christianity; against them were
directed her combat of suffering and prayer. "I heard
terrible threats that I was to be carried off again,
whether I would or not. A man stood before me and said:
'Dead or alive, she must go!'—I cast myself into my
Saviour's arms, crying to him piteously. Then came other
pictures: I beheld an informer gathering up all that was
said in the little town; I saw people coming and going,
tormenting me with questions and raillery; cunning visitors,
and false friends near me who did me much harm. These
were true torments. The priests I saw in deep sleep;
whatever they did appeared like a spider's web. I saw on
all sides increasing malice, cunning, and violence which, at
last, frustrated their own designs, failed in their ends, and
completely baffled one another. In terror I beheld myself
abandoned by all my friends. Then I saw a troop of men
in a distant meadow, about a hundred of them with a lead-
er, and I thought to myself that this must be the place in
which Our Lord once fed the seven thousand people. Our
Lord came to meet me. With Him were all His disciples from
among whom He chose twelve. I saw Him looking from one to
another. I recognized them all, the old men full of simplicity, the young robust and sun-burnt. He sent them off in
all directions, following them in spirit to distant nations. I
thought, 'Ah! what can such a handful do among such
multitudes!'—The Lord answered: 'Their voice sounds
far and near. So also in these days many are sent. Whoever they may be, men or women, they can do the same.
Behold to what multitudes these twelve have borne salvation! They whom I send in your day will do the same,
no matter how poor or despised they may be!'—I felt that
this vision was for my encouragement."

If she saw in spirit a new attack, she strengthened herself for it by prayer. "What can creatures do to me?" she said. "If they want to tear this body to pieces, I shall deliver it up for Thee, my Saviour! Lord, I am Thy handmaid!"—Then she had a vision in which was shown her how much good she could do in her state of abandonment. —"I found myself in a vast region belonging not to earth. The ground which bore me, or over which I floated, was like a veil of gauze, and below I saw the earth dark as night with pictures here and there. Around where I stood were troops of translucent spirits ranged in choirs; they were not the saints, but praying souls, who offered petitions from below and received gifts from on high. They prayed themselves; they offered the prayers of others: they implored the assistance of the more elevated choirs who answered such requests, sending more or less help, coming and going in the light. These elevated choirs were the saints. They that surrounded me seemed to be souls whom the Lord willed should see the dangers that menaced the earth and offer prayers to avert them. All professions, all stations in life, seemed to have their praying souls, who exercised a most beneficent influence. I prayed, too, for I saw innumerable miseries. God sent help by His saints and the effect was instantaneous —obstacles opposed to evil; undertakings turning out well, though apparently by chance; changes wrought in souls, etc.; the dying converted and admitted to the Sacraments; people in danger on land and water—all saved by prayer. I saw what might prove fatal to certain individuals suddenly snatched out of their path, and all by the power of prayer. I adored the justice of God!"

She beheld her own position under the figure of a lamb. —"I saw a broad country spreading out before me like a map, with forests and meadows, flocks and shepherds,

Just in front of me was a shepherd with a numerous flock of sheep, and behind them came the shepherd-boys. The former discharged his duties a little carelessly, but the latter were more active. The flock was in good condition. There was one lamb, sleeker and fatter than the others; there was something remarkable about it, the sheep pressed around it. They passed a clump of high trees among which lay a fierce wolf and a second one a little further on; they were wolves, and yet they were like men too. The wolves appeared to understand each other; they often ran together and lay in wait for the lamb. I trembled for the poor little thing, and I could not understand how the shepherd could be so negligent. One of the boys seemed attentive to it, but he could not do much for it, although he was faithful to the portion of the flock intrusted to him. Several times when the wolves attempted to seize it the sheep gathered bleating around it. To my amazement the shepherd made no effort to protect it. Everything seemed to be against it. It was in an exposed position, and once the wolves were on the point of carrying it off; again they caught it by the throat, tore off a piece of its flesh, and were about to strangle it, when the others ran to the rescue. The pity I felt made me understand that there was question of myself. Suddenly there came a man from above, the wolves fled, and I saw that I had the man's bones by me (1). I wondered that his body was in one place, his spirit in another. Then the shepherd's boy came up and brought the lamb back."

The lamb, so little cared for by the shepherds, was helped by some blessed soul who had suffered at a remote period, in the same place and under the same circumstances as Sister Emmerich herself.

(1) Relics-

On October 9th, she related the following : " There was a holy widow by me who had lived at the manor in Dül-men, and who had died in prison. She conversed with me a long time ; we have not yet finished our conver-sation. She spoke of her time and imprisonment, as if in the present ; justice and faith were proscribed terms in her day and, therefore, had she suffered. She told me her family name, she was of the house of Galen. She showed me the prisons, partly subterranean, in which she and her relatives were confined. She spoke much of my own his-tory, saying that all things happen according to the de-signs of God, and that I should never say anything but what is inspired at the moment. ' How wonderfully,' she said, ' hast thou faced the danger! Hadst thou known it be-forehand, thou wouldst have died of fright. Other wonders will be effected. Unbelief is at its height, unheard-of con-fusion will reign ; but after the storm, faith will be re-estab-lished !'—The lady seemed to know me well. She explained to me many things in my life, consoled and encouraged me, saying that I had nothing to fear. She spoke of the state of the clergy, also of relics. ' It would be well,' she said, ' if they were collected together and deposited in some church. They do, indeed, exercise a beneficent influ-ence wherever they are, but the little respect shown them is very injurious. The dust in which they lie ought to be buried in blessed ground. There are still many relics at Dülmen Manor.'

" The lady wore a robe, open at the neck, crossed in front and falling behind in folds with a train, the sleeves tight with trimming around the wrists gathered and starch-ed, over which fell a part of the sleeve. She died innocent, imprisoned by an association, or secret tribunal which, at that time, was the cause of many evils and inspired great terror. It was something like the Free-masons, but more violent."

Oct. 21st—" The good lady again appeared to me, conversed a long time, and repeated that she was of the family of Galen. She does not protect as sacred relics do, but she helps, she warns. She told me not to mind, for my persecutors fear me more than I do them. They attack me boldly because nothing is done to oppose them."

" I met a man who also belonged to the time of the good lady of ' The Vehme ' (1). I saw him in Dülmen Manor, whither he used often to go; but once he stayed too long, which circumstance led to his death. He was one of the most distinguished men of the country, and one of the heads of the secret tribunal...... He was secretly very pious and good. He often received warnings on the iniquities and cruelties of the tribunal. He tried to prévent them by means of the good lady who gave notice to its intended victims and saved as many as she could. Once he remained too long with her planning projects of this kind. This roused the suspicions of some wicked men, who plotted to put him to death.

" I beheld secret meetings at night, sinister-looking men introduced into this country, and going furtively from place to place. Then I had a vision of a castle and garden this side of Münster, an old building with towers. Here dwelt the good man. He was in the garden, wrapped in a mantle as if about to set out for the assembly, when three men in disguise fell upon him, stabbed him, and dragged him into an alley. The blood flowed in streams from his wounds and the men tried to wash away the stains, but in vain. They filled a sack with the blood-stained earth and carried it to Dülmen Manor with the body. They deposited

(1) The secret tribunal mentioned above.

them in a vault by the church where were the remains of
many who had been killed in the same way. He belonged to
the Droste family. . . . The lady told me that it was well for
him to die when he did, for he was pious and his conscience
was in a good state. 'Fear not,' she said to me, 'things
must be as they are. Thy persecutors have neither right nor
reason to do thee harm. Let nothing disquiet thee! If
thou art questioned, answer only what comes to thy mind at
the moment !' "

Sister Emmerich in her humility was often occupied
with this thought : " For what have I, poor sinner, deserved
that my persecutors should render themselves so guilty
on my account ?"—and although God had given her the consolation of knowing that she was not responsible, she begged for special sufferings to expiate their offence. From
the last week in October, she was a prey to interior abandonment, whilst her frame was consumed by fever, her
tongue adhered to her palate, and she had not the strength
to reach the water placed at her side ; the pain in her
wounds often drew tears, and sometimes made her swoon
away. These were sufferings she had voluntarily embraced
for the good of her neighbor. In her distress, she was consoled by an apparition of Blessed Nicholas von der Flue, who
said to her : " I shall be thy very good friend, I shall help
thee a little," and he held out to her a little bunch of herbs the
smell of which gave her strength. " Thou sufferest," he said,
"in every member of thy body, because the faults for which
thou dost atone are so manifold."

On the nineteenth Sunday after Pentecost is read the
Gospel of the wedding-feast and the nuptial robe. That
night Blessed Nicholas was her guide in the following
vision:—

"I saw Blessed Nicholas as a great, tall man with hair

like silver. He wore a low notched crown, sparkling with precious stones; his tunic, which descended to the ankles, was white as snow and he held in his hand another crown higher than his own and set with jewels. I asked him why he held that resplendent crown instead of the bunch of herbs. He spoke earnestly and in few words of my death, of my destiny, and said that he would take me to a great wedding-feast. He placed the crown on my head, and I flew with him into the palace which I saw in the air above me. I was to be a bride, but I was so timid and ashamed that I knew not what to do. It was a wedding of wonderful magnificence. I beheld the manners and customs of all classes of society on the occasion of a marriage festival, and the action of deceased ancestors upon their descendants. First of all was the banquet for the clergy. Here I saw the Pope, and Bishops with their croziers and episcopal robes, and many others of the clergy, high and low. Above each one, in an upper choir, were the saints of his race, his ancestors, his patrons and the protectors of his charge, who acted through him, judging and deciding. At this table there were also spiritual affianced of the highest rank. With my crown on my head, I had to join them as their equal, which filled me with confusion. They were all still living, though as yet they had no crowns. Above me stood the one who had invited me and, as I was so abashed, he managed everything for me. The dishes on the table looked like earthly food, but they were not such in reality. I saw through everything, I read all hearts. Back of the banquet-hall were many different rooms filled with people, and there were new arrivals at every moment. Many among the ecclesiastics seated at the banquet were ordered out as unworthy, for they had mixed with worldlings, had served them rather than the Church. The worldlings were punished first, then the ecclesiastics were banished to other apartments, more or less remote. The number of the just was very small. This was the first table and the first hour.

" The clergy withdrew and another table was prepared at which I did not sit. I stood among the spectators, Blessed Nicholas still above me to help me. Emperors, kings, and sovereign princes placed themselves at table, great lords served them, and above were the saints reckoned among the ancestors of each. To my great embarrassment, some of the kings noticed me, but Nicholas came to my aid and always answered for me. They sat not long at table. They were all alike, their actions imperfect, weak and inconsistent; if one happened to be a little superior to his fellows it was not through virtue. Some came not quite up to the table, and all were sent away in their turn.

" I remember in particular the Croy family. They must have had among them a holy stigmatisée, for she said to me, 'See, there are the Croys !'

" Then came the table of the distinguished nobility, and I saw among others the good Vehme lady hovering over her family.

" Then came the table of the wealthy citizens, and I cannot describe the frightful state of this class. Most of them were sent away and cast with those of the nobility who were as bad as themselves, into a hole like a sewer where they splashed about in mud and filth.

" After these came a class of a little better standing, honest old citizens and peasants. There were many good people here, among them my own family. My father and mother stood above my other relatives. Then came the descendants of Brother Klaus (Blessed Nicholas), right good, strong tradesmen ; but some of them were rejected. Then

came the poor and the crippled from among whom many
pious people were excluded, as well as the bad. I had
much to do with them. Above them I saw numbers of persons and tribunals. I cannot recount all. When the six
tables were over, the holy man brought me back again to my
bed from which he had taken me. I was very weak, quite unconscious; I could neither speak nor make a sign, I seemed
about to die. Klaus signified to me that my life would be
short, without however specifying any particular time for
its close."

November 8th—"Again I had a great vision of persecution and I beheld my miseries increase. I saw my enemies watching that no one should help me, and gathering
up all that was said and done against me. The devil,
furious with me, was rushing with open jaws on certain
persons to confuse them and chase them away; but what
hurt me most, was that my nearest friends reproached and
tormented me with inconsiderate advice and accusations.
They that were willing to help me were few and they could do
nothing. My persecutors assailed me in my abandonment,
and I was deprived of spiritual and corporal assistance.
My enemies loaded me with trials hitherto unknown. 'Where,'
they asked, 'are your ghostly Superiors? where your spiritual directors? Have they ceased to interest themselves in
you? Who among the clergy are your protectors?'—Their
words tortured me, drove me almost wild, and the desertion
of my dearest friends afflicted me keenly. When I
was almost in despair Nicholas von der Flue appeared.
He told me to thank God for showing me these things,
to arm myself with patience, and especially to avoid
anger in my replies which should be reserved; that the
trial would be shorter, if borne well; and, finally, that I
still had much to suffer from my friends who would injure

me and exact things of me, though not with a bad intention. If I endured this patiently, I should profit by it. He promised that the trial would not last long and that he would help me. Then he gave me his own little prayer on paper which I was to say. I had made use of it from my youth. It ran thus : ' Lord, detach me from myself,' etc. He gave me also a picture about the size of my hand. On top was a sun, and underneath the word, *Justice*, from which I understood that Divine Justice would end my persecution. At the bottom was a face full of benevolence with the word *Mercy*, and this gave me the assurance that I should soon receive help from the Divine Mercy. Under the face was a coffin with four lighted tapers."

Her vision was soon realized. One week after the Landrath's injurious pamphlet, her Superiors and friends urged her to appeal to a higher tribunal, and to lodge a formal complaint against him and the treatment she had received during imprisonment (1). The affair was pressed on all sides; but Sister Emmerich, in obedience to her angelic director, declined taking such a step. She saw the sufferings now prepared for her under the image of a thorn-hedge which she had to cross.

" The sight of it terrified me," she said. " but my guide encouraged me—' How many hast thou not already crossed ! Wilt thou despair at the end ?'—I knelt and prayed and, by virtue of my prayer, I crossed the hedge, I know not how. I felt invisible assistance. Then I saw three men coming toward me who tried to make me say what I would do to the Landrath. I told them that I would read his pamphlet to see if it were in accordance with his character, and that, if my Superiors questioned me, I should tell the truth. I was told also that my wounds would

(1) "I see, on account of this writing," she said, " my enemies contending; they separate, they are dissatisfied. The Landrath stands alone."

bleed next Good-Friday and again on another day; that
enemies were waiting for this event; but they would
never see it, as they sought not the truth.

"I beheld crowds of children who came from Münster
with some grown people to see the *impostor ;* but they were
all kind to me, they loved the *impostor* very much. It
seemed as if I taught them something. Several saints
were round me in this vision and, what pleased me greatly,
St. Francis dressed in a long, coarse robe was among
them, his forehead very broad, his jaws hollow, his chin
large. He consoled me, and told me not to complain, that
he, too, had been persecuted. He had kept his wounds
very secret, but the blood from his side often streamed
down to his feet. Although some had seen his wounds,
they did not in consequence believe. It is better to believe and not to see, for seeing does not make them believe
who have not the gift of faith. He (St. Francis) was tall,
thin, vigorous, his hollow cheeks ruddy as of one interiorly inflamed, and he had black eyes. I saw no beard. He
was not infirm, but very winning and sprightly."

When Sister Emmerich was informed of her Superior's
desire that she should appeal to a higher court, she suddenly closed her eyes, and fell into ecstasy, her countenance becoming very grave. She afterward said:—" I invoked God,
the Father. I begged Him to look upon His Son who satisfies
for sinners at every moment, who every moment offers
Himself in sacrifice, that He might not be too severe toward
that poor, blind Landrath, but to assist and enlighten him
for the love of His Son. At the same instant, I saw a vision
of Good-Friday, the Lord sacrificing Himself upon the cross,
Mary and the disciples at its foot. This picture I saw
over the altar at which priests say Mass. I see it at all
hours of the day and night. I see, too, the whole parish,

how the people pray, well or badly, and how the priest
fulfils his duties. I see first the church here, then the
churches and parishes all around, as one sees near him a
fruit-tree lit up by the sun, and in the distance others
grouped together like a wood. I see Mass celebrated at
all hours of the day and night throughout the world, and
in some far-off regions with the same ceremonies as in the
times of the Apostles. Above the altar, I see a heavenly
worship in which an angel supplies all that the priest
neglects. I offer my own heart for the want of piety among
the faithful and I beg the Lord for mercy. I see many
priests performing this duty pitiably. Some, mere formalists,
are so attentive to the outward ceremonies as to neglect
interior recollection ; they think only of how they appear
to the congregation, and not at all of God. The scrupulous
ever long to feel their own piety. I have had these impressions since childhood. Often during the day I am absorbed in
this far-off gazing on the Holy Sacrifice ; if I am spoken to
my answer comes as from a person who interrupts not his
own work to answer a child's questions. Jesus loves us
so much that He constantly renews His work of Redemption. The Mass is the hidden history of Redemption, Redemption become a Sacrament. I saw all this in my earliest youth and I used to think every one did the same."

That afternoon, still in ecstasy, she said :—"They call
me disobedient, but I dare not do otherwise. They want
me to complain ! When it is too late, they will help me ! I
see what trouble the wicked enemy gives himself to bring
about a lawsuit ; he wants me to lodge a complaint, he cannot harm me in any other way. I see that if there is a
suit, I shall die and all will be hushed up, and that is what
the devil is after. My guide has said to me : ' Thy best
friends want thee to begin a lawsuit, but beware of doing

so ! Forget not that the signs thou bearest are not signs of accusation, but of reconciliation. They have not been given to thee for strife, but for pardon. Write two letters in thy prayer-book, an L. (*liebe*, *love*) and a V. (*vergiss nicht*, forget not). Let *them* complain, but thou not!"

How faithfully she obeyed her guide's instructions, we see from the Pilgrim's notes, a few days later: " She suffers intensely, she vomits blood, her forehead is inflamed, and the pains of her wounds are so violent that the bed shakes under her quivering limbs. She will not be helped by relics now; she wants to endure her pain for the poor souls and for her enemies."

These poor souls thanked her the following night. " I was the occasion," she said, " of a very great procession of the purified souls. They were known to me, they prayed for me. I took the heavy crucifix from the Coesfeld church, detached the figure, and carried it. I was the only living being there. The souls wore not the clothes of their own time, still all were clothed differently and their countenances were different. They went barefoot, some whiter or grayer than others. I went with the procession out of the gate, and I had much communication with the poor souls. I went to two Jesuits to whom I had confessed in my youth. One lived with his pious sisters who sold coffee, but privately ; it was not a public store. I often bought coffee there after the first Mass. The spirit of the old man pointed out the little house to me and remarked how changed all was now. He told me that he remembered me distinctly, that he had always wished me well, and that he prayed for me. The other also spoke with me."

The evil consequences that would result from any action she might take against the commission were shown her by her angel. She saw that after the unfavorable impression of the commission produced on the public mind by the Landrath's pamphlet, her enemies would willingly carry her off from Dülmen under pretence of a new investigation. All the details of their plans were shown her as if being actually executed; and this made her suffer so much the more acutely as she was forced to bear it in silence. " God alone can help me," she said weeping ; " I have neither consolation nor help beside." She heard in her visions the words : "This is a warning of what they will do," and she beheld the sufferings by which she would avert the dangers.— " Thou mayest ward off the sufferings awaiting thee from thy enemies by prayer ; but they will be replaced by others and by annoyances from thy friends," said her Heavenly Spouse to her one day. " Thou wilt often be almost in despair."—and the very next morning, Gertrude loaded her with reproaches, such as "she gave away to the poor all that they had, she was a spendthrift, their affairs were every which way, and she was ruled by the evil spirit !"

" I found her very weak," says the Pilgrim, " her cheeks stained with tears ; she vomited blood, she was consumed by thirst, and she could not drink. The evil one tormented her. As soon as Gertrude began her reproaches, he showed himself visibly.—' When I was alone and in prayer,' she said, 'I was freed from his presence or, better still, when I took up my relics ; but, if I laid them aside, there he was again ! I struggled with him all day. When the Pilgrim tried to comfort me, the apparition became more frightful. It was the same demon who was always present in Mersmann's house among the commissioners.'—When, at last, the enemy was forced to retire, she saw the road she had yet to travel before reaching the Heavenly Jerusalem. It was a rugged path broken up by precipices over which both friends and enemies had stretched nets to ensnare her; scraps of writing were attached to many of them as if to warn her. She read: ' Be silent! Turn aside! Suffer patiently! Look not back! Look straight ahead! Do not lose sight of Me too often!' which last words gave rise to a conversation with her Spouse from which she gathered charity and patience. ' Yes, I see it!' she exclaimed, ' He shows me what I have already surmounted!'—'And who has guided thee thus far ?' said He to her. ' How canst thou complain ? O thou forgettest Me too often!'—'Ah! my well-beloved Spouse, I understand all now. All things are for the best. I would rather be despised and ill-treated with Thee than rejoice with the world!'

"Some days after, when I was in distress, the evil spirit again placed before me various pictures of the sufferings in store for me; he showed them as quite unbearable, and I was on the point of yielding. Then I thought, I will make an effort and flee away, but I could not. I sank back, because I was acting on my own light. I was at last worn out with the struggle, and I said, ' Now I will bear my misery with my Lord Jesus!' At the same moment the Lord appeared to me pale and exhausted, dragging His cross up Golgotha and sinking under the weight. I flew to Him, conscious of how I had wronged Him, I acknowledged my sin, and took one end of His cross on my shoulders. Now had I strength and vigor, because I acted for Jesus. He showed me what He endured for me, and my cowardice confounded me; but thanks to Him, I again have courage!"

"On the Feast of St. Cecilia, my cowardice again forced itself upon me and I felt remorse for not having been more patient during the investigation. I invoked St. Cecilia for consolation, and she came to me instantly through the air. O heart-rending sight! Her head half-severed from her body, lay on her left shoulder ! She was short, slight and delicate, black hair and eyes, and a fair complexion. She wore a yellowish white robe, with large heavy golden flowers, the same in which she had been martyred. She spoke as follows :—

" ' Be patient ! God will forgive thy fault, if thou dost repent. Be not so troubled for having spoken the truth to thy persecutors. When one is innocent, he may speak boldly to his enemy. I, too, reproached my enemies. When they spoke to me of blooming youth and the golden flowers on my robe, I replied that I esteemed them as little as the clay of which their gods were formed and that I expected gold in exchange for them. Look ! with this wound, I lived three days and tasted the consolation of Jesus Christ's servants. I have brought thee patience, this child in green. Love him, he will help thee !' She disappeared and I wept with joy. The child sat down by me on the bed and stayed with me. He sat uncomfortably on the edge, kept his little hands in his sleeves, and hung his head with a mournful but kind air, asking for nothing, complaining of nothing. His demeanor touched and consoled me more than I can say. I remember having had the patience-child by me once before. When the people from Holland tormented me almost to death, the Mother of God brought him to me. He said : ' See, I allow myself to be taken on either arm, nursed or put on the floor, I am always satisfied—do thou the same !' Since that time, even in my waking state I see that child, seated near me, and I have *really* acquired patience and peace."

She endured in vision torments equivalent to exterior persecution to satisfy the justice of God.

Nov. 13th—"I saw myself carried by shouting and hooting enemies up a high scaffold which was so narrow

that I could hardly lie on it. I was in danger of falling
and breaking my neck. My enemies were triumphant at
the sight. I lay in agony, until at last the Mother of God
appeared in the form of her statue of Einsiedeln, and made
the scaffold broad enough for me to walk on it. When I
descended unexpectedly, my enemies were filled with confusion."

Nov. 25th—" I found myself again on an enclosed scaffold in whose centre was an opening through which one beheld a dark prison. All was still, I saw no one and it seemed
as if I were about to perish secretly by falling through the
hole. Then Sts. Frances and Louisa appeared, they who had
so often helped me. They raised a plank and showed me
a ladder which, as soon as I stepped upon it, sank with
me to the ground, and I escaped. Then an old nun of our
convent washed my soiled feet; but the marks of the wounds
were not removed, and I drew my feet away in confusion."

Nov. 27—" That I might see what dangers I had escaped, I was taken by my guide into an empty four-cornered
house like a barn. On one side stood a great cauldron
as large as my room, under which blazed a fire. I was to be
thrown into the kettle. First came all the young people
I knew with sticks and shavings, but their fire soon
burned out. Then came all the married people and old
women I had ever known. They built a blazing fire
with great logs, but it also went out without even catching
all round though some embers lay smouldering. I was
not yet thrown into the cauldron. After them came the
nuns and made a fire in a most ridiculous way. They
heaped up slyly all kinds of trash, reeds, withered leaves,
dry herbs, nothing but hollow worm-eaten things which
they could bring easily and secretly. They were praying
all the time and running into the church. No one wanted

her neighbor to see what she did, and yet all were doing the same thing. It was most amusing to see them making the fire. I recognized each one's peculiar style. I saw in particular Sister Soentgen. She piled up a good deal of wood, so that some of the smouldering sticks were relighted. Then the nuns left the house one after another, and I, too, retired. Soon, however, I returned. Now came people of all sorts in vehicles, among them some doctors, who made observations, setting the cauldron on the fire and feeling again and again if the water was getting hot. Then Sister Soentgen came back, stirred up the fire, and spoke so sweetly that I also ran and brought a log of wood for it. Then came spies, among them the Landrath; they seized me suddenly and threw me into the cauldron. I was frightened to death. I thought I should die. They repeatedly drew me half out and plunged me in again up to the neck, sometimes forcing me down to the very bottom where I awaited my death in agony. Then came my friends, Frances and Louisa, to take me out, but I insisted on remaining till the end. At last, however, they took me under the arms and lifted me out, a proceeding which the *cooks* unwillingly allowed. They went away saying : ' We shall try it in another place, there are too many people here.'—I saw them go to an upper, retired chamber in which they wanted to shut me up, but they did not succeed.

" I thought that, to comfort me in my frightful agony, Blessed Louisa took me to Rome and left me in a great cave, where I saw numerous bones of the saints, bones of the arms and smaller ones arranged in order, and many little pots, urns, and flasks of various shapes, containing dried blood of the saints. I had never before seen such things. I found bones of which I have little particles, and also blood belonging to the saints of whom I have relics. The cave was quite

bright, lit up by these sacred objects. I arranged and venerated them; and I was thinking how I should get out, when
the soul of a woman I had once known appeared to me.
She told me that I must end her sufferings. She had sought
me long and only now found me. During life she had refused
a poor pregnant woman a piece of buttered bread which she
craved and which she might easily have spared her. For
this she was now devoured by insatiable hunger. She begged
me to help her. Then appeared, also, the soul of the other
poor woman entreating me earnestly in behalf of her neighbor. I had once known her too. As I was still in the relic
cave, I knew not where I could get bread and butter,
although I was eager to help the poor soul. Then a beautiful, shining youth appeared and pointed to a corner of the
cave where was what I wanted : an oval loaf, long as my
hand and two fingers thick. It was of a pale yellow color
not like our bread. It looked as if it had been rolled up
in something and baked under the ashes. By it stood a
pot of melted butter and a knife. I tried to spread the
butter thickly on the bread but it always ran back into the
pot ; and, at last, the whole thing fell from my hands into the
dirt. Then the youth said : ' See, that is because you always
want to do too much (1),' and he bade me scrape up the
butter and clean it. When I gave the bread to the woman,
she thanked me, saying that she would soon be in a better
state and then she would pray for me.—Then came another
woman carrying a small bag of salt. She had been a little
niggardly. She told me with tears that she had once refused
a little salt to a poor woman, and now for punishment she
had to beg salt. She asked me to give her some, and the

---

(1) These souls appeared to Sister Emmerich in a place to which she had been transported in spirit. She could aid them, as she was still living. Weight and measure had
to be observed, since satisfaction must be proportioned to the debt. To give to one soul
more than is necessary is to take away from another. Sister Emmerich participates in
the merits of the holy martyrs which they acquired during their mortal career.

youth showed me where to get it. It was very different
from our salt, damp, coarse, and yellow. I took one of the
smallest grains to fill up the measure. But every time I laid
it on the pile it fell off, and again did I receive the same
reproof. When I had given her the salt, she disappeared
satisfied, promising to pray for me. Darkness reigned in
the cave, the sacred things alone shone brightly. The
youth then took me to the place where the martyrs suffered
and to a charnel-house, such as I had seen before, to assure
me that all was real, and then he brought me back to my
bed."

Nov. 28th—"I saw a great conflagration. The Landrath's
house was all on fire. Sparks and burning beams flew
around wounding people far and near, but not setting anything on fire. I was sorry for the man's misfortune; but I
soon found out that I and not he was to be the sufferer.
An enormous firebrand, like a burning flitch of bacon, was
carried by the wind over my head; but a soul warded it off
and it fell to the ground. She said: ' It does not burn me.
I have had to undergo a very different fire, but now I am well-
off.' Then I saw, to my great joy, that it was the soul of an old
peasant-woman who was very fond of me in my childhood, and
who had often complained to me of the trouble her daughter
gave her. I had shown her affection and cleaned her when
covered with vermin. This soul had been thirty years out of
the body; she was extraordinarily bright and beautiful. She
thanked me with a frank and joyous air, and told me how
rejoiced she was to be able to help me now in return for
what my prayers had done for her. She bade me be comforted; that I had, it was true, still much to suffer, but
that I should accept all quietly and uncomplainingly from
God; that she would help and protect me as far as she
could. ' And,' she added, ' I am not the only one who

helps thee. Ah! thou hast so many protectors! See, all for
whom thou hast prayed, whom thou hast assisted—all will
help thee in thy need.' Then she pointed to many souls that
I knew; they were in various situations, and all were going
to protect me. I cannot say enough of the joy and satisfaction I felt on beholding the splendor and beauty of this old
woman whom we used to call *Aunty.*

"But I saw all this time the Landrath's house burning
more fiercely, and I felt that it was a picture of the consequences of his wickedness, of the ruin and unhappiness in store
for him. I pitied him from my heart, and I begged the soul to
pray and get prayers that God might not punish him for
the evil he had done or still would do me. I begged that he
might be treated as if he had loaded me with benefits and,
on this condition, I would accept all sufferings. She promised and disappeared.

" Afterward I had to carry the Landrath up a mountain,
which greatly fatigued me. I had already had to do this for
many others. Long ago, even before he came to see me, I
had to carry the Pilgrim in vision, which labor represents
the exertion necessary to lead a soul into the way of salvation. When St. Francis Xavier was sent to convert the pagans, he often carried black men on his shoulders in vision."

In the first week of Advent, Sister Emmerich had her last
vision relating to her persecutors. " I had to struggle all night,
I am worn out with the sad pictures I saw. My guide took me
all around the earth through immense black caverns built
by the powers of darkness, and filled with people wandering
about in sin. It was as if I went over all the habitable points
of the globe and saw nothing but sin. I often saw new
troops of men falling from on high into the blindness of vice.
I saw nothing good. I saw, in general, more men than
women, the children were few. Often when I was over-

come by the sight, my guide brought me for a little while out
into the light, into a meadow or beautiful region where the
sun shone, but where there were no people ; afterward I
had to return into the darkness and see again the malice,
blindness, pride, deceit, envy, avarice, discord, murders,
luxury, snares, passions, the horrible wickedness of men—
all plunging them into greater misery, deeper darkness. I
was under the impression that whole cities were built upon
a thin crust which would soon cave in and precipitate them
into the abyss. I saw people digging ditches for one another's
destruction; but there were no good people here, none falling
into the ditches. All these wicked people were in a great dark
place, running about at random as in a great fair, grouping
together, and enticing one another to sin. Sometimes the
darkness grew deeper, and the road led down a steep
crag, frightful to behold, extending around the whole earth.
I saw people of all nationalities, all costumes, and all
sunk in crime. At times I awoke in terror, and saw the
moon shining brightly in at my window. I groaned in anguish, and begged God to send me no more such frightful
pictures ; but I had soon again to descend into those terrible regions of darkness and behold their abomination. Once
I found myself in a sphere so horrible that I thought myself
in hell, and I began to weep aloud. My guide said : 'I am
by thee, hell cannot be where I am.' Then turning longing-
ly to the poor souls in purgatory, I was transported into the
midst of them. It seemed like a place near the earth, and
there too I saw inexpressible torments; but they were God-
fearing souls who sinned not, who perpetually sighed,
hungered, thirsted for deliverance. They could all see
what they longed for and for which they had to wait in
patience ; their suffering was full of resignation ; their
acknowledgment of their faults and their utter inability to

help themselves peculiarly touching. I saw all their sins. They were in different depths, different degrees of abandonment ; some up to the neck, some to the breast, etc., and they implored aid. After I had prayed for them, I awoke and again begged God to deliver me from these visions. But scarcely had I fallen asleep than I was lead once more into the dark regions. Satan threatened me and placed horrible pictures before me. Once I met an insolent devil who said something like the following : 'There was no necessity for your coming down here and seeing everything—now you'll go up above, boast of your trip, and write something about it!' I told him to cease his stupid talk. Once I thought I saw a great, wicked city being undermined by devils who were already far advanced with the work. I thought as it had so many heavy buildings, it must now soon fall in. I had often felt that Paris would sink in, for I see so many caves under it, but not cut out purposely like those in Rome."

" At last, I reached a large place like one of our own cities. In it was a little more light, and there I was shown a horrible sight, Our Lord Jesus Christ crucified! My whole soul shuddered, for the executioners were men of our own time, and Our Lord was suffering much more cruelly from them than He did from the Jews. Thank God, it was only a picture!--' So would they,' said my guide, ' now treat the Lord, could He still suffer.'—I saw with horror among His tormentors men whom I knew, even priests. This place was connected with the dark regions by many veins and ramifications. I saw, too, my own persecutors and how they would treat me, if I fell into their hands ; they would by torture try to make me confirm their false statements."

The remembrance of this horrible vision made her heart beat with fright. Nothing could induce her to give it

entire ; she concluded with these words : " My guide said to
me, ' Now hast thou seen the horrible blindness and darkness of men.   Murmur no more at thy own lot, but pray !
Thy lot is very sweet.'—This vision was followed by that in-
quietude I so often feel, that of being accountable for something since so many sins are committed on my account.
The dread of disobedience haunts me.   My guide said : ' It
is pride that makes thee think that only good should happen
through thee !   And if thou are not obedient, it is my fault
and not thine !' "

Some days later, she said : " My persecutors will now
leave me in peace.   I saw that they had a mind to use
violence, but they were suddenly seized with fright and
became disunited.   I saw it under the picture of a fire
breaking out among them.   One mistrusts the other and
fears being betrayed.   My Spouse has told me that I will not
yield to impatience.   I shall have a little repose to finish
reading the last five leaves of my great book.   I must have
rest that I may leave its contents after me.   I have still
much, very much to do !"

On Dec. 14th, she had a vision of an ecclesiastical investigation that would be instituted after her death.   Whilst in
ecstasy, she related to the Pilgrim : " I saw the clergy
receiving from Rome letters commissioning them to proceed
to an investigation in due form.   I saw after this a church
in which there were no seats.   It seemed to me that it had
once been desecrated, but was now restored.   It was a solid,
angular old building, but beautiful ; no hollow wooden ornaments about it, no sham gold.   The clergy entered in silence.
With their exception, there was no one in the church but
the saints and my own soul.   They drew a coffin from one
of the vaults, carried it before the altar, opened it as if about
to make a trial of something, and left it open whilst they

celebrated High Mass. Then they cut from one of the hands a consecrated finger, for in the coffin was the body of a holy Bishop. They laid the relic on the altar and replaced the coffin in the vault. I felt that they were coming to me with the relic, and I ran off home. They came, and were very strict and grave. I know not what they did to me, for I was on high as if in a beautiful meadow, and st ll at the same time up in the clouds, by the old Bishop whose finger had been cut off. It was wrapped in red velvet and one of the clergy carried it on his breast. I was now suddenly united to my body again by the holy Bishop, and I arose and looked in amazement at all the gentlemen. After the investigation, I again saw the clergy in the church from which they had taken the finger. They now put it back into the coffin under the altar, and a great thanksgiving was celebrated.—The church was full of people and there were also many saints and souls present, with whom I sang in Latin.

"Afterward I had a vision of a new convent. Still it was as if it all took place after my death. Had I lived longer, they would have made me undergo a great trial; so I must die first. The end that they propose can be as well attained after my death as before. I saw also that after my death, some one will cut off one of my hands, and here and there changes will be quietly made in the churches in which relics will be more honored and again exposed for public veneration."

When the Pilgrim mentioned this vision to Sister Emmerich's confessor, he remarked: "She has often enjoined upon me when she thought herself dying and I carried her the Sacraments, she being in ecstasy, to cut off one of her hands after her death. I know not why she said this unless she intended to intimate that it would retain the power of recognizing relics.   She often told me that even after death, she would be obedient to my orders in quality of confessor. And of the priest's consecrated fingers she says that were his body fallen to dust and his soul in hell, yet will the consecration still be recognized in the bones of the fingers. They will burn with an altogether peculiar fire, so ineffaceable is the mark."

CHAPTER XL.

MIRACULOUS EFFECTS OF THE•CRUSTS THAT FELL FROM
SISTER EMMERICH'S STIGMATA.   DECEMBER
28, 1818 (1).

On the evening of Dec. 15th, as Sister Emmerich lay in
ecstasy, the Pilgrim placed on her breast a little parcel, containing a relic, previously designated by her as belonging to
St. Ludger, and the crusts that had fallen from her own
wounds.   She was instantly aware of his action and, without awaking from ecstasy, she exclaimed: "Ah! what a
good shepherd!   He has come over the broad waters!   His
body lies in the old church in my country.   It is he from
whom they took the finger yesterday.   But there is another
person!   I have not seen her for a long time.   Strange!
There is something in it I cannot understand!   She has the
stigmata, she is an Augustinian!   She is clothed as I used
to be and as I still am, partly as a little nun.   It is singular!   She must be still alive, she is hidden in some corner.
I cannot understand it!   How much she has suffered!   I
can take her for a model, for all my sufferings are nothing
to hers!   And, strange to say, she is outwardly joyous!
No one knows what she endures.   It would seem almost
as if she knew it not herself!

"I see by her so many poor people and children.   I think
I know them.   Some one must have hidden this person from
me.   My friends and acquaintances must know her.   Ah! how
her heart is wounded!   It is encircled by a crown of thorns

(1) Thus the Pilgrim headed his notes of Dec. 15, 16, 17, 1819.   The author retains
it, as he considers the fact of Sister Emmerich's having this remarkable vision just at
the close of the terrible sufferings of this period, most significant.

full of sharp points. She has very curious surroundings, and how many people are secretly spying and calumniating her! How bright and joyous she is under it! She bounds along like a deer! She is truly an example for me. Now I see clearly how miserable I am!"

After these words, the Pilgrim retired leaving the crusts in the parcel! Next morning, she related the following: "I had last night a most wonderful vision which I cannot understand. There must be a person hidden here who is frequently placed in circumstances similar to mine. She had the stigmata, too, but she has now lost them. I watched her all night in her pains. She must have lived in our convent, for I saw around her all the nuns excepting myself. No one ever guessed the terrible secret suffering that oppressed her, as she was always so cheerful. I cannot imagine what it all means. I have never had such graces or such sufferings, and I could not help feeling very much ashamed at my own cowardice. Perhaps, before my time, such a person lived in our convent; but the circumstances are so like unto my own that it puzzles me. I cannot understand it, it is all very strange!"

The Pilgrim here remarked: "Perhaps, it was a picture of yourself, of how you would have supported your sufferings, were you perfect; and you may also have seen graces received of which you may have been unconscious or forgetful."

She thought that this might possibly be the case and, at the Pilgrim's request, she continued the recital of this vision of herself.

"I saw a religious who had been very ill even before her entrance, forced to leave her convent. From the very beginning of her novitiate, she was a prey to indescribable secret sufferings. Once I saw her heart sur-

rounded by roses which changed suddenly to thorns and
tore it cruelly, whilst sharp points and darts entered her
breast. People far and near suspected her, calumniated
her in the most odious manner. All their thoughts
against her, though not passing into deeds, flew toward her
like steel-pointed arrows and wounded her on all sides. Plots
hatched afar entered her flesh like sharp darts, and once I
saw her heart literally cut to pieces. Still was she cheerful,
kind toward all as if unconscious of her wrongs. My compassion for her was so great that I felt her pains in my own
breast. Her soul was perfectly transparent and, when
fresh sufferings assailed her, I saw in her fiery red rays
and wounds, especially in her breast and heart. Around
her head was a crown of thorns of three different kinds of
branches: one of small white flowers with yellow stamens;
the second with flowers like the first, but longer leaves;
the third of roses and buds. She often pressed it down on
her head, and then the thorns penetrated more deeply.

"I saw her at work in the convent, going here and there,
the birds lighting familiarly upon her shoulders. Sometimes she stood perfectly rigid or lay prostrate on the
ground, when a man often came and bore her to her cell.
I could never see into her cell, he seemed to put her in
through the wall. A protecting spirit was ever by her,
whilst the devil constantly prowled around, stirred up
minds against her, raised loud noises in her room, and even
assaulted her person; but she seemed to be always abstracted, her mind elsewhere. I saw her sometimes in the
church, mounting in the most extraordinary manner upon
the altar, clambering up the walls and windows where she
had any cleaning to do. She was raised and upheld
by spirits in places where another could not possibly
stand. On several occasions, I saw her in two places at

once : in the church before the Blessed Sacrament and, at the same time, either up stairs in her cell, in the kitchen, or elsewhere, and once I saw evil spirits maltreating her most cruelly. She used to be surrounded by the saints, and sometimes she held the Infant Jesus in her arms for hours together. When with her sister-religious, He was always at her side. Once I saw her at table and weapons of all kinds being hurled at her; but she was shielded by the blessed who crowded around her. I saw her at another time making hosts, although quite ill, and a blessed spirit aiding her. Once, when she lay sick and neglected, I saw two of the deceased religious making up her bed and carrying her here and there. They lifted her from her bed and placed her in the middle of the room where she lay on her back without support in the air ; some one entered the room unexpectedly and she fell heavily to the floor. I saw her very often reduced to extremity by the use of natural remedies, and then I saw the apparitions with which she was favored : a beautiful woman all resplendent with light, or a youth like my Celestial Spouse who brought her remedies in little phials, or herbs, or morsels of something which they put on a little shelf at the head of her bed. Once, as she knelt by her table, rigid in ecstasy, she received from an apparition a little statue of Mary; and at another time, her Heavenly Affianced placed on her finger a ring containing a precious stone on which was carved a figure of His Blessed Mother. After some time her Affianced returned and took it away from her. I often saw blessed spirits laying pictures and all sorts of things on her breast when she was ill, and taking them away when she got better ; and I often beheld her miraculously protected from imminent and serious danger. One day she stood by the trap-door of the drying-loft, helping to raise a basket of wet linen, whilst another sister worked the rope below. When the basket had almost reached the top, she made an effort to draw it toward her with one hand, the other grasping the rope. Just then the devil raised a frightful din in the court-yard. The sister below turned her head and slackened her hold on the rope to the imminent peril of the one above who was nearly precipitated, basket and all, upon her companion. Had not God protected her and allowed some one to seize the rope, she would certainly have been killed; as it was, she dislocated her hip from which accident she afterward endured terrible tortures. I saw her wonderfully protected by her angel on many other occasions and under circumstances perilous to both soul and body, and I beheld her driven almost to despair by her persecutors. Once, when sick unto death, she was borne away from her convent by two persons who would never have succeeded in preserving her life during the short journey, had not some more powerful beings come to their aid.

" I saw her when out of her convent dressed as I was at that time, a prey to secret sufferings, but favored by the same graces as before. She was often without assistance and sick unto death.

" Again, I saw her at the hermitage where she fainted. She was brought home to her lodgings by a friend who discovered the cross on her breast. And again, I saw her in two places at one and the same time, lying in bed and walking around her room, several persons keeping watch at the door. I saw her very ill in bed, her whole person rigid, her arms extended, her color brilliant as a rose. A resplendent cross descended from on high toward the right of the bed. On it was the Saviour from whose Wounds shot luminous red rays piercing her hands, feet, and side.

From each wound darted three rays fine as the finest thread, which united in a point as they entered her body. The three from the Wound of the Side were larger and further apart than the others and terminated in a point like a lance. At the instant of contact, I saw drops of bloods spurting from her hands, feet, and right side. When the circumstance became known, the whole town was in excitement, but soon the affair was hushed up and kept secret. I saw her confessor ever true to her, but timid, scrupulous, and suspicious, submitting her to endless trials. An Ecclesiastical Commission was deputed to examine into her case. It was conducted most rigorously, and I rejoiced to see the members soon convinced of her truth. I saw her afterward undergoing the surveillance of some citizens during which she was, as usual, supported by supernatural beings, her angel ever by her side. Later, I saw near her a man writing in secret; but he was not an ecclesiastic.

"I saw her subjected to another investigation which began with every appearance of good faith and kindness, but the devil was at the bottom of it. She was often in danger of death during it, but she was supported and strengthened by heavenly apparitions. Her persecutors did not want to allow her to return to her friends and there were others expecting her, desiring to have her in other places. She was betrayed and ill-treated. Her heart was torn by men's malice, but she was throughout the whole affair, cheerful, even gay, so much so that even the nurse guessed nothing of what she endured interiorly. I saw her, thanks to supernatural intervention, restored to her own home. I saw her afterward in still greater danger, her enemies assembled for the purpose of carrying her off by force; but they disputed among themselves and gave up their design. I saw her chief persecutor entering her presence in a rage as if about to attack her, when suddenly, by some interior movement, he became calm and withdrew. Meanwhile her sister, whose hidden malice and perversity were quite incomprehensible, caused her great anxiety. I saw her spiritual relations with certain ecclesiastics.

" She excited my pity. I felt her sufferings in my own breast, and I wanted to ask her how she could bear so many afflictions. I inquired of my guide if I might question her, if I might speak familiarly with her, and he said I might. Then I asked how she could support her secret sufferings so uncomplainingly, to which she answered in these few words : ' *As you do !*'—which greatly astonished me. I saw once that the Mother of God also endured incomprehensible sufferings in secret.

" Then I saw that this person once lived with a mantuamaker, a good though strict women. I saw her once take off a garment in the street and bestow it upon a poor beggar. The devil laid snares for her ; he did not approach her himself, but he sent wicked men, among them a married man ; but she understood not the drift of their intentions. Three different times I saw the evil one attempting her life. Twice he tried to hurl her down the ladder which led to the garret in which she slept. She used to rise by night to pray, and twice I beheld a horrible black figure push her to the edge of the landing ; but her angel interposed and saved her. On another occasion, as she was making the Way of the Cross in a lonely place near the river, I saw the enemy trying to cast her into a deep pit near the citadel ; but again her angel rescued her. I saw her conversing frequently and lovingly with her dear Celestial Affianced, to whom one day she pledged her troth, though I cannot say whether there was an exchange of rings or not. Their interviews were full of childlike simplicity. Once I saw her at mid-day absorbed in prayer, languishing with divine love, in the Jesuits' church, Clara Soentgen by her side.—A resplendent youth, her Affianced, issued from the Blessed Sacrament in the tabernacle and presented her two crowns, one of roses, the other of thorns. She chose the latter. He placed it on her head and she pressed it down to her own great pain. She was so absorbed as not to perceive that the sacristan was rattling his keys to attract her attention. Clara Soentgen may have seen something strange in her exterior, but the interior signification was unknown to her. She herself was unconscious of her blood having flowed until one of her companions remarked to her that her binder was stained with iron-mould (1). She hid these effusions of blood until after she entered the convent when they became known to one of the sisters. I saw her at Clara Soentgen's, where she gladly gave all that she earned to maintain the household in peace.

" Again, I beheld her working in the fields. So great was her desire to enter a convent that she fell sick. She firmly resolved to go. She had constant vomitings and went about so sad that her mother anxiously questioned her as to the cause; on learning it she expressed disapprobation, saying that such a project was not feasible on account of her daughter's poverty and delicate health. When she informed her father of it, he also disapproved and reprimanded her severely. But she told her parents that God was rich, He would help her. She fell ill, and I saw her confined to her bed. About noon, one day, when no one was home but her mother, I saw her lying, as I thought, asleep, the sun shining through her little window. A man and two female religious radiant with light entered her room. They approached her bed bearing a large

(1) " Binder," a pointed covering for the forehead, worn by peasants.

book written upon parchment in letters of red and gold, and bound in yellow with clasps. The frontispiece was a picture of a man, and there were several other pictures in it. They presented it to her, saying, if she would study it, she would learn all that a religious ought to know. She replied that she would be only too glad to do so, and she took it on her knees. It was in Latin, but she understood it all and read it eagerly. She took this same book with her to the convent and often studied it earnestly; whenever she had perused a certain portion of it, it was withdrawn from her. Once I saw it lying on her table whence some of the religious tried to steal it away, but they could not remove it. I saw her in another part of the convent when the priest found her in prayer perfectly unconscious of all around, as if paralyzed. I saw Our Lord appear to her on the Feast of St. Augustine, make the sign of the cross on her breast, and then give her a cross which she pressed to her heart before returning it to Him. It was white and soft like wax. After this she was sick unto death till Christmas, and she received all the Sacraments. She dreamed that she saw Mary sitting under a tree at Bethlehem; she conversed with her and ardently longed to die and remain with Our Lady. But Mary told her that she, too, had longed to die with her Divine Son, but she had to live and suffer many years after His death. Then she awoke.

"I saw the luminous cross descending toward her and her reception of the stigmata. I saw her during the investigation and I understood that she was far advanced in the reading of her book. I saw her afterward in the house in which I now am and in Mersmann's house where, too, she had the book. She was often in danger of death from which, however, she was always supernaturally saved. Lastly, I saw her future. There was an ecclesiastical inquiry, and they seemed to be drawing up papers concerning her. (1)"

June 15, 1821.—On this day Sister Emmerich had a vision of St. Ludgarde. She saw a series of pictures drawn from her own life.

"I had also visions of the life of a person who, as I afterward discovered, was none other than myself. Sometimes they were presented in union with those of St. Ludgarde's life that I might note the points of resemblance in God's gifts to each and the manner of their bestowal. From her infancy this person was persecuted by the evil one. She used to pray in the fields in places in which she instinctively felt the influence of a malediction, the presence of the powers of darkness. The devil at such times raged around the child, struck her, and hurled her to the ground; at first she ran away in terror but soon returned, animating her courage by faith and confidence in God. 'How canst thou chase me away, miserable wretch! There is nothing in common between us. Thou hast never had any power over me, neither shalt thou have it in this place!'—and kneeling down again in the same spot, she continued her prayer until Satan withdrew. Unable to make her relax her fervor, he urged her to weaken and destroy her health by excessive austerities, but the child defied him and redoubled her mortifications. One day, her mother left her alone, charging her to mind the house, and the demon sent an old woman from the neighborhood to tempt her. Having some bad object in view, the old woman said to the child: 'Go get some ripe pears from my garden! Be quick before your mother comes back!'—Off she ran in all haste. A plough half-hidden under the straw lay in her path. She

(1) The Pilgrim was so astonished at her words that he wrote in his journal : " Ah ! If we had not these hateful interruptions ! If we could only get her whole history from her own lips, what a treasure should we possess ! What a faithful portrait of this admirable soul !"

Stumbled and struck her breast so violently against it that she fell senseless to the ground. Her mother returning home, found the child in this condition and brought her to her senses by a sound correction. But the child long felt the effects of the accident.

" I saw how Satan misled the mother. For a long time she had erroneous ideas of her child, and often punished her undeservedly ; but the little girl bore all patiently, offered it to God, and so overcame the enemy.

" I saw her praying at night and the devil inciting a boy to distract her in an unseemly manner ; but she drove him off and continued her prayer.

" I saw the devil cast the child down from a high ladder, but her angel protected her ; and once, as she crept along the narrow edge of a deep ditch, to avoid treading on the wheat he tried to push her in, but again she escaped the danger.—Once Satan threw her into a pond about twelve feet deep and thrust her to the bottom three times, but her angel brought her each time to the surface.

" I saw the child, on another occasion, about stepping into her little bed, her heart raised to God in prayer, when the evil one from under the bed seized her by the ankles with icy-cold hands and tumbled her over on the floor. I remember very well that she was neither terrified nor did she cry aloud ; she remained quite still and, though no one had ever taught her to do so, she redoubled her prayers and conquered her enemy.

" She was always surrounded by suffering souls who were visible to her ; she prayed for them earnestly, notwithstanding the devil's attacks. Last night, during this vision, the soul of a peasant-woman came to me and thanked for her deliverance.

" I saw the child, now arrived at girlhood, attacked by a

young man instigated thereto by the devil; but she was protected by the ministry of two angels.

"I saw her praying in the cemetery of Coesfeld. The devil dashed her from side to side and, as she returned home, he cast her into a tan-pit.

"I beheld all the attacks, all the persecutions levelled against her in the convent. I saw Satan cast her down the trap-door where she remained hanging by both hands in a most wonderful manner. I never saw him rouse in her the least temptation contrary to purity, indeed he never even attempted to do so. I saw the investigation to which she was subjected and Satan taking an active part in the whole affair. I should not have comprehended how she could have endured so much, had I not seen angels and saints constantly by her. I saw, too, the interior dispositions of all the assistants, their continual touching of her wounds, and I heard their discourse. They gave her repose neither by day nor by night, for they were continually approaching her with a light. I saw their rage when they could discover nothing. When the Landrath said to her: 'I have caught Lambert, he has confessed all! You also must now do the same!'—he was truly frightful to behold. He was furious and, at the same time, so pressing, so insinuating, that he was on the point of drawing from her a word that might have served her enemies' purposes; but I saw a spirit on such occasions laying his hand on her lips. I saw the Abbe Lambert sad unto death, but trying to overcome himself to the great advantage of his soul. I saw that his time of life will be short. I saw the Pilgrim's book from which many things were taken for publication."

CHAPTER XLI.

ADVENT AND CHRISTMAS, 1819.—JOURNEYS IN VISION TO A
JEWISH CITY IN ABYSSINIA AND TO THE MOUNTAIN
OF THE PROPHETS, *via* THIBET.—LABORS FOR
CHILDREN.—MYSTICAL SUFFERINGS.

On the first Sunday of Advent, 1819, a poor old Jewess
came begging an alms of Sister Emmerich for her sick
husband; she was kindly received and to a few silver
pieces Sister Emmerich added words that both touched and
consoled her. It was not the first time the poor woman
had sought the couch of suffering for relief in her own sorrows, and she had never come in vain. On this occasion,
the invalid was seized with such compassion for the poor
Jews that she turned to God with ardent prayers for their
salvation. She was most wonderfully heard. Shortly
after, she related the following vision in which her task was
assigned for the beginning of the ecclesiastical year, *prayer*
not only for the poor Jewess, but also for her whole race.

"It seemed to me that the old Jewess Meyr, to whom I
had often given alms, died and went to purgatory, and that
her soul came back to thank me as it was through me that
she was led to believe in Jesus Christ. She had
reflected that I had so often given her alms, although no one
gives to the poor Jews; and she had thereby felt a desire
spring up in her heart to die for Jesus, if faith in
Jesus were the true faith. It was as if her conversion
had already taken place or would take place, for I felt
impelled to give thanks and to pray for her. Old Mrs. Meyr

was not dead. But her soul had been disengaged from the body in sleep that she might inform me that, if she died in her present sentiments, she would go to purgatory. Her mother, she said, had also received an impression of the truth of Christianity, and she certainly was not lost. I saw the soul of her mother in a dark, gloomy place, abandoned by all. She was as if walled up, unable to help herself or even to stir, and all around her, above and below, were countless souls in the same condition. I had the happy assurance that no soul was lost whom ignorance alone hindered from knowing Jesus, who had a vague desire to know Him, and who had not lived in a state of grievous sin. The soul of the Jewess said that she was going to take me to the native place of her family whence her maternal ancestors had been banished for some crime.

" She would take me also to a city of her people among whom some were very pious, but as they had no one to instruct them, they remained in error. She said I should try to touch their hearts. I went with her willingly. The soul was far more beautiful than the poor old woman who is still living. My angel was at my side and, when the Jewess made little mistakes, he appeared to shine more brilliantly and corrected them. Then she appeared to see him too, for she would ask eagerly, ' Who told you that ? Was it the Messiah ? '—We journeyed over Rome and the sea and through Egypt where I did not see any great waters—only in the middle of the country a great white river which often overflows and fertilizes the soil. All was sand and sand-hills, which the winds scattered around. In this desert are immense stone buildings, high, thick, massive, such as are nowhere else. They are not houses but they are full of great caves and passages where rest numbers of dead bodies. They are very different from the subterra-

nean tombs of Rome. The bodies are all swathed like little infants, hard, stiff, dark brown, and tall; ungraceful figures
are sculptured on the monuments. I went into one and
saw the bodies, but not one was luminous. We went on
further and further south over sand deserts where I saw
spotted beasts, like great cats, running nimbly, and here and
there round buildings on high hills covered with straw, with
towers and trees above. We went up higher and higher
over white sand and green stone polished like glass, into a
region of steep and rugged mountains. I was surprised to
see so many fertile places among the rocks. At last we
reached a large, strange-looking Jewish city, like nothing
I had ever seen before in the narrowness, obscurity,
and intricacy of its streets and houses. The mountains
and rocks appeared as if about to topple over. The whole
place was pierced with caves, grottos, and fissures over which
one must either climb or go around them. It is less a city
than an enormous group of mountains covered with houses,
towers, square blocks of stone, and it is full of caves and
excavations. We did not touch the earth, though we did
not go over the houses either, but moved between them along
the walls, always mounting higher and higher. It seemed
to me that it was all hollow and might cave in at any moment.
There are no Christians, but on the distant part of the mountain are people who are not Jews. I saw on one side a high
quadrangular stone building with round holes in the top covered with iron bars which I took for a Jewish synagogue.
Here and there were houses with gardens on shelving rocks
lying above and behind them. The soul of the old Jewess
Meyr told me on the way that it was true that in former
times the Jews, both in our country and elsewhere, had
strangled many Christians, principally children, and used
their blood for all sorts of superstitious and diabolical prac-

tices. She had once believed it lawful; but she now knew
that it was abominable murder. They still follow such
practices in this country and in others more distant; but
very secretly, because they are obliged to have commercial
intercourse with Christians. We entered the city near the
gate through a long, narrow, dangerous court between two
rows of houses which looked like an open street, but which
really ended in an angle full of caves and windings leading
into the heart of the rocks. All sorts of figures were cut
out in them. I had a feeling that murders had been committed here and that few travellers left them alive. I did
not go into them, they were too frightful. I know not how
we got out of the court again.

" The soul of the Jewess Meyr said that she would take
me now to a very pious, almost saintly family, upon whom
the people all looked as upon their hope; they even expect
from them a deliverer, perhaps the Messiah. ' They are
very good,' she said, ' and so are all their connections.' She
wanted me to see them. We crossed the mountainous city
which we had entered at the north, and mounted toward the
east, till we reached a level place whence we had a view of
the eastern side. There was a row of houses running
toward the south at the end of which stood a large, solid
building overtopped by mountains and gardens. The soul
told me that seven sisters dwelt here, the descendants of
Judith. The eldest, still unmarried, was also named Judith,
and all the inhabitants of the city hope that some day she
will do for her people what Judith did for their ancestors.
She dwells in the large stone castle at the end of the
place. The soul begged me to be kind to them for they
know not the Messiah, and to touch their hearts as I had
touched hers. I forgot to say that it was night when we
entered the city. I saw men sleeping in the caves and

corners, and among them many good, simple-hearted people,
very different from our Jews, franker and nobler. They were
like gold compared with lead or copper; still there was also a
great deal of superstition, crime, horrible filthiness among
them and even something like witchcraft.

" We went into the first house at the corner, which belonged to one of the seven sisters. We passed through a round
vestibule and entered a square apartment, the bed-chamber
of the owner, who had a hooked nose. The soul of the
Jewess again praised her excellent qualities ; but, whenever
she said anything inexact, my guide drew near, that is he
appeared and corrected it. She would then ask, ' Was it
the Messiah who told you that ?'—I answered, ' No, His
servant.'—As I looked upon Judith's sleeping sister, I suddenly became conscious that she was not good. I saw that
she was a wicked adulteress who secretly admitted strangers.
She appeared aware of our presence, for she sat up, looked
around in alarm, and then arose and went about the house.
I said to the soul that now she saw that this woman misbe-
haved. She was greatly surprised, and asked if the Messiah
had told me that too. We went into the houses of the
other sisters, who also had hooked noses, but not all equally
so, and all were better than the first. I cannot now remember how it was that I found them alone, for all were married
and some had children. They wanted for nothing. Their
houses were richly carpeted and furnished, beautiful shining
lamps hanging in the rooms ; but all lived upon their sister
Judith's generosity. The sixth sister was not at home. She
was with her mother who lived in a small house just in front
of Judith's. We went in by a little round court and saw the
mother, an old Jewess at her window. She was complaining
angrily to her sixth daughter that Judith gave her less than
the others, that she even gave more to her bad sister, and

had turned her, her mother, out of doors. It was horrible to see the old Jewess in such a rage.

"We left them quarrelling, and went to see Judith herself in the castle before which stretched a deep broad chasm. I could not look down it steadily. A bridge with an iron railing spanned it, the flooring being only a grating through which at a frightful depth could be seen all kinds of filth, bones, and rubbish. I tried to cross, but something held me back. I could not enter without Judith, so I had to wait; such were my orders. Morning began to dawn, and I saw that the side of the mountain on which we then were, was more pleasant and fertile than the north side by which we had ascended, and I noticed that the castle gate was fastened by a huge beam shaped like a cross. This fact very much surprised me. Suddenly Judith, returning from distributing alms in the city, stood before the bridge. She is about thirty years old, unusually tall and majestic. I never before saw a woman of such vigor and courage, so heroic and resolute; she has a noble countenance, her nose just slightly hooked, hardly enough so, however, to be perceptible. Her whole person, her gestures breathe something elevated, something extraordinary; but, at the same time, she is simple, pure, and sincere. I° loved her from the first. She wore a mantle. Her dress from the neck to the waist was most proper, tight as if laced, especially over the breast; she looked as if she had on a stout corset under her long, striped, many-colored robe. She had something like a gold chain around her neck and large pearls in her ears. A kind of variegated turban was wound around her head, and over it was thrown a veil. A tolerably large basket hung in full view upon her arm, the rods of which were black, the hoops white. She was returning home from one of her nocturnal expeditions when she caught sight of me on the bridge. She appeared startled, took a step backward, but did not run. She exclaimed :—' O My God! what askest Thou of me ? Whence is this to me ?'—but soon she recovered herself and asked who I was and how I came there. I told her that I was a Christian and a religious, that I had been brought thither because of s me good people sighing for salvation, but who were without instruction. When she found that I was a Christian, she sh wed surprise at my having come so far by a route so dangerous. I told her that curiosity had not impelled me, but that the soul by me had led me thither, in order to touch her heart. ' This is,' I said, ' the anniversary of the coming of Christ, the Messiah ; it is a yearly festival.' I added that she should reflect upon the miserable condition of her race and turn to the Redeemer, etc. Judith was deeply affected, she became gradually convinced that she was conversing with spirits. It seemed to me that she either said or thought that she would find out whether I was a natural or a supernatural being, and she took me with her to the house. A narrow path led over the bridge which could, however, be enlarged. When we reached the huge crossbeam that barred the gate, she touched something, the gate flew back, and we passed through a court-yard into which several gates opened ; all around stood statues of various kinds, chiefly old yellow busts. We entered an apartment in which some women were sitting cross-legged on the ground before a long, narrow table about as high as a foot-stool ; they were taking something, and Judith thought that she would now put me to the test. She made me enter first. I did so and went around behind the women, who did not appear to see me ; but, when Judith entered, they arose and passed before her bowing slightly as a mark of respect. Then she took a plate, passed around the women,

and presented it to me, holding it against my breast, for
she wanted to find out whether I was a spirit or not. Now,
when she saw me decline her offer and that none of the
women appeared to see me, she became very serious and
went with me into her own room. She acted like a person
who half-believes herself alone, who wants to convince herself that it is so, but who at the same time doubts it. She spoke
timidly, but not fearfully. She is, in very deed, a Judith,
most courageous! Her room was simple, some cushions
lying around, and several old busts on the wall. Here
we conversed a long time. I spoke of her wicked sister.
Judith was exceedingly distressed and desirous of remedy-
ing the disorder. Then I mentioned her mother whom I
had seen in such a passion, and she told me that, on account of her temper, she had had to build her the little dwelling adjoining the castle; that she was very angry at being sent
away, and at her giving more to one than to another, for all
shared her bounty, as she, Judith, was not willing that they
should live by usury. She took them money every night.
Many others of the city lived at her expense, for her
father had left a great treasure of which no one living knew
but herself. He had loved her tenderly and left her
everything. The people built their hopes upon her.
Her secret alms made them see in her something superhu-
man, for they knew not of the treasure. They had once
been greatly oppressed by war when she had done all in her
power for them; and so her deceased father (as she called
him) left her the treasure. All wished her to marry, hoping that a deliverer would be born from her; but she instinctively shrank from marriage. My appearance made
upon her an impression such as she had never before
known, and she felt that the Messiah might, indeed, be
already come in Christ. She desired to inquire further

into it, and, if she were convinced, she would strive to lead
her people to salvation. She knew well that all would follow
her, and she thought perhaps that was what they expected of her. After conversing in this strain, she took a lamp,
led me into a kind of cave by a secret trap-door in the floor
of her room, and showed me the immense treasure. I never
before saw so much gold. The whole cave was lined with
it and there was, besides, an enormous quantity of precious
stones, one could hardly enter without stepping on them.
She then took me all over the house. In one room were
seated a number of old men, some of them Moors, wearing
frontlets and turbans, their robes bordered with fur;
they smoked long pipes, and they were drinking like the
women in the other room. In another room were both men
and women. We went up to the second story and into a
large apartment singularly arranged. Around the walls
and over the doors were yellow busts of venerable, old,
bearded men. The furniture was odd-looking, antique and
artistically carved, reminding me of the Jesuit church at
Coesfeld, though the carving here was more elaborate. In
the middle of the room hung a large lamp and I think seven
others around it, and there was also something like an altar
with rolls of parchment on it. The whole room was wonderful! Near it was another where lay numbers of
decrepit men, as if being cared for. Then we went up on
the roof. Back of the house on a terraced slope was the
garden with large spreading trees carefully trimmed. We
went up on this side and Judith pointed out in the distance a ruined building with crumbling towers, remarking
that it had been the boundary of her nation's possessions
before they had been conquered by a neighboring people
and driven back. They still feared a renewal of their
misfortune of which these walls stood as a perpetual me-

morial. I saw them and water also in the distance. We mounted higher across deep ravines and strange buildings, the rocks at times jutting out over one another as if the trees and houses on them were about to fall. We went to another part of the city where rose a steep rock like a high wall. Steps were cut in it, and here and there gushed limpid springs. Judith told me that there was a tradition of this city's having suffered extremely from drought. A strange man, a Christian, came and struck the rock with his staff, when water gushed forth. It used to be conducted by pipes, but they were not now in existence. All the springs, excepting this one, had ceased to flow. Judith left me by the fountain; she returned home and I continued my journey. We took no leave of each other. It was all like a dream to her and she parted from me as if she no longer saw me. My road went up, up. I saw trees with large yellow fruits lying underneath, fertile fields, beautiful flowers, and bees in hives different from ours. They were square, tapering upward, black, and smeared with something. I was now far past the Jewish mountain, and I saw men who lived under large spreading trees like houses. They had few movables. Some of them were spinning and I saw, here and there, a kind of loom. Their flocks, animals like those of the Magi, grazed around. There were also animals like great jackasses, all very tame. Some of these people lived in tents; but they stayed not long in any one place, they were continually moving. Clambering over bushes and stones, I came to a large subterranean cavern in good condition supported by short square pillars on which were all kinds of figures and inscriptions; in it was something like an altar, a large stone, above it and on either side great holes like ovens. I wondered why the people did not use this beautiful hall. They are good, simple creatures and they doubt not that their faith is the right one. At last, I crossed the sea and returned home."

June 21, 1820.—" Last night I took another long jour- ney to the high mountain-city and Judith's castle. I did not find her sisters in the houses leading to the castle. I know not where they are. I know that she had promised faithfully to put an end to the disorders of one of them. All the rest was as before, only it was later in the day, and there were numbers of strange Jews up-stairs praying in the synagogue. I went to Judith who was sit- ting in her room reading a book. There was something about her inexpressibly grand, noble, and touching. I gazed upon her with delight. I have no doubt that she will become a Christian, if God gives her the opportunity, and then the greater part of her people will follow her. I cannot look upon this woman in her beauty, her majesty, her courage, her tenderness of heart, her humility, without great love and hope. I saw her once more in my illness before the last, but I forgot to mention it. I have fin- ished the journey that relates to her."

In the second week of Advent, Sister Emmerich was taken by her angel to the highest peak of a mountain in Thibet, quite inaccessible to man. Here she saw Elias guard- ing the treasures of knowledge communicated to men by the angels and prophets since the creation. She was told that the mysterious prophetic book in which she had been al- lowed to read, belonged here. This was not her first visit. She had often been brought hither by her angel, and also to the terrestrial Paradise not far distant. These places seem- ed to be closely connected, as in both she met the same holy custodians. Her own prophetic light gave her a cer- tain right to participate in the riches preserved in them and she had need of the supernatural gifts there bestowed upon her for the continuance of her expiatory task. She could retain only a general impression of what she saw which she reproduced in very imperfect sketches.

Dec. 9, 1819—"Last night I journeyed over different parts of the Promised Land. I saw it just as it was in Our Lord's time. I went first to Bethlehem, as if to announce the coming of the Holy Family, and then I followed a route already well known to me and saw pictures of Our Lord's public life. I saw Him distributing the bread by the hands of two of His disciples, and then explaining a parable. The people sat on the slope of a hill under tall trees which bore all their leaves on top like a crown. Underneath were bushes with red and yellow berries, like bramble-berries. A stream of water ran down the hill and branched off into other small streams. I gathered some of the grass. It was soft, fine as silk, like thick moss. But when I tried to touch other objects, I could not. I found they were only pictures of times long past, though the grass I really felt. The Lord was, as usual, in a long, yellowish woollen tunic. His hair, parted in the middle, fell low upon His shoulders. His face was peaceful, earnest, and beaming with light, His forehead very white and shining. The two who distributed the bread broke it into pieces which the men, women, and children ran to receive; they ate and then sat down. Behind the Lord was a brook. I saw many other pictures as I passed rapidly from place to place. Leaving Jerusalem I went toward the east, and met several great bodies of water and mountains which the Magi had crossed on their journey to Bethlehem. I came also to countries in which many people lived, but I did not enter them. I travelled mostly over deserts. At last, I reached a very cold region, and I was led up higher and higher. Along the mountain-chain from west to east, was a great road over which troops of men were

travelling. They were diminutive, but very active, and they
carried little standards. I saw some of another race, very
tall; — they were not Christians. Their road led down the
mountain. But mine led up to a region of incredible beauty,
where the air was balmy, and vegetation green and luxuriant—flowers of marvellous loveliness, charming groves,
dense woods. Numbers of animals sported around apparently harmless. No human beings inhabited this region, no
man had ever been there, and from the great road only
clouds could be seen. I saw herds of nimble animals with
very slender legs like young roebucks; they had no horns,
their skin was clear brown with black spots. I saw a short
black animal something like the hog, and others like great
goats, but still more like the roebucks; they were tame,
bright-eyed, and nimble. I saw others like fat sheep with
wigs of wool and thick tails; others like asses, but spotted;
flocks of little yellow nanny-goats and herds of little horses;
great long-legged birds running swiftly; and numbers of lovely
tiny ones of all colors, sporting in perfect freedom, as if
ignorant of man's existence. From this paradise I mounted
still higher, as if through the clouds, and, at last, came to
the summit of the mountain, where I saw wonders! It was
a vast plain, surrounding a lake, in which was a green island connected with the shore by a strip of verdant land.
The island was surrounded by great trees like cedars. I
was taken up to the top of one of them. I held on firmly to
the branches, and saw the whole island at once. There
were several slender towers with a little portico on each as
if a chapel were built over the gate. These porticoes were
all covered with fresh verdure, moss or ivy; for the vegetation here was luxuriant. The towers were about as high
as bell-towers, but very slender, reminding me of the tall
columns in the old cities I had seen on my journey. They

were of different forms, cylindrical and octagonal; the former
built of huge stones, polished and veined with moon-shaped
roofs; the latter, which had broad, projecting roofs were covered with raised figures and ornaments by means of which one
might climb to the top. The stones were colored brown, red,
black, and arranged in various patterns. The towers were not
higher than the trees, on one of which I stood, though they
seemed to be equal to them in number. The trees were a kind
of fir with needle-shaped leaves. They bore yellow fruit
covered with scales, not so long as pine-apples, more like
common apples. They had numerous trunks covered toward
the root with gnarled bark, but higher up it was smoother;
they were straight, symmetrical, and stood far enough apart
not to touch. The whole island was covered with verdure,
thick, fine, and short, not grass, but a plant with fine curled
leaves like moss, as soft and nice as the softest cushion.
There was no trace of a road or path. Near each tower
was a small garden laid off in beds with a great variety of
shrubs and beautiful blooming trees—all was green, the
gardens differing from one another as much as the towers.
As from my tree I glanced over the island, I could see the
lake at one end, but not the mountain. The water was
wonderfully clear and sparkling. It flowed across the island
in streams which were lost underground.

" Opposite the narrow slip of land in the green plain was
a long tent of gray stuff inside of which, at the further end,
hung broad colored stripes, painted or embroidered in all
kinds of figures. A table stood in the centre. Around it
were stone seats without backs; they looked like cushions
and they, too, were covered with living verdure. In the
middle and most honorable seat, behind the low, oval, stone
table, was a manly, holy, shining figure sitting cross-legged
in eastern fashion, and writing with a reed on a large roll of

parchment. The pen looked like a little branch. Right and
left lay great books and parchment rolls on rods with
knobs at either end. By the tent was a furnace in the
earth, like a deep hole, in which burned a fire whose flames
rose not above its mouth. The whole country was like a
beautiful green island up in the clouds. The sky above was
indescribably clear, though I saw only a semicircle of bright
rays, much larger however than we ever see. The scene
was inexpressibly holy, solitary, charming! Whilst I
gazed upon it, it seemed as if I understood all that it signified. But I knew that I should not be able to remember it.
My guide was visible until we reached the tent, and then
he disappeared.

"As I gazed in wonder, I thought, 'Why am I here?
And why must I, poor creature, see all this?'—And the
figure from the tent spoke : ' It is because thou hast a share
in it!'—This only surprised me more, and I descended or
rather I floated down to where he sat in the tent. He
was clothed like the spirits I am accustomed to see, his
look and bearing like John the Baptist or Elias. The books
and rolls were very old and precious. On some of them were
metallic figures or ornaments in relief : for instance, a man
with a book in his hand. The figure told me, or informed me
in some way, that these books contained all the holiest things
that had ever come from man. He examined and compared
all, and threw what was false into the fire near the tent. He
told me that he was there to guard everything until the
time would come to make use of it, which time might have
already come, had there not been so many obstacles. I
asked if he did not feel tired waiting so long. He replied :
' In God there is no time !' He said that I must see everything, and he took me out and showed me around. He said
also that mankind did not yet deserve what was kept there.

The tent was about as high as two men, as long as from here to the church in the city, and about half as broad. The top was gathered into a knot and fastened to a string which went up and was lost in the air. I wondered what supported it. At the four corners were columns that one could almost span with both hands; they were veined like the polished towers and capped by green knobs. The tent was open in front and on the sides. In the middle of the table lay an immense book that could be opened and shut; it seemed to be fastened to the table and it was to this the man referred to see if the others were right. I felt there was a door under the table and that a sacred treasure was kept there. The moss-covered seats were placed far enough from the table to allow one to walk around between them and it; behind them lay numbers of books, right and left, the latter destined for the flames. He led me all around them, and I noticed on the covers pictures of men carrying ladders, books, churches, towers, tablets, etc. He told me again that he examined them and burned what was false and useless; mankind was not yet prepared for their contents, another must come first. He took me around the shore of the lake. Its surface was on a level with the island. The waters at my feet ran under the mountain by numerous channels and reappeared below in springs. It seemed as if all this quarter of the world received thereby health and benediction; it never overflowed above. The descent of the mountain on the east and south was green and covered with beautiful flowers; on the west and north there was verdure, but no flowers. At the extremity of the lake, I crossed over without a bridge, and went all around among the towers. The ground was like a bed of thick, firm moss, as if hollow underneath. The towers arose out of it, and the gardens around them were watered by rivulets which flowed either to or from the lake, I know not which. There were no walks in the gardens, though they were all laid out in order. I saw roses far larger than ours, red, white, yellow, and dark, and a species of lily, very tall flowers, blue with white streaks, and also a stalk as high as a tree with large palm leaves. It bore on the top a flower like a large plate. I understood that in the towers were preserved the greatest treasures of creation, and I felt that holy bodies rested in them. Between two of them, I saw standing a singular chariot with four low wheels. It had two seats and a small one in front. Four persons could easily be accommodated and, like everything else on the island, it was all covered with vegetation or green mould. It had no pole. It was ornamented with carved figures so well executed that, at first sight, I thought them alive. The box was formed of thin metallic open worked figures; the wheels were heavier than those of Roman chariots, yet it all seemed light enough to be drawn by men. I looked at everything closely, because the man said : ' Thou hast a share herein, and thou canst now take possession of it.' I could not understand what share I had in it. ' What have I to do,' I thought, ' with this singular looking chariot, these towers, these books ?' I had a deep feeling of the sanctity of the place. I felt that with its waters the salvation of many generations had flowed down into the valleys, that mankind itself had come from this mountain, and had sunk ever lower, lower, and lower, and I also felt that heaven's gifts for men were here stored, guarded, purified, and prepared. I had a clear perception of it all ; but I could not retain it, and now I have only a general impression.

"When I re-entered the tent, the man again addressed me in the same words : ' Thou hast a part in all this, thou

canst even take possession of it !'—And, as I represented to
him my incapacity, he said with calm assurance: ' Thou wilt
soon return to me !' He went not out of the tent whilst I
was there, but moved around the table and the books.
The former was not so green as the seats, nor the
seats as the things near the towers, for it was not so
damp here. The ground in the tent and everything
it contained were moss-grown, table, seats, and all.
The foot of the table seemed to serve as a chest to hold something sacred. I had an impression that a holy body reposed
therein. I thought there was under it a subterranean
vault and that a sweet odor was exhaled from it. I felt
that the man was not always in the tent. He received me
as if he knew me and had waited for my coming. He told
me confidently that I should return, and then he showed me
the way down. I went toward the south, by the steep
mountain, through the clouds, and into the delightful region
where there were so many animals. There was not a single one up above. I saw numerous springs gushing from
the mountain, playing in cascades, and running down in
streams. I saw birds larger than geese, in color like a par-
tridge, with three claws in front of the foot and one behind,
a tail somewhat flat, and a long neck. There were other
birds with bluish plumage very like the ostrich, but rather
smaller. I saw all the other animals.

"In this journey I saw many more human beings than
in the others. Once I crossed a small river which I felt
flowed from the lake above. I followed it awhile, and then
lost sight of it. I came to a place where poor people of
various races lived in huts. I think they were Christian
captives. I saw brown-complexioned men with white ker-
chiefs on their head, bringing food to them in wicker baskets; they reached it to them the whole length of their

arm, and then fled away in fright as if exposed to danger. They lived in rude huts in a ruined city. I saw water in which great, strong reeds grew, and I came again to the river which is very broad here and full of rocks, sandbanks, and beautiful green weeds among which it danced. It was the same river that flowed from the mountain and which, as a little stream, I had crossed higher up. A great many dark-complexioned people, men, women, and children in various costumes were on the rocks and islets, drinking and bathing. They seemed to have come from a distance. It reminded me of what I had seen at the Jordan in the Holy Land. A very tall man stood among them, seemingly their priest. He filled their vessels with water. I saw many other things. I was not far from the country where St. Francis Xavier used to be. I crossed the sea over innumerable islands. "

Dec. 22d—" I know why I went to the mountain. My book lies among the writings on the table and I shall get it again to read the last five leaves. The man who sits at the table will come again in due time. His chariot remains there as a perpetual memorial. He mounted up there in it and men, to their astonishment, will behold him coming again in the same. Here upon this mountain, the highest in the world, whose summit no one has ever reached, were the sacred treasures and secrets concealed when sin spread among men. The water, the island, the towers, are all to guard these treasures. By the water up there are all things refreshed and renewed. The river flowing from it, whose waters the people venerate, has power to strengthen; therefore is it esteemed more highly than wine. All men, all good things have come down from above, and all that is to be secured from destruction is there preserved.

" The man on the mountain knew me, for I have a share

in it. We know each other, we belong together. I cannot express it well, but we are like a seed going through the
whole world. Paradise is not far from the mountain. Once
before I saw that Elias lived in a garden near Paradise."

Dec. 26th—"I have again seen the Prophet Mountain.
The man in the tent reached to a figure floating over him
from heaven leaves and books, and received others in return.
He who floated above reminded me very much of St. John.
He was more agile, pleasing, and lighter than the man in
the tent, who had something sterner, more energetic and
unbending about him ; the former was to the latter as the
New to the Old Testament, so I may call one John, the
other Elias. It seemed as if Elias presented to John revelations that had been fulfilled and received new ones from him.
Then I suddenly saw from the white sea a jet of water shoot
up like a crystal ray. It branched into innumerable jets
and drops like immense cascades, and fell down upon different parts of the earth, and I saw men in houses, in huts, in
cities all over the world enlightened by it. It began at once
to produce fruit in them."

Dec. 27th, Feast of St. John the Evangelist, Sister Emmerich beheld St. Peter's basilica shining like the sun, its rays
streaming over all the world. "I was told," she said, "that
this referred to St. John's Apocalypse. Various individuals
would be enlightened by it and they would impart their
knowledge to the whole world. I had a very distinct vision,
but I cannot relate it."

During the octave she had constant visions of the
Church, of which, however, she could relate but little. Nor
could she give a clear idea of the connection existing
between them and the Prophet Mountain, but we may
infer from the Pilgrim's notes that they formed a cycle of
visions singularly grand.

"I saw St. Peter's. A great crowd of men were trying to pull it down whilst others constantly built it up again. Lines connected these men one with another and with others throughout the whole world. I was amazed at their perfect understanding. The demolishers, mostly apostates and members of the different sects, broke off whole pieces and worked according to rules and instructions. They wore white aprons bound with blue riband. In them were pockets and they had trowels stuck in their belts. The costumes of the others were various. There were among the demolishers distinguished men wearing uniforms and crosses. They did not work themselves, but they marked out on the wall with a trowel where and how it should be torn down. To my horror, I saw among them Catholic priests. Whenever the workmen did not know how to go on, they went to a certain one in their party. He had a large book, which seemed to contain the whole plan of the building and the way to destroy it. They marked out exactly with a trowel the parts to be attacked, and they soon came down. They worked quietly and confidently, but slyly, furtively, and warily. I saw the Pope praying, surrounded by false friends who often did the very opposite to what he had ordered, and I saw a little black fellow (a laic) laboring actively against the Church. Whilst it was thus being pulled down on one side, it was rebuilt on the other, but not very zealously. I saw many of the clergy whom I knew. The Vicar-General gives me great joy. He went to and fro, coolly giving orders for the repairing of the injured parts. I saw my confessor dragging a huge stone by a roundabout way. I saw others carelessly saying their breviary and, now and then, bringing a little stone under their cloak or giving it to another as something very rare. They seemed to have neither confidence, earnestness, nor method. They hardly knew what was going on. It was lamentable ! Soon the whole front of the church was down; the sanctuary alone stood. I was very much troubled and I kept thinking, ' Where is the man with the red mantle and white banner whom I used to see standing on the church to protect it ?' Then I saw a most majestic lady floating over the great square before the church. Her wide mantle fell over her arms as she arose gently on high, until she stood upon the cupola and spread it over all the church like golden rays. The destroyers were taking a short repose, and when they returned they could in no way approach the space covered by the mantle. On the opposite side, the repairs progressed with incredible activity. There came men, old, crippled, long-forgotten, followed by vigorous young people, men, women, children, ecclesiastic and lay, and the edifice was soon restored. Then I saw a new Pope coming in procession, younger and far sterner looking than his predecessor. He was received with pomp. He appeared about to consecrate the church. But I heard a voice proclaiming it unnecessary as the Blessed Sacrament had not been disturbed. The same voice said that they should solemnly celebrate a double feast, a universal jubilee and the restoration of the church. The Pope, before the feast began, instructed his officers to drive out from the assembled faithful a crowd of the clergy both high and low, and I saw them going out, scolding and grumbling. Then the Holy Father took into his service others, ecclesiastic and lay. Now commenced the grand solemnity in St. Peter's. The men in white aprons worked on when they thought themselves unobserved, silently, cunningly, though rather timidly."

Dec. 30th—" Again I saw St. Peter's with its lofty copola on whose top stood Michael shining with light. He wore a blood-red robe, a great banner in his hand. A desperate struggle was going on below—green and blue combatants against white, and over the latter, who seemed to be worsted, appeared a fiery red sword. None knew why they fought. The church was all red like the angel, and I was told that it would be bathed in blood. The longer the combat lasted, the paler grew the color of the church, the more transparent it became. Then the angel descended and approached the white troops. I saw him several times in front of them. Their courage was wonderfully aroused, they knew not why or how, and the angel struck right and left among the enemy who fled in all directions. Then the fiery sword over the victorious whites disappeared. During the engagement the enemy's troops kept constantly deserting to the other side; once they went in great numbers.

"Numbers of saints hovered in the air over the combatants, pointing out what was to be done, making signs with the hand, etc., all different, but impelled by one spirit. When the angel had descended, I beheld above him a great shining cross in the heavens. On it hung the Saviour from whose Wounds shot brilliant rays over the whole earth. Those glorious Wounds were red like resplendent door-ways, their centre golden-yellow like the sun. He wore no crown of thorns, but from all the Wounds of His Head streamed rays Those from His Hands, Feet, and Side were fine as hair and shone with rainbow colors ; sometimes they all united and fell upon villages, cities, and houses throughout the world. I saw them here and there, far and near, falling upon the dying, and the soul entering by the colored rays into the Saviour's Wounds. The rays from the Side spread over the Church like a mighty current lighting up every part of it, and I saw that the greater number of souls enter into the Lord by these glittering streams. I saw also a shining red heart floating in the air. From one side flowed a current of white light to the Wound of the Sacred Side, and from the other a second current fell upon the Church in many regions; its rays attracted numerous souls who, by the Heart and the current of light, entered into the Side of Jesus. I was told that this was the Heart of Mary. Besides these rays, I saw from all the Wounds about thirty ladders let down to the earth, some of which, however, did not reach it. They were not all alike but narrow and broad, with large and small rounds, some standing alone, others together. Their color corresponded to the purification of the soul, first dark, then clearer, then gray, and, at last, brighter and brighter. I saw souls painfully climbing up. Some mounted quickly, as if helped from above, others pressed forward eagerly but slipped back upon the lower rounds, whilst others fell back entirely into the darkness. Their eager and painful efforts were quite pitiful. It seemed as if they who mounted easily as if helped by others, were in closer communication with the Church. I saw, too, many souls of those that fell on the battle-field taking the path leading into the Body of the Lord. Behind the cross, far back in the sky, I saw multitudes of pictures representing the preparation begun ages ago for the work of Redemption. But I cannot describe it. It looked like the stations of the Way of Divine Grace from the Creation to the Redemption. I did not always stand in the same place. I moved around among the rays, I saw all. Ah, I saw inexpressible, indescribable things! It seemed to me that the Prophet Mountain drew near the cross whilst at the same time it remained in its own position, and I had a view of it as in the first vision. Higher up and back of it were gardens full of shining animals and plants. I felt that it was Paradise.

" When the combat on earth was over, the church and
the angel became bright and shining, and the latter
disappeared; the cross also vanished and in its place stood
a tall, resplendent lady extending over it her mantle of
golden rays. There was a reconciliation going on inside,
and acts of humility were being made. I saw Bishops and
pastors approaching one another and exchanging books.
The various sects recognized the Church by her miraculous
victory and the pure light of revelation they had seen
beaming upon her. This light sprang from the spray of
the fountain gushing from the Prophet Mountain. When
I saw this reunion, I felt that the kingdom of God was near.
I perceived a new splendor, a higher life in all nature, and
a holy emotion in all mankind as at the time of the Saviour's birth. I felt so sensibly the approach of the kingdom of God that I was forced to run to meet it uttering
cries of joy (1).

" I had a vision of Mary in her ancestors. I saw their
whole stock, but no flower on it so noble as she. I saw her
come into this world. How, I cannot express, but in the
same way as I always see the approach of the kingdom of
God with which alone I can compare it. I saw it hastened
by the desires of many humble, loving, faithful Christians.
I saw on the earth many little luminous flocks of lambs
with their shepherds, the servants of Him who, like a
lamb, gave His Blood for us all. Among men reigned
boundless love of God. I saw shepherds whom I knew,
who were near me, but who little dreamed of all this, and I
felt an intense desire to arouse them from their sleep. I rejoiced like a child that the Church is my mother, and I had
a vision of my childhood when our school-mastei used to
say to us: ' Whoever has not the Church for his mother,

(1) **This she** really did in her vision, praying in a loud voice.

looks not upon God as his father!'—Again I was a child,
thinking as then, 'The church is stone. How, then, can
it be thy mother! Yet, it is true, it is thy mother!'—and
so I thought that I went into my mother whenever I entered the church, and I cried out in my vision, 'Yes, she is,
indeed, thy mother!'—Now I suddenly saw the Church as a
beautiful, majestic lady, and I complained to her that she allowed herself to be neglected and ill-treated by her servants.
I begged her to give me her son. She put the Child Jesus
into my arms, and I talked to Him a long time. Then I
had the sweet assurance that Mary is the Church; the
Church, our mother; God, our father; and Jesus, our
brother—and I was glad that when a child I had gone into the stone mother, into the church, and that, through
God's grace, I had thought: 'I am going into my holy
mother!'—"Then I saw a great feast in St. Peter's which,
after the victorious battle, shone like the sun. I saw numerous processions entering it. I saw a new Pope, earnest and energetic. I saw before the feast began a great
many bad Bishops and pastors expelled by him. I saw
the holy Apostles taking a leading part in the celebration.
I saw the petition: 'Lord, Thy kingdom come,' being verified. It seemed as if I saw the heavenly gardens coming
down from above, uniting with pure places on earth, and
bathing all in original light. The enemies that had fled
from the combat were not pursued; they dispersed of their
own accord."

These visions upon the Church were soon absorbed in
one great contemplation of the Heavenly Jerusalem.

"I saw in the shining streets of the city of God brilliant palaces and gardens full of saints, praising God and
watching over the Church. In the Heavenly Jerusalem
there is no Church, Christ Himself is the Church. Mary's

throne is above the city of God, above her are Christ and
the Most Holy Trinity, from whom falls upon Mary a
shower of light which then spreads over all the holy city.
I saw St. Peter's basilica below the city of God, and I ex-
ulted at the thought that, in spite of all men's indifference,
it ever receives the true light from on high. I saw the
roads leading to the Heavenly Jerusalem and pastors conducting therein perfect souls among their flocks ; but these
roads were not crowded.

"I saw my own way to God's city and I beheld from it,
as from the centre of a vast circle, all whom I had ever
helped. There I saw all the children and poor people for
whom I had made clothes, and I was surprised and amused
to see what varied forms I had given them. Then I saw
all the scenes of my life in which I had been useful, if only
to a single person, by counsel, example, assistance, prayer,
or suffering ; and I saw the fruit they had drawn from it
under the symbol of gardens planted for them which they
had either cared for or neglected. I saw every one upon
whom I had ever made an impression and what effect it
produced."

The fact of Sister Emmerich's retaining the liveliest remembrance of those actions most dear to her in her natural
state, is quite characteristic of her, so simple and yet so
heroic. Her labors for the sick and the poor ever constituted her greatest delight. Day and night, awake or in vision,
in the midst of her sufferings, she was constantly occupied
in works of this kind, and great was her delight when she
finished some pieces of clothing for her needy clients. We
shall give the Pilgrim's remarks on this subject just as they
fell from his own pen :—

"Nov. 18th—I found her mending some coarse woollen
stockings to be given away. I thought it all a waste of time

and I said so to her, whereupon she gave me a beautiful instruction on the way to perform charity."

"Dec. 12th—She was unusually gay this morning, working away at little caps and binders, made out of all kinds of scraps, for poor women and children at Christmas. She was enchanted with her success, laughed and seemed perfectly radiant. Her countenance shone with the purity of her soul; she even looked a little mischievous as if about to introduce some one who had lain concealed. She says she is never so happy as when working for little children. This joyousness was, however, accompanied by a peculiar sensation—she was, as it were, absent and beholding an infinity of things against her will. She recollected herself repeatedly, glancing around her little room as if to assure herself that she was really there; but soon it all disappeared again and she was once more surrounded by strange scenes."

Dec. 14th—" Last night I saw a woman of this place who is near her accouchement. She confided to a friend her destitute condition, not having clothes in which to wrap the child. I thought, ' Ah! if she would only come to me !'— Her friend said to her, ' I shall see if I can get you something,' and to-day she came to tell me of the poor creature's distress. I was so glad to be able to provide for her wants."

We turn again to the Pilgrim's journal and find the following:—

" Dec. 13th—She was very bright again to-day, making clothes for poor infants. Nothing pleases her more than to receive some cast-off garments and old scraps for this purpose. Her money has also been again miraculously multiplied. For two days she knew not what to do, having only four thalers left. She recommended the affair to God when, all at once, she found ten in small change. She thinks their being in small change signifies that she should make use of them right away. She is surprised at the quantity of work she has finished. Her scraps and old pieces are dearer to her than the most costly treasures, though she is so rapt in contemplation during her work that she sees the scissors moving as if in a dream, and she often thinks she is cutting up the wrong thing."

" Dec. 18th—When I entered she was talking to her little niece about poor children; she was quite bright, although suffering a good deal. She said to the child : 'Last night I saw a child in a new jacket, but it had only one sleeve.'— ' Yes,' replied the child, ' it was little Gertrude. You gave her some stuff for a jacket, but there was not enough for both sleeves ; she told me so in school to-day.' Tears sprang to the invalid's eyes, and she told me that she always felt such consolation in speaking to the innocent child that she could hardly restrain herself ; she was sometimes obliged to send her away that she might not witness her emotion."

" Dec. 20th—She finished her work to-day with great effort and the help of God. She put herself to much trouble, she has everything in perfect order. ' I have nearly all my gifts ready,' she said, ' for mid-winter, then I shall have to begin again. I am not ashamed to beg for the poor. Little Lidwina used to do it. I have seen her in her room on the ground-floor ; it was about twice as large as mine, the miserable walls of clay, all was very poor. On the right of the door stood her bed around which hung a black woollen cloth like a curtain. Opposite the bed were two little square windows with round panes opening upon a court, and against the wall, between the windows, stood a kind of little altar with a cross and ornaments. Good Lidwina lay patiently in the dark corner with no feather bed, only a heavy, black quilt. She wore a black mantle which covered her all over even her hands, and she looked very sick, her face was full

of fiery red marks. I saw her little niece by her, a remark-
bly good and amiable child, about as large as my niece.
She waited on her so compassionately! Lidwina sent her
to beg some meat for the poor, and she brought back a
shoulder of pork and some pease; then I saw her in the çorner
to the left of the door, where the fireplace was, cooking
both in a great pot or kettle. Then I had another picture,
Lidwina looking for her Heavenly Spouse whom she saw
coming. I saw Him, too, He was mine also. But a man
who had hid len himself between the door and her bed distracted her, and she was so worried that she began to weep.
I had to laugh, for the same thing often happened to me
too. I saw that her lips were greatly swollen."

Dec. 21st—"When I felt the cold last night, I thought
of the freezing poor, and then I saw my Spouse who said:
'Thou hast not the right kind of confidence in me. Have
I ever let thee freeze? Why dost thou not give thy extra
beds to the poor? If thou hast need of them again, I shall
give them back to thee.'—I was ashamed of myself and I
resolved, in spite of Gertrude, to give away the beds not in
use."—That very evening she did so, saying: 'If my relations want to visit me, they may sleep on straw, or stay at
home.' "

Dec. 22d—"She cried out in ecstasy: 'There I see all
the children for whom I have ever made anything! They
are so merry, they have all the things, they all shine—my
little Boy is there, too. Come here, dear little one. sit there,'
and she pointed to a seat. 'O how I thirst for my Saviour!
It is a burning thirst, but it is sweet—the other thirst is
disgusting. O what thirst Mary must have had for her
Child! Still she had Him only nine months under her heart,
and I can receive Him so often in Holy Communion! Such
food is upon earth, and yet many die of hunger and thirst!

The land in which this blessing is given to man is just as desolate and poor as the rest of the world! But the blessed let nothing go to loss. Wherever a church once existed, it still exists. O how many churches I see around Bethlehem and in the whole world, floating in the air above the places on which they formerly stood! Feasts are still celebrated in them. There is the church in which Mary's Conception was so magnificently celebrated. Mary's spotlessness consists in this that she had in her no sin, no passion; her sacred body never endured sickness. She possessed, however, no grace without her own co-operation, excepting that by which she conceived the Lord Jesus."

After this she had a vision of how the " Little Boy," had been the constant companion of her life :—

" What I now saw in vision, once really happened ; for the little Boy used to work with me when I was a child (1).

" When I was ten years old, He said to me : ' Let us go see how the little crib looks that we made years ago !'—' Where can it be ?' I thought. But the little Boy said I had only to go with Him, we should soon find it. When we did so we saw that the flowers (2) of which we had made it, had formed garlands and crowns, some only half-finished. The little Boy said, ' The pearls are still wanting in front. ' Only one small circlet of pearls was entirely finished and I slipped it on my finger. But, to my great distress and fright, I could not get it off. I begged the little Boy to do so, for I was afraid I should not be able to work with it on. He succeeded, and we put everything back again. But I think it was only a picture, I do not remember it as a real event. After I had grown up I got sick. I wanted to go to the convent; but as I was so poor, I became sad. The little Boy

(1) The particulars are given in one of the first chapters.
(2) Symbols of suffering.

said that that was nothing, His Father had enough, the Christ-Child had nothing either, and that I should one day enter a convent. I did, indeed, enter; it was a joyful time! As a nun, I was sick and in distress because I had nothing. I used to say, 'Now, see how it is! Thou wast to have care of all, I was always to have enough; and now Thou stayest away, and I get nothing!'—Then the little Boy came that night with gold, pearls, flowers, and all kinds of precious things. I knew not where to put them all. Twice again I received such things in vision, but I know not what has become of them. I think they were symbolical of the gifts I was to receive and which were miraculously multiplied; as, for example, Herr von Galen's present and the coffee on St. Catherine's day. I used to be sick all the time; well for a couple of days, then sick again, and in this state I saw many things with the Child Jesus and many cures. Then I was out of the convent very ill, often in intense agony and distress; but the little Boy always came with help and advice. Lastly, I had a vision of the future. The little Boy took me again to see the garlands and flowers of the crib in a kind of sacristy, where they lay in a casket, like golden crowns and jewels. He again said, 'Only some pearls are wanting, and then all will be used in the Church.'—I understood that I am to die, as soon as all the pearls will have been added."

In Advent she had her usual visions of Mary and Joseph journeying from Nazareth to Bethlehem :—

Nov. 27th—"I went to Bethlehem, and thence I journeyed a good distance to meet the Mother of God and Joseph. I knew they would go into a stable, and I hurried on joyously to meet them. Again I saw them coming with the ass, as peaceful and calm, as lovely as ever, and I was so glad to see it all once more as I had done in my childhood.

I went a long way back and found the stable, and on looking behind I saw Joseph and Mary far away with the ass,
shining with light. It seemed as if a luminous disc surrounded the Holy Family as they moved forward in the
darkness. Anne and Joachim had prepared all things
for the holy Virgin's delivery, and they hoped she would come
back in time to make use of them. But Mary knew that she
would not be delivered in her parents' house and with wonderful humility, she took of all that had been prepared but
two pieces, for she had an inexpressible feeling that she
must and should be poor. She could have no outward
show, for she had all within herself. She knew, or felt, or
saw in some unknown way that, as through a woman, sin
had entered the world, so by a woman was the expiation to
come, and it was in this sentiment that she exclaimed, ' I am
the handmaid of the Lord !' She always followed an interior voice which in moments of grace urged her irresist.
ibly. This same voice has often called me to make long
journeys, and never in vain."

Dec. 13th—" Last night I was near Bethlehem in a low,
square hut, a shepherd's hut, occupied by an old couple.
They had partitioned off a corner for themselves on the left
by a slanting black mud-wall. By the fire-place stood
some crooks, and a few plates hung on the wall. The
shepherd came out of his apartment and pointed to another
just opposite, where sat Mary and Joseph in silence on the
ground against the wall. Mary's hands were joined on her
breast; she wore a white robe and veil. I stayed by them
awhile reverently. At the back of the house was a bush."

Dec. 14th—" I went from Flamske to the Promised
Land, as I had often done when a child, and I ran to meet
Mary. I was in such a hurry, so eager for the coming of
the Christ-Child, that I flew through Jerusalem and Beth-

lehem with streaming hair. I wanted to get them a right good lodging for the night, and I found one not far from the first which I met on my entrance. I went into a shepherd's hut back of which was a sheep-fold. The shepherd and his wife were both young. I saw the Holy Family arrive late at night. The shepherd gently reproached St. Joseph for travelling at so late an hour with Mary. Mary sat sideways on the ass on a seat with a resting-place for the feet. She was very near the birth of the Christ-Child. They left the ass at the door, and I think the shepherd took it into the sheep-stable. They were treated kindly. They went into a separate apartment and made some arrangements. They had brought some small fine loaves with them, but I never saw them eat much. I spoke quite simply with the Mother of God and, as I had my work with me, I said to her : ' I know well that thou needest nothing from me, but still I may make something for poor children. Be so good as to point out the most needy.' She told me to go on quietly with my work and that she would do as I requested. Then I went over into a dark corner where no one could see me, and worked away diligently. I finished many things, and watched the Holy Family preparing for their departure."

Dec. 16th—"I journeyed quickly on to Bethlehem although I was quite fatigued, and I hurried to a shepherd's cot, one of the best in sight of Bethlehem. I knew that Mary would arrive there that night. I saw her and Joseph in the distance. She was on the ass and shining with light. The interior of the cot was like the others ; on one side of the fire-place all sorts of vessels and pastoral utensils, on the other an apartment in which I thought Mary and Joseph would lodge. There was an orchard near by and back of it the sheep-fold which was not enclosed, the roof

supported only by stakes. The shepherd and his wife were
young and very hospitable. When I first appeared, they
asked what I wanted, and I told them that I had come to
wait for Joseph and Mary who would arrive there that day.
They replied that that had happened long ago, and that it
would never happen again. They were a little short with
me. But I said that it happened every year, for the feast was
kept in the Church. Then they grew quite clever and
obliging. I sat down in a corner with my work. They
had to pass me often, and they wanted to give me a light,
but I assured them that I needed none, I could see very
well. The reason they said that the event was passed and
would not again be repeated was that, on entering the house,
I, too, had thought: ' How is this ? These people were here
long ago, and they are still here ! They cannot still be
alive !' Then I said to myself: ' Why, what foolish
questioning ! Take things as thou findest them !' This reassured me, but the people had met my doubt by a similar
one. It was like a mirror, reflecting these words : ' What-
soever you would that men should do unto you, do ye also
unto them.'

" When Joseph and Mary arrived, they were kindly received. Mary got off the ass, Joseph brought in his bun-
dles, and both went into the little room on the right.
Joseph sat down on his bundle, and Mary on the ground
against the wall. These young people were the first to offer them anything ; they set before them a little wooden
stool on which stood flat oval dishes. On one were small
round loaves, on the other small fruit. Mary and Joseph
did not touch them, though Joseph took some and went
out with it ; I think there was a beggar outside. The ass
was tied before the door. Although they ate not, yet they
received the gifts humbly and gratefully. I always wonder-

ed at their humility in taking whatever was given them. I drew near to them timidly, rendered them homage, and begged the Blessed Virgin to ask her Son at His birth, not to let me do or desire anything but His most holy will. I spoke of my work, that she might tell me how to do it and distribute it. She bade me go on, soon all would be right. Then I sat down timidly in my little corner and sewed, but I did not stay until the Holy Family left.

" My guide took me through a wilderness some distance from Bethlehem toward the south, and it seemed to be in our own time. I saw a garden with trees shaped like a pyramid, their leaves fine and delicate, and there were lovely green plots with little flowers. In the centre, on a column around which twined a luxuriant vine, stood a small eight-cornered church covered with the vine branches. At some distance, only the leaves could be seen, but a nearer view disclosed bunches of grapes an ell long. It was wonderful how the branches supported their weight. The vine itself was as thick around as a small arm. From the eight sides of the little church, which had no doors and whose walls were transparent, ran pathways. In the church was an altar on which were three pictures of the holy season (Advent) : one was Mary and Joseph's journey to Bethlehem ; another the Child Jesus in the crib ; the third, the Flight into Egypt. They seemed to be living representations. On the eight sides, hovered twelve of the ancestors of Mary and Joseph who had celebrated these scenes. My guide told me that a church once stood here in which the relations of the Holy Family and their descendants always celebrated these holy feasts. It had been destroyed, but the feast will continue to be celebrated in the spiritual church until the end of time. Then he brought me back quickly.

" My state on these days is very singular. I seem not to be
on the earth. I see around, far and near, people and pictures, men dying of spiritual famine, evils everywhere ;
I see people here in our own country, or in the islands, or
under tents, or in forests—I see them learning in one place,
forgetting in another, but everywhere misery and blindness.
When I look up to heaven, how poor and senseless seem
these people ! They are sunk in impurity, they interpret
everything in a wrong sense. Then I try to push them on
to God—it is all dark and obscure, and I feel a deep,
deep disgust for life. Everything earthly is abominable,
and violent hunger seizes me ; but it is not disgusting, it is
sweet. Corporal hunger is so disgusting !"

Dec. 23d—"I met Mary and Joseph near Bethlehem
just about dusk. They were resting under a tree by the
roadside. Mary got down from the ass and Joseph went
alone into the city to seek a lodging in one of the nearest
houses. The city had no gate here, the road passed through
a broken part of the wall. Joseph hunted in vain for a lodging, for crowds of strangers were in Bethlehem. I stayed
with the Mother of God. When Joseph came back he told
the Blessed Virgin that he could find no place near, and
both returned to Bethlehem, Mary on foot and Joseph leading the ass. They went first to be enrolled. The man made
some remarks to Joseph about bringing his wife, saying it
was unnecessary, and Joseph blushed before Mary fearing
she might think he had a bad name here. The man said also
that, as there was such a crowd in this quarter, they would
do well to go elsewhere, and they would certainly find
lodgings. They went along timidly. The street was rather
a country-road than a street, for the houses stood on hills.
On the opposite side, where they were far apart, there was
a beautiful, widespreading tree, the trunk smooth, the

branches forming a shelter. Joseph left Mary and the ass under this tree, and set off again in search of lodgings. Mary leaned at first against the tree, her loose robe falling in full folds around her, a white veil covering her head. The ass stood with his head turned toward the tree. Many passed on various errands, looked at Mary, but knew not that their Redeemer was so near! She waited so patiently, so quietly, so humbly! Ah! she had to wait a long time! At last she sat down, her feet crossed under her, her hands joined on her breast, her head bowed. Joseph returned disappointed, he had found no lodgings. Again he set out in another direction, and again Mary waited patiently; but he was unsuccessful as before. Then he remembered a place near by where the shepherds sometimes sought shelter. They, too, could go there, and even if the shepherds came, they need not mind them. They started and turning to the left, followed a lonely road which soon became hilly. Before a small rising stood a clump of trees, pines or cedars, and others with leaves like box. In the hill was a grotto or cave, the entrance closed by a gate of twigs. Joseph entered and began to clear away the rubbish, whilst Mary stayed outside with the ass. Joseph then brought her in. He was very much troubled. The grotto was but ten feet high, perhaps not that much, and the place where the manger stood was slightly raised. Mary sat down on a mat and rested against her bundle. It was, perhaps, nine o'clock when they entered this grotto. Joseph went out again and came back with a bundle of sticks and reeds, and a box with a handle containing live coals which he poured out at the entrance and made a fire. They had everything necessary for that purpose, as well as various other utensils, though I did not see them cooking or eating. Joseph again went out, and on his return he wept. It must

now have been about midnight. For the first time I
saw the Blessed Virgin kneeling in prayer, after which
she lay down on the mat, her head on her arm, the
bundle for a pillow. Joseph remained humbly at the entrance of the grotto. In the roof, a little to one side, were
three round air holes with gratings. On the left of the
grotto was another apartment cut out of the rock or hill,
the entrance broader than the first and opening on the
road that led to the fields where the shepherds were.
There were small houses on the hills and sheds built of
twigs or branches supported by four, six, and eight posts.

" After this I had quite a different vision. I saw Bethlehem as it now is ; one would not know it, so poor and desolate has it become. The Crib is now in a chapel under the
earth and Mass is still read there ; it is larger than it used to
be, and it is covered with all kinds of white marble ornaments and figures. Above it stands a church like an old
ruined convent, but Mass is celebrated only in the grotto of
the Crib. I saw over it in the air a beautiful spiritual church.
It was eight-cornered and had but one altar. Above it
were choirs of saints. On the altar was a representation of
the Crib before which shepherds knelt, and through the air
came little lambs like little white clouds in the picture.
The officiating priest was a kind looking old man with white
hair and a long beard. He wore a very wide antique vestment,
a cowl over his forehead and around his face. It was Jerome. Incense was used during the ceremony more frequently than with us. Holy Communion was administered, and
I saw, as among the Apostles, a little body, like a tiny body
of light, entering the mouth of the communicants. There
were about six priests performing the ceremony, and when
it was over they ranged before the altar, face to face as in
choir, and chanted. Then the scene changed. Jerome re-

mained alone, and the body of the church was filled with nuns of different Orders. They ranged in three ranks as in choir and chanted. I saw the Annonciades among them and Jane, who told me that, from her childhood, she had seen these mysteries thus represented and also the great good resulting from them to mankind. It was for this reason she had founded her Order. She was now present with all her faithful nuns to continue the celebration of this feast almost forgotten by men. She exhorted me to reflect upon what had given birth to her charity and teach it also to my spiritual children. She told me many more things of the same kind that I intend to leave after me to my sisters in religion. May God grant it! I saw also at the feast Frances and other nuns whom I knew."

On the evening of Dec. 23d, the Pilgrim and Father Limberg spent two hours at Sister Emmerich's bedside whilst she lay in ecstasy (1) The former wrote: "She experienced violent pains in her limbs and particularly in her wounds. She bore them joyously, though at times she was unable to repress her groans; her hands and feet quivered with pain, the former opening and closing convulsively. She has made all her presents, finished all her work, sorted and put away all the scraps and ends of thread that were left. When this was done, she sank exhausted under her pains which were to form her own Christmas gift at the Infant's Crib. These pains are always shown to her under the

---

(1) The Pilgrim was deeply touched by what he saw and heard. He began his entry in his journal by these words :—

"Whilst I write, I am saddened at the thought of the miseries by which we are surrounded. The darkness of our understanding prevents our calmly receiving and clearly recording the heavenly secrets revealed to us by this simple, childlike soul so favored by God. I can reproduce very imperfectly mere shadows, as it were, of those visions which prove the reality, in an ever eternal present, of God's relations with man obscured by sin. And even this has to be effected hastily and even stealthily. I cannot express what I feel! They who have for years stifled and mocked at this grace, they who recognize it and yet persecute her, who know neither how to seek nor how to appreciate it, will weep with me when the mirror that reflects it shall have been obscured by death !

"Infant Jesus, my Saviour, give me patience !"

form of flowers.   She said : ' Dorothea is going with me to
the Crib, she has come for me.   She told me that she had
often been blamed for ornamenting the altar so profusely
with flowers, but that she had always answered : " Flowers
wither.   God takes from them the color and fragrance that
He once gave , so, too, may sin wither ! May whatever is
good be offered to Him, since it is from Him !' Dorothea
used to be taken to the Crib in spirit, and she offered everything to the Lord in sacrifice.   The Pilgrim, too, must
take all his sufferings to the Infant Jesus, all his weaknesses, all his faults, and he must take nothing back. He
must begin all over, and ask the Child Jesus for a burning
love that he may taste the consolations of God.   I see also
St. Jerome.   He lived here a long time, and obtained from
God such a fire of love that it almost consumed him.'

   " O who can tell the beauty, the purity, the innocence of
Mary !   She knows everything. and yet she seems to know
nothing, so childlike is she.   She lowers her eyes and,
when she looks up, her glance penetrates like a ray, like a
pure beam of light, like truth itself !   It is because she is
perfectly innocent, full of God, and without returns upon
self.   None can resist her glance.

   " I see the Crib and above it, celebrating the feast, are
all the blessed who adored the Child Jesus at His birth, all
who ever venerated the Holy Place, and all who have gone
there even only in devout desire.   They celebrate in a
wond rful spiritual church the eve of the Redeemer's birth ;
they represent the Church and all who desire the sacred
spot to be honored, the holy season celebrated   Thus acts
the Church Triumphant for the Church Militant; and thus
should the Militant act for the Church Suffering.   O how
indescribably beautiful it is !   What a blessed certainty !
I see these spiritual churches all around, far and near, for

no power can destroy the altar of the Lord. Where it is
no longer visible, it stands invisibly cared for by blessed
spirits. Nothing is perishable that is done in the Church
for the love of Jesus! Where men are no longer worthy
to celebrate, the blessed do it in their stead and all hearts
that turn to the service of God are there present. They find
a holy church and a heavenly feast, though their corporal
senses perceive it not ; they receive the reward of their
piety.

"I see Mary in heaven on a magnificent throne offering
to her Divine Son, sometimes as a new-born babe, sometimes as a youth, and again as the Crucified Saviour, all
hearts that have ever loved Him, that have ever united in
celebrating His feast. . . . . ."

Here Sister Emmerich was radiant with joy, her speech,
her glance, full of animation, and she expressed herself so
intelligently and with so much ease even upon the most
hidden and sublime subjects that the Pilgrim was lost in
amazement. His words but faintly reproduce those of this
inspired soul, who spoke not so much in glowing colors as
in fiery flames.

" See," she exclaimed, " how all nature sparkles and ex-
ults in innocence and joy! It is like a dead man rising
from the gloom and decay of the grave, which proves that
he not only lives, youthful, blooming, and joyous, but that he
is also immortal, innocent, and pure, the sinless image of his
Maker ! All is life, all is innocence and thankfulness ! Oh,
the beautiful hills, around which the trees stretch their
branches as if hastening to strew at the feet of their new-
born Saviour the perfumes, flowers, and fruits from Him received ! The flowers open their cups to present their varied forms, their colors, their perfumes to the Lord who will
so soon come to tread among them. The springs murmur

their desires, and the fountains dance in joyous expectation, like children awaiting their Christmas gifts. The birds warble notes of joy and gladness, the lambs bleat and skip, all life is filled with peace and happiness. In the veins of all flow quicker, purer streams. Pious hearts, earnest, longing hearts now throb instinctively at the approach of Redemption. All nature is astir. Sinners are seized with sadness, repentance, hope ; the incorrigible, the hardened, the future executioners of the Lord, are anxious and fearful, they cannot comprehend their own uneasiness as the fulness of time draws near. The plenitude of salvation is in the pure, humble, merciful heart of Mary, praying over the Saviour of the world incarnate in her womb, and who, in a few hours, like light become flesh, will enter into life, into His own inheritance, will come among His own who will receive Him not. What all nature now proclaims before my eyes when its Creator comes to abide with it, is written in the books upon the Mountain wherein truth will be preserved until the end of time. As in the race of David the Promise was preserved in Mary until the fulness of time; as this race was cared for, protected, purified, until the Blessed Virgin brought forth the Light of the world ; so that *holy man* purifies and preserves all the treasures of creation and thePromise, as also the essence and signification of all words and creatures until the fulness of time. He purifies all, erases what is false or pernicious, and causes the stream to flow as pure as when it first issued from God, as it now flows in all nature. Why do seekers seek and find it not ? Here let them see that good ever engenders good, and evil brings forth evil, if it be not averted by repentance and the Blood of Jesus Christ. As the blessed in heaven, the pious on earth, and the poor souls work together, helping, healing through Jesus Christ, so do I now see the same in all nature. It is inexpressible! Every simple-hearted man who follows Jesus Christ receives that gift, but it is through the marvellous grace of this season. The devil is chained in these days, he crawls he struggles; therefore I hate all crawling things. The hideous demon is humbled, he can do nothing now. It is the unending grace of this holy season."

Two days after, she related the following:—

"I saw St. Joseph going out in the evening with a basket and vessels, as if to get food. No words can express his simplicity, gentleness, and humility. I saw Mary kneeling in ecstasy in the same place as before, her hands slightly raised. The fire was still burning, and on a shelf was a little lamp. The grotto was full of light. There were no shadows, but the lamp looked dull like a flambeau in the sunlight, for its flame was material. Mary was alone. I thought then of all I wanted to bring to the Crib of the expected Saviour. I had a long journey to make through places I had often seen in the Life of the Lord, in all of which I saw care, trouble, anguish of soul. I saw Jews plotting in their synagogues and interrupting their service. I went also to a place in the environs where sacrifices were being offered in a pagan temple in which was a frightful idol with wide jaws. They put into it flesh offered in sacrifice, when the monster instantly fell to pieces. Fear and confusion seized the worshippers, who fled in all directions.

"I went also into the country of Nazareth, to Anne's house, just one moment before the Saviour's birth. I saw Anne and Joachim asleep in separate apartments. A light shone over Anne, and she was told in a dream that Mary had brought forth a son. She awoke and hurried to Joachim whom she met coming to her; he, too, had had the

same dream. They prayed together praising God, their
arms raised to heaven. The rest of their household, likewise experienced something extraordinary. They came to
Anne and Joachim whom they found filled with joy. When
they heard of the birth, they thanked God with them for
the new-born child. They did not know for certain that
He was the Son of God ; but they knew that it was a child
of salvation, a child of promise. They had an intuitive assurance of it, although they could not express it. They
were, besides, struck by the wonderful signs in nature, and
they looked upon that night as holy. I saw pious souls
here and there around Nazareth, rising up awakened by a
sweet interior joy and, whether knowingly or otherwise,
celebrating with prayer the entrance of the Word made
Flesh into the life of time.

" My whole way on that marvellous night lay through
the most varied scenes—people in all countries flocking together, some joyous, some prayerful, others uneasy and
sad. My journey was rapid toward the east, though a little more to the south than when I went to the Mountain of
Elias. In an old city I saw a large open square surrounded by huge, half-ruined columns and magnificent buildings
in which was extraordinary commotion. Men and women
flocked together. Crowds were coming in from the country
and all were gazing up at the sky. Some looked through
tubes about eight feet long, with an opening for the eye,
others pointed out something in the air, and all uttered
such exclamations as, ' What a wonderful night ! '—They
must have observed a sign in the heavens, perhaps a com-
et, which was, without doubt, the cause of their excitement,
though I do not remember having seen anything of it.

" I hastened on to a place where people with their
priests were drawing water on the banks of their sacred

river. They were more numerous than before—it seemed to be a feast. It was not night when I arrived, it was noonday (1). I could not speak to all whom I knew. I spoke to some who understood me and were deeply moved. I told them they should no longer draw the sacred water, but that they should turn to their Saviour who was born. I know not how I said it, but they were surprised and impressed, and some, especially the most pious and reflective, were a little frightened, for there were very, very pure and deeply sensitive souls among them. These latter I saw going into their temples, in which I could see no idols, though there was something like an altar; they all knelt, men, women, and children. The mothers placed their little ones before them and held up their tiny hands as if in prayer. It was a truly touching sight!

"I was led back to the Crib. The Saviour was born! The holy Virgin sat in the same place, wrapped in a mantle and holding on her lap the Infant Jesus swathed in ample bands, even His face was covered. Both were immovable and seemed to be in ecstasy. Two shepherds were standing timidly at some distance, and some were looking down through the air-holes in the roof. I adored in silence! When the shepherds went away, St. Joseph entered with food in a basket and carrying on his arm something like a coverlet. He set them down, and drew near to Mary who placed the Infant in his arms. He held It with unspeakable joy, devotion, and humility. I saw that he did not know It to be the Second Person of the Divinity, although he felt that It was the Child of Promise, the Child that would bring salvation into the world, that It was a holy Child.

(1) It must have been, the hour there (India) corresponding to our midnight. Sister Emmerich beheld Christ's birth in Bethlehem at our midnight and all the events there as night scenes; but, on arriving in India, the time of Nativity changes in her vision to the real time, the hour it really was at the Ganges when her soul arrived here.

" I knelt and begged the Mother of God to lead to her Son all who I knew had need of salvation, and immediately I saw in spirit those of whom I was thinking—my thought was the sign that she had heard my prayer. I thought of Judith on the mountain and, all at once, I saw her in her castle, in the hall in which the lamps hung, and there were many people present, among them some strangers. It looked like a religious reunion. They seemed to be consulting together about something and they were much agitated. I saw, too, that Judith remembered my apparition and that she both desired and feared to see me again. She thought if the Messiah were really come, and if she could be quite sure of what the apparition had said to her, she would do what she had promised, in order to help her people.

" It was day. Mary sat cross-legged in her usual place busied apparently with a piece of linen, the Child Jesus lay at her feet swathed, but His face and hands free. Joseph was at the entrance opposite the fire-place making something like a frame to hang vessels on, and I stood by the ass thinking : ' Dear old man, you need not finish your work, you must soon go.' Now came in two old women from Mary's country who seemed to be old acquaintances, for they were kindly received, though Mary did not rise. They brought quite a number of presents—little.fruits, ducks, large birds with red, awl-shaped beaks, which they carried under their arms or by the wings, some small oval loaves about an inch thick, and lastly, some linen and other stuff. All were received with rare humility and gratitude. They were silent, good, devout woman. They were deeply affected as they gazed down upon the Child, but they did not touch Him. They withdrew without farewells or ceremony. I was looking at the ass; its back was very broad, and I said to myself, ' Good beast, thou hast borne many bur-

dens !'—I wanted to feel it, to see if it were real, and I
passed my hand over its back.   It was just as soft as silk,
it reminded me of the moss I had once felt.   Now came
from the country of the shepherds, where the gardens and
the balsam-hedges are, two married women with three little
girls about eight years old.   They seemed to be strangers,
people of distinction, who had come in obedience to a miraculous call.   Joseph received them very humbly.   They
brought presents of less size than the others, but of greater
value : grain in a bowl, small fruits, a little cluster of thick
three-cornered golden leaves on which was a stamp like a
seal.   I thought how wonderful !   That looks just like the
way they represent the eye of God ! But no ! how can I
compare the eye of God with red earth !'—Mary arose and
placed the Child in their arms.   They held Him awhile, and
prayed in silence with hearts raised to God, and then they
kissed the Child. Joseph and Mary conversed with them and,
when they departed, Joseph accompanied them a little distance.   They appeared to have travelled some miles and
secretly, for they avoided being seen in the city.   Joseph
behaved with great humility during such visits, retiring
and looking on from a distance.

   " When Joseph went out with the ladies, I prayed and
confidently laid open my miseries to Mary.   She consoled
me, though her answers were very brief; for instance,
three words upon three points.   This manner of communicating is very difficult to explain.   It is an intuitive perception something like the following : when Mary, for example, wanted to say; ' These sufferings will strengthen
thee spiritually, thou wilt not yield to them, they will make
thee more clear-sighted, will render thee victorious,' I perceived nothing but the meaning of these words under the
figure of a palm-tree which is said to become more elastic,

more vigorous by the pressure of a weight upon it. In the same way, she told me something like the following : ' The struggle with thy sister will be painful, a sharp combat is before thee. Be comforted ! With the trial and the suffering thy supernatural strength will increase. The sharper thy sufferings, the more clearly, the more profoundly, wilt thou understand. Think of the profit thou wilt derive from it !'—I received this last instruction under the perception of the principle by which the purity of gold is increased under the hammer, or the polish of a mirror is produced. Then she told me that I must tell all, keep nothing back, even if it seemed to me of small importance. Everything has its end. I must not allow myself to be discouraged by the thought that I do not rightly comprehend. I must tell all even if my words appear useless and unconnected. A change will come over many Protestants after my death, and the conviction of the truth of my state will contribute greatly thereto ; consequently I must keep nothing back."

On Christmas-Eve she was shown in a vision new sufferings in store for her. The following is her account of it :—

" There came three holy nuns, among them Frances of Rome, who brought me a clean white robe with a scalloped border ; on the left side was a red heart surrounded by roses. I touched them and the thorns pricked me to blood. The nuns threw the robe around me quickly, saying that I must wear it until the new-year when it would be exchanged for a gray one with a heavy iron cross. If at the new-year I returned the present one spotless, the cross on the second one would, perhaps, be much lightened. I thought this referred to my death, and I said, ' Is it true that I am going to die ?'—But they answered, ' No, thou hast still much to suffer,' and then they disappeared. My guide announced those bitter sufferings in severe words that cut into my soul like swords. He told me that I should not succumb, that I drew them on myself by undertaking so much for others, that I should be more moderate, not so eager to do so much good, that Jesus alone can do such things. Then sharp pains racked me until two hours past midnight. I lay upon a harrow covered with thorns that penetrated into my very bones."

She had at short intervals three attacks of these same sufferings. On Dec. 29th, the Pilgrim found her quite changed in appearance by physical and mental pain, her features drawn, her forehead knit, her whole frame twitching convulsively. "I have not slept all night," she said, "I am almost dead; still I had exterior consolation. The sweetness of suffering spread itself through my inmost soul, it came from God. The Blessed Virgin also consoled me. I saw her inexpressible sufferings on the night the Lord was seized, and particularly that caused her by Peter's denial. I saw how she lamented it to John; it was only to him that she told her grief. I asked her why my sister's state gave me so much pain, wounded me so deeply, yes, almost distracted me, whilst I supported courageously far worse than it. I was told: 'As thou dost perceive light from the relics of the saints by thy intuition of the union existing among Christ's members, so dost thou perceive more clearly the blindness, the anger, the disunion of thy sister's state, because it comes from the root of thy sinful flesh in fallen Adam, in a direct line through thy ancestors. Thou dost feel their sins in thy flesh through thy parents and earliest ancestors. It is sin proceeding from the share thou hast in the fall.'—I suffered, I watched, I fainted away, I regained consciousness, I counted the hours, and when morning dawned I cried out to my Spouse not to

abandon me. I saw Him taking leave of His Mother. I saw
Mary's grief. I saw Him upon the Mount of Olives, and He
said to me : ' Dost thou wish to be treated better than Mary,
the most pure, the most beloved of all creatures ? What
are thy sufferings compared with hers ? '—Then He showed
me endless miseries, the dying unprepared, etc., and my
guide said to me : ' If thou wouldst help them, suffer for
them, else how can justice be satisfied ? '—He showed me
future sorrows, and told me that few pray and suffer to
avert evils. I became thankful and courageous, I suffered
joyously for I had seen *Him !* He again said, ' See, how
many dying souls ! in what a state ! '—and showed me a dying priest of my own country, one who had fallen so low
that he could not receive Holy Communion with faith and
purity of heart. I did not know him. My guide said,
' Suffer for all these until mid-day '—Then I suffered joyously. I still suffer, but I shall soon be relieved."

" Toward noon her countenance changed, the heart-rending expression faded, her pains seemed to leave her gradually like water evaporating under the sun's rays. Her
drawn features relaxed and precisely at noon, became
sweet and peaceful as those of a sleeping child—the paroxysm had passed. Her members became torpid, and she fell
into a state of insensibility exempt from suffering.

" The last evening of the year she was completely absorbed by her journey to the Heavenly Jerusalem, and she occasionally repeated some verses from the Breviary referring
to the City of God. Once she said : ' I must be trodden
under foot, my garden is too flourishing, it will produce
nothing but flowers.'—She beheld herself in all possible
situations, her heart cruelly lacerated. She exclaimed : ' O
how much that person afflicts me ! I can hardly endure
the sight of her sufferings ! I beg God to hide them from me !'

"On the night of January, 1820, the three little nuns came again and took off her white robe, which was still spotless. They put on her the promised gray one with the heavy black cross which she was to wash white with her tears. A number of poor souls came to thank her for their deliverance, among them an old woman of her own hamlet for whom she had prayed much. She felt that she had delivered them through the spotlessness of her white robe, and that affected her deeply. 'When I received the gray robe,' she said, 'I saw again all the torments in reserve for me. I had, besides, an apparition of St. Teresa, who consoled me greatly by speaking of her own sufferings. She also reassured me on the score of my visions, telling me not to be troubled but to disclose all; that with her it so happened that the more open she was in this respect the clearer did her visions become. My Spouse also spoke lovingly with me and explained the gray robe.—" It is of silk," He said, "because I am wounded in my whole person, and thou art not to tear it by impatience. It is gray, because it is a robe of penance and humiliation." He told me, too, that when I was sick, He was satisfied with me; but that when I was well, I was too condescending. He said, moreover, that I should tell all that was shown me even though I might be ridiculed for it, for such was His will. Everything is of use. Then I felt as if I were borne from one bed of thorns to be laid on another, but I offered all for the poor souls.' "

January 2d—the Pilgrim found her enduring a martyrdom. "It would be vain," he writes, "to attempt a description of her sufferings. To understand it even slightly, one would have to watch the various phases of her inexplicable state." The cause of her pains none could divine. Her life glided by in this daily struggle without

sympathy or support. She never appeared to lose the remembrance of her thorny crown; even when the rest of
her person became rigid, she retained command over her
head, supporting it in such a way that the thorns might
not penetrate too deeply. Sometimes her whole body was
slashed and torn with whips, her hands were tied, she was
bound with cords; the torture she endured forced the cold
sweat from every pore, and yet she related all without a sign
of impatience. Suddenly she extended her arms in the form
of a cross with an effort so violent that one would have
thought the distended nerves were about to snap. She
lowered them again, her head gradually sank upon her
breast as if she were dead, her limbs were motionless, she
lay like a corpse. 'I am with the poor souls,' she murmured,
and on returning to consciousness, she related the following
though with an effort :—

" 'I have had three violent attacks, and I have suffered
everything just as my Spouse did in His Passion. When
I was about to yield, when I groaned in agony, I beheld
the same suffering undergone by Him. Thus I went
through the whole Passion as I see it on Good-Friday. I
was scourged, crowned with thorns, dragged with ropes,
I fell, I was nailed to the cross, I saw the Lord descend
into hell, and I, too, went to purgatory. I saw many
detained therein; some I knew, others I knew not. I saw
souls saved who had been buried in darkness and forgetfulness, and this afforded me consolation.

" 'The second attack I endured for all that were not in a
state to bear patiently what falls to their lot, and for the
dying who were unable to receive the Blessed Sacrament.
I saw many whom I helped.

" 'The third attack was for the Church. I had a vision
of a church with a high, elaborate tower, in a great city

on a mighty river (1). The patron of the church is
Stephen by whom I saw another saint who was martyred
after him. Around the church I saw many very distinguished people, among them some strangers with aprons and
trowels who appeared about to pull down the church with
the beautiful tower and slate roof. People from all parts
were gathered there, among them priests and even religious,
and I was so distressed that I called to my Spouse for
assistance. Xavier with the cross in his hand had once
been all powerful, the enemy ought not to be allowed to
triumph now! Then I saw five men going into the church,
three in heavy antique vestments like priests, and two very
young ecclesiastics who seemed to be in Holy Orders. I
thought these two received Holy Communion, and that they
were destined to infuse new life into the Church. Suddenly a flame burst from the tower, spread over the roof, and
threatened to consume the whole church. I thought of
the great river flowing by the city—could they not extinguished the flames with its waters? The fire injured many
who aided in the destruction of the church and drove them
away, but the edifice itself remained standing, by which I
understood that the Church would be saved only after a great
storm. The fire so frightful to behold indicated in the first
place, a great danger; in the second, renewed splendor after
the tempest. The Church's destruction is already begun
by means of infidel schools.

"I saw a great storm rising in the north and sweeping in
a half-circle to the city with the high tower, and then off
to the west. I saw combats and streaks of blood far and
wide in the heavens over many places, and endless woes and
misery threatening the Church, the Protestants everywhere
laying snares to entrap her. The servants of the Church

---

(1) These details point to Vienna, the Austrian capital.

are so slothful. They use not the power they possess in the priesthood! I shed bitter tears at the sight."—She wept whilst recounting this vision, imploring Almighty God to deliver her from such spectacles. She mourned also over the flocks without shepherds, and counselled prayer, penance, and humility to avert a portion of the impending danger.

END OF VOLUME I.

If you have enjoyed this book, consider making your next selection from among the following . . .

Prices guaranteed through December 31, 1989.

At your bookdealer or direct from the publisher.

Prices guaranteed through December 31, 1989.